Understanding Unix®/Linux Programming

Bruce Molay
Harvard University

Prentice
Hall

Pearson Education, Inc.
U   ey 07458

b11421848

Library of Congress Cataloging-in-Publication Data

CIP data on file

Vice President and Editorial Director, ECS: *Marcia Horton*
Senior Acquisitions Editor: *Petra Recter*
Editorial Assistant: *Renee Makras*
Vice President and Director of Production and Manufacturing, ESM: *David W. Riccardi*
Executive Managing Editor: *Vince O'Brien*
Assistant Managing Editor: *Camille Trentacoste*
Production Editor: *Lakshmi Balasubramanian*
Director of Creative Services: *Paul Belfanti*
Creative Director: *Carole Anson*
Cover Art: *Gerald Bustamante/SIS, Inc.*
Art Director: *Jayne Conte*
Art Editor: *Gregory Dulles*
Manufacturing Manager: *Trudy Pisciotti*
Manufacturing Buyer: *Lisa McDowell*
Marketing Manager: *Pamela Shaffer*
Marketing Assistant: *Barrie Reinhold*

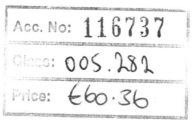

© 2003 Pearson Education, Inc.
Pearson Education, Inc.
Upper Saddle River, NJ 07458

UNIX is a registered trademark of the Open Group in the US and other countries.

Printed in the United States of America

10 9 8 7 6 5 4

ISBN 0-13-008396-8

Pearson Education Ltd., *London*
Pearson Education Australia Pty. Ltd., *Sydney*
Pearson Education Singapore, Pte. Ltd.
Pearson Education North Asia Ltd., *Hong Kong*
Pearson Education Canada, Inc., *Toronto*
Pearson Educación de Mexico, S.A. de C.V.
Pearson Education—Japan, *Tokyo*
Pearson Education Malaysia, Pte. Ltd.
Pearson Education, Inc., *Upper Saddle River, New Jersey*

To Marcia and Ira

Preface

Understanding Unix Programming

EXPLAINING UNIX

I wrote this book to explain how Unix works and to show you how to write system programs for Unix. Unix, still evolving after 30 years, has grown more complex, but it has not gotten more complicated. Its fundamental structure and design principles still apply. By understanding the structure, principles, and history, you will be able to read, enhance, and add to the vast accumulated literature of Unix programs. You also will have a lot of fun.

To make the ideas really clear, I present them in many forms: pictures, analogies, pseudocode, real code, experiments, exercises, and anecdotes. These explanations evolve from actual, useful problems and projects.

WHO IS PREPARED FOR THIS BOOK?

You must know how to program in C. If you know C++, you should be able to follow the code and adapt quickly. You have to know about arrays, structs, pointers, and linked lists and be able to understand, and write, code that uses these.

You need not have used Unix, nor do you need to know about the internals of an operating system. In each chapter, we start with the user-level features of Unix. The question, "What does that do?" at the user level leads inevitably to the system-level question, "How does it work?"

You need to have access to a Unix system and a sense of adventure.

WHAT'S IN IT FOR ME?

This book explains the components of a Unix system, what they do, the theory of how they work, and how to program using those components. You will also see how all these components fit together to form a coherent, intelligible operating system.

This book is based on a course, *Unix Systems Programming*, which I have taught at the Harvard Extension School since 1990. Students have described, on course evaluations and by e-mail years later, what the course gave them. One student said the course gave him "the keys to the kingdom." He understood Unix at the user, programming, and theory levels well enough to feel he could go anywhere and make sense of most problems. A physician in the course liked the case-study approach, comparing it to the way medical interns learn by working real problems.

Another student, one who went on to be a project leader at the Open Software Foundation, said the course taught him the ideas and skills he needed for that job.

FOR WHICH VERSION OF UNIX IS THIS WRITTEN?

Almost all of them, including GNU/Linux. The focus of the book is the structure and skills that form the basis of all versions of Unix, not the specific variations from one dialect to the next. Once you understand the main ideas, those details are easy to pick up.

Acknowledgements

This book was made possible with the help of many people.

At Prentice-Hall, I thank Petra Recter for offering this opportunity and for guiding the project, and I thank Gregory Dulles for working with me on the illustrations.

For their thoughtful, encouraging remarks and concrete suggestions, I thank the reviewers of drafts of the book: Ben Abbott, John B. Connely, Geoff Sutcliffe, Louis Taber, Sam R. Thangiah, and Lawrence B. Wells. For pivotal information about graphics software, I thank Peggy Bustamante and Amit Chatterjee. For untold conversations and moral and practical support throughout this project, I thank Yuriko Kuwabara.

I thank the many students and teaching assistants in *Unix Systems Programming* whose questions and remarks in class discussions and in tutorial conversations helped shape the outline, explanations, metaphors, and images that form this book. I especially thank Larry deLuca for his years as a teaching assistant and for the material of Chapter 13.

Table of Contents

Table of Illustrations

Unix Systems Programming
The Big Picture

OBJECTIVES

Ideas

- A Unix system contains user programs and the system kernel.
- The Unix kernel is a collection of specific subsystems.
- The kernel manages all programs and access to resources.
- Communication between processes is an important aspect of Unix programs.
- What is systems programming?

Commands

- bc
- more

1.1   INTRODUCTION

What is systems programming? What is Unix systems programming? Where are we going in this book? In this chapter, we look at the big picture, figuratively and literally.

We begin by examining the role of an operating system and what it means to write programs that work directly with the operating system. Moving quickly from generalities, we look at Unix programs that use operating-system services and then go on to write our own version of one. Finally, we look at a diagram that represents a Unix computer. The diagram and the technique of dissecting programs form the basis for this book.

1.2   WHAT IS SYSTEMS PROGRAMMING?

1.2.1   The Simple Program Model

You may have written scientific programs, financial programs, graphics programs, and text-processing programs. There are many sorts of programs. Many programs are based on the model in Figure 1.1:

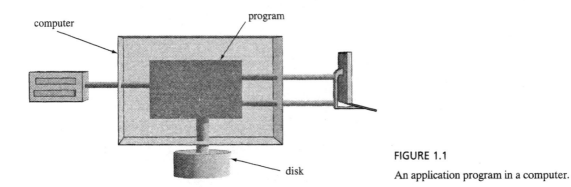

FIGURE 1.1

An application program in a computer.

A program is a piece of code that runs in a computer. Data go into the program, the program does something with the data, and data come out of the program. A human may type at a keyboard and display, the program may read or write to a disk, the program may send data to a printer. The possibilities are numerous.

In this model of a program, one writes clear, sensible code such as,

```
/* copy from stdin to stdout */
main()
{
    int c;
    while( ( c = getchar() ) != EOF )
        putchar(c);
}
```

This code corresponds to a visual model depicted in Figure 1.2:

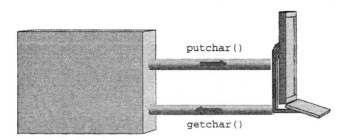

FIGURE 1.2

How application programs see user I/O.

The figure is based on the notion that the keyboard and screen are both connected to the program. On a simple personal computer, this model is pretty close to reality. The keyboard and video display are plugged into the motherboard of the computer. The processor chip and the memory chips are plugged into the motherboard. Simple strips of metal connect these components. You can open the case and see lines on the printed circuit board that correspond to the lines in the figure.

1.2.2 Face Reality

What if you log into a multiuser system, like a typical Unix machine? In that case, the simple model of keyboard and monitor wired to the CPU is false. The real picture is closer to the following image shown in Figure 1.3.

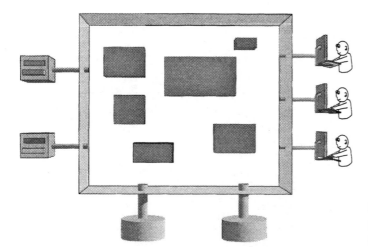

FIGURE 1.3

Reality: many users, programs, and devices.

That is, there are several keyboards and displays, there may be several disks, one or more printers, and there are certainly several programs running at once.

Nonetheless, programs that get input from *the keyboard* and send output to *the display* or to *the disk* work fine. Programs can assume the simple model and still get the correct result.

Something more complicated, though, is going on. Somehow all these various keyboards are connected to the various programs. Somehow there are lots of connections inside that machine. If you were to open the case and look for lines on the motherboard, would you see something like Figure 1.4?

Not likely. Wiring it would be a nightmare. It would not even work, since different programs come and go as different users log in and out. There must be a different model of what goes on inside a multiuser, multitasking computer.

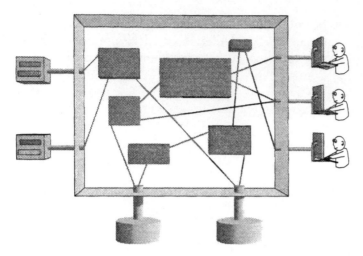

FIGURE 1.4

How are they all connected?

1.2.3   The Role of the Operating System

The role of an operating system is to manage and protect all the resources and to connect the various devices to the various programs. In physical terms, an operating system does in software what those wires on the PC motherboard do in hardware.

The tangle of wires shown in the previous figure is replaced with the model in Figure 1.5.

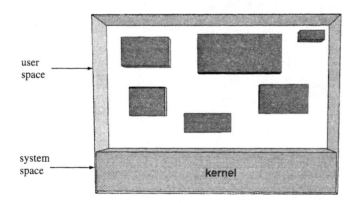

user space

system space   kernel

FIGURE 1.5

An operating system is a program.

The operating system is a program. The code for the operating system, like the code for any running program, resides in the computer's memory. The memory also contains other programs—programs users write and run. The operating system connects those programs to the outside world.

1.2.4   Providing Services to Programs

Now that we have seen the problem (how can multiple users connect to multiple processes?) and the outline of the solution (have a master program manage all the connections), we start to fill in the details.

First, some vocabulary. The computer memory provides *space* to store programs and data, just the way an attic provides space to store clothes and other things. The part of the computer memory where the operating system is stored is called *system space*, and the part of the memory that contains user programs is called *user space*.

The operating system is called the *kernel*; the wires from the keyboards and screens are connected to the computer: See Figure 1.6.

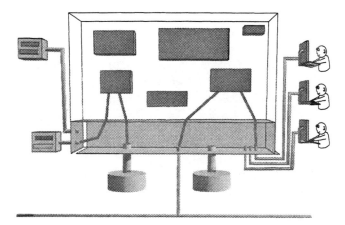

FIGURE 1.6

The kernel manages all connections.

Notice that the place where the wires connect is in system space; thus, the kernel is the only program with access to those devices.

User programs get data by asking the kernel. The kernel transfers data from the keyboard to the program and transfers data from the program to the wire that runs to the display. Similarly, the kernel has sole access to the hard disk, printers, network cards, and all other peripheral devices. If a program wants to connect to or control any of those things, it needs to ask the kernel.

The connecting lines in the picture represent these virtual wires the kernel provides. Access to these external objects are *services* the kernel provides to user programs.

We now have a context in which to explain systems programming and the content of this book. Regular application programs may be written as though they had direct connections to the terminals, disks, and printers. System programs work in this larger model—the world of resources and kernel services. We shall study what services the kernel provides, the structure of those services, and how to write programs that work in this larger context.

1.3 UNDERSTANDING SYSTEMS PROGRAMMING

The kernel provides access to system resources. System programs use those services directly. What are those services and how can we learn to use them?

1.3.1   System Resources

Processors

A program is a set of instructions; a processor is the hardware that executes instructions. Processors are also called processing units. Some computers contain several processors. The kernel assigns processors to programs, and the kernel starts, pauses, resumes, and ends the execution of a program on a processor.

Input/Output

All data that flow in and out of programs go through the kernel. Data coming in from and going out to users at terminals travel through the kernel. Data that come in from disks and go out to disks pass through the kernel. This centralization ensures that data are transferred correctly—data go to the right place; efficiently—no extra time is wasted getting information from one place to another, and securely—no process is able to look at information it is not supposed to see.

Process Management

Unix uses the term process to refer to a program in action. A process consists of memory, open files, and other system resources a program needs to run. Just as a program can ask the kernel for data, a program can ask the kernel for processes. The kernel creates new processes. The kernel schedules processes and arranges for them to work cooperatively.

Memory

The computer's memory is a resource. Programs may request additional memory to store information. The kernel keeps track of which processes are using which sections of memory and protects the memory of one process from being damaged by another process.

Devices

One can attach all sorts of devices to a computer. Tape drives, CD players, mice, scanners, and video cameras are examples of devices. Communicating with a device can be complicated. The kernel provides access to devices and takes care of the complexities. When a program wants to take a picture using a camera attached to the computer, it asks the kernel for access to that resource.

Timers

Some programs depend on time. They may perform an operation at set intervals; they may need to wait a while and then do something; they may need to know how much time some operation has taken. The kernel makes timers available to processes.

Interprocess Communication

In the real world, people need to communicate, so they use telephones, e-mail, paper mail, radio, television, and other means to transfer information. In a computer system that runs several programs at once, processes need to communicate. The kernel provides various forms of *interprocess communication*. Like the phone system and the postal service, these communication systems are resources.

Networking

A network connecting computers is a broader form of interprocess communication. A network allows processes on different computers, even on different operating systems, to exchange data. Network access is a kernel service.

1.3.2   Our Goal: Understanding Systems Programming

We just listed many types of services and access the kernel provides to system programs. What are the details of each type of service? How does data get from a device to the program and back? We want to understand what the kernel is doing, how it does it, and how to write programs that use those services.

1.3.3   Our Method: Three Simple Steps

We shall learn about Unix services by

1. Looking at "real" programs
   We shall study standard Unix programs to see what they do and how they are used in practice. We shall see what system services these programs use.
2. Looking at the system calls
   We shall next learn about the system calls we use to invoke these services.
3. Writing our own version
   Once we understand the program, what system services it uses, and how those services are used, we are ready to write our own system programs. These programs will be extensions of existing programs or ones that use similar principles.

We shall study Unix system programming by asking, over and over, the following three questions:

> What does that do?
> How does that work?
> Can I try to do it?

1.4   UNIX FROM THE USER PERSPECTIVE

1.4.1   What Does Unix Do?

Our first step in learning about any aspect of Unix is to ask *What does it do*? We first ask that question about Unix as a whole. What does a Unix user see? What does the system look like to someone sitting down at a Unix terminal?

As we take this quick tour of what Unix does, we can start wondering how it works.

1.4.2   Log In—Run Programs—Log Out

Using Unix is easy. You log in, run some programs, and then log out. You *log into* the system by typing a username and password:

```
Linux 1.2.13 (maya) (ttyp1)

maya login: betsy
Password: _
```

After you log in, you run programs. There are all sorts of programs. You can run a program to read and send e-mail. You can run a program to compute the positions of planets or values of mutual funds. You can run programs to play games.

Running programs is also pretty easy. The system prints a *prompt* on your screen. You type in the name of the program you want to run. The computer runs the program. When the program is done, the system prints another prompt on the screen.

Even nice-looking graphical desktops fit this description. The screen with its icons and menus is a prompt, and clicking on an icon or menu item is equivalent to typing a command name. Behind the graphical interface is software that associates text names of image files with text names of programs.

When you are done running programs, you *log out*:

```
$ exit
```

Depending on the configuration of your account, you may be able to log out by typing *logout* or by pressing Ctrl-D.

How Does That Work?

That all looks pretty easy, but what is going on? How does this all work?

What does it mean to be *logged in*? With a personal computer, one is used to the idea of *the person using the computer* the same way one thinks about the person using the family car. On a Unix machine many people, even hundreds of people, can be logged in at the same time. How does the system know who is logged in and where they are logged in?

Let us describe this process in more detail. If your name and password are accepted, the system starts up a program called a shell and connects you to that shell. Each logged-in user is connected to a different shell process.

Figure 1.7 is a picture of someone logged into a Unix system.

The computer is the box at the left part of the picture; the user is the person sitting at the keyboard and screen. Inside the computer is memory that holds the kernel and user processes. The user's connection to the system is controlled by the kernel. The kernel transfers data between the user and the shell.

The shell prints a *prompt* to tell the user it is ready to run a program. In these examples, the prompt is the dollar-sign character. Prompts may be any string of characters. The user types the name of a program, and the kernel sends that input to the shell.

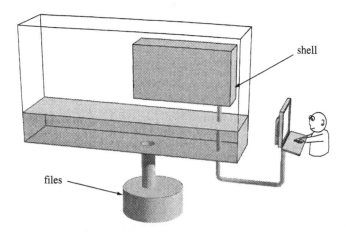

shell

files

FIGURE 1.7

A user logged into a computer.

For example, to run the program that prints the current time and date, a user types the command date:

```
$
$ date
Sat Jul 1 21:34:10 EDT 2000
$ _
```

The program called date is run, it prints out the date, then the shell prints a new prompt.

To run another program, just type the name. Many Unix systems have a program called fortune. Here is an example:

```
$ fortune
Algol-60 surely must be regarded as the most important
programming language yet developed.
               -- T. Cheatham
$ _
```

When you log out, the kernel disposes of the shell process it had assigned to you.

How does the kernel create this shell process? How does the shell process take the name of a program and run the program for you? How does the shell know when that program is done? Logging in and running programs is not as simple as it first appears. We study the details in Chapter 8.

1.4.3   Working with Directories

When you are logged in, you can work with your files. Your files may contain e-mail, images, program source code, executable programs, and all sorts of data. Files are organized into directories.

A Tree of Directories

Unix organizes files into a tree-structured directory system and provides commands to view and navigate this system.

Here is a diagram of a directory tree:

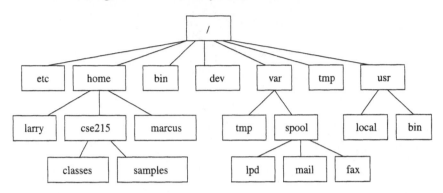

FIGURE 1.8

Part of the directory tree.

The top of the file system is called **/**. **/** contains several directories. This directory is called the *root directory* because the entire tree of directories grows from it.

Typical Unix systems have directories at this root level called /etc, /home, /bin, and some other standard names. Each user is assigned, in this tree, a home directory to store personal files. On many systems, user directories are subdirectories of /home.

Unix provides several commands for working with this directory structure. There are programs for creating new directories, for deleting directories, for *moving around* through the tree, and for examining what a directory contains. Log in and try these commands yourself.

Commands for Working with Directories

ls - list directory contents

The ls command lists the contents of a directory. If you just type ls, you are shown the contents of the current directory. If you type ls dirname, you are shown the contents of the specified directory. For example, you can type

    ls /etc

to see the files and directories stored in the /etc directory. Similarly, you can type

    ls /

to see what files and directories are stored in the root directory.

cd - change to a different directory

Use the cd command to move into a different directory. When you log into the system, you are in your home directory. You can leave your home directory and visit other parts of the tree by changing into other directories. For example, you type

```
cd /bin
```

to visit the directory that contains many system programs. Once in `/bin`, you can type `ls` to see what files and directories are there. From any directory, you can move up one level in the tree by typing the command

```
cd ..
```

Regardless of how far you roam, you can jump back to your home directory by typing just

```
cd
```

`pwd` - print path to current directory

The `pwd` command tells you where you are in the directory tree. It prints the *path* from the root of the directory system to your current location. For example,

```
$ pwd
/home/cse215/samples
```

shows that the path from the root of the tree to our current directory is to enter the directory called home, then from there enter the subdirectory called `cse215`, and so on.

`mkdir`, `rmdir` - make and remove directories

Use `mkdir` to create a new directory. For example,

```
$ cd
$ mkdir jokes
```

makes a directory called `jokes` under your home directory. You are not allowed to create new directories in the directories of other users.

   To delete a directory, use the `rmdir` program. For example,

```
$ rmdir jokes
```

removes the directory called `jokes` if it contains no files or directories. You have to delete or move the contents of a directory before you can delete it.

   Directory Commands: How Do They Work?   We have seen how a hard disk appears to be a tree of directories, each linked to one above it and each containing any number of directories below it. Each directory can contain files. A user can *travel* through this structure, changing from one directory to another, creating new directories here and there, and deleting directories.

   How does this all work, though? A hard disk is just a stack of metal platters that can store patterns of magnetism. Where are the directories? What does it mean for you to be "in your home directory"? What does it mean for you to be in another directory?

Lots of people can be logged into one Unix machine, and all those people can be in different directories or all in the same directory if they please. Does it get crowded if they all jam into one directory?

How can one write programs that navigate through this structure? What role does the kernel play in creating this tree model?

1.4.4   Working with Files

Directories provide a storage system for files. Users have personal files they store in and below their home directories. The system has files it stores in system directories.

What can a user do with files? We begin by looking at some basic operations.

Commands for Working with Files

Names of Files - a brief introduction

Files have names. On most versions of Unix, filenames can be quite long, up to about 250 characters. Filenames may contain any character except for the "/" character. They may contain upper and lower case letters, and the difference matters. They may contain punctuation marks, spaces, tabs, and even carriage returns.

cat, more, less, pg - examine file contents

A file contains data. Use the commands cat, more, or less to view the contents of a file. cat displays the entire contents of a file:

```
$ cat shopping-list
soap
cornflakes
milk
apples
jam
$
```

If a file is longer than a screenful, you can use more to page through the file one screen at a time:

```
$ more longfile
```

At the end of each screenful, you may press the space bar to see the next screenful, the Enter key to see the next line, or the "q" key to quit. The commands less and pg are available on some systems; they are similar to more.

cp - make a copy of a file

To make a copy of a file, use the cp command. For example,

```
$ cp shopping-list last.week.list
```

makes a new file called last.week.list and copies the contents of shopping-list into that new file.

rm - delete a file

To remove a file from a directory, use the rm command. For example,

```
$ rm old.data junk shopping.june1992
```

removes three files.

Unix does not have an undelete feature. Many people can use the system at the same time. When you delete a file, the system may immediately give that disk space to another user. Disk space that only seconds ago contained your term paper may now contain source code to someone else's C program.

mv - rename or move a file

To rename a file or to move a file to a different directory, use the mv command. For example,

```
$ mv prog1.c first_program.c
```

changes the name of prog1.c to first_program.c.

You can also move a program to a different directory by giving a directory name as the last argument:

```
$ mkdir mycode
$ mv first_program.c mycode
```

lpr, lp - print file on paper

You can print a file on paper by using the lpr command. The simplest form is

```
$ lpr filename
```

which sends the named file to the default printer. Many systems have more than one printer, and the lpr command has a more complicated form that allows you to specify which printer you want to use. Please see the documentation for your local system for details. On some systems, the command may be lp.

File Commands: How Do They Work?   Users think of a file as a bunch of information, usually a document. A document contains page after page of line after line of characters. How are these stored on a disk? How does one make a copy of a file? How can a file be moved from one directory to another? How does the system rename a file? For that matter, how does a file have a name? You, the reader, have a name; where do you keep it? Unix has to address all these questions. You, as a system programmer, need to understand how it all works.

File Permission Attributes

You have some files, other users have their files, and the people who run the system have their system files. You may not want people to change or perhaps even read your files. The people who run the system do not want users to change system files or make a mess of system directories.

To allow users to control access to their files, Unix assigns to each file several attributes. A file has an *owner*, and a file has *file permission attributes*. The owner of a file is a user on the system. You are the owner of files you create. Other users own files they create.

Every file has three groups of file permission attributes. The `ls -l` command shows attributes of a file:

```
$ ls -l outline.01
-rwxr-x---    1 molay      users     1064 Jun 29 00:39 outline.01
```

This is the *long* version of the output of `ls`. The `-l` is called a *command line option*. You modify the behavior of Unix commands by specifying these options when you run the command. This longer, optional output from `ls` includes the permission information, the name of the owner of the file, the size of the file, and the modification date and time. The string of dashes and letters at the left side of the output of `ls -l` represents the file permission bits.

Every file has an owner and three groups of file permission attributes:

```
- r w x    r w x    r w x      r: read, w: write, x:execute
  user     group    other
```

The world of users is divided into three categories: the user who owns the file, the group to which the user belongs, and the other people. Users in each of these three categories may be granted access to read the file, write to the file, or execute the file. These nine attributes are independent. You may, for example, give other people permission to modify a file but not to read it. You can even deny *yourself* permission to read one of your own files.

File Permissions: How Do They Work? How do permission bits work? How do you set up these permission attributes? How does Unix enforce these policies? Where are these permission bits stored? We explore and explain these topics in later chapters.

1.5 UNIX FROM THE LARGER PERSPECTIVE

1.5.1 Connections between Users and Programs

In the previous section, we looked at the user view of what Unix *does*, and we began to ask how it works. A user logs in, runs programs, works with files and directories, and logs out. At the same time, though, lots of other users can log in, run programs, work with their files and directories, and log out. Users can work with the same files and directories, users can send e-mail or instant messages to one another. Each user works in a private space, but that private space is part of a larger system.

We shall explore how this all works and see how to write programs that work in this larger system. What is this *larger system*? This larger system is one that consists of more than one user, more than one program, more than one computer, and the connections among these people, programs, and computers.

We now look at three examples to see some of the ideas and questions that arise in this larger view of programming.

1.5.2   Internet Bridge Tournaments

A lot of people play bridge on the Internet. People sit down at their computers, connect to a bridge site, and look for a game. Once the players join a game, four people sitting at computers around the world look at screens that show a common table, share common decks of cards, and each can see what he or she has been dealt. Here is a simple picture:

FIGURE 1.9

Four people play bridge over the Internet.

Figure 1.9 shows four people, each at a computer, each computer connected to a single communication line: the Internet.

This picture is missing the bridge table, so we add that in Figure 1.10.

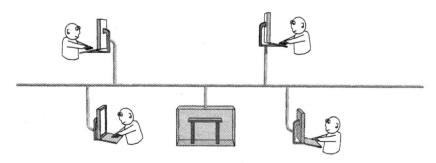

FIGURE 1.10

The bridge table on a server computer.

There is now, on the network, a fifth entity. This *bridge table* contains the decks of cards that are used in the games. It is the *surface* on which the visible cards are displayed. It is the *place* people gather around in order to play a game.

When cards are dealt in a physical game, actual cards are passed from one person to another. When cards are dealt in this virtual game, what gets passed from where and to whom? Where are the cards? What does it mean to hold cards in your hand? How can a program prevent two people from being dealt the same cards? In the real world, that is not a big problem; in the virtual world, cards lack the physical integrity that prevents one from being in two places at once.

Figure 1.11 shows some of the communication paths:

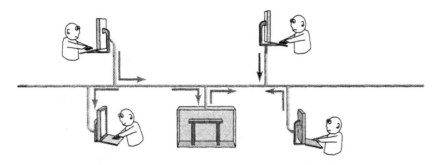

FIGURE 1.11

Separate programs send messages to each other.

This bridge example introduces the following three topics, which are important in much Unix system programming:

Communication

How does one user or process communicate with another user or process?

Coordination

Two players can not take cards from the deck at the same time. How can a program establish coordination between processes so they share resources correctly?

Network Access

In this example, programs on separate user computers communicate over the Internet. How can a program connect to other programs using the Internet? How does a program gain access to the Internet?

1.5.3   bc: The Secret Life of a Unix Desk Calculator

Every version of Unix comes with a calculator program called bc, a simple, text-based calculator with two fascinating characteristics. To start the program, just type

```
$ bc
```

There is no prompt, no version number, no sign-on message. It just sits there waiting to do some math. Type in an expression and press the Enter key:

```
2+3*4+5*10
```

bc prints out the correct answer. It knows to do multiplication before doing addition. To exit from bc, press Ctrl-D.

One fascinating thing about bc is that it can handle very large integers, such as

```
9999999999999999999 * 8888888888888888888
88888888888888888887111111111111111111112
```

You can use exponents to generate really big numbers:

```
3333 ^ 44
1011006158449564099500589848918228579482240528849807070336511179476 9\
4389041106492529115438146889072194814220900468838187035540915541156 3\
21805747562427309521
```

If you raise 3333 to the exponent 44, you get a number represented by two-and-a-half lines of decimal digits. Experiment with bc to see how large a number bc can handle.

bc is also a programming language with variables, loops, and a C-like syntax. For example, the following code is acceptable to bc:

```
x = 3
if ( x == 3 ){
    y = x * 3;
}
y
```

Here is the other interesting thing about the bc program. bc is not a calculator; it does not do any calculations. To see what is going on, try this:

```
$ bc
2 + 3
5
<-- press Ctrl-Z here

Stopped
$ ps
PID    TTY    S           TIME CMD
25102 ttyp2   T        0:00.02 bc
27081 ttyp2   T        0:00.01 dc -
27560 ttyp2   I        0:00.59 -bash
27681 ttyp2   T        0:00.00 bc
$ fg
<-- press Ctrl-D here
```

The ps program lists the processes you are running. This display shows four processes. One is "-bash," a log-in shell. There are two programs running called bc and one that says dc -. What is this dc program?

The on-line manual is provided with most versions of Unix. To read the manual page about the dc command, type

```
$ man dc
User Commands dc(1)

NAME
     dc - desk calculator

SYNOPSIS
     dc [ filename ]

DESCRIPTION
     dc is an arbitrary precision arithmetic package. Ordinarily
     it operates on decimal integers, but one may specify an
     input base, output base, and a number of fractional digits
     to be maintained. The overall structure of dc is a stacking
     (reverse Polish) calculator. If an argument is given, input
     is taken from that file until its end, then from the standard
     input.
```

This page comes from the SunOS 5.8 manual; most versions of Unix come with a similar description of this command. This page says dc is a calculator. Furthermore, it says that dc is a stacking, reverse-Polish calculator. It expects the user to type in the numbers first and the operation later. Adding 2 + 3 looks like the following:

```
2
3
+
p
5
```

That is, you push a 2 on the stack, then you push a 3 on the stack, then you add the top two items on the stack, then you print the value that is on the top of the stack. If dc is a calculator, and dc is a stack-based calculator, who is bc, and why is dc running?

The answer becomes clear if you read the manual for bc. The manual says that bc is a preprocessor for dc.[1] bc is a parser. It communicates with a process running dc through a communication system called *pipes*, shown in Figure 1.12.

User input such as "2 + 2" flows into the bc process. bc translates that into the stack syntax and sends it to dc. dc does the math and sends back the result. bc then formats that result for the end user. The user thinks bc is a calculator.

---

[1]The GNU version of bc uses an internal stack-based calculator instead of dc.

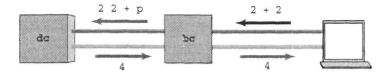

FIGURE 1.12

Programs send messages to each other.

This bc/dc example is another program that, like Internet bridge, involves different processes and some sort of communication and cooperation. The separate programs work together as a system; each part does one specific task. Each part is clearly separate from the others; the interprocess communication is as much a part of the system as the individual programs are.

The similarities between Internet bridge and the bc/dc system are the fundamental principles of Unix system programming. Learning Unix system programming, therefore, consists of learning how to build these separate programs and how to build the connections and cooperation.

1.5.4   From bc/dc to the Web

It is a short step from the bc/dc pair to the World Wide Web. In the bc/dc pair, bc is the user interface and dc is the engine that does the work. With the World Wide Web, the browser is the user interface and the Web server does the work. The architecture is exactly the same:

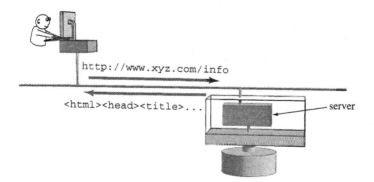

FIGURE 1.13

Separate programs send messages to each other.

The user interacts with the browser. The browser is not where the Web pages are; the Web pages are on servers. The servers speak a terse, text-based language called HTTP, just as dc speaks a terse, text-based language called RPN. The user agent (bc, or the browser) translates user input (2 + 3, mouse clicks) into the terse, text-based language and sends the request to the engine (dc, the web server). The user agent (bc, browser) receives the reply from the server and formats it for the user.

There is no conceptual difference between the original bc/dc model and the World Wide Web. It is probably no coincidence that the Web first grew up on Unix systems.[2]

1.6   CAN I TRY TO DO ONE?

We have now looked at the first two questions. We looked at several aspects of Unix and asked, "What does that do?" We have asked, "How does that work?" In a few cases, such as bc/dc, we saw at least a partial answer.

The third question in our approach is "Can I try to do one?" In this section, we write a version of the Unix more program.

First, "What does more do?"

more displays a file one screenful at a time. Most Unix systems come with a large text file called /etc/termcap used by some editors and video games. If you want to page through this file, you can type

```
$ more /etc/termcap
```

You will see the first screenful of the file. At the bottom of the screen, the more program will print, in reverse video, the percentage of the file you have seen. You may press the space bar to see the next page, you may press the Enter key to see the next line, you may press the letter "q" to quit, and you may press "h" to see the help screen.

Notice that you do not have to press the Enter key after pressing the space bar or "q" or "h." The program responds at once.

The three ways to invoke more from the command line are as follows:

```
$ more filename
$ command | more
$ more < filename
```

In the first case, more displays the contents of the named file. In the second case, the program specified by *command* runs, and its output is displayed page by page. In the third case, more displays the contents of what it reads from standard input. Standard input happens to be attached to the specified file.

Second, "How does more work?"

After running more a few times, we can guess that the logic probably goes something like this:

```
+----> show 24 lines from input
| +--> print [more?] message
| |    Input Enter, SPACE, or q
| +--  if Enter, advance one line
+----  if SPACE
       if q --> exit
```

---

[2]By the way, it was Amy Chused, a student in my course, who pointed out the connection between bc/dc and all TCP/IP client-server programming.

Our program should be flexible about input, just like the real more. That is, if the user specifies a filename on the command line, we read from that file. If no filename is specified on the command line, the program reads from standard input.

Here is a first draft of our own version of more:

```
/* more01.c - version 0.1 of more
 *          read and print 24 lines then pause for a few special commands
 */
#include        <stdio.h>

#define PAGELEN 24
#define LINELEN 512

void do_more(FILE *);
int see_more();

int main( int ac , char *av[] )
{
        FILE *fp;
        if ( ac == 1 )
                do_more( stdin );
        else
                while ( --ac )
                        if ( (fp = fopen( *++av , "r" )) != NULL )
                        {
                                do_more( fp ) ;
                                fclose( fp );
                        }
                        else
                                exit(1);
        return 0;
}
void do_more( FILE *fp )
/*
 * read PAGELEN lines, then call see_more() for further instructions
 */
{
        char    line[LINELEN];
        int     num_of_lines = 0;
        int     see_more(), reply;

        while ( fgets( line, LINELEN, fp ) ){           /* more input    */
                if ( num_of_lines == PAGELEN ) {        /* full screen?  */
                        reply = see_more();             /* y: ask user   */
                        if ( reply == 0 )               /*    n: done     */
                                break;
                        num_of_lines -= reply;          /* reset count   */
                }
                if ( fputs( line, stdout ) == EOF )     /* show line      */
                        exit(1);                        /* or die         */
                num_of_lines++;                         /* count it       */
        }
```

```
        }
        int see_more()
        /*
         *      print message, wait for response, return # of lines to advance
         *      q means no, space means yes, CR means one line
         */
        {
                int     c;
                printf("\033[7m more? \033[m");              /* reverse on a vt100  */
                while( (c=getchar()) != EOF )                     /* get response */
                {
                        if ( c == 'q' )                  /* q -> N                  */
                                return 0;
                        if ( c == ' ' )                  /* ' ' => next page    */
                                return PAGELEN;          /* how many to show    */
                        if ( c == '\n' )                 /* Enter key => 1 line */
                                return 1;
                }
                return 0;
        }
```

The code consists of three functions. The main function decides whether to read data from a file or from standard input. Having settled on an input stream, main passes that input stream to the function called do_more to display that stream screenful by screenful. The do_more function, in turn, displays a screenful of text and then calls the function see_more to ask the user what to do next.

Compile and run it as follows:

```
$ cc more01.c -o more01
$ more01 more01.c
```

This program works pretty well. The program displays 24 lines of the file and prints, in eye-catching reverse video, the prompt |more?|. Press the Enter key to advance the display one line. This program needs more work.

In particular, the |more?| message stays on the screen and scrolls up with the text. Also, if you press the space bar or the "q" key, nothing happens until you press Enter. That's not so good. Also, the little |more?| message is still there.
Writing a version of more illustrates the basic fact about Unix programming:

> **Unix programming is not as difficult as you think it is, but it is not as easy as you first imagine.**

The program performs a clearly defined task. The logic behind that task is pretty clear from its action. Devising an algorithm that performs that action is not all that tricky.

Then we begin to see subtle problems. How do we get the program to respond to keystrokes without having to press Enter? How do we figure out the percent of the file we have displayed? How do we erase the |more?| prompt after the user presses a key?

That cannot be too tricky, but first we need to finish comparing other features. How well does our program handle input streams? The main function checks the number of command-line arguments. If no filenames are specified on the command line, the program reads from standard input. That makes it possible to put more at the end of a pipeline, as in

$ **who | more**

This *pipeline* runs the who command to list all users on the system and sends that list of users into the more command. The more program displays 24 lines at a time, a useful thing if the number of users exceeds 24. Let us test our program, not with who, but with ls:

$ **ls /bin | more01**

We expect to see the contents of the /bin directory, 24 lines at a time.

When you run this, you will see that more01 does *not* pause after 24 lines. What could have gone wrong? Here is the reason. Our more01 program reads and prints 24 lines of input from the ls command. When more01 reads the 25th line, it prints the more? prompt and waits for user input. Our program waits for the user to press the space bar, the Enter key or the letter "q."

Where does that user input come from? The program uses getchar, which reads from standard input. But the notation

$ **ls /bin | more01**

attaches the standard input of more01 to the output of ls. Our version of more tries to read user commands from the same stream as the data. The following picture shows the situation:

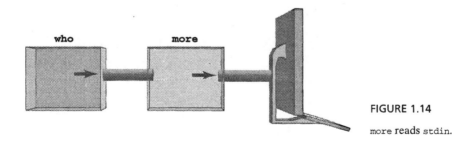

FIGURE 1.14

more reads stdin.

How does the real more solve this problem? That is, how can the program read data from standard input and still get user input from the keyboard? The answer is to read from the keyboard directly. Figure 1.15 illustrates what the real version of more does.

There is a special file in every Unix system called /dev/tty. This file is actually a connection to the keyboard and screen. Even if the user changes the standard input or standard output of a program by using the < or > characters, the program can still communicate with the terminal by reading and writing data to the /dev/tty file.

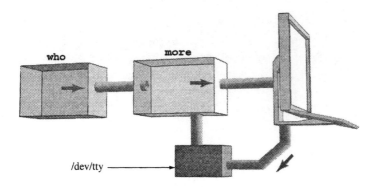

/dev/tty

FIGURE 1.15

who reads user input from a terminal.

The diagram shows more has two sources of input. The standard input of the program is attached to the output of who. But more also reads data from /dev/tty. more reads lines from the file and displays them on the screen. When it needs to ask the user whether to display one more line, one more page, or to quit, it reads the input from /dev/tty.

With this new knowledge, we can enhance more01.c to more02.c:

```
/* more02.c - version 0.2 of more
 *      read and print 24 lines then pause for a few special commands
 *      feature of version 0.2: reads from /dev/tty for commands
 */
#include        <stdio.h>

#define PAGELEN 24
#define LINELEN 512

void do_more(FILE *);
int see_more(FILE *);

int main( int ac , char *av[] )
{
        FILE *fp;

        if ( ac == 1 )
                do_more( stdin );
        else
                while ( --ac )
                        if ( (fp = fopen( *++av , "r" )) != NULL )
                        {
                                do_more( fp ) ;
                                fclose( fp );
                        }
                        else
                                exit(1);
        return 0;
}
void do_more( FILE *fp )
```

```
/*
 * read PAGELEN lines, then call see_more() for further instructions
 */
{
        char    line[LINELEN];
        int     num_of_lines = 0;
        int     see_more(FILE *), reply;
        FILE    *fp_tty;

        fp_tty = fopen( "/dev/tty", "r" );              /* NEW: cmd stream  */
        if ( fp_tty == NULL )                           /* if open fails    */
                exit(1);                                /* no use in running*/

        while ( fgets( line, LINELEN, fp ) ){           /* more input       */
                if ( num_of_lines == PAGELEN ) {        /* full screen?     */
                        reply = see_more(fp_tty);       /* NEW: pass FILE * */
                        if ( reply == 0 )               /*    n: done       */
                                break;
                        num_of_lines -= reply;          /* reset count      */
                }
                if ( fputs( line, stdout ) == EOF )     /* show line        */
                        exit(1);                        /* or die           */
                num_of_lines++;                         /* count it         */
        }
}
int see_more(FILE *cmd)                                 /* NEW: accepts arg */
/*
 * print message, wait for response, return # of lines to advance
 * q means no, space means yes, CR means one line
 */
{
        int     c;
        printf("\033[7m more? \033[m");                 /* reverse on a vt100  */
        while( (c=getc(cmd)) != EOF )                   /* NEW: reads from tty */
        {
                if ( c == 'q' )                         /* q -> N              */
                        return 0;
                if ( c == ' ' )                         /* ' ' => next page    */
                        return PAGELEN;                 /* how many to show    */
                if ( c == '\n' )                        /* Enter key => 1 line */
                        return 1;
        }
        return 0;
}
```

Compile and test this version:

```
$ cc -o more02 more02.c
$ ls /bin | more02
```

This version, `more02.c` can read data from standard input and still read commands from the keyboard. Notice how trying to write a standard Unix program led us to learn about the file called `/dev/tty` and its role as a direct connection to the user's terminal.

Our program still needs work. We still have to press the Enter key to get the program to respond. Also, the "q" and space characters show up on the screen. Somehow, the real version of `more` changes input so characters are delivered immediately to the program; the Enter key is not needed. The real `more` also arranged it so characters you type do not show up. If you press "q", the program quits, but you do not see the letter "q" on the screen.

Instant Input: How Does That Work?

It turns out that connections to terminals have settings. You can adjust the settings of the connection so characters are delivered as they are typed instead of only after the user presses Enter. You can adjust the settings so the characters the user types do not show up on the screen. You can adjust all sorts of settings that control the way the terminal delivers data to your program.

As we delve into this problem, more details emerge in our picture. Now, it looks like the following:

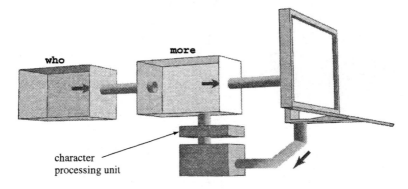

FIGURE 1.16

The connection to the terminal has settings.

The new item in this picture is the control unit added to the connection to `/dev/tty`. That control unit lets a programmer adjust how the connection between the program and the terminal works, the way dials and switches on a radio let you adjust how the connection between the tuner and the speaker works.

To write a complete, smoothly operating version of `more`, we need to study that connection control unit and how to program it.

We also need to answer some other questions. How do we find the percent of the file shown? The real version of `more` displays the percent of the file the user has seen. How can we add that feature? The operating system knows how large the file is. We just need to learn how to ask the operating system for that information.

What about the reverse video? What about the number of lines? Some displays use different methods to create reverse-video text. Different displays have different numbers of lines. A fixed size of 24 lines and the vt100-specific reverse-video codes lack flexibility. How can we write a version of more that works for any terminal type and any number of lines? We need to learn about terminal screen control and attributes.

1.7 A LOT OF QUESTIONS AND A MAP

1.7.1 What Now?

We have defined the project for this book. Unix is an operating system that allows several people to use the system at the same time. Users can run programs and work with files and directories. These programs can communicate with one another, within one computer, and across networks. Users run programs to manage their files, process data, transfer and transform data, and communicate with other users.

How do all these programs work? What do the programs do? What does the operating system do? As we explored the main features of the system, we asked many questions.

We now begin to answer these questions. Our case study of the more command demonstrates the approach we shall take. We look at a real program, study what it does, and then try to write our own version of it. In the process, we discover more details of how Unix works and learn to use those principles.

1.7.2 And Now for the Map

We need a map for our journey. Here it is:

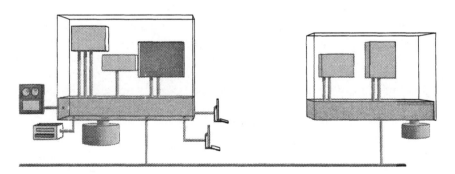

FIGURE 1.17

A diagram of the main structure of a Unix system.

This diagram of a Unix system depicts the main structure of any Unix system. The memory is divided into system space and user space. The kernel and its data structures occupy system space. User processes live in user space. Some users connect to the system through terminals; the lines to these terminals connect to the kernel. Files are stored in a file system on a disk. Devices of various sorts are attached to the kernel and made available to user processes. Finally, there is a network connection. Some users connect to the system through a network connection.

In each section of the book, we focus on parts of this diagram. We zoom in on each component to explore services the kernel offers and to explain the logic and data structures the kernel uses to provide those services.

By the end of the book, you will have studied each part of this picture and will have seen all the ideas and techniques needed to write complete Unix system programs—Internet bridge, for example.

1.7.3   What Is Unix? History and Dialects

This book explains basic ideas and structures of Unix and shows how to write programs that work in a Unix system. But what is Unix? Where did it come from? What exactly can you expect from this book?

First, where did Unix come from? Unix started as a kernel and set of tools created around 1969 at Bell Laboratories by a few computer scientists to solve specific technical problems. Unix was not a commercial product. In fact, during the 1970s, Bell Labs distributed Unix software, including complete source code, to schools and research centers for nominal fees. Researchers at Bell Labs and many other computer scientists spent years learning from, improving, and adding to the original programs. During the 1980s, several companies licensed Unix source code and built customized versions of the system. The two main centers of Unix development were AT&T and the University of California at Berkeley. AT&T developed a version called System V, and UCB developed versions collectively called BSD. Most varieties of Unix derived from one or both of these main versions. Over the years, ownership passed, in a sequence of sales, from AT&T through a sequence of companies, UCB stopped working on Unix, and various groups tried to reconcile and standardize the system.

Independent of deals and standards, the basic design and principles of Unix spread through academic and commercial computing. Different dialects and models of the system evolved. Some versions include specialized features, like real-time processing. Through all these adaptations and changes, Unix always retained a core architecture and consistent set of functions. Although the exact internal structure and set of tools in a version of Unix from AT&T in 1980 differ from those in a version of Unix written in Helsinki in 1991, system programs written for that 1980 version can, with minimal changes, compile and run on the Finnish version.

What, then, is Unix? The term a *Unix system*, increasingly is used to refer to systems that follow the core structure and provide the functions common to all these variations. Some systems look like and work like Unix, but are not derived from AT&T or UCB code. The GNU/Linux combination of tools and kernel is a well-known Unix-like system. One formal description of the system interface is called POSIX. To understand, read, and write Unix programs, you need to know more than a single standard, though.

Unix has a long and varied history; how much of Unix can you expect to learn about from one book? We concentrate on structure, principles, and techniques common to all Unix systems. Some details are left out, some operations are duplicated, and all ideas are explained in practical contexts.

I do not include every detail, and sometimes I suggest you check local documentation. This book is not a comprehensive reference on every aspect of every version of

Unix. In fact, exploring and using on-line documentation to learn about your system is an essential part of knowing about Unix.

Sometimes I describe different functions that do the same thing. One cause of duplication of functions is the decentralized growth of Unix. Different groups, like the ones at AT&T and UCB, sometimes devised different solutions to the same problem. Another cause of duplicate functions is normal growth. When people replace a Unix service, such as alarm timers, with a more flexible version, they do not want to break existing programs, so they rarely remove the older, simpler interface. Sometimes I mention one solution, sometimes more than one. As you study Unix programs, you will encounter these various solutions. Studying various approaches can clarify the fundamental ideas and help you adapt to local variations.

Finally, I present Unix in the context of actual software projects. Unix is a system of ideas and techniques created by people building solutions to real problems. We start with real problems and see how the ideas provide solutions. Unix makes sense when you see how the pieces work as a system.

SUMMARY

- A computer system includes several types of resources such as disk storage, memory, peripheral devices, and network connections. Programs use these resources to store, transfer, and process data.
- Computer systems that run several programs for several users at the same time require a central management program. The Unix kernel is a program that schedules programs and controls access to resources.
- User programs ask the kernel for access to resources.
- Some Unix programs consist of separate programs that share or exchange data.
- Writing systems programs requires an understanding of the structure and use of kernel services.

C H A P T E R   2

Users, Files, and the Manual
who Is First

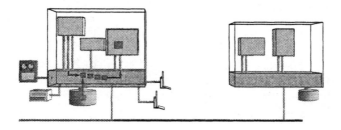

OBJECTIVES

Ideas and Skills

- The role and use of on-line documentation
- The Unix file interface: open, read, write, lseek, close
- Reading, creating, and writing files
- File descriptors
- Buffering: user level and kernel level
- Kernel mode, user mode, and the cost of system calls
- How Unix represents time, how to format Unix time
- Using the utmp file to find list of current users
- Detecting and reporting errors in system calls

System Calls and Functions

- open, read, write, creat, lseek, close
- perror

Commands

- man
- who
- cp
- login

2.1   INTRODUCTION

Who else is using the system? Is it crowded? Is my friend logged on? Every multiuser computer system has a who command. The command tells you who else is using the computer. How does it work?

In this chapter, we explore the who command in Unix. In doing so, we learn how to use Unix to process files. In addition to learning about Unix, we shall see how to learn *from* Unix. That is, we see how to use a Unix system as a reference manual about itself.

2.2   ASKING ABOUT who

Recall this picture of a Unix system:

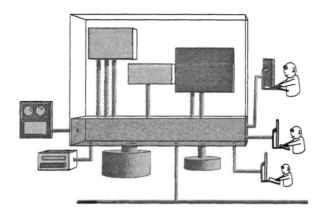

FIGURE 2.1

Users, files, processes, devices, and kernel.

The large box is computer memory; it is divided into user space and system space. Users connect to the system from terminals. This system has two hard disks, shown as large cylinders, and one printer. Various programs are running in user space. These programs communicate to the outside world through the kernel. The lines from the processes to the kernel represent these communication channels.

For our first project, we shall study the who command. We ask,

1. What does who do?
2. How does who work?
3. Can I write who?

2.2.1   Commands Are Programs

Before we start, it is important to know that almost all Unix commands, like who and ls, are simply programs written by a variety of people, usually in C. When you type ls, you are asking your shell to run the program named ls. The ls program lists the names of files in the directory. If you do not like what ls does, you can write your own version of the command and use it instead.

Adding new commands to Unix is easy. You write a new program and have the executable file stored in one of the standard system directories such as /bin, /usr/bin, /usr/local/bin. Many Unix commands began life as a program someone wrote to solve a particular problem. Others found it useful, and it gradually found its way onto more and more Unix machines. Perhaps your version of who will someday be the standard.

2.3   QUESTION 1: WHAT DOES who DO?

If we want to know who is using the system, we type the command who:

```
$ who
heckerl      ttyp1      Jul 21 19:51    (tide75.surfcity.com)
nlopez       ttyp2      Jul 21 18:11    (roam163-141.student.ivy.edu)
dgsulliv     ttyp3      Jul 21 14:18    (h004005a8bd64.ne.mediaone.net)
ackerman     ttyp4      Jul 15 22:40    (asd1-254.fas.state.edu)
wwchen       ttyp5      Jul 21 19:57    (circle.square.edu)
barbier      ttyp6      Jul  8 13:08    (labpc18.elsie.special.edu)
ramakris     ttyp7      Jul 13 08:51    (roam157-97.student.ivy.edu)
czhu         ttyp8      Jul 21 12:47    (spa.sailboat.edu)
bpsteven     ttyp9      Jul 21 18:26    (207.178.203.99)
molay        ttypa      Jul 21 20:00    (xyz73-200.harvard.edu)
$
```

Each line represents one log-in session. The first item on the line is the *username* of the user, the next column is the name of the terminal at which the user is logged in, the third part tells when the person logged in, and the last part tells from where the user logged in. Some versions of who do not show the name of the remote computer unless you request it.

2.3.1   Reading the Manual

Running who provides some information about what the command does. To learn a lot more about what a command does, consult the on-line manual.

Every Unix system comes with documentation for all commands. Once, Unix came with a printed manual with a page or two for each command. Now, the manual is on the disk, and the command to read a page from the manual is man.[1] To read the manual page on the who command, type

```
$ man who
who(1)                                                              who(1)

NAME

   who - Identifies users currently logged in

SYNOPSIS

   who [-a]   |[-AbdhHlmMpqrstTu] [file]

   who am i

   who am I

   whoami
```

---

[1] Some Unix software supplements the traditional man documentation with references using the info system or with a linked collection of HTML pages.

The who command displays information about users and processes on the local system.

STANDARDS

Interfaces documented on this reference page conform to industry standards as follows:

who: XPG4, XPG4-UNIX

Refer to the standards(5) reference page for more information about industry standards and associated tags.

OPTIONS

-a Specifies all options; processes /var/adm/utmp or the named file with all options on. Equivalent to using the -b, -d, -l, -p, -r, -t, -T, and -u options.

more (10%)

All manual pages, often called *manpages*, have the same basic format. The top line tells the name of the command and the section of the manual in which it appears. This example shows who (1); the command is called who and the section number is 1. Section 1 contains documentation for all the user commands. Check the manual on your system to see what the other sections of the manual contain.

The NAME section of a manpage contains the name of the command and a one-line summary of what the command does.

The SYNOPSIS section shows how to use the command. It shows what to type and lists the arguments and options the command accepts. An *option* is usually a dash followed by one or more letters. These *command line options* affect how the command operates.

Manpages use square brackets ([-a]) to indicate items that may be included but are not required by the command. This page for who shows that you can type who by itself, you can type who -a (pronounced *who dash a*), or you can type who followed by a dash and any combination of AbdhHlmMpqrsTu, followed by a filename if you like.

The manpage also shows who accepts the following three other forms:

```
who am i
who am I
whoami
```

You can read about these alternate forms in the manual, or you can try them.

The DESCRIPTION section describes what the command does. These descriptions vary from command to command and from one flavor of Unix to another. Some are terse, but precise. Some contain more details and several examples. In any case, they describe all the features of the command and are the authoritative reference.

The OPTIONS section lists each of the command-line options and what each does. Back in the *Olden Days*®, each Unix command was simple. Each did one thing and had one or two options. Over the years, many commands developed new features, each activated by a different command-line option. Some commands, like this version of who, have accrued a lot of options.

The SEE ALSO section contains a list of related topics in the manual. Some manpages contain a BUGS section.

2.4   QUESTION 2: HOW DOES who DO IT?

We saw that who displays information about the users who are currently logged in. The manpage describes all the things who can do and how to get it to do them. How does who work? How does who do it?

You might suspect a system program like who uses special system functions. It might involve advanced administrator privileges. You might need to get a system developer kit, including a CD-ROM, thick books, and secret codes. It might run into money.

Actually, complete documentation of the operation of the who command is on the system itself. You simply need to know where to look.

Learning about Unix from Unix

You can learn about any Unix command by using these four techniques:

- Read the manual
- Search the manual
- Read the .h files
- follow SEE ALSO links

We shall use all these techniques to learn about the who command.

Read the Manual

To learn about who, type

$ **man who**

and page down to the DESCRIPTION section. This paragraph appears in the SunOS manpage:

```
DESCRIPTION
     The who utility can list the  user's  name,  terminal  line,
     login  time,  elapsed  time  since  activity occurred on the
     line, and the process-ID of the command interpreter  (shell)
     for   each  current  UNIX  system  user.   It  examines  the
     /var/adm/utmp file to obtain its information.   If  file  is
     given,  that file (which must be in utmp(4) format) is exam-
     ined.  Usually, file will be /var/adm/wtmp, which contains a
     history  of all the logins since the file was last created.
```

That tells the whole story. who examines the /var/adm/utmp file to obtain its information. It appears, from this description, that the list of current users is stored in a file. who just reads the file. How do we learn about this file? We can search the manual.

Search the Manual

The man command allows you to search the manual for keywords. Use the -k option for searching. To find out more about 'utmp', type

```
$ man -k utmp
endutent        getutent (3c)   - access utmp file entry
endutxent       getutxent (3c)  - access utmpx file entry
getutent        getutent (3c)   - access utmp file entry
getutid         getutent (3c)   - access utmp file entry
getutline       getutent (3c)   - access utmp file entry
getutmp         getutxent (3c)  - access utmpx file entry
getutmpx        getutxent (3c)  - access utmpx file entry
getutxent       getutxent (3c)  - access utmpx file entry
getutxid        getutxent (3c)  - access utmpx file entry
getutxline      getutxent (3c)  - access utmpx file entry
pututline       getutent (3c)   - access utmp file entry
pututxline      getutxent (3c)  - access utmpx file entry
setutent        getutent (3c)   - access utmp file entry
setutxent       getutxent (3c)  - access utmpx file entry
ttyslot         ttyslot (3c)    - find the slot in the utmp file of the
                                  current user
updwtmp         getutxent (3c)  - access utmpx file entry
updwtmpx        getutxent (3c)  - access utmpx file entry
utmp            utmp (4)        - utmp and wtmp entry formats
utmp2wtmp       acct (1m)       - overview of accounting and
                                  miscellaneous accounting commands
utmpd           utmpd (1m)      - utmp and utmpx monitoring daemon
utmpname        getutent (3c)   - access utmp file entry
utmpx           utmpx (4)       - utmpx and wtmpx entry formats
utmpxname       getutxent (3c)  - access utmpx file entry
wtmp            utmp (4)        - utmp and wtmp entry formats
wtmpx           utmpx (4)       - utmpx and wtmpx entry formats
$
```

This output was generated on a SunOS machine. The output is likely to be different on different installations. Each line of output lists the topic, the title of the manpage, and a brief description. The entry marked utmp with the label utmp and wtmp entry formats looks like what we need. Some of the other entries sound useful, and we might visit them later.

The notation utmp (4) means the manpage for utmp is in section 4 of the manual. Include that number when using the man command:

```
$ man 4 utmp
utmp(4)                                                           utmp(4)

NAME
     utmp, wtmp - Login records
```

```
SYNOPSIS

   #include <utmp.h>

DESCRIPTION

   The utmp file records information about who is currently using the
   system.
   The file is a sequence of utmp entries, as defined in struct utmp in the
   utmp.h file.

   The utmp structure gives the name of the special file associated with
   the user's terminal, the user's login name, and the time of the login
   in the form of time(3). The ut_type field is the type of entry, which
   can specify several symbolic constant values. The symbolic constants
   are defined in the utmp.h file.

   The wtmp file records all logins and logouts.  A null user name
   indicates a logout on the associated terminal.  A terminal referenced
   with a tilde (~) indicates that the system was rebooted at the
   indicated time. The adjacent pair of entries with terminal names
   referenced by a vertical bar (|) or a right brace (}) indicate the
   system-maintained time just before and just after a date command has
   changed the system's time frame.

   The wtmp file is maintained by login(1) and init(8).  Neither of these
   pro-grams creates the file, so, if it is removed, record keeping is
   turned off. See ac(8) for information on the file.

FILES

   /usr/include/utmp.h

   /var/adm/utmp
```

more (88%)

We are closing in quickly on how who works. The first manpage said who reads the utmp file. This manpage, the one for utmp says the utmp file is *a sequence of* utmp *entries as defined in* struct utmp *in the* utmp.h file. The file is a sequence of records, an array, each of a structure defined in utmp.h. Where is this utmp.h file?

We are in luck. The FILES section of the manpage tells us. It says the file is /usr/include/utmp.h.

Before we advance to the next technique (read the .h files), notice some of the other information on this manpage. This page mentions a wtmp file that records all logins and logouts. It refers to commands called login(1), init(8), and ac(8). These might be interesting topics to pursue later.

Learning about Unix from the manual is like searching the Web for a particular subject. As you read various pages, you find other links that introduce you to related, interesting, and useful topics. We have our mission, though, so we study the <utmp.h> file.

Read the .h files

The manpage for utmp says the structure of the records in the utmp file is described in /usr/include/utmp.h. On most Unix machines, the header files for system information are stored in the directory called /usr/include. When the C compiler sees a line such as

```
#include   <stdio.h>
```

it looks for that file in /usr/include. We use more to read the file:

```
$ more /usr/include/utmp.h

   . . .

#define UTMP_FILE           "/var/adm/utmp"
#define WTMP_FILE           "/var/adm/wtmp"

#include <sys/types.h>   /* for pid_t, time_t */

/*
 * Structure of utmp and wtmp files.
 *
 * Assuming these numbers is unwise.
 */
#define ut_name ut_user                         /* compatibility */
struct utmp {
        char    ut_user[32];          /* User login name */
        char    ut_id[14];            /* /etc/inittab id- IDENT_LEN in
                                       * init */
        char    ut_line[32];          /* device name (console, lnxx) */
        short   ut_type;              /* type of entry */
        pid_t   ut_pid;               /* process id */
        struct exit_status {
            short         e_termination;  /* Process termination status */
            short         e_exit;         /* Process exit status */
        } ut_exit;                    /* The exit status of a process
                                       * marked as DEAD_PROCESS.
                                       */
        time_t  ut_time;              /* time entry was made */
        char    ut_host[64];          /* host name same as
                                       * MAXHOSTNAMELEN */
};
/* Definitions for ut_type                                           */

utmp.h  (60%)
```

After skipping messages and other introductory material, we find this structure definition. Log-in records, it appears, consist of eight members. The ut_user array stores the user log-in name. The ut_line array stores the *device*, which means the terminal from which the user connected. A few lines later in the struct are ut_time to store the log-in time and ut_host to store the name of the remote computer.

This struct contains other members. These do not correspond to items who displays, but they may come in handy in some situations.

The structure of the utmp record on your system may be different from this one. The utmp.h file on your system, though, will describe the format of the utmp data on your system. The names of the fields in the structure are usually the same across flavors of Unix, but the line marked "compatibility" shows that they vary sometimes. Header files are usually well commented, and the comments contain useful information.

2.4.1   We Now Know How who Works

By reading the on-line manual on the topics of who and utmp and by reading the header file /usr/include/utmp.h, we learned how who works. who reads structures from a file. The file contains one structure for each log-in session. We know the exact layout of the structure. The flow of information is shown in Figure 2.2.

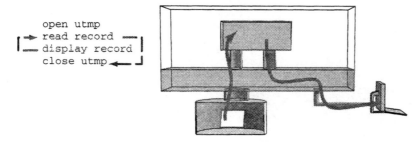

```
        open utmp
      read record
      display record
        close utmp
```

FIGURE 2.2

Data flow in the who command.

The file is an array, so who must read the records and print out the information. The simplest logic would be to read and print them one by one. Could it be that easy?

We have not looked at the source code for a version of who, but we have been able to learn all about the command from the on-line information. The manual tells us what the command does, and the header files show the data structure it uses.

The only way to see if you really understand something is to try it yourself.

2.5   QUESTION 3: CAN I WRITE who?

In the next part of this chapter, we craft a program that works just like who. We continue learning from on-line documentation, and we test our program by comparing its output to the output of the version of who on our system. Our analysis of the program so far shows that there are only two tasks we need to program:

• Read structs from a file
• Display the information stored in a struct

2.5.1   Question: How Do I Read Structs from a File?

You use `getc` and `fgets` to read chars and lines from a file. What about structs of raw data? We could use `getc` to read in a struct char by char, but that sounds tedious. We want to read in complete structs from the disk.

Let's Read the Manual!

We want to find manpages about `file` and `read`. The `-k` option accepts only one keyword, so we pick one of the keywords and try

```
$ man -k file
```

to see what topics show up. There are a *lot* of topics about files. On my system, that command just printed out 537 lines. We want to search those 537 lines for lines that contain the word "read." The Unix command called `grep` prints out lines that contain a specified pattern. We use `grep` in a pipeline as follows:

```
$ man -k file | grep read
_llseek (2)             - reposition read/write file offset
fileevent (n)           - Execute a script when a channel becomes readable
                          or writable
gftype (1)              - translate a generic font file for humans to read
lseek (2)               - reposition read/write file offset
macsave (1)             - Save Mac files read from standard input
read (2)                - read from a file descriptor
readprofile (1)         - a tool to read kernel profiling information
scr_dump, scr_restore, scr_init, scr_set (3) - read (write) a curses
screen from (to) a file
tee (1)                 - read from standard input and write to standard
                          output and files
$
```

The most promising item in this list is `read(2)`. The others all sound like they are about other topics.

Look at the manpage in section 2 about `read`:

```
$ man 2 read
READ(2)                     System calls                     READ(2)

NAME
        read - read from a file descriptor

SYNOPSIS
        #include <unistd.h>

        ssize_t read(int fd, void *buf, size_t count);

DESCRIPTION
        read() attempts to read up to count bytes from file
        descriptor fd into the buffer starting at buf.
```

If count is zero, read() returns zero and has no other
results. If count is greater than SSIZE_MAX, the result
is unspecified.

RETURN VALUE

On success, the number of bytes   read   is   returned   (zero
indicates   end of file), and the file position is advanced
by this number.   It is not an   error   if   this   number   is
smaller   than the number of bytes requested; this may happen for example because fewer bytes are actually available
right   now (maybe because we were close to end-of-file, or
because we are reading from a pipe, or from   a   terminal),
or   because read() was interrupted by a signal.   On error,
-1 is returned, and errno is set   appropriately.   In   this
case   it is left unspecified whether the file position (if
any) changes.

This system call allows us to read a specified number of bytes from a file into a buffer.
We want to read one struct at a time, so we can use   `sizeof(struct utmp)`   to specify
the number of bytes to read. This manpage says that `read` reads from a file descriptor.
How do we get one of those? Looking through the `read` manpage, we see the following
in the last part:

RELATED INFORMATION (called SEE ALSO in some versions)

Functions: fcntl(2), creat(2), dup(2), ioctl(2), getmsg(2), lockf(3),
lseek(2), mtio(7), open(2), pipe(2), poll(2), socket(2), socketpair(2),
termios(4), streamio(7), opendir(3) lockf(3)

Standards: standards(5)

This page contains a reference to `open(2)`. Running

    man 2 open

reveals how `open` works. The page for `open` refers to `close`. By examining the on-line
manual, we find the three pieces we need to read structs from a file.

2.5.2   Answer: Use `open`, `read`, and `close`

We can use these three system calls to extract log-in records from the utmp file. The
manual pages for these topics can be pretty dense. These calls have many options and
some complex behavior when used with pipes, devices, and other sources of data. The
basic facts are distilled and presented below.

Opening a file: `open`

The `open` system call creates a connection between a process and a file. That connection is called a *file descriptor* and is depicted in Figure 2.3 as a tunnel from the process
to the kernel.

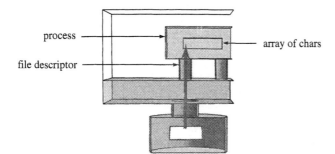

process —

file descriptor —

array of chars

FIGURE 2.3

A file descriptor is a connection to a file.

The basic usage of the open call is as follows:

open		
PURPOSE	Creates a connection to a file	
INCLUDE	#include <fcntl.h>	
USAGE	int fd = open(char *name, int how)	
ARGS	name	name of file
	how	O_RDONLY, O_WRONLY, or O_RDWR
RETURNS	-1	on error
	int	on success

To open a file, specify the name of the file and the type of connection you want. The three types are a connection for *reading*, a connection for *writing*, and a connection for *reading and writing*. The header file /usr/include/fcntl.h contains the definitions of O_RDONLY, O_WRONLY, and O_RDWR.

Opening a file is a kernel service. The open system call is a request from your program to the kernel. If the kernel detects an error, it returns the value −1.

There are many sorts of errors. The file might not exist. It might exist, but you might not have permission to read it. It might be in a directory to which you do not have access. The manpage for open lists all the errors. We examine error handling later in this chapter.

What if the file is already open? That is, what if another process is working with the file? Unix does not prevent several processes from opening the same file at the same time. If it did, two different users could not run who at the same time.

If things go well, the kernel returns a small positive integer. This number is called a *file descriptor* and is the identifier for the connection. You may open several files at the same time. Each connection is assigned a unique file descriptor. Your program may even open the same file several times; each connection is assigned a different file descriptor.

You use the file descriptor for all operations on the connection.

Reading Data from a File: read

You can read data from a file descriptor into a process:

read	
PURPOSE	Transfer up to qty bytes from fd to buf
INCLUDE	#include <unistd.h>
USAGE	ssize_t numread = read(int fd, void *buf, size_t qty)
ARGS	fd source of data buf destination for data qty number of bytes to transfer
RETURNS	-1 on error numread on success

The read system call asks the kernel to transfer *qty* bytes of data from the file descriptor *fd* to the array *buf* in the memory space of the calling process. The kernel does what it can and returns a result. If the request fails, read returns −1. Otherwise, the call returns the number of bytes transferred.

Why would you get fewer bytes than the number you ask for? The file might not have as many bytes as you ask. For example, if you ask for 1000 bytes and the file only contains 500 bytes, you are likely to get 500 bytes. When you reach end of file, read returns zero, since there are no more bytes to read.

What sort of errors can read encounter? The manpage lists the errors available on your system.

Closing a File: close

When you are done reading or writing data to a file descriptor, you close it. The close call is as follows:

close	
PURPOSE	Closes a file
INCLUDE	#include <unistd.h>
USAGE	int result = close(int fd)
ARGS	fd file descriptor
RETURNS	-1 on error 0 on success

The `close` system call hangs up the connection specified by file descriptor *fd*. `close` returns -1 on error. For example, trying to close a file descriptor that does not refer to an open file is an error. Other errors are described in the manual.

2.5.3   Writing `who1.c`

We are almost there. We have an idea of how who works, and we have the three system calls we need to connect to a file, extract chunks of data from a file, and close a file. The top-level code looks like the following:

```
/* who1.c  - a first version of the who program
 *               open, read UTMP file, and show results
 */
#include        <stdio.h>
#include        <utmp.h>
#include        <fcntl.h>
#include        <unistd.h>

#define SHOWHOST            /* include remote machine on output */

int main()
{
        struct utmp     current_record; /* read info into here       */
        int             utmpfd;         /* read from this descriptor */
        int             reclen = sizeof(current_record);

        if ( (utmpfd = open(UTMP_FILE, O_RDONLY)) == -1 ){
                perror( UTMP_FILE );    /* UTMP_FILE is in utmp.h    */
                exit(1);
        }
        while ( read(utmpfd, &current_record, reclen) == reclen )
                show_info(&current_record);
        close(utmpfd);
        return 0;                        /* went ok */
}
```

This program implements the logic outlined earlier in the chapter. The while loop reads records, one by one, from the file descriptor into current_record. A function called show_info displays the log-in information. The program loops until read returns anything but a complete record. Finally, it closes the file and returns.

The call to perror is a handy way to report system errors. We look at that later in the chapter.

2.5.4   Displaying Log-In Records

Here is the code for a first draft of show_info, the function to display the information in the utmp records:

```
/*
 *  show info()
 *       displays contents of the utmp struct in human readable form
```

```
 *          *note* these sizes should not be hardwired
 */
show_info( struct utmp *utbufp )
{
        printf("%-8.8s", utbufp->ut_name);       /* the logname  */
        printf(" ");                             /* a space      */
        printf("%-8.8s", utbufp->ut_line);       /* the tty      */
        printf(" ");                             /* a space      */
        printf("%10ld", utbufp->ut_time);        /* login time   */
        printf(" ");                             /* a space      */
#ifdef   SHOWHOST
        printf("(%s)", utbufp->ut_host);         /* the host     */
#endif
        printf("\n");                            /* newline      */
}
```

We specify field widths to printf in this program to match the widths of the strings in the output of the system version of who. This program prints out the ut_time member as a long int. The header file declares it to be a time_t value, but we do not know what that is yet.

Compile and run it:

```
$ cc who1.c -o who1
$ who1
           system b  952601411  ()
           run-leve  952601411  ()
                     952601416  ()
                     952601416  ()
                     952601417  ()
                     952601417  ()
                     952601419  ()
                     952601419  ()
                     952601423  ()
                     952601566  ()
LOGIN      console   952601566  ()
           ttyp1     958240622  ()
shpyrko    ttyp2     964318862  (nas1-093.gas.swamp.org)
acotton    ttyp3     964319088  (math-guest04.williams.edu)
           ttyp4     964320298  ()
spradlin   ttyp5     963881486  (h002078c6adfb.ne.rusty.net)
dkoh       ttyp6     964314388  (128.103.223.110)
spradlin   ttyp7     964058662  (h002078c6adfb.ne.rusty.net)
king       ttyp8     964279969  (blade-runner.mit.edu)
berschba   ttyp9     964188340  (dudley.learned.edu)
rserved    ttypa     963538145  (gigue.eas.ivy.edu)
dabel      ttypb     964319455  (roam193-27.student.state.edu)
           ttypc     964319645  ()
```

```
rserved   ttypd   963538287  (gigue.eas.ivy.edu)
dkoh      ttype   964298769  (128.103.223.110)
          ttypf   964314510  ()
molay     ttyq0   964310621  (xyz73-200.harvard.edu)
          ttyq1   964311665  ()
          ttyq2   964310757  ()
          ttyq3   964304284  ()
          ttyq4   964305014  ()
          ttyq5   964299803  ()
          ttyq6   964219533  ()
          ttyq7   964215661  ()
cweiner   ttyq8   964212019  (roam175-157.student.stats.edu)
          ttyqa   964277078  ()
          ttyq9   964231347  ()
$
```

Compare the output of our program with the output of the system version of who:

```
$ who
shpyrko   ttyp2   Jul 22 22:21     (nas1-093.gas.swamp.edu)
acotton   ttyp3   Jul 22 22:24     (math-guest04.williams.edu)
spradlin  ttyp5   Jul 17 20:51     (h002078c6adfb.ne.rusty.net)
dkoh      ttyp6   Jul 22 21:06     (128.103.223.110)
spradlin  ttyp7   Jul 19 22:04     (h002078c6adfb.ne.rusty.net)
king      ttyp8   Jul 22 11:32     (blade-runner.mit.edu)
berschba  ttyp9   Jul 21 10:05     (dudley.learned.edu)
rserved   ttypa   Jul 13 21:29     (gigue.eas.ivy.edu)
dabel     ttypb   Jul 22 22:30     (roam193-27.student.state.edu)
rserved   ttypd   Jul 13 21:31     (gigue.eas.harvard.edu)
dkoh      ttype   Jul 22 16:46     (128.103.223.110)
molay     ttyq0   Jul 22 20:03     (xyz73-200.harvard.edu)
cweiner   ttyq8   Jul 21 16:40     (roam175-157.student.stats.edu)
$
```

Our version looks promising, but it is not an exact match. There are some wrinkles to iron out. We printed all the same usernames who lists, we have the correct terminal names, we have the correct remote hostnames, but there are two problems.

What We Need to Do

- Suppress blank records
- Get the log-in times correct

2.5.5 Writing who2.c

Version 2 of our who program includes fixes for the two problems we saw in version 1. Again, we solve these problems by reading the manual pages and the header files.

Suppressing Blank Records

The real version of who lists usernames of users logged into the system. Our version lists what it finds in the utmp file. The utmp file seems to have records for all terminals, even unused ones. We have to change our program so it does not print records for unused terminal lines. How can we tell which utmp records do not represent active sessions?

A simple solution (and it does not work) is to skip entries with a blank username. That handles most of the cases, but does not screen out the entry with *user* LOGIN at the line for the *console*. A better solution (and it does work) is only to print out utmp records that represent users logged into the system.

Examining the /usr/include/utmp.h file, we find the following:

```
/*         Definitions for ut_type                                    */

#define EMPTY            0
#define RUN_LVL          1
#define BOOT_TIME        2
#define OLD_TIME         3
#define NEW_TIME         4
#define INIT_PROCESS     5        /* Process spawned by "init" */
#define LOGIN_PROCESS    6        /* A "getty" process waiting for login */
#define USER_PROCESS     7        /* A user process */
#define DEAD_PROCESS     8
```

This list looks helpful. Each record has a member called ut_type. The values for that member are listed, with symbolic names, in the header file. Type 7 looks like our lucky number. If we make the following minor change to our show_info function, those blank records should vanish:

```
show_info( struct utmp *utbufp )
{
        if ( utbufp->ut_type != USER_PROCESS )        /* users only ! */
                return;
        printf("%-8.8s", utbufp->ut_name);            /* the username  */
```

Displaying Log-in Time in Human-Readable Form

We now work on the problem of presenting the time in a format that makes sense to people. We start by searching the manual and header files. Manpages on the topic of time vary a lot among versions of Unix. Typing

```
$ man -k time
```

returns many entries. On one machine, I got 73, and on another I got 97. You could eyeball a list that long, or you could filter the output. These filters zoomed in pretty well:

```
$ man -k time | grep transform
$ man -k time | grep -i convert
```

The manual led to some useful header files. /usr/include/time.h was informative on several Unix systems. Explore your system for facts about time. Here are the facts:

How Unix Stores Times: the time_t *Data Type*

Unix stores times as the number of seconds since midnight, Jan 1, 1970, G.M.T. The time_t data type is an integer that stores a number of seconds. Unix uses this format for many applications. ut_time in the utmp records represents the log-in time as the number of seconds since the beginning of *the Epoch.*

Making a time_t *readable:* ctime

The function that converts a number of seconds since the start of Unix time into a sensible format is ctime, described in section 3 of the manual:

```
$ man 3 ctime
CTIME(3)                Linux Programmer's Manual              CTIME(3)

NAME
       asctime,  ctime,  gmtime,  localtime,  mktime  - transform
       binary date and time to ASCII

SYNOPSIS
       #include <time.h>

       char *asctime(const struct tm *timeptr);

       char *ctime(const time_t *timep);

       struct tm *gmtime(const time_t *timep);

       struct tm *localtime(const time_t *timep);

       time_t mktime(struct tm *timeptr);

       extern char *tzname[2];
       long int timezone;
       extern int daylight;

DESCRIPTION
       The ctime(), gmtime() and localtime() functions all take
       an argument of data type time_t which represents calendar
       time.  When interpreted as an absolute time value, it rep-
       resents the number of seconds elapsed since 00:00:00 on
       January 1, 1970, Coordinated Universal Time (UTC).

   ...

       The ctime() function converts the calendar time timep into
       a string of the form

           "Wed Jun 30 21:49:08 1993\n"
```

> The abbreviations for the days of the week are Sun,
> Mon, Tue, Wed, Thu, Fri, and Sat. The abbre-
> viations for the months are Jan, Feb, Mar, Apr,
> May, Jun, Jul, Aug, Sep, Oct, Nov, and
> Dec. The return value points to a statically allocated
> string which might be overwritten by subsequent calls to
> any of the date and time functions. The function also

This is exactly what we need. We have a `time_t` value in the `utmp` records. We want a string that looks like

```
Jun 30 21:49
```

`ctime(3)` is a function that takes a pointer to a `time_t` and sends back a pointer to a string that looks like

```
Wed Jun 30 21:49:08 1993\n
    ^^^^^^^^^^^^
```

Notice that the string we want for who is embedded in the string `ctime` returns. This coincidence makes coding the date part of who particularly simple. We call `ctime` and print out the 12 characters starting at offset 4 in the result. `printf("%12.12s", ctime(&t) +4)` does just that.

Putting It All Together

We now know how to suppress empty records, and we know how to display the `ut_time` value as a readable date. Here is the finished version of `who2.c`:

```c
/* who2.c  - read /etc/utmp and list info therein
 *         - suppresses empty records
 *         - formats time nicely
 */
#include        <stdio.h>
#include        <unistd.h>
#include        <utmp.h>
#include        <fcntl.h>
#include        <time.h>

/* #define      SHOWHOST */

void showtime(long);
void show_info(struct utmp *);

int main()
{
        struct utmp     utbuf;          /* read info into here */
        int             utmpfd;         /* read from this descriptor */
```

```
          if ( (utmpfd = open(UTMP_FILE, O_RDONLY)) == -1 ){
                  perror(UTMP_FILE);
                  exit(1);
          }

          while( read(utmpfd, &utbuf, sizeof(utbuf)) == sizeof(utbuf) )
                  show_info( &utbuf );
          close(utmpfd);
          return 0;
  }
  /*
   *      show info()
   *                      displays the contents of the utmp struct
   *                      in human readable form
   *                      * displays nothing if record has no user name
   */
  void show_info( struct utmp *utbufp )
  {
          if ( utbufp->ut_type != USER_PROCESS )
                  return;

          printf("%-8.8s", utbufp->ut_name);      /* the logname   */
          printf(" ");                            /* a space       */
          printf("%-8.8s", utbufp->ut_line);      /* the tty       */
          printf(" ");                            /* a space       */
          showtime( utbufp->ut_time );            /* display time */
  #ifdef SHOWHOST
          if ( utbufp->ut_host[0] != '\0' )
                  printf(" (%s)", utbufp->ut_host);/* the host     */
  #endif
          printf("\n");                           /* newline       */
  }

  void showtime( long timeval )
  /*
   *      displays time in a format fit for human consumption
   *      uses ctime to build a string then picks parts out of it
   *      Note: %12.12s prints a string 12 chars wide and LIMITS
   *      it to 12chars.
   */
  {
          char    *cp;                     /* to hold address of time     */
          cp = ctime(&timeval);            /* convert time to string      */
                                           /* string looks like           */
                                           /* Mon Feb  4 00:46:40 EST 1991 */
                                           /* 0123456789012345.            */
          printf("%12.12s", cp+4 );        /* pick 12 chars from pos 4     */
  }
```

Testing who2.c

We compile and run who2.c. For variety, we turn off the SHOWHOST setting. We run the
system who and compare outputs:

```
$ cc who2.c -o who2
$ who2
rlscott   ttyp2    Jul 23 01:07
acotton   ttyp3    Jul 22 22:24
spradlin ttyp5     Jul 17 20:51
spradlin ttyp7     Jul 19 22:04
king      ttyp8    Jul 22 11:32
berschba ttyp9     Jul 21 10:05
rserved   ttypa    Jul 13 21:29
rserved   ttypd    Jul 13 21:31
molay     ttyq0    Jul 22 20:03
cweiner   ttyq8    Jul 21 16:40
mnabavi   ttyx2    Apr 10 23:11
$ who
rlscott       ttyp2        Jul 23 01:07
acotton       ttyp3        Jul 22 22:24
spradlin      ttyp5        Jul 17 20:51
spradlin      ttyp7        Jul 19 22:04
king          ttyp8        Jul 22 11:32
berschba      ttyp9        Jul 21 10:05
rserved       ttypa        Jul 13 21:29
rserved       ttypd        Jul 13 21:31
molay         ttyq0        Jul 22 20:03
cweiner       ttyq8        Jul 21 16:40
mnabavi       ttyx2        Apr 10 23:11
$
```

Pretty close. Different versions of who use different column widths. Changing the column widths will make our output match the output of the system version perfectly. You
may need to make similar adjustments to get it to work on your system.

   Some versions of who print out the hostname of the remote system if there is one.
Some versions do not print out the remote hostname. These adjustments are cosmetic.
The program produces an accurate list of users, their terminal lines, and log-in times.

2.5.6   A Look Back and a Look Forward

We began the chapter with a simple question, "How does the Unix who command
work?" We followed three steps. First, we learned what the command does. Then we
found out, by reading about the technical details, how it works. Then, we wrote our own
version to see if we really understood how it works.

   In the process of following these three steps, we learned how to use the Unix
manual and the header files. Writing our own version led to deeper understandings.
The structure of the utmp file became clearer. We saw that logging in actually involves

making an entry in a log. We learned how Unix stores times. This knowledge will be useful when learning about other parts of Unix.

Finally, we read about related topics. The manual page for the utmp file refers to a wtmp file. The manual page for ctime refers to other time-related functions. These connections reveal more about the structure of the system.

2.6   PROJECT TWO: WRITING cp (READ AND WRITE)

In who we read from a file. How do we write to a file? To learn about writing to files, we devise a version of the Unix cp command.

2.6.1   Question 1: What Does cp Do?

cp makes a copy of a file. The typical usage is

```
$ cp source-file target-file
```

If there is no target file, cp creates it. If there is a target file, cp replaces the contents of that file with the contents of the source file.

2.6.2   Question 2: How Does cp Create and Write?
Creating/Truncating a File

One method to create or rewrite a file is the creat system call. The summary is

	creat	
PURPOSE	Create or zero a file	
INCLUDE	#include <fcntl.h>	
USAGE	int fd = creat(char *filename, mode_t mode)	
ARGS	filename:	the name of the file
	mode:	access permission
RETURNS	-1	on error
	fd	on success

The creat system call opens *filename* for writing. If there is no file with that name, the kernel creates the file. If there *is* a file with that name, the kernel discards its contents, truncating the file to a size of zero.

If the kernel creates the file, it sets the permission bits for the file to the value specified by the second argument[2], for example,

```
fd = creat("addressbook", 0644);
```

---

[2]Actually, the permission bits are modified by the umask of the process. See Chapter 3.

creates or truncates a file called addressbook. If the file does not exist, the permission bits are set to rw-r--r--. (See Chapter 3 for details.) If a file with that name exists, the file is now empty, the permission mode does not change. In either case, *fd* represents a file open for writing only.

Writing to a File

You send data to an open file with the write system call:

write	
PURPOSE	Send data from memory to a file
INCLUDE	#include <unistd.h>
USAGE	ssize_t result = write(int fd, void *buf, size_t amt)
ARGS	fd a file descriptor buf an array amt how many bytes to write
RETURNS	-1 on error num written on success

The write system call copies data from process memory to a file. If the kernel is unable or unwilling to copy the data, write returns −1. If the kernel transfers data, write returns the number of bytes it transferred.

Why would the number of bytes transferred differ from the number of bytes requested? There are several reasons. The system might impose a limit on the maximum file size a user could create, or the disk might be nearly full. If the request would exceed the limit or space, the write system call writes as many bytes as possible and then stops. Your programs should always compare the number of bytes you ask to send to the file to the number of bytes that actually go to the file. If these numbers differ, the program must respond in a sensible way.

2.6.3   Question 3: Can I Write cp?

We now test our understanding by writing a version of cp. A program outline is as follows:

```
    open sourcefile for reading
    open copyfile   for writing
+-> read from source to buffer -- eof? -+
|__ write from buffer to copy           |
                                        |
    close sourcefile    <--------------+
    close copyfile
```

Figure 2.4 shows the players and the flow of data:

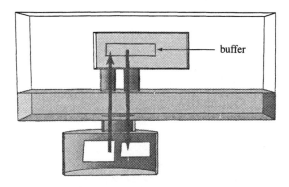

buffer

FIGURE 2.4

Copying a file by reading and writing.

The files are on the disk, with the original file on the left and the copy on the right. The process is living in user space. A buffer is a chunk of memory inside the process. The process has two file descriptors. Bytes are read from the original file into the buffer and then written from the buffer to the copy.

Finally, here is code that implements the picture:

```
/** cp1.c
 *      version 1 of cp - uses read and write with tunable buffer size
 *
 *      usage: cp1 src dest
 */
#include        <stdio.h>
#include        <unistd.h>
#include        <fcntl.h>

#define BUFFERSIZE      4096
#define COPYMODE        0644

void oops(char *, char *);

main(int ac, char *av[])
{
        int     in_fd, out_fd, n_chars;
        char    buf[BUFFERSIZE];
                                                /* check args    */
        if ( ac != 3 ){
                fprintf( stderr, "usage: %s source destination\n", *av);
                exit(1);
        }
                                                /* open files    */

        if ( (in_fd=open(av[1], O_RDONLY)) == -1 )
                oops("Cannot open ", av[1]);

        if ( (out_fd=creat( av[2], COPYMODE)) == -1 )
                oops( "Cannot creat", av[2]);

                                                /* copy files    */
```

```
            while ( (n_chars = read(in_fd , buf, BUFFERSIZE)) > 0 )
                    if ( write( out_fd, buf, n_chars ) != n_chars )
                            oops("Write error to ", av[2]);
            if ( n_chars == -1 )
                            oops("Read error from ", av[1]);

                                                    /* close files  */

            if ( close(in_fd) == -1 || close(out_fd) == -1 )
                    oops("Error closing files","");
    }

    void oops(char *s1, char *s2)
    {
            fprintf(stderr,"Error: %s ", s1);
            perror(s2);
            exit(1);
    }
```

Compile and test the program:

```
$ cc cp1.c -o cp1
$ cp1 cp1 copy.of.cp1
$ ls -l cp1 copy.of.cp1
-rw-r--r--   1 bruce     bruce        37419 Jul 23 03:12 copy.of.cp1
-rwxrwxr-x   1 bruce     bruce        37419 Jul 23 03:08 cp1
$ cmp cp1 copy.of.cp1
$
```

This seems to work. The cmp utility compares two files and reports differences. There are no differences between these files, so the report shows nothing.

How well does our program respond to errors? First we try to copy a nonexistent file, and then we try to write over a directory. The result is as follows:

```
$ cp1 xxx123 file1
Error: Cannot open  xxx123: No such file or directory
$ cp1 cp1 /tmp
Error: Cannot creat /tmp: Is a directory
```

Test other error situations. Read the manpages for the system calls to see what errors might arise and try to generate them. Be sure you do not clobber any files you want to keep.

2.6.4   Unix Programming Seems Pretty Easy

who is a program that reads from a file and formats the data. cp is a program that reads from one file and writes to another file. Both programs use the same basic system calls to connect to and transfer data in and out of files. The manual and the header files provided us with all the facts we needed to understand and write these programs.

This Unix programming does not seem too hard. Are we missing some underlying issues? Sort of. Along with the three questions we asked when learning about Unix and Unix programming is one more question: *How can I make this run better?*

2.7   MORE EFFICIENT FILE I/O: BUFFERING

cp1 contains a symbol BUFFERSIZE, the size of the array that holds bytes as they travels from source file to the copy. The value is 4096. We raise an important question: Does the size of the buffer matter?

2.7.1   Does the Size of the Buffer Matter?

You bet it does. If you use a ladle to transfer soup from one pot to another, a larger ladle requires fewer transfers and less time.

Consider a file that is 2500 bytes long. Here are some facts:

```
Ex: Filesize = 2500 bytes

If buffer = 100 bytes then
copy requires 25 read() and 25 write() calls

If buffer = 1000 bytes then
copy requires 3 read() and 3 write() calls
```

Changing buffer size from 100 to 1000 reduces the number of read and write system calls from 50 to 6. Does that matter?

The following table shows execution time for cp1 copying a 5-megabyte file with various values of BUFFERSIZE:

buffersize	execution time in seconds
1	50.29
4	12.81
16	3.28
64	0.96
128	0.56
256	0.37
512	0.27
1024	0.22
2048	0.19
4096	0.18
8192	0.18
16384	0.18

System calls consume time. A program that makes a lot of system calls runs slower and takes time other users might want to use.

2.7.2   Why System Calls Are Time Consuming

Why is a system call time consuming? Figure 2.5 shows the flow of control:

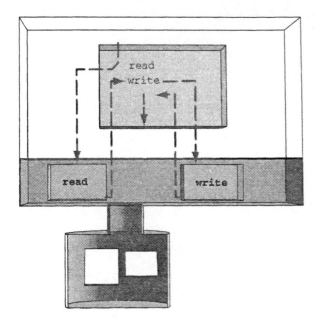

FIGURE 2.5

Control flow during system calls.

Here we see system memory with a process floating around in user space and the kernel rooted in system space. The disk is accessible to the kernel.

Our program cp1 wants to read data, so it makes the read system call to ask the kernel for data. The code that actually transfers the data from the disk to the process is part of the kernel. Therefore, control jumps from your code in user space to kernel code in system space. The CPU now executes the kernel code to transfer data. Executing code to transfer data takes time.

Not only does transferring data take time, but jumping into and out of the kernel takes time. The CPU runs in *supervisor mode* with a special stack and memory environment when executing kernel code and runs in *user mode* when executing user code.

Kernel functions must have access to the disk, the terminals, the printers, and other resources. User functions must **not** have access to those resources. Therefore the computer actually operates in different modes. When running in user mode, the computer is limited to a certain segment of memory in user space. When running in kernel mode, the computer has access to all of memory. The details of changing modes depend on the processor. Each CPU has its own notions of supervisor mode and user mode, and each version of Unix has to adapt its model of user mode and kernel mode to match the capabilities of the CPU.

Consider Clark Kent and Superman. When he changes from user mode (Clark Kent) to kernel mode (Superman), he has to find a phone booth, change his clothes, take off his glasses, and restyle his hair. Superman then performs some task, which takes time. And changing back to user mode takes time. The more frequently Clark Kent performs mode changes, the more time he uses, and the less time he has to be a reporter or fight crime.

Your program is no different. The more time the CPU spends executing kernel code and changing into and out of kernel mode, the less time it has to run your code or provide system services. Because of this cost in time, some system calls are said to be *expensive*. What does the expense of reading and writing data tell us about our version of who?

2.7.3 Does This Mean That who2.c Is Inefficient?

Yes! One system call for each utmp record makes as much sense as buying a pizza one slice at a time or buying eggs one at time. If you are going to make fried eggs for three people at breakfast, you could drive to the store, buy one egg, drive back, fry it, then serve it. After doing the first egg, you could drive to the store, buy another egg, drive back, fry it, then serve it. Finally, you could drive out to buy the third egg and realize why eggs come in those handy cartons.

A better idea is to read in a bunch of records at once. Then, as with eggs in a carton, process the ones in your local storage one by one. The egg carton is called a buffer. Here is pseudocode for the getegg method using buffered egg input:

```
getegg(){
        if ( eggs_left_in_carton == 0 )
                refill carton at store
                if ( eggs_at_store == 0 )
                        return EndOfEggs
                eggs_left_in_carton = 12
        }
        eggs_left_in_carton--;
        return one egg;
}
```

Each call to getegg fetches one egg, but not from the store. Only when the carton runs out does this function make a trip to the store. What does this have to do with Unix programming?

Look in /usr/include/stdio.h for the code for getc. Some versions of Unix implement getc as a macro using the same logic as getegg.

2.7.4 Adding Buffering to who2.c

We make who2.c much more efficient by using buffering to reduce system calls. The idea presented in the getegg function can be translated into code. Figure 2.6 shows how it works:

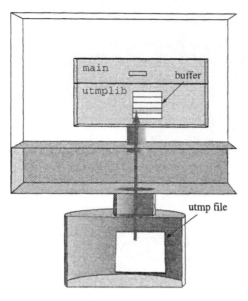

File buffering with utmplib

main calls a function
in utmplib.c to get the
next struct utmp.

Functions in utmplib.c read
structs 16 at a time from the
disk into an array.

The kernel is called
only when all 16 are
used up.

utmp file

FIGURE 2.6

Buffering disk data in user space.

We create an array that holds 16 utmp structs. That array is marked *buffer* in the lower box in the process. That array holds a bunch of structs inside the process, the same way an egg carton holds a bunch of eggs inside your house. We write a function called utmp_next to dispense utmp records from the buffer.

We modify main to get structs from our user-space buffer by calling our own user-space function utmp_next. When all the structs in the buffer have been processed, only then does utmp_next call read to ask the kernel for 16 more utmp records. This new model cuts the number of read system calls by a factor of 16.

This 16-struct buffer and the functions to load it from the disk and to dispense structs to main are encapsulated in a file called utmplib.c.

The Code for utmplib.c

The file utmplib.c, shown here, implements utmp record buffering:

```
/* utmplib.c  - functions to buffer reads from utmp file
 *
 *      functions are
 *              utmp_open( filename )   - open file
 *                      returns -1 on error
 *              utmp_next( )            - return pointer to next struct
 *                      returns NULL on eof
 *              utmp_close()            - close file
 *
```

```
 *          reads NRECS per read and then doles them out from the buffer
 */
#include         <stdio.h>
#include         <fcntl.h>
#include         <sys/types.h>
#include         <utmp.h>

#define NRECS    16
#define NULLUT   ((struct utmp *)NULL)
#define UTSIZE   (sizeof(struct utmp))

static  char    utmpbuf[NRECS * UTSIZE];                 /* storage      */
static  int     num_recs;                                /* num stored   */
static  int     cur_rec;                                 /* next to go   */
static  int     fd_utmp = -1;                            /* read from    */

utmp_open( char *filename )
{
        fd_utmp = open( filename, O_RDONLY );            /* open it      */
        cur_rec = num_recs = 0;                          /* no recs yet  */
        return fd_utmp;                                  /* report       */
}

struct utmp *utmp_next()
{
        struct utmp *recp;
        if ( fd_utmp == -1 )                             /* error ?      */
                return NULLUT;
        if ( cur_rec==num_recs && utmp_reload()==0 )    /* any more ?    */
                return NULLUT;
                                        /* get address of next record   */
        recp = ( struct utmp *) &utmpbuf[cur_rec * UTSIZE];
        cur_rec++;
        return recp;
}

int utmp_reload()
/*
 *      read next bunch of records into buffer
 */
{
        int     amt_read;
                                                /* read them in         */
        amt_read = read( fd_utmp , utmpbuf, NRECS * UTSIZE );

                                                /* how many did we get? */
        num_recs = amt_read/UTSIZE;
                                                /* reset pointer        */
        cur_rec  = 0;
        return num_recs;
}
```

```
utmp_close()
{
        if ( fd_utmp != -1 )                    /* don't close if not   */
                close( fd_utmp );               /* open                 */
}
```

utmplib.c contains the buffer and variables and functions to manage data flow through the buffer. The variables num_recs and cur_rec record how many structs are in the buffer and how many have been used.

Each time a record is fetched, utmp_next checks if the cur_rec counter has reached the number of records in the buffer. If there are no unused records, utmp_next reloads the buffer from the disk. Before returning a record, utmp_next increments cur_rec.

utmplib.c provides a clear interface of access functions, hiding the internal details of the storage location and format of utmp records. utmp_next simply returns pointers to structures.

Here is the revised version of main:

```
/* who3.c - who with buffered reads
 *          - surpresses empty records
 *          - formats time nicely
 *          - buffers input (using utmplib)
 */
#include         <stdio.h>
#include         <sys/types.h>
#include         <utmp.h>
#include         <fcntl.h>
#include         <time.h>

#define SHOWHOST

void show_info(struct utmp *);
void showtime(time_t);

int main()
{
        struct utmp     *utbufp,        /* holds pointer to next rec    */
                        *utmp_next();   /* returns pointer to next      */

        if ( utmp_open( UTMP_FILE ) == -1 ){
                perror(UTMP_FILE);
                exit(1);
        }
        while ( ( utbufp = utmp_next() ) != ((struct utmp *) NULL) )
                show_info( utbufp );
        utmp_close( );
        return 0;
}
/*
 *      show info()
 ...
```

Instead of calling `open`, `read`, and `close`, this revised version calls equivalent functions in the buffering module. The display functions in `show_info`, though, are unaffected.

2.8 BUFFERING AND THE KERNEL

Buffering is an extremely useful idea. The principle is clear: read data in big chunks into a region in your memory space, and then process smaller pieces as you need them.

2.8.1 If Buffering Is So Smart, Why Doesn't the Kernel Do It?

It does. Jumping in and out of kernel mode takes time, but transferring data between the hard disk and memory takes eons by comparison. To save time, the kernel keeps copies of disk blocks in memory. Figure 2.7 illustrates.

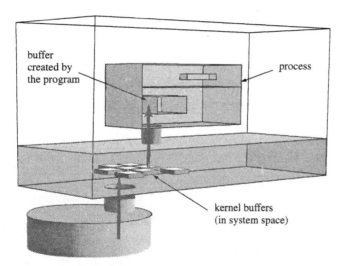

FIGURE 2.7

Buffering disk data in the kernel.

A disk is a collection of blocks of data, just as the `utmp` file is a collection of log-in records. Kernel buffers contain copies of some disk blocks just as our `utmp` buffers contain copies of `utmp` records. The kernel copies blocks from the disk into kernel buffers. When a process asks for data from a specific file, the kernel copies data from a kernel buffer into the buffer in the process. The kernel does not copy directly from the disk to user space.

What if the requested chunk of data is not in a kernel buffer? The kernel suspends the requesting process and adds the requested block to its shopping list. The kernel then finds other processes that are ready to do some work and lets those processes run.

Sometime later, the kernel moves the requested data from the disk into a kernel buffer. The kernel can now further copy the data into a buffer in user space and then wake the sleeping process.

Understanding the principles of *kernel buffering* changes how we understand the read and write system calls. The read call copies data into a process from a kernel buffer, and write copies data from the process to a kernel buffer. Transferring data between kernel buffers and the disk is different from the read and write calls.

The kernel can copy the data to the disk whenever it gets around to it. Like outgoing letters you stack up on a hallway table, data written by processes accumulates in kernel buffers waiting for the kernel to copy them to the disk. It is possible, and certainly happens, that those blocks of data never get to the disk. If the system is shut off abruptly, without giving the kernel a chance to copy buffered blocks to the disk, the updates or additions to the file are lost.

Consequences of Kernel Buffering

- Faster "disk" I/O
- Optimized disk writes
- Need to write buffers to disk before shutdown

2.9   READING AND WRITING A FILE

Our first program, who, reads from a file. Our second program, cp, reads from one file and writes to another file. Are there programs that read and write the same file?

2.9.1   Logging Out: What It Does

What happens when you log out? One thing that happens is the system changes a record in the utmp file. The output of who1 shows that utmp may contain records for unused terminal lines. Experiment to see how it works. Try this:

1. Log in twice, using two telnet windows, to one machine.
2. Use the who1 program we wrote to see the contents of utmp.
   Note what terminal lines you are using.
3. Log out of one of your sessions.
4. Run who1 again to see what happened to those two utmp records.

You will see that one of the records that contained your username has changed. Notice that ut_time is changed. What does the new time represent? On some systems, the username is blanked out. Did it make any other changes to the record? What about the remote hostname?

2.9.2   Logging Out: How It Works

It looks pretty simple. The program that removes your name from the log has to do the following:

1. Open the utmp file.
2. Read the utmp file until it finds the record for your terminal.

3. Write a revised utmp record in its place.

4. Close the utmp file.

Consider the four steps, one by one.

Step 1: Open the utmp file

The log-out program reads from utmp (it has to locate the record for your terminal) and also writes to utmp (it has to replace that record), so the log-out program must open the file for reading *and* writing:

```
fd = open(UTMP_FILE, O_RDWR);
```

Step 2: Find the record for your terminal

That is pretty easy. A while loop can read one utmp record at a time (or use buffering) and compare the ut_line member with the name of your terminal. It goes something like the following:

```
while( read(fd, rec, utmplen) == utmplen )   /* get next record */
    if ( strcmp(rec.ut_line, myline) == 0 ) /* what, my line?  */
        revise_entry();                      /* remove my name  */
```

Step 3: Write a revised utmp record in its place

The log-out program revises the record, then writes the revised record back to the file. The log-out program changes the ut_type value from USER_PROCESS to DEAD_PROCESS. Some versions of the program may blank out the username and hostname fields and replace the ut_time value with the log-out time. It is easy to code those changes.

Now for the big question: How do we write the revised record back to the file? If we just call write, our code updates the *next* record. That happens because the kernel keeps track of our *current position* in the file and advances the current position each time bytes are read or written to the file. Having just found the utmp record for your terminal, the current position is at the start of the next record. This raises an important question:

Q: *How can a program change the current read-write position in a file?*
A: *The* lseek *system call.*

We look at lseek in the next section.

Step 4: Close the file

Call close(fd).

2.9.3 Moving the Current Position: lseek

Unix maintains a *current position* for each open file as shown in Figure 2.8.

Each time you read bytes from a file, the kernel reads the data at the current position and then advances the current position by the number of bytes it read. The same position is used for writing data to a file. Each time you write bytes to a file, the kernel

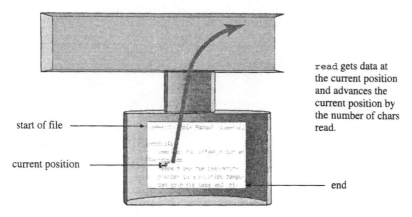

read gets data at
the current position
and advances the
current position by
the number of chars
read.

start of file

current position

end

FIGURE 2.8

Every open file has a current position.

puts them in the file at the current position and then advances the current position by that many bytes.

The current position belongs to the connection to the file, not to the file. For example, if two programs open the same file at the same time, each connection has its own current position. The programs can read or write different parts of the file.

The lseek system call lets you change the current position of an open file as follows:

lseek	
PURPOSE	Set file pointer to specified offset in file
INCLUDE	#include <sys/types.h> #include <unistd.h>
USAGE	off_t oldpos = lseek(int fd, off_t dist, int base)

ARGS	fd: file descriptor
	dist: a distance in bytes
	base: SEEK_SET => start of file
	  SEEK_CUR => current position
	  SEEK_END => end of file

RETURNS	−1 on error or the previous position in the file

lseek sets the current position for open file *fd* to the position defined by the pair *dist* and *base*. The *base* may be (0) start of file, (1) current position, or (2) end of file. The distance is a number of bytes relative to the base.

For example, the code

```
lseek(fd, -(sizeof(struct utmp)), SEEK_CUR);
```

moves the current position a distance sizeof(struct utmp) bytes *before* the current position. Notice that the distance can be negative. The code

```
lseek(fd, 10 * sizeof(struct utmp), SEEK_SET);
```

sets the current position to the start of the 11th utmp record in the file, and the code

```
lseek(fd, 0, SEEK_END);
write(fd, "hello", strlen("hello"));
```

sets the current position to the end of file and writes a string there.

Finally, notice that lseek(fd, 0, SEEK_CUR) returns the current position.

2.9.4   Code to Log Out from a Terminal

We now have all the pieces we need to write a function that marks a terminal record in utmp as logged out:

```
/*
 * logout_tty(char *line)
 *    marks a utmp record as logged out
 *    does not blank username or remote host
 *    returns -1 on error, 0 on success
 */
int logout_tty(char *line)
{
    int         fd;
    struct utmp rec;
    int         len = sizeof(struct utmp);
    int         retval = -1 ;                         /* pessimism */

    if ( (fd = open(UTMP_FILE,O_RDWR)) == -1 )        /* open file */
        return -1;

    /* search and replace */
    while ( read(fd, &rec, len) == len)
        if ( strncmp(rec.ut_line, line, sizeof(rec.ut_line)) == 0)
        {
            rec.ut_type = DEAD_PROCESS;                    /* set type */
            if ( time( &rec.ut_time ) != -1 )             /* and time */
                if ( lseek(fd, -len, SEEK_CUR)!= -1 )    /* back up  */
                    if ( write(fd, &rec, len) == len )   /* update   */
                        retval = 0;                      /* success! */
            break;
        }
    /* close the file */
    if ( close(fd) == -1 )
        retval = -1;
    return retval;
}
```

This code checks for errors from every system call it makes. Your systems programs must always check every system call for errors. These programs may be modifying files and data structures the system depends on. Leaving files inconsistent or incomplete can have serious consequences. On the other hand, some of the sample programs in this text will omit some error checking to make the main system calls and program logic clear and visible.

Speaking of errors, we now look at error handling and reporting.

2.10   WHAT TO DO WITH SYSTEM-CALL ERRORS

When open cannot open a file, it returns -1. When read cannot read data, it returns -1. When lseek cannot seek, it returns -1. System calls return -1 when something goes wrong. Your programs should test the return value of every system call they make and take intelligent action when errors occur.

What can go wrong? Every system call has its own set of errors. Consider the open system call. The file might not exist, you might not have permission to open it, or you might have too many files open. How does your program tell which of several possible errors is the one that happened?

How to Identify What Went Wrong: errno

The kernel tells your program the cause of the error by storing an error code in a global variable called errno. Every program contains this variable.

The manpage for errno(3) and the file <errno.h> include the error-code symbols and numeric codes. Here are a few examples:

```
#define EPERM       1       /* Operation not permitted */
#define ENOENT      2       /* No such file or directory */
#define ESRCH       3       /* No such process */
#define EINTR       4       /* Interrupted system call */
#define EIO         5       /* I/O error */
```

Different Responses to Different Errors

You can use these symbols in your program to identify what went wrong and take appropriate action, as in the following code:

```
#include   <errno.h>

extern int errno;

int sample()
{
    int fd;
    fd = open("file", O_RDONLY);
    if ( fd == -1 )
    {
        printf("Cannot open file: ");
        if ( errno == ENOENT )
            printf("There is no such file.");
        else if ( errno == EINTR )
            printf("Interrupted while opening file.");
```

```
else if ( errno == EACCESS )
    printf("You do not have permission to open file.");
...
```

The action your program takes should depend on what went wrong. For example, if open fails because the file does not exist, you might ask the user for a different file-name. On the other hand, if the program has too many files open (EMFILE), the program could close some files and try again. In this case, the user does not need to know about the error or the corrective action.

Reporting Errors: `perror(3)`

If you want to print a message describing the error, you *could* test the value of errno and print different messages for different values. The sample function above does that. Instead, though, it is easier to use the library function perror(string). perror(string) looks up the error code and prints, to standard error, the string you pass it and a descriptive message.

This revised version of sample uses perror:

```
int sample()
{
    int fd;
    fd = open("file", O_RDONLY);
    if ( fd == -1 )
    {
        perror("Cannot open file");
        return;
    }
    ...
```

When an error occurs in the call to open, you will see messages such as

```
Cannot open file: No such file or directory
Cannot open file: Interrupted system call
```

The first part of the output is the string you pass to perror, and the rest of the output is the text description that corresponds to the error code in errno.

SUMMARY

MAIN IDEAS

- The who command reports the list of current users by reading a system logfile.
- Unix systems store data in files. Unix programs transfer data into and out of files using six system calls:

```
open(filename, how)
creat(filename, mode)
read(fd, buffer, amt)
```

```
write(fd, buffer, amt)
lseek(fd, distance, base)
close(fd)
```

- A process reads and writes data through *file descriptors*. A file descriptor identifies a connection between a process and a file.
- Each time a program makes a system call, the computer has to change from user mode to kernel mode and execute kernel code. Programs run more efficiently if they minimize the number of system calls.
- Programs that read and write data can reduce the number of system calls by storing data in buffers and calling the kernel when write buffers are full or read buffers are empty.
- The Unix kernel uses buffers inside kernel memory to reduce the number of times it has to transfer data to and from the disk.
- Unix stores times as the number of seconds since the beginning of Unix time.
- When Unix system calls encounter an error, the system sets the global variable errno to an error code and returns the value -1. System programs can use the value in errno to diagnose the error and take appropriate action.
- Much of the information summarized in this section is available on the system. Extensive manual pages explain what commands do and describe, in many cases, *how* they work. Header files contain the definitions of data structures, the values of symbolic constants, and the function prototypes used to build system tools.

EXPLORATIONS

2.1 *The* w *command* Unix has a command called w that is related to who. Try the command, and read the manpage. What information does w provide that who does not? How much of that information is in the utmp file? What does the other information mean? Try to find sources for the other pieces of information.

2.2 *Crashes and* utmp When you log in, your username, terminal, the time, and your remote host are recorded in the utmp file. When you log out, the record is cleared. What happens if the system crashes? Clearly, the utmp file is left containing the list of users logged in at the time of the crash. When the system starts again, the information in the utmp file is not accurate. What does Unix do about the utmp file when the system starts? Does it create it with entries for all the available terminal lines? Does it create an empty file and allow terminal line entries to accumulate? Look for answers to this question by searching the manual, header files, and start-up scripts. You can experiment on your own machine.

2.3 Test cp1 by copying a file to /dev/tty: cp1 cp1.c /dev/tty. The destination file is the terminal. Our program opens, writes to, and closes the terminal using exactly the same system calls it uses to send data to a disk file. Now, copy from the terminal to a disk file using cp1 /dev/tty file1. Your keyboard now becomes the input file. You need to indicate you are done typing by pressing the Enter key and then typing Ctrl-D.

2.4 The standard C file functions fopen, getc, fclose, and fgets are all part of a system for buffered input and output to files. These functions use a struct of type FILE to provide an intermediate layer similar to the one the utmplib module provides. Find the definition of

FILE in the header files, describe the members of the struct, and compare them to the variables in utmplib.c.

2.5 *Writing kernel buffers to disk* How can you be sure that data you write to the disk really get there? We have said that the kernel is free to copy data when it gets around to it. Explore the manual to learn what system calls and programs are used to ensure buffers are copied to the disk.

2.6 *Opening the same file several times* Unix allows many processes to open a file at once. Unix also allows one process to open the same file several times. Experiment with opening the same file several times by creating a file containing some random text and then writing a program that does the following:

(a) Opens the file for reading, then

(b) Opens the same file for writing, then

(c) Opens the same file for reading.

You should now have three file descriptors. The program should now

(d) read 20 bytes using the first fd and print what you get

(e) write the string "testing 1 2 3 ... " using the second fd,

(f) read 20 bytes using the third fd and print what you get.

2.7 *Learning about the manual* The man command tells you about all Unix commands, system calls, system devices, and other topics. What command do you use to learn about the man command? How many sections are there in the manual on your version of Unix? What are they?

2.8 *Exploring the* utmp *file* The utmp file, we saw in our early experiments, contains some records that do not correspond to current log-in sessions. What other sorts of records are contained in the file? What do they represent?

2.9 *Jumping off the end of a file* lseek allows you to set the current position to locations after the end of the file. For example,

```
lseek(fd,100,SEEK_END)
```

moves the position 100 bytes past the end of a file.

What happens if you read data after the end of a file? What happens if you write data after the end of a file? Try some large values, something like writing "hello" 20,000 bytes after the end of a file. Check the size of the file with ls -l, and check the size of the file with ls -s. What is going on?

PROGRAMMING EXERCISES

2.10 *Identity crisis* The manual page for who lists who am i as an acceptable usage of the command. It also lists whoami. Modify who2.c so it supports the who am i usage. Experiment with the command whoami and read the manpage. How does it differ from who am i? Write a program that works like whoami.

2.11 What does the standard cp do if you try to copy a file onto itself? For example: cp file1 file1. What do you think is the correct action? Modify cp1.c to handle that situation.

2.12 *Files vs. API's* We created utmplib.c to improve efficiency, but it has an additional effect. That other effect is replacing a file of data with a set of functions, an *API*. This API returns all utmp structs, even the ones that do not represent logged-in users. The who command only wants to see records that represent active sessions. Modify utmplib.c so it only returns records of active sessions. How does this change affect the rest of the who3.c code. Is this change a good idea? Why or why not?

2.13 *Buffering and seeking* The `logout_tty` function in the text uses `lseek` to back up one record so it can rewrite a record. Notice that `logout_tty` does not use buffering to read the `utmp` file. The program would be more efficient if it used buffering.

   (a) Explain what problems would arise if we *had* mixed `lseek` with calls to the functions in `utmplib.c`.

   (b) Add a new function to `utmplib.c` called

```
utmp_seek(record_offset,base)
```

   that changes the current position for calls to `utmp_next` in the same way that `lseek` changes the current position for calls to `read`. This new function moves the current position to *record_offset* records relative to *base* where *base* is SEEK_SET, SEEK_CUR, or SEEK_END. Note the argument is measured in `utmp` records, not in bytes.

   (c) Modify `logout_tty` to use this modified version of `utmplib.c`.

2.14 *Examining utmp* The `who1` program lists every entry in the `utmp` file. That was not our intention, but it provided a handy tool for examining the contents of utmp. Make `who1` even more useful by adding code to it that prints out all the other fields in the struct. The `ut_type` field is particularly useful. Modify the program so it allows the user to override the default `utmp` file by specifying a filename on the command line. You can now use this tool to examine the `wtmp` file.

2.15 *Preventing file destruction* The standard version of `cp` silently overwrites existing files. That is, if you have a file called `file2`, and you type

   $ `cp file1 file2`

   you destroy the original contents of `file2`. The standard version of `cp` supports a `-i` option that causes the program to ask you before writing over a file. Add that feature to the `cp1.c` code.

PROJECTS

Based on the material in this chapter, you can learn about and write versions of the following Unix programs:

```
ac, last, cat, head, tail, od, dd
```

A FINAL PUZZLER: THE `tail` COMMAND

We learned a lot by looking at a few commands. Consider one more command. We are almost out of time, so you will have to work on this one yourself.

The `lseek` system call allows you to move the current position anywhere in a file. The call `lseek(fd,0,SEEK_END)` moves the current position to the end of the file.

The `tail` command displays the last ten lines of a file. Try it. `tail` has to move, not to the end of a file, but to a spot ten lines before the end of a file. The `distance` argument to `lseek`, though, is in units of characters.

How can `tail` work? Design your own version. Think about buffering to make your program efficient. Read the manual page to see all the options `tail` supports. How would those work? Designing this program seems, like `who` and `cp`, to be a straightforward project.

The source code to two versions of `tail` are available on the Web site for the book. One is the GNU version, the other is from BSD. They use completely different techniques. Before you peek at those solutions, try to write one yourself.

# CHAPTER 3

Directories and File Properties Looking through ls

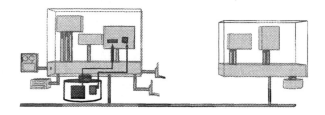

OBJECTIVES

Ideas and Skills

- A directory is a list of files
- How to read a directory
- Types of files and how to determine the type of a file
- Properties of files and how to determine properties of a file
- Bit sets and bit masks
- User and group ID numbers and the passwd database

System Calls and Functions

- opendir, readdir, closedir, seekdir
- stat
- chmod, chown, utime
- rename

Commands

- ls

3.1   INTRODUCTION

We know how to read and write the contents of files. Files have more than contents, though. A file has an owner, a modification time, a size, a type, and other attributes. Names of files are listed in directories, just as names of people are listed in telephone books. How can we determine names and properties of files?

The ls command lists the names in a directory and reports information about files. We study ls as a way to learn more about directories and file types and properties.

3.2   QUESTION 1: WHAT DOES ls DO?

3.2.1   ls Lists Names of Files and Reports File Attributes

Type the command ls to see what it does:

```
$ ls
Makefile      docs       ls2.c      s.tar      statdemo.c  tail1.c
chap03        ls1.c      old_src    stat1.c    tail1
$
```

The default action of ls is to list the names of the files in the current directory. ls sorts the names in alphabetical order. Some versions of ls arrange the names in columns, some versions need to be asked to (using the –c option).

ls can display more than just the names of files. When given the -l command-line option, ls presents information about each of the files, using the *long format*:

```
$ ls -l
total 108
-rw-rw-r--   2 bruce    users        345 Jul 29 11:05 Makefile
-rw-rw-r--   1 bruce    users      27521 Aug  1 12:14 chap03
drwxrwxr-x   2 bruce    users       1024 Aug  1 12:15 docs
-rw-r--r--   1 bruce    users        723 Feb  9  1998 ls1.c
-rw-r--r--   1 bruce    users       3045 Feb 15 03:51 ls2.c
drwxrwxr-x   2 bruce    users       1024 Aug  1 12:14 old_src
-rw-rw-r--   1 bruce    users      30720 Aug  1 12:05 s.tar
-rw-r--r--   1 bruce    support      946 Feb 18 17:15 stat1.c
-rw-r--r--   1 bruce    support      191 Feb  9  1998 statdemo.c
-rwxrwxr-x   1 bruce    users      37351 Aug  1 12:13 tail1
-rw-r--r--   1 bruce    users       1416 Aug  1 12:05 tail1.c
$
```

Each line of output represents one file and includes several attributes of the file.

3.2.2   Listing Other Directories, Reporting on Other Files

A Unix system has many directories, each with its own collection of files. What if you want information about other directories and the files in those directories? You ask ls for information about files in other directories by specifying directory names and filenames on the command line:

Asking ls about Other Directories and Their Files	
Example	Action
ls /tmp	list names of files in /tmp directory
ls -l docs	show attributes of files in docs directory
ls -l ../Makefile	show attributes of ../Makefile
ls *.c	list names of files matching pattern *.c

If an argument is a directory, ls lists its contents. If an argument is a file, ls lists its name or attributes. Command-line options affect what ls does and what it shows.

3.2.3   Popular Command-Line Options

The manual page for ls lists many command-line options. Some popular ones are given in the following table:

Command	Action
ls -a	shows "."-files
ls -lu	shows last-read time
ls -s	shows size in blocks
ls -t	sorts in time order
ls -F	shows file types

A Remark on Dot-Files

The -a option requires explanation if you are new to Unix. Unix implements the concept of *hidden files* by using a simple convention. The convention is that ls does not list the name of a file if the first character of the filename is a dot. Nothing in the operating system (i.e., the kernel) knows or cares about a concept of hidden files. It is purely a convention that ls follows and users depend on.

Some programs use dot filenames in a user's home directory to store user preferences. These configuration files are easy to edit if you need to, but you do not have to see them all the time.

3.2.4   Answer One: A Summary

Experimenting with ls and reading the manual page, we find ls does two things:

Lists the contents of directories
Displays information about files

Notice that `ls` does one thing for a directory and a different thing for files. `ls` figures out if a command-line argument is a file or a directory. How does that work? If we are to write a version of `ls`, we need to master three skills:

- How to list the contents of a directory
- How to obtain and display properties of a file
- How to determine if a name refers to a file or a directory

3.3   BRIEF REVIEW OF THE FILE SYSTEM TREE

Before we focus on those three projects, let us take a look at the big picture of how Unix organizes files on a disk.

A disk is organized as a tree of directories, each of which contains files or directories. Figure 3.1 uses little rectangles to indicate files inside directories and uses lines to show how a directory is connected to directories below and above it:

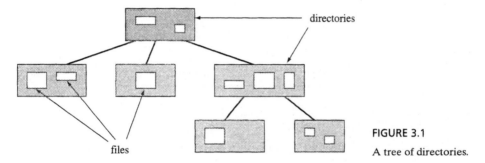

FIGURE 3.1

A tree of directories.

In Unix, every file on the system is located somewhere in a single tree of directories. There are no separate drives or volumes. Just the opposite in fact, the directories on physically separate disks and partitions are seamlessly subsumed into this single tree. Even floppy disks, CD-ROMs, and other removable drives appear as subdirectories somewhere on the tree.

This simplicity simplifies writing `ls`. We only have to think about directories and files, not partitions and volumes.

3.4   QUESTION 2: HOW DOES `ls` WORK?

`ls` produces a list of filenames. How complicated can it be? A first guess is

```
        open directory
+-> read entry         -end of dir?-+
|__ display file info                |
        close directory   <------------+
```

This outline looks just like the logic for who. The main difference is that the who program opens and reads from a file, and the `ls` program opens and reads its data from a directory. How much different is reading a directory from reading a file? What is a directory, anyway?

3.4.1   What Is a Directory, Anyway?

Answer A directory is a kind of file that contains a list of names of files and directories. A directory is like the utmp file (see Chapter 2) in some ways; it consists of a sequence of records, each record with a clearly defined and completely documented structure. Each record in a directory represents one item—a single file or a single directory.

Unlike a regular file, a directory is never empty. Every directory contains two specific items—. and ..—called *dot* and *dotdot*, respectively. *dot* is the name of the current directory, and *dotdot* is the name of the directory one level up.

3.4.2   Do open, read, and close Work for Directories?

Answer 1 In the *Olden Days*® there was no other way. Try these commands on your system:

```
$ cat /
as'.a'asa..a'bw.tagsb'c{
quota.userc'{
      quota.group'esbetce''sbtmp''"sbdev"      sbmnt    '    wcsbin   '2
    sbopt2
        '8
          sbusr8
            '9
              sbvar9
(many lines of hard-to-read data omitted)

$ more /tmp
/tmp is a directory
$ od -c /dev
0000000   360 001  \0  \0 024  \0 001  \0   .  \0  \0  \0 360 001  \0  \0
0000020   001 200  \0  \0 002  \0  \0  \0 024  \0 002  \0   .   .  \0  \0
0000040   002  \0  \0  \0 001 200  \0  \0 361 001  \0  \0 030  \0  \a  \0
0000060     M   A   K   E   D   E   V  \0 361 001  \0  \0 001 200  \0  \0
0000100   362 001  \0  \0 030  \0 004  \0   k   l   o   g  \0  \0  \0  \0
0000120   362 001  \0  \0 001 200  \0  \0 363 001  \0  \0 030  \0 004  \0
0000140     k   c   o   n  \0  \0  \0  \0 363 001  \0  \0 001 200  \0  \0
0000160   364 001  \0  \0 030  \0  \a  \0   k   b   i   n   l   o   g  \0
0000200   364 001  \0  \0 001 200  \0  \0 365 001  \0  \0 030  \0 004  \0
0000220     k   m   e   m  \0  \0  \0  \0 365 001  \0  \0 001 200  \0  \0
0000240   366 001  \0  \0 024  \0 003  \0   m   e   m  \0 366 001  \0  \0
```

These examples show some interesting things. First, cat and od are able to read directories just as they read regular files. These two programs use the standard file-access calls: open, read, and close. Therefore, directories *can* be read as plain files.

Second, more refuses to show you the directory. more knows the argument refers to a directory and will not display the contents. more can display the contents of a directory, but does not think you want to see it. Some versions of cat will, like this version of more, tell you the file is a directory and not display the contents.

Finally, these examples show that directories do not contain plain text. A directory consists of a sequence of structs.

Answer 2 It is a bad idea to use open, read, and close to list contents of directories. Unix supports many types of directories and can read disks using Apple HFS format, ISO9660, VFAT format, NFS directories, and various flavors of Unix directories. Using read to process each type would require knowing the format of the records for each type of directory.

3.4.3 OK, OK, How Do I Read a Directory?

We check the manual. A search for the keyword *direct* using

```
$ man -k direct
```

finds 81 entries on one system. Filtering that output for keyword *read* yields

```
$ man -k direct | grep read
DXmHelpSystemDisplay (3X)   - Displays a topic or directory of the
   help file in Bookreader.
opendir, readdir, readdir_r, telldir, seekdir, rewinddir, closedir (3)  -
   Performs operations on directories
$
```

which looks perfect. The first screen of the manpage shows

```
$ man 3 readdir
opendir(3)                                                    opendir(3)

NAME

opendir, readdir, readdir_r, telldir, seekdir, rewinddir, closedir -
Performs operations on directories

LIBRARY

Standard C Library (libc.a)

SYNOPSIS

#include <sys/types.h>
#include <dirent.h>

DIR *opendir (
   const char *dir_name );

struct dirent *readdir (
   DIR *dir_pointer );

int readdir_r (
   DIR *dir_pointer,
   struct dirent *entry,
   struct dirent **result);

long telldir (
   DIR *dir_pointer );
```

```
void seekdir (
  DIR *dir_pointer,
  long location );

void rewinddir (
  DIR *dir_pointer );

int closedir (
  DIR *dir_pointer );
```

[more] (11%)

Reading through the manpage, we find that getting data from a directory is similar to getting data from a file. opendir opens a connection to a directory, readdir returns a pointer to the next item in the directory, and closedir shuts down the connection. seekdir, telldir, and rewinddir are similar to lseek. Figure 3.2 shows what is going on.

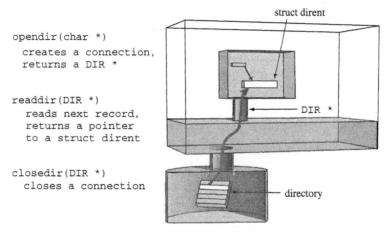

```
opendir(char *)
  creates a connection,
  returns a DIR *

readdir(DIR *)
  reads next record,
  returns a pointer
  to a struct dirent

closedir(DIR *)
  closes a connection
```

struct dirent

DIR *

directory

FIGURE 3.2

Reading entries from a directory.

Reading the Contents of a Directory

A directory is a list of files, more precisely, a sequence of records, each a *directory entry*. We read the entries by calling readdir. Each call to readdir returns a pointer to the next record, a variable of type struct dirent. The components of this structure are described in some manpages and in the header file /usr/include/dirent.h.

For example, a Sun OS manpage for dirent begins

```
File Formats                                          dirent(4)

NAME
    dirent - file system independent directory entry

SYNOPSIS
    #include <dirent.h>
```

DESCRIPTION
> Different file system types may have different directory entries. The dirent structure defines a file system independent directory entry, which contains information common to directory entries in different file system types. A set of these structures is returned by the getdents(2) system call.
>
> The dirent structure is defined:

```
struct  dirent {
        ino_t           d_ino;
        off_t           d_off;
        unsigned short  d_reclen;
        char            d_name[1];
};
```

Each dirent struct contains a member called d_name. This member stores the filename. Notice that the length of the d_name array is defined as one on this system. What is going on here? One char only gives space for a terminating null character.

3.5 QUESTION 3: CAN I WRITE ls?

Here is the logic for listing a directory:

```
main()
        opendir
        while ( readdir )
                print d_name
        closedir
```

The complete code for ls1.c is

```
/** ls1.c
 **     purpose   list contents of directory or directories
 **     action    if no args, use .  else list files in args
 **/
#include        <stdio.h>
#include        <sys/types.h>
#include        <dirent.h>

void do_ls(char []);

main(int ac, char *av[])
{
        if ( ac == 1 )
                do_ls( "." );
        else
```

```
                    while ( --ac ){
                            printf("%s:\n", *++av );
                            do_ls( *av );
                    }
        }

        void do_ls( char dirname[] )
        /*
         *      list files in directory called dirname
         */
        {
                DIR               *dir_ptr;               /* the directory */
                struct dirent     *direntp;               /* each entry    */

                if ( ( dir_ptr = opendir( dirname ) ) == NULL )
                        fprintf(stderr,"ls1: cannot open %s\n", dirname);
                else
                {
                        while ( ( direntp = readdir( dir_ptr ) ) != NULL )
                                printf("%s\n", direntp->d_name );
                        closedir(dir_ptr);
                }
        }
```

Compile and run the code, and then compare its output with the output of the
ls installed on the system:

```
$ cc -o ls1 ls1.c
$ ls1
.
..
s.tar
tail1
Makefile
ls1.c
ls2.c
chap03
old_src
docs
ls1
stat1.c
statdemo.c
tail1.c
$ ls
Makefile     docs       ls1.c      old_src     stat1.c     tail1
chap03       ls1        ls2.c      s.tar       statdemo.c  tail1.c
$
```

3.5.1 How Did We Do?

Not bad for a first try. This version 1.0 `ls` lists files in a directory, but it needs work in the following areas:

(a) Not Sorted
Our list of filenames is not sorted alphabetically. *Fix:* We could read all the file-names into an array and then use `qsort` to sort the array.

(b) No Columns
Standard `ls` arranges the list of files in columns. Some versions arrange the list across then down, and some versions arrange the list down then across. *Fix:* Read the list of names into an array and then figure out column widths and heights.

(c) Lists '.' files
This version displays the names of dot files. The standard version of `ls` only shows these if the -a option is specified. *Fix:* It should be easy to suppress these names and add the -a option.

(d) No -l info
The standard `ls` displays information about a file if the user specifies the -l op-tion, ours does not. *Fix:* Adding -l is not so easy. The `dirent` structure defined in <dirent.h> has only a few members. Nowhere in the `dirent` struct is the size of the file, the owner, or any of the other properties. If information about files is not stored in the directory, where is that information stored?

3.6 PROJECT TWO: WRITING `ls` `-l`

We saw that `ls` does two different types of things: `ls` lists directories, and `ls` displays in-formation about files. We then discovered these two actions are unrelated. A directory contains little more than names of files. Finding and displaying information about files is a completely separate project. We pursue it using the standard three questions.

3.6.1 Question 1: What Does `ls` `-l` Do?

Here is sample output:

```
$ ls -l
total 108
-rw-rw-r--    2 bruce     users          345 Jul 29 11:05 Makefile
-rw-rw-r--    1 bruce     users        27521 Aug  1 12:14 chap03
drwxrwxr-x    2 bruce     users         1024 Aug  1 12:15 docs
-rw-r--r--    1 bruce     users          723 Feb  9  1998 ls1.c
-rw-r--r--    1 bruce     users         3045 Feb 15 03:51 ls2.c
drwxrwxr-x    2 bruce     users         1024 Aug  1 12:14 old_src
-rw-rw-r--    1 bruce     users        30720 Aug  1 12:05 s.tar
-rw-r--r--    1 bruce     support        946 Feb 18 17:15 stat1.c
-rw-r--r--    1 bruce     support        191 Feb  9  1998 statdemo.c
```

```
-rwxrwxr-x    1 bruce     users       37351 Aug  1 12:13 tail1
-rw-r--r--    1 bruce     users        1416 Aug  1 12:05 tail1.c
-rw-r--r--    1 cse215    cscie215      574 Feb  9  1998 writable.c
$
```

Each line consists of the following seven fields:

mode	The first character in each line represents the *type* of the file. A "-" indicates a regular file, and a "d" indicates a directory. There are other types of files. You can learn a lot about Unix by understanding the file types.
	The remaining nine characters in this first column represent the access permissions. Permission to read, write, and execute a file can be set on or off for three classes of users: user, group, and everyone else. In the previous sample output, all the files and directories are readable by every class of user, but the files are only writable by the user who owns the files. The compiled file tail1 is executable by everyone.
links	A link is a reference to a file. This topic is discussed in the next chapter.
owner	Each file belongs to a user. The username of the owner is shown.
group	Each file belongs to a group of users, too. Some versions of ls show the name of the group.
size	The number of bytes in the file is in column five. Notice that directories in this example all have the same size. Storage for directories is allocated in blocks, so the size of a directory is always a multiple of 512. For regular files, the size represents the number of bytes of data in the file.
last-modified	The next field consists of three strings representing the last-modified time. For newer files, the output includes the month, day, and time. For older files, ls shows the month, day, and year. Why is that a useful system? How old is *old enough* to warrant showing the year?
name	The name of the file is shown.

3.6.2   Question 2: How Does ls -1 Work?

How can we get information about a file? Let us search the manual. The search

```
$ man -k file | grep -i information
```

ought to find useful reference material, but is disappointing on many versions of Unix. Many versions, it turns out, use the term *file status* rather than *file information* or *file properties*. The system call that retrieves file status is called stat.

3.6.3   Answer: The `stat` Call Gets File Information

Figure 3.3 shows how `stat` works:

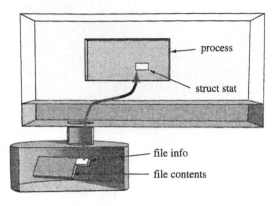

`stat(name,ptr)`

copies information about
"name" from the disk into
a struct inside the calling
process.

process

struct stat

file info

file contents

FIGURE 3.3

Reading file properties using `stat`.

A file is stored on the disk. A file has contents, and a file has a set of attributes: size, owner ID, etc. A process wants information about a file. The process defines a place to store file information, defines a buffer of type `struct stat`, and then asks the kernel to copy file information from the disk to the buffer:

stat		
PUPOSE	Obtain information about a file	
INCLUDE	#include <sys/stat.h>	
USAGE	int result = stat(char *fname, struct stat *bufp)	
AGRS	fname	name of file
	bufp	pointer to buffer
RETURNS	-1	if error
	0	if success

`stat` copies information about file *fname* into the structure pointed to by *bufp*. The following example shows how to use `stat` to find the size of a file:

```
/* filesize.c - prints size of passwd file */
#include <stdio.h>
#include <sys/stat.h>

int main()
{
```

```
        struct stat infobuf;                  /* place to store info */

        if ( stat( "/etc/passwd", &infobuf) == -1 )   /* get info */
               perror("/etc/passwd");
        else
               printf(" The size of /etc/passwd is %d\n", infobuf.st_size );
}
```

stat copies the information about the file into the struct called infobuf, and the program then reads the size of the file from the st_size member of the struct.

3.6.4   What Other Information Does **stat** Provide?

The manual page for stat and the header file /usr/include/sys/stat.h describe the
members of struct stat:

st_mode	type and permissions
st_uid	ID of owner
st_gid	ID of group
st_size	number of bytes in file
st_nlink	number of links to file
st_mtime	last content-modified time
st_atime	last-accessed time
st_ctime	last properties-changed time

The struct contains some other items, but these attributes are the ones ls -1 displays.
The next sample program, fileinfo.c, retrieves and prints those attributes:

```
/* fileinfo.c - use stat() to obtain and print file properties
 *             - some members are just numbers...
 */
#include <stdio.h>
#include <sys/types.h>
#include <sys/stat.h>

int main(int ac, char *av[])
{
        struct stat info;          /* buffer for file info */

        if (ac>1)
                if( stat(av[1], &info) != -1 ){
                    show_stat_info( av[1], &info );
                    return 0;
                }
                else
                    perror(av[1]);   /* report stat() errors  */
        return 1;
}
show_stat_info(char *fname, struct stat *buf)
/*
```

```
             * displays some info from stat in a name=value format
             */
            {
                    printf("   mode: %o\n", buf->st_mode);        /* type + mode */
                    printf("  links: %d\n", buf->st_nlink);       /* # links     */
                    printf("   user: %d\n", buf->st_uid);         /* user id     */
                    printf("  group: %d\n", buf->st_gid);         /* group id    */
                    printf("   size: %d\n", buf->st_size);        /* file size   */
                    printf("modtime: %d\n", buf->st_mtime);       /* modified    */
                    printf("   name: %s\n", fname );              /* filename    */
            }
```

Compile and run `fileinfo`, and then compare the output with that from `ls -1`:

```
$ cc -o fileinfo fileinfo.c
$ ./fileinfo fileinfo.c
   mode: 100664
  links: 1
   user: 500
  group: 120
   size: 1106
modtime: 965158604
   name: fileinfo.c
$ ls -l fileinfo.c
-rw-rw-r--    1 bruce      users          1106 Aug  1 15:36 fileinfo.c
```

3.6.5   How'd We Do?

links, *size*, and *name* worked perfectly. *modified-time* is a `time_t`. We can use `ctime` to convert this value into a string containing the month, day, time, or year.

We print *mode* as a number, but `ls` prints the value as

```
-rw-rw-r--
```

user and *group* are numbers in the struct, but `ls` prints a username and a group name. To complete the project of writing `ls -1`, we have to learn how to convert the mode, the user, and the group from numbers to strings.

3.6.6   Converting File Mode to a String

How are the file type and permission bits stored in the `st_mode` member? How can we extract those attributes and present them as a sequence of 10 characters? What is the connection between the octal number `100664` and the string `-rw-rw-r--`?

Answer: st_mode is a 16-bit quantity. Separate attributes are encoded in substrings of these 16 bits. Figure 3.4 shows five coding substrings:

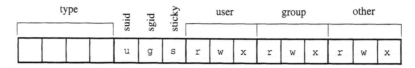

FIGURE 3.4

File type and access coding.

The first four bits represent the type of the file. Four bits can contain 16 possible patterns of 1s and 0s. Each of these 16 patterns can correspond to a file type. At least seven file types exist now.

The next three bits are used for special attributes of a file. Each bit corresponds to a special attribute; a '1' turns the attribute on, a '0' turns it off. These *set-user-ID*, *set-group-ID*, and *sticky* bits will be discussed later.

Finally, there are three sets of permission bits, one set specifying access by the user that owns the file, one set specifying access by members of the group of the file, and the last set specifying access by all other people on the system. For each class of user, there are three bits indicating if the file may be read, written, and executed. A value of '1' in a spot indicates the permission is granted, and a value of '0' in the spot indicates permission is denied.

Subfield Coding Is Not Magic

Packing special meanings into subfields of larger strings is a common technique. The idea is used in the following examples:

Examples of Subfield Coding	
617-495-4204	area, exchange, line
027-93-1111	social security number
128.103.33.100	IP numbers

How to Read Subfields: Masking

How can you determine whether the telephone number 212-333-4444 is in the 212 area code? That is easy: You look at the first three digits and compare that substring to the string 212. *Another technique* is to zero out all digits but the first three and then compare the result to 212-000-0000.

The technique of zeroing out digits so only a subfield shows through is called *masking*. Think of putting a mask over your face to obscure all features except for your eyes or perhaps your eyes and mouth. We can use a set of masks to translate st_mode into the string displayed by ls -l.

Subfield coding is a common, important technique in systems programming. You need to know four things to understand subfield coding and masking.

Thing One: The Concept of Masking

Masking a value is zeroing out bits in the number so only a subfield is unaffected.

Thing Two: An Integer is Just a String of Bits

Integers are stored in the computer as a sequence of bits. Figure 3.5 shows how the decimal value 215 is expressed as a sequence of 1s and 0s using binary (base-2) notation: What is the decimal expression for the second value, 00011010?

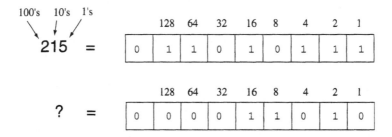

FIGURE 3.5

Translating between decimal and binary.

Thing Three: The Technique of Masking

The *bitwise and* operation, **&**, causes one value to mask another. Figure 3.6 shows a value of 100664 octal (base 8) being masked with bits including the user-writable bit: Notice how other 1's in the original number are converted to 0's by the mask.

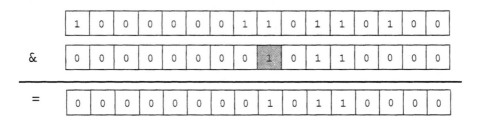

FIGURE 3.6

Applying a bitmask.

Thing Four: Using Base 8

Working with masks in binary is tedious, particularly for masks 16 or 32 bits long. Just as we group large decimal numbers into three-digit bunches (e.g., 23,234,456,022) for ease of reading, we group large binary numbers into three-digit bunches and convert each bunch into a single octal digit (0 through 7).

For example, we can bunch digits in the binary number 1000000110110100 into threes as 1,000,000,110,110,100 and translate each bunch to get 0100664, which is easier to comprehend.

Using Masking to Decode File Types

The type of the file is coded in the first four bits of the mode. We can use masks to decode the information. Specifically, we use a mask to zero all but the first four bits, then compare the result to codes for each file type.

These definitions are in <sys/stat.h> or in a file it includes:

```
#define S_IFMT      0170000      /* type of file */
#define   S_IFREG   0100000      /*   regular */
#define   S_IFDIR   0040000      /*   directory */
#define   S_IFBLK   0060000      /*   block special */
#define   S_IFCHR   0020000      /*   character special */
#define   S_IFIFO   0010000      /*   fifo */
#define   S_IFLNK   0120000      /*   symbolic link */
#define   S_IFSOCK  0140000      /*   socket */
```

The symbol S_IFMT is a mask that selects the first four bits; the value of the mask is 0170000. Convince yourself this mask selects the correct set of bits by converting octal digits back to three bits. The code for a regular file (S_IFREG) is 0100000; the value for a directory is 0040000. For example, the code fragment

```
if ( (info.st_mode & 0170000) == 0040000 )
        printf("this is a directory.");
```

checks whether the mode specifies a directory by masking all but the file-type field and comparing that result to the directory code.

If you do not want to write code to mask and test, you can instead use macros in <sys/stat.h>:

```
/*
 *      File type macros
 */

#define S_ISFIFO(m)     (((m)&(0170000)) == (0010000))
#define S_ISDIR(m)      (((m)&(0170000)) == (0040000))
#define S_ISCHR(m)      (((m)&(0170000)) == (0020000))
#define S_ISBLK(m)      (((m)&(0170000)) == (0060000))
#define S_ISREG(m)      (((m)&(0170000)) == (0100000))
```

These macros allow you to write code such as

```
if ( S_ISDIR(info.st_mode) )
        printf("this is a directory.");
```

Using Masking to Decode Permission Bits

The low nine bits in the mode represent the read, write, and execute permission for each class of user. ls converts those nine 1s and 0s into a string of dashes and letters.

Each bit has a mask available through `<sys/stat.h>`. The following code takes a simple, but readable, approach—test each bit separately:

```
/*
 * This function takes a mode value and a char array
 * and puts into the char array the file type and the
 * nine letters that correspond to the bits in mode.
 * NOTE: It does not code setuid, setgid, and sticky
 * codes
 */
void mode_to_letters( int mode, char str[] )
{
    strcpy( str, "----------" );        /* default=no perms */
    if ( S_ISDIR(mode) )  str[0] = 'd';  /* directory?       */
    if ( S_ISCHR(mode) )  str[0] = 'c';  /* char devices     */
    if ( S_ISBLK(mode) )  str[0] = 'b';  /* block device     */

    if ( mode & S_IRUSR ) str[1] = 'r';  /* 3 bits for user  */
    if ( mode & S_IWUSR ) str[2] = 'w';
    if ( mode & S_IXUSR ) str[3] = 'x';

    if ( mode & S_IRGRP ) str[4] = 'r';  /* 3 bits for group */
    if ( mode & S_IWGRP ) str[5] = 'w';
    if ( mode & S_IXGRP ) str[6] = 'x';

    if ( mode & S_IROTH ) str[7] = 'r';  /* 3 bits for other */
    if ( mode & S_IWOTH ) str[8] = 'w';
    if ( mode & S_IXOTH ) str[9] = 'x';
}
```

Decoding Bits and Writing `ls`

We are pretty close to knowing enough to write a version of `ls` with the correct long format. We can print out the file size, links, and name correctly. We can take the mode and convert it into the standard sequence of letters and dashes. The date can be converted from a `time_t`, via `ctime`, into a string. What about the strings for owner and group?

3.6.7   Converting User/Group ID to Strings

The owner and group of the file are stored as numbers, a *user ID* and a *group ID*. `ls`, though, prints out the username and the group name. What is the connection between a UID and a username?

Searching the manual for *username*, *uid*, and *group* turns up wildly different results from one version of Unix to the next. See what you find. Here are the facts:

Fact One: `/etc/passwd` Is the List of Users

How do you log into a Unix machine? The system asks you for a username then asks you for a password. The system then decides if that username/password pair is acceptable. How does it know?

The traditional system for recording username and passwords is a file called /etc/passwd. This file is a list of all the users on the system. The file looks like this:

```
root:WPA4d1OwUxypE:0:0:root:/root:/bin/bash
bin:*:1:1:bin:/bin:
daemon:*:2:2:daemon:/sbin:
smith:x1mEPcp4TNokc:9768:3073:James Q Smith:/home/s/smith:/shells/tcsh
fred:mSuVNOF4CRTmE:20359:550:Fred:/home/f/fred:/shells/tcsh
diane:7oUS8f1PsrccY:20555:550:Diane Abramov:/home/d/diane:/shells/tcsh
ajr:WitmEBWylar1w:3607:3034:Ann Reuter:/home/a/ajr:/shells/bash
```

This plain-text file is the list of users and information about the users. Each line in the file represents information about one user. The fields in the line are separated by colons. The first field is the username, the second field is the encrypted password,[1] the third field is the user ID, and the fourth field is the group to which the user belongs. The other fields are the *Real Name* of the user, the home directory for the user, and the path to the program the user uses as a shell. The passwd file is publicly readable. For more detail, search the manual for the keyword passwd.

This looks perfect. Search the file for a record with the user ID, and then take the first field from the line. The technique is not perfect, though: searching through /etc/passwd is a bit tedious, and the method does not work on many networked systems.

Fact Two: /etc/passwd Is Not Always the Complete List of Users

Every Unix system has an /etc/passwd file, but on many Unix systems this file does not include all users. Networked installations want to let their users log into any machine on the network with the same username and password. To make this possible using /etc/passwd, the system administration would need to add each user and current password to the /etc/passwd file on every machine on the network. When a user changed a password, that change would have to be distributed to every /etc/passwd on the network. If one machine was down, it could get out of sync with the rest of the machines.

One solution is to install a minimal /etc/passwd on each machine for stand-alone operation but keep the full list of users in a network-accessible database. New users and password changes are recorded in this central database. All programs that need user information consult the central database. A system for centralized network information is called NIS. The manual should have more information.

Fact Three: getpwuid Provides Access to the Complete List of Users

The library function getpwuid provides access to the database of user information. If your system uses the passwd file, getpwuid looks there, and if your system uses a central database, getpwuid talks to that database. Using getpwuid assures portable code.

getpwuid takes a UID as argument and returns a pointer to a struct passwd, defined in /usr/include/pwd.h as follows:

---

[1]Many systems store the encrypted passwords in a *shadow* file to increase security.

```
/* The passwd structure.   */
struct passwd
{
    char *pw_name;                    /* Username.   */
    char *pw_passwd;                  /* Password.   */
    __uid_t pw_uid;                   /* User ID.   */
    __gid_t pw_gid;                   /* Group ID.   */
    char *pw_gecos;                   /* Real name.   */
    char *pw_dir;                     /* Home directory.   */
    char *pw_shell;                   /* Shell program.   */
};
```

This function and this struct definition provide just what we need to fill in the username in the long format for `ls`. The simple solution is

```
/*
 * returns a username associated with the specified uid
 * NOTE: does not work if there is no username
 */
char *uid_to_name( uid_t uid )
{
    return getpwuid(uid)->pw_name ;
}
```

This function is simple but not robust. If `uid` is not associated with a username, `getpwuid` returns the `NULL` pointer. In that case, there is no `pw_name` member to dereference. How can that happen? The regular version of `ls` has a solution to this problem.

Fact Four: Some UIDs Do Not Correspond to Lognames

Say you have an account on a particular Unix machine with the username `pat` and user ID 2000. When you create files, those files are owned by you. That is, the `stat` system call returns a struct for your files with the number 2000 in the `st_uid` field. That number is an attribute of the file.

Then you move to another town. The system administrator deletes your line in the `passwd` file, removing the association between the number 2000 and the username `pat`. When a program passes the number 2000 to `getpwuid`, `getpwuid` passes back `NULL`.

The standard version of `ls` handles this case by printing out the UID if there is no corresponding username.

What would happen, though, if a new user were added to the system and assigned your old UID? Any files you left around on the system are now owned by that user. That user has permission to read, write, and delete those files.

For the final task, how do we convert the group ID to a group name? What is a group? What is a group ID?

Fact Five: `/etc/group` Is the List of Groups

Consider a Unix machine at a business. People are organized into departments and share projects. There may be a group of people in sales, a group in management, etc.

Consider a school. Some people are teachers, some are students, some are administrators. People may be grouped by being in the same course or the same department.

Unix provides a system for defining groups and assigning users to groups. The file /etc/group is a plain-text file that looks like the following:

```
root::0:root
other::1:
bin::2:root,bin,daemon
sys::3:root,bin,sys,adm
adm::4:root,adm,daemon
uucp::5:root,uucp
mail::6:root
tty::7:root,tty,adm
lp::8:root,lp,adm
```

The name of the group is the first field, the group password (a rarely used item) is the second field, the group ID number is the third field, and the fourth field is a comma-separated list of usernames. These users belong to the group.

Fact Six: A User Can Belong to More than One Group

The passwd file contains fields for the UID and GID for each user. The group specified in the passwd file entry is the primary group for a user, but a user may belong to other groups. Adding a username to an entry in /etc/group adds that user to that group. In the example above, you can see that user adm belongs to the groups called sys, adm, tty, and lp . This list is used with the permission bits for group access. For example, if a file belongs to the group called lp and is group writable, then user adm may modify that file.

Fact Seven: getgrgid Provides Access to the List of Groups

On a networked system, the data in /etc/group can also be moved to a central database. As with the list of user information, Unix provides functions that provide access to the group list regardless of the implementation. The manual page for getgrgid explains the details and related functions. For our purposes, we use code that looks like this:

```
/*
 * returns a groupname associated with the specified gid
 * NOTE: does not work if there is no groupname
 */
char *gid_to_name( gid_t uid )
{
    return getgrgid(gid)->gr_name ;
}
```

3.6.8 Putting It All Together: ls2.c

We examined each item in the output of ls -l. For each one, we now know what the field means and how to convert the value into a form people understand. The program ls2.c is the result:

```
/* ls2.c
 *      purpose  list contents of directory or directories
 *      action   if no args, use .  else list files in args
 *      note     uses stat and pwd.h and grp.h
 *      BUG: try ls2 /tmp
 */
#include        <stdio.h>
#include        <sys/types.h>
#include        <dirent.h>
#include        <sys/stat.h>

void do_ls(char[]);
void dostat(char *);
void show_file_info( char *, struct stat *);
void mode_to_letters( int , char [] );
char *uid_to_name( uid_t );
char *gid_to_name( gid_t );

main(int ac, char *av[])
{
        if ( ac == 1 )
                do_ls( "." );
        else
                while ( --ac ){
                        printf("%s:\n", *++av );
                        do_ls( *av );
                }
}

void do_ls( char dirname[] )
/*
 *      list files in directory called dirname
 */
{
        DIR             *dir_ptr;               /* the directory */
        struct dirent   *direntp;               /* each entry    */

        if ( ( dir_ptr = opendir( dirname ) ) == NULL )
                fprintf(stderr,"ls1: cannot open %s\n", dirname);
        else
        {
                while ( ( direntp = readdir( dir_ptr ) ) != NULL )
                        dostat( direntp->d_name );
                closedir(dir_ptr);
        }
}

void dostat( char *filename )
{
        struct stat info;

        if ( stat(filename, &info) == -1 )                      /* cannot stat */
```

```
                    perror( filename );                    /* say why      */
            else                                  /* else show info        */
                    show_file_info( filename, &info );
    }
    void show_file_info( char *filename, struct stat *info_p )
    /*
     * display the info about 'filename'.  The info is stored in struct at
*info_p
     */
    {
            char    *uid_to_name(), *ctime(), *gid_to_name(), *filemode();
            void    mode_to_letters();
            char    modestr[11];

            mode_to_letters( info_p->st_mode, modestr );

            printf( "%s"     , modestr );
            printf( "%4d "   , (int) info_p->st_nlink);
            printf( "%-8s "  , uid_to_name(info_p->st_uid) );
            printf( "%-8s "  , gid_to_name(info_p->st_gid) );
            printf( "%8ld "  , (long)info_p->st_size);
            printf( "%.12s ", 4+ctime(&info_p->st_mtime));
            printf( "%s\n"   , filename );
    }
    /*
     * utility functions
     */

    /*
     * This function takes a mode value and a char array
     * and puts into the char array the file type and the
     * nine letters that correspond to the bits in mode.
     * NOTE: It does not code setuid, setgid, and sticky
     * codes
     */
    void mode_to_letters( int mode, char str[] )
    {
        strcpy( str, "----------" );              /* default=no perms */

        if ( S_ISDIR(mode) )  str[0] = 'd';    /* directory?        */
        if ( S_ISCHR(mode) )  str[0] = 'c';    /* char devices      */
        if ( S_ISBLK(mode) )  str[0] = 'b';    /* block device      */

        if ( mode & S_IRUSR ) str[1] = 'r';    /* 3 bits for user   */
        if ( mode & S_IWUSR ) str[2] = 'w';
        if ( mode & S_IXUSR ) str[3] = 'x';

        if ( mode & S_IRGRP ) str[4] = 'r';    /* 3 bits for group */
        if ( mode & S_IWGRP ) str[5] = 'w';
        if ( mode & S_IXGRP ) str[6] = 'x';

        if ( mode & S_IROTH ) str[7] = 'r';    /* 3 bits for other */
```

```
        if ( mode & S_IWOTH ) str[8] = 'w';
        if ( mode & S_IXOTH ) str[9] = 'x';
}
#include        <pwd.h>

char *uid_to_name( uid_t uid )
/*
 *      returns pointer to username associated with uid, uses getpw()
 */
{
        struct  passwd *getpwuid(), *pw_ptr;
        static  char numstr[10];

        if ( ( pw_ptr = getpwuid( uid ) ) == NULL ){
                sprintf(numstr,"%d", uid);
                return numstr;
        }
        else
                return pw_ptr->pw_name ;
}

#include        <grp.h>
char *gid_to_name( gid_t gid )
/*
 *      returns pointer to group number gid. used getgrgid(3)
 */
{
        struct group *getgrgid(), *grp_ptr;
        static  char numstr[10];

        if ( ( grp_ptr = getgrgid(gid) ) == NULL ){
                sprintf(numstr,"%d", gid);
                return numstr;
        }
        else
                return grp_ptr->gr_name;
}
```

And here it is in action, followed by the output of the system version of ls:

```
$ ls2
drwxrwxr-x   4 bruce      bruce            1024 Aug  2 18:18 .
drwxrwxr-x   5 bruce      bruce            1024 Aug  2 18:14 ..
-rw-rw-r--   1 bruce      users           30720 Aug  1 12:05 s.tar
-rwxrwxr-x   1 bruce      users           37351 Aug  1 12:13 tail1
-rw-rw-r--   2 bruce      users             345 Jul 29 11:05 Makefile
-rw-r--r--   1 bruce      users             723 Aug  1 14:26 ls1.c
-rw-r--r--   1 bruce      users            3045 Feb 15 03:51 ls2.c
-rw-rw-r--   1 bruce      users           27521 Aug  1 12:14 chap03
drwxrwxr-x   2 bruce      users            1024 Aug  1 12:14 old_src
drwxrwxr-x   2 bruce      users            1024 Aug  1 12:15 docs
-rwxrwxr-x   1 bruce      bruce           37048 Aug  1 14:26 ls1
```

```
-rw-r--r--   1 bruce    support        946 Feb 18 17:15 stat1.c
-rwxrwxr-x   2 bruce    bruce        42295 Aug  2 18:18 ls2
-rw-r--r--   1 bruce    support        191 Feb  9 21:01 statdemo.c
-rw-r--r--   1 bruce    users         1416 Aug  1 12:05 tail1.c
$ ls - l
total 189
-rw-rw-r--   2 bruce    users          345 Jul 29 11:05 Makefile
-rw-rw-r--   1 bruce    users        27521 Aug  1 12:14 chap03
drwxrwxr-x   2 bruce    users         1024 Aug  1 12:15 docs
-rwxrwxr-x   1 bruce    bruce        37048 Aug  1 14:26 ls1
-rw-r--r--   1 bruce    users          723 Aug  1 14:26 ls1.c
-rwxrwxr-x   2 bruce    bruce        42295 Aug  2 18:18 ls2
-rw-r--r--   1 bruce    users         3045 Feb 15 03:51 ls2.c
drwxrwxr-x   2 bruce    users         1024 Aug  1 12:14 old_src
-rw-rw-r--   1 bruce    users        30720 Aug  1 12:05 s.tar
-rw-r--r--   1 bruce    support        946 Feb 18 17:15 stat1.c
-rw-r--r--   1 bruce    support        191 Feb  9  1998 statdemo.c
-rwxrwxr-x   1 bruce    users        37351 Aug  1 12:13 tail1
-rw-r--r--   1 bruce    users         1416 Aug  1 12:05 tail1.c
$
```

How'd We Do?

ls2 displays information about files in the standard ls -l format. The output looks good. The columns line up perfectly, and the translation from internal bit patterns and ID numbers to readable strings is almost complete.

The program needs more work. The *real* version prints a total line at the top. What does that mean? Furthermore, it still does not sort filenames, nor does it handle the -a option, nor does it arrange filenames in columns, and it assumes each of its arguments is a directory name.

ls2 has an even more serious bug: It does not list information about files in other directories correctly. Try the command: ls2 /tmp to see the problem. Correcting this error is left as an exercise.

3.7 THE THREE SPECIAL BITS

The st_mode member of the stat structure contains sixteen bits. Four are used for the type, and nine are used for access permission. The three other bits are used to activate special properties of a file.

3.7.1 The Set-User-ID Bit

The first of the three special bits is called the *set-user-ID* bit. It is the solution to an important question:

> *How can a regular user change his or her password?*

That's easy, use the passwd command! But, how does the passwd command work? Note the owner and file permission bits for the file of passwords:

```
$ ls -l /etc/passwd
-rw-r--r--   1 root     root           894 Jun 20 19:17 /etc/passwd
```

Changing your password means changing your record in that file, but *you do not have permission to write to that file*. Only the user named root has write permission. How does using the passwd program give you the right to change a file you are not allowed to change? Do you see the problem?

The solution is to give permission to the program, not to you. The program you use to change your password, /usr/bin/passwd or /bin/passwd, is owned by root and has the *set-user-ID bit set*. The permission bits appear as

```
$ ls -l /usr/bin/passwd
-r-sr-xr-x   1 root      bin          15725 Oct 31  1997 /usr/bin/passwd
```

That SUID bit tells the kernel to run the program as though it were being run by the owner of the program. The name *set user ID* comes from the fact that the bit causes the kernel to set the *effective user ID* to the user ID of the owner of the program.

User root owns /etc/passwd so a program running as root can modify the file.

Doesn't That Mean I Can Change Passwords of Other Users?

No. The passwd program knows who you are. It uses the getuid system call to ask the kernel for the user ID you used when you logged in. passwd has permission to rewrite the entire password file, but will only change the record for the user running the program.

Other Uses for the Set-User-ID Bit

The SUID bit is used for any program that provides controlled access to a file or other resource. Consider a print-spooling system. Many users want to print files, but the printer can only print one file at a time. The Unix lpr command can copy your file to a directory where it will wait its turn to be printed. It would be risky to permit all users to copy files to this spool directory and update lists of files to print. Instead, the lpr program is owned by root or lpr and has the set-uid bit turned on. When you, a regular user, use lpr , the program runs with the effective user ID of root or lpr and can modify the contents of the spool directory and any associated files. Programs to remove print jobs from the print queue are also set-uid programs.

Computer games that update databases of top-scoring players or read files of secret maps are marked to run as the user who owns the database or the secret files. Any user can play the game, but only the game can update the score list and read the maps.

A Mask to Test for the SUID Bit

A program can test whether a file has the set-user-ID bit on by using the mask defined via <sys/stat.h>. The definition is

```
#define S_ISUID       0004000        /* set user id on execution */
```

You can translate that to binary to verify that it selects the first of the three special bits.

3.7.2   The Set-Group-ID Bit

The second special bit sets the *effective group ID* of a program. If a program belongs to group *g* and the *set group ID* bit is set, the program runs as though it were being run by a member of group *g*. This bit grants the program the access rights of members of that group.

A programmer can test the bit with the following mask:

```
#define S_ISGID          0002000           /* set group id on execution */
```

3.7.3 The Sticky Bit

This bit has two completely different uses, one for files and one for directories. First, the file use. In the *Olden Days*® Unix handled the problem of running several programs at the same time through a technique called *swapping*. Consider the following situation: Your computer has 1 megabyte of user space, and you are running three programs, each of which uses half a megabyte of memory. Obviously, only two of them can be in memory at once. Where does the kernel put programs that are not running at a particular instant? In the old days, the kernel stored the entire program on a section of a hard disk reserved for swapping. When it was time for that program to run again, the kernel would *swap out* one of the other programs and then *swap in* the one that was about to run.

Loading a program from the *swap device* was faster than loading a program from the regular section of the disk. On the regular section of the disk, a program might be fragmented, that is, split into many small sections scattered across the disk. On the swap device, the program was never fragmented.

Now, consider a program that people used a lot, like an editor, compiler, or computer game. If a copy of that program were kept on the swap device, the kernel could load it faster. The *sticky bit* told the kernel to keep the program on the swap device even if nobody was using it right now. The name comes from the fact that the program sticks to the swap device the way chewing gum sticks to your shoe.

Swapping entire programs in and out of memory is no longer necessary. A technique called virtual memory allows the kernel to move programs in and out of memory in small sections, called pages. The kernel no longer needs to load the entire block of code to run a program.

The sticky bit has a different meaning when applied to a directory. This meaning also involves something sticking around. Some directories are designed to hold temporary files. These scratch directories, notably /tmp, are publicly writable, allowing any user to create and *delete* any files there. The sticky bit overrides the publicly writable attribute for a directory. Files in the directory may only be deleted by their owners.

3.7.4 The Special Bits and `ls -l`

As we have just seen, each file has a type and 12 attribute bits, but `ls` uses only nine spots to display these 12 attributes. How does it manage?

The manpage on `ls` should have all the details, but the example

```
-rwsr-sr-t   1 root      root        2345 Jun 12 14:02 sample
```

shows how the letter *s* is used in place of the letter *x* to indicate that the user and group-executable bits have been augmented by the set-user and set-group ID bits. The *t* at the end indicates that the sticky bit is on.

3.8   SUMMARY OF ls

We now have a working version of ls that lists files in a directory and displays information about those files. In the process of seeing what ls does, how ls works, and writing our own version, we have had to make sense of many aspects of Unix design. Here is a list of the main topics:

Directories and Files

Unix stores data in files. A directory is a special kind of file; a directory contains a list of names of files. A directory even contains a name for itself. Unix provides a set of functions to open, read, seek, and close directories. It does not provide a write function.

Users and Groups

Each person who uses the system is assigned a username and a user ID number. People use their username to log in and communicate with other users; the system uses the UID to identify the owner of files. People belong to groups. Each group has a group name and a group id number.

File Attributes

Every file has a collection of properties. A program can obtain the list of properties for a file by using the stat system call.

File Ownership

Every file has an owner. Unix records the UID of the owner as a property of the file. A file belongs to a group. Unix records the GID of the group as a property of the file.

Access Permissions

Users may read, write, and execute files. Each file has a set of permission bits that determine which users may perform which operations. Permission to read, to write, and to execute a file may be controlled on three levels: user, group, and other.

3.9   SETTING AND MODIFYING THE PROPERTIES OF A FILE

ls -l reports several properties of a file. How are these properties established? Can they be changed? If so, how? If not, why not? We examine the properties displayed in the *long format*,

```
-rw-r--r--    1 bruce    users       3045 Feb 15 03:51 ls2.c
```

from left to right, considering each of the attributes in turn.

3.9.1   Type of a File

A file has a type. It can be a regular file, a directory, a device file, a socket, a symbolic link, or a named pipe.

Establishing the Type of a File   The type of the file is established when the file is created. For example, the `creat` system call creates a regular file. Different system calls are used to create directories, devices, and the like.

Changing the Type of a File   It is not possible to change the type of a file. In stories, pumpkins turn into coaches, but nobody ever explained where the seeds and pulp go.

3.9.2   Permission Bits and Special Bits

Every file has nine permission bits and three special bits. These bits are established when the file is created and can be modified by making the `chmod` system call.

Establishing the Mode of a File   The second argument to `creat` specifies the permission bits you want set when the file is created. For example,

```
fd = creat( "newfile", 0744 );
```

creates `newfile` and requests an initial set of permission bits `rwxr--r--`.

The second argument to `creat` is a request, not an order. The kernel takes the mode requested in `creat` and applies a mask. The result is the bits actually set. The mask is called the *file-creation mask* and specifies which bits should be turned *off*.

For example, if you want to prevent programs from creating files that can be modified by the group or by others, you want to turn off the bits `----w--w-`, which equal 022 in octal. The `umask` system call, for example,

```
umask( 022 );
```

sets the file-creation mask to turn off those two bits. Masks are commonly used to turn on bits and to select bits. Here, the mask specifies which bits to turn off. Yes, it is backwards.

Changing the Mode of a File   A program can modify the permission bits and special bits by making the `chmod` system call. The two examples,

```
chmod( "/tmp/myfile", 04764 );
```
and
```
chmod( "/tmp/myfile", S_ISUID | S_IRWXU | S_IRGRP|S_IWGRP | S_IROTH );
```

have identical effects. In the first case, the new set of bits is expressed in octal, and in the second case, the masks from `<sys/stat.h>` are combined with the bitwise or operator into a single value. The second case allows the meaning of the bits to change in the future without breaking your program. The number of existing programs that use the explicit octal form make it unlikely that anyone will change the meaning of the bits. The mode requested by `chmod` is not affected by the *file-creation mask*.

In sum, we have the following table:

chmod	
PURPOSE	Change permission and special bits for a file
INCLUDE	`#include <sys/types.h>` `#include <sys/stat.h>`
USAGE	`int result = chmod(char *path, mode_t mode);`
ARGS	path path to file mode new value for mode
RETURNS	-1 if error 0 if success

A Shell Command to Change Permission and Special Bits   The shell command `chmod` is a regular Unix command-line program for modifying the permission and special bits. `chmod` allows the user to specify the bit pattern in octal (e.g., *04764*) or in symbolic notation (e.g., *u=rws g=rw o=r*).

3.9.3   Number of Links to a File

The meaning of this attribute will be explained in the next chapter. In brief, though, the number of links is simply the number of times the file is referenced in directories. If a file appears in three places in various directories, the link count is 3.

To increase the link count, create more references. (You can use `link`.) To decrease the link count, remove references. (You can use `unlink`.)

3.9.4   Owner and Group of a File

Each file has an owner. Internally Unix records the owner of a file as a user ID number and the group of a file as a group ID number.

Establishing the Owner of a File   In simple terms, the owner of a file is the user who creates it. But, people do not create files, the kernel does. The kernel creates a file when a process executes the `creat` system call. In reality, then, when the kernel creates a file, it sets the owner of the file to be the effective user ID of the process that calls `creat`. The effective user ID of the process usually is the user ID of the person running the process. If the program has the set-user-ID bit set, though, the effective user ID is the user ID of the person who owns the program. Got it?

Establishing the Group of a File   Under ordinary circumstances, the group of a file is set to the effective group ID of the process that creates the file. Under nonordinary circumstances, the group ID of a file is set to the group ID of the parent directory.

Huh? It is sort of like getting your nationality from your place of birth instead of from the people who created you. It makes some sort of sense.

Changing the Owner and Group of a File   A program can modify the owner and group of a file by making the chown system call. For example,

```
chown( "file1", 200, 40 );
```

changes the user ID to 200 and the group ID to 40 for the file called file1. If either argument is -1, that attribute is not modified. Normally, users do not change the owner of a file. The superuser may set the user ID and the group ID for any file to any value. This call is typically used to set up and manage user accounts. The owner of a file can change the group ID of a file to any group to which that user belongs.

In sum, we have the following table:

chown		
PURPOSE	Change owner and or group ID of a file	
INCLUDE	#include <unistd.h>	
USAGE	int chown(char *path, uid_t owner, gid_t group)	
ARGS	path	path to file
	owner	user ID for file
RETURNS	group	group ID for file
	-1	if error
	0	if success

Shell Commands to Change User and Group ID for Files   The shell commands chown and chgrp are regular Unix command-line programs for modifying the user ID and group ID for files. These programs allow users to change the user and group IDs for several files in one command. The manpage contains all the details.

The chown and chgrp commands allow the user to specify the IDs as numbers or as usernames and group names.

3.9.5   Size of a File

The size of a file, directory, and named pipe represents the number of bytes stored. Programs can increase the size of a file by adding more data to it. Programs can zero the size of a file by using creat. Programs may not shorten a file to a nonzero length.

3.9.6   Modification and Access Time

Each file has three timestamps: the time the file was last modified, the time the file was last read, and the time the file properties (such as owner ID or permission bits) were last changed. The kernel automatically updates these times as programs read and write the file. It may seem odd, but you can write programs that set the modification and access times to arbitrary values.

Changing Modification and Access Times of a File   The `utime` system call
sets the modification and access times for a file. To use `utime`, create a struct containing two `time_t` elements, one for the access time and one for the modification
time, then call `utime` with the name of the file and a pointer to that struct. The kernel sets the access time and the modification time for that file to the values you
specify.

In sum, we have the following table:

	utime
PURPOSE	Change access and modification time for files
INCLUDE	`#include <sys/time.h>` `#include <utime.h>`
USAGE	`#include <sys/types.h>` `int utime( char *path, struct utimbuf *newtimes )`
ARGS	`path` path to file `newtimes` pointer to a struct utimbuf see utime.h for details
RETURNS	`-1` if error `0` if success

Why would you want to change modification or access times? `utime` is particularly useful when retrieving files from backups and archives. Consider a backup copy of a
set of files. On the backup disk or tape, those files are marked with their original modification times. When a program restores a file from a backup, it sure would be nice if it
came back with its modification time intact. That way, you would know that it was, for
example, the version from last April.

For that reason, the program that copies the files from the backup medium does
two things. First, it copies the data into a new file. Then, it changes the modification and
access times to match those on the backup disk. That way your restored files have the
same contents and the same properties of those on the backup.

Shell Commands to Change Modification and Access Times   The shell command `touch` is a regular Unix command-line program for setting the modification and
access times for files. The manpage contains all the details.

3.9.7   Name of a File

When you create a file, you give it a name. The `mv` command allows you to change the
name of a file. `mv` also allows you to move a file from one directory to another.

Establishing the Name of a File   The creat system call sets the name and the initial mode of a file.

Changing the Name of a File   The rename system call changes the name of a file. It takes two arguments, the old name and the new name:

rename	
PURPOSE	Change name and/or move a file
INCLUDE	#include <stdio.h>
USAGE	int result = rename(char *old, char *new)
ARGS	old old name of file or directory new new pathname for file or directory
RETURNS	-1 if error 0 if success

SUMMARY

MAIN IDEAS

- A disk contains files and directories. Files have contents and properties. Directories also have contents and properties. A file can contain any sort of data. A directory can only contain a list of file names.
- The names in a directory refer to files and to other directories. The kernel provides system calls for reading the contents of directories, for reading the properties of files, and for modifying most attributes of files.
- The type of a file, the access permissions, and three special attributes are stored as bit patterns in an integer. Bit masks are a technique for examining bit patterns.
- The owner and group of a file are stored as numbers. The correspondence between these numbers and user names and group names is established by the passwd and group databases.

WHAT NEXT?

A directory is a list of files and directories. Directories are linked together into a tree. How does this tree work? How are directories linked together? In the next chapter, we examine the internal structure of the directory tree.

VISUAL SUMMARY

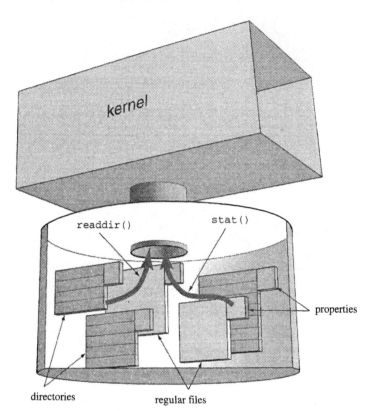

FIGURE 3.7

A disk contains files, directories, and their properties.

EXPLORATIONS

3.1 *Length of d_name[ ]* In the definition of the `struct dirent`, the length of the `d_name[]` character array is 1 on some systems and 255 on some others. What is the actual length? Why these weird numbers? Why not define it as a `char *` ?

3.2 *Protecting Files from Yourself* The protection mode `------rwx`, which you can set with the command `chmod 007 filename`, is legal, but bizarre. It grants permission to read, write, and execute `filename` to everyone on the system, but not to the owner of a file nor to members of the group of the file. Assign a file this mode. Can you read it? Experiment with various combinations to figure out the logic the kernel uses when it determines if the `open` system call should be allowed access to a file. If you have access to kernel sources, find the code that enforces file permissions and see if your guess was correct.

3.3 *IDs and usernames* Each user has a username, and each username has an associated user ID. Is it possible for two different usernames to have the same user ID? Is it possible for the same username to have two different user IDs? If you have root access to a machine, you can experiment with various combinations. Create two different users with the same user ID but with different usernames and passwords. Can they modify each other's files? What does `who` show? What does `ls -l` show? What does the command `id` show? What about e-mail? What do the results of these experiments tell you about how some of these commands work?

Can you think of any situations where multiple usernames with the same user ID would be useful?

3.4 *Special Bits and Directories* Directories, like all Unix files, have a full set of permission bits, including a set-user-ID bit and a set-group-ID bit. Here is a puzzle. If you turn on the *set-group-ID* bit for a directory, does it have any effect? If so, what and why? If not, could you think of some use for this bit?

3.5 *Executable Content vs. Executable Permission* Every file has three execute permission bits, one for the owner, one for the group, and one for the rest of the world. You can set the execute permission bit for any file, even for plain-text files that contain lists of things to pick up at the grocery store.

On the other hand, a file containing executable code, such as an `a.out` file created by compiling a C program, can have its execute bits turned off. Explain the difference between the ideas of executable content and execute permission for a file. Are they related? Read about the `file` command.

3.6 *Lognames and UIDs* Each user has a username and a number, the UID. Why? Wouldn't it be simpler to record the username of the user as the owner of a file? Why not have a single identifier for each user? What are the problems with two systems of identification? What are the advantages of having two systems? If you were designing your own operating system, what would you do?

3.7 The manual page for `dirent`, shown in the text, refers to a system call named `getdents(2)`. What does that call do, and what is its relation to `readdir`?

3.8 The sample listing of `ls -l` shows directories with permission mode `drwxr-xr-x`, typically. From left to right, this pattern means the item is a directory, that the owner of the file may read, write, and execute the directory, and that group members and anyone else may read or execute the directory.

What does the "execute" permission mean for a directory? A file may contain machine-language code or code in a scripting language. It makes sense to mark such files as "executable"; the computer can execute the machine language directly, or it can run an interpreter to execute the script. A directory is just a list of files and cannot be run.

What does the execute bit mean for a directory? Why is it useful? You can experiment by using `chmod` to turn off the execute bit for a directory and seeing what happens.

3.9 *Owning your terminal* Users connect to the system through terminals or through terminal emulation programs. Each terminal appears as a file in the `/dev` directory. Type `ls -l /dev/tty* | more`. This command shows all the terminal devices and their properties. Like regular files, files that represent terminals have an owner. The owner of a terminal is the user logged in at that terminal. Terminal devices not in use are owned by `root`.

The owner of the terminal is changed by the `login` program. Find source code to the `login` program, and locate in the code where the ownership is changed. What program changes the ownership back to root when you log out?

PROGRAMMING EXERCISES

3.10 Add multicolumn output to `ls1.c`. Experiment with the standard version of `ls` to see what it does. You will see the column width depends on the length of the file names in the listing. Also, the columns are as equal in length as possible. Finally, the width of the display depends on the width of your terminal window. How does `ls` figure that out?

3.11 *The ls2 bug* Modify `ls2.c` so it works correctly when the name of a directory is given as a command-line argument.

3.12 Modify the `ls2.c` program so it handles the `suid`, `sgid`, and sticky bits correctly. Read the manual to be sure you handle all possible combinations.

3.13   The standard `cp` utility allows the second argument to be a directory name. In that situation, the file is copied to a file with the same name in the directory. That is,

```
$ cp file1 /tmp
```

has the effect of typing

```
$ cp file1 /tmp/file1
```

Modify the `cp1.c` program in Chapter 2 to behave this way.

3.14   Sometimes you need to copy all the files in a directory. You might need to make a backup of a set of files. Modify the `cp1.c` program in Chapter 2 so that if given two directory names as arguments, it copies all the files in the first directory into the second directory, giving each copy the same name as the original.

3.15   Modify `ls1.c` so it sorts the list of files. Standard `ls` supports a `-r` option to print the list in reverse order. Add that option.

Some versions of `ls` support a `-q` option for "quick" output. This option causes `ls` not to sort the list. This option is useful when a directory contains an enormous number of files, so many that even a quick sort takes significant time.

3.16   Draw a picture with 16 little boxes and fill in the 1s and 0s for the mode for a directory with permission modes of `rwxr-x--x`.

3.17   *Locking the Barn* If you turn off the read permission for a file, you cannot open the file for reading. What if you have already opened the file for reading and then turn off the read permission from another terminal? Do subsequent `read` calls fail? Write a program that opens a file for reading, reads a few bytes, then calls `sleep(20)` to wait for 20 seconds then reads more. During that 20 seconds, make the file unreadable. What happens? Explain what read permission really means.

3.18   *Recursive* `ls` Standard `ls` supports the `-R` option. This option lists the contents of a directory and the contents of all directories below it. Try it. Modify `ls2.c` to support the `-R` option.

3.19   *Showing Access Times* Standard `ls` supports a `-u` option to display the time of last access instead of the time of last modification. What happens if you use `-u` without using `-l`? Modify `ls2.c` to support the `-u` option.

What is the point of allowing a user to specify `-u` without `-l` ? Hint: read about the `-t` option.

3.20   Write a simple version of `chown` that accepts a username or user ID number and an arbitrary number of filenames on the command line. How do you translate the username into a user ID? What if there is no user with the specified username on the system? Note: to test your program, you need to run as the superuser.

3.21   The time of last access for a file is useful information. Backing up files is a good idea, but reading a file for backup changes the time of last access for the file. It would be nice to have a backup program that copies a file but leaves the time of last access unchanged. Furthermore, it would be nice if the copy had the same modification time and same last access time as the original. Write a version of `cp` that does these two things.

3.22   Your terminal device is a file that programs use to get data from you and send data to you. When a program reads from the terminal device, it gets data from your keyboard. When a program writes to the terminal device, those bytes are sent to your screen. The `st_mtime` setting for the terminal file represents the time of last modification of that file. Write a program called `lastdata` that lists all current users and displays for each user the time when the terminal was last modified. Use the same format as `who`.

PROJECTS

Based on the material in this chapter, you can learn about and write versions of the following Unix programs:

```
chmod, file, chown, chgrp, finger, touch
```

CHAPTER 4

Focus on File Systems
Writing `pwd`

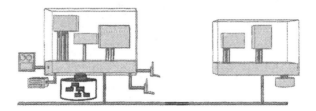

OBJECTIVES

Ideas and Skills

- User's view of the Unix file system tree
- Internal structure of Unix file system: inodes and data blocks
- How directories are connected
- Hard links, symbolic links: ideas and system calls
- How `pwd` works
- Mounting file systems

System Calls and Functions

- `mkdir, rmdir, chdir`
- `link, unlink, rename, symlink`

Commands

- `pwd`

4.1 INTRODUCTION

Files contain data. Directories are lists of files. Directories are organized into a tree-like structure. Directories can contain other directories. What does it mean for a file to be "in a directory"? When you log into a Unix machine, you are "in your home directory." What does it mean for a person to be "in a directory?"

This tree-like structure is a fiction. A hard disk is really a stack of metal platters, each with a magnetically responsive coating. How does this stack of spinning metal appear to be a tree of files, properties, and directories?

To answer these questions, we shall write a version of the pwd command. pwd reports your current location in the directory tree. The sequence of directories and subdirectories from the top of the tree to your location is called the *path* to your working directory. To write pwd, we have to understand how files and directories are stored and organized. We explore the structure of a file system by starting with what it looks like to users, then by looking at the internal structure, and finally by studying the system calls and how to use them.

4.2   A USER'S VIEW OF THE FILE SYSTEM

4.2.1   Directories and Files

Users look at a Unix disk and see a tree of directories. Each directory can contain files and other directories. Figure 4.1 is a sketch of a tiny section of the tree.

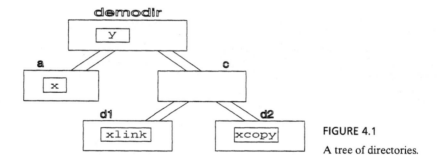

FIGURE 4.1

A tree of directories.

We start by building this directory structure, and by doing so, introduce Unix commands for managing these trees of files and directories.

4.2.2   Directory Commands

We can build the tree with this sequence of commands:

```
$ mkdir demodir
$ cd demodir
$ pwd
/home/yourname/experiments/demodir
$ mkdir b oops
$ mv b c
$ rmdir oops
$ cd c
$ mkdir d1 d2
$ cd ../..
$ mkdir demodir/a
```

We could have used many other sequences of commands; the one shown here is intentionally complicated to include several approaches.

Read through the example, drawing the tree as you go. The example uses a few basic commands. mkdir creates a new directory or directories with the specified names. What happens if you try to create a directory that has a name already taken by a file or directory? rmdir removes a directory or directories. What if you try to remove a directory that contains subdirectories? mv renames a directory; it can also move a directory from one place to another.

cd is different. It does not do anything to a directory; instead, cd affects you, the user. cd moves you from one directory to another, as though you were walking from one room into another room. pwd prints out the *path* to the current directory. In the example, we start in the subdirectory called demodir, which is a subdirectory of experiments, which is below yourname, which is below home, which is below the *root directory*, designated with the single slash (/).

4.2.3   File Commands

We now create some files in this directory tree:

```
$ cd demodir
$ cp /etc/group x
$ cat x
root::0:
bin::1:bin,daemon
users::200:
$ cp x copy.of.x
$ mv copy.of.x y
$ mv x a
$ cd c
$ cp ../a/x d2/xcopy
$ ln ../a/x d1/xlink
$ ls > d1/xlink
$ cp d1/xlink z
$ rm ../../demodir/c/d2/../z
$ cd ../..
$ cat demodir/a/x
(what appears here?)
```

This sequence of file operations is also intentionally complicated to demonstrate various commands and operations. Step through the commands, drawing the files as you go. Predict what the last command in the sequence produces. This example uses the most common file-handling commands. cp makes a copy of a file. We wrote a version of cp in an earlier chapter. cat copies the contents of the file to standard output. mv renames a file, as shown in the first example, and moves a file to a different directory, as shown in the second example. rm deletes a file. Notice how directory paths may include ".." and multiple elements. The notation ".." stands for the directory one level up, also known as the *parent directory*. A sequence of slash-separated directory names specifies a path to follow that leads to the named object. In particular, note the roundabout path used to remove the file called z.

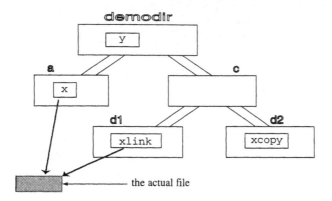

FIGURE 4.2
Two links to the same file.

Copying, examining, and renaming files are standard operations on any computer system. The next command, ln, is not so common but is an essential part of Unix. In this example, we take an existing file, ../a/x and make a link to it. The link is called d1/xlink. Look at Figure 4.2 to see where these two items live. The thing called x is in the demodir/a directory, and the thing called xlink lives in the demodir/c/d1 directory. Both x and xlink are called *links*. A link is a pointer to a file. Both ../a/x and d1/xlink point to the same data on the disk. As an example, the next command ls > d1/xlink replaces the contents of the xlink file with the output of ls. What happens when you cat the file ../a/x?

4.2.4   Tree Commands

Several Unix commands operate on entire tree structures. Here are some examples:

```
ls -R
```

The ls command can list the contents of an entire tree. The -R option tells ls to list the contents of the specified directory and all its subdirectories. In an earlier chapter, we wrote a version of ls. How much more work is it to add this recursive descent feature?

```
chmod -R
```

The chmod command changes the permission bits of files. The -R option tells chmod to apply the changes to all files in subdirectories.

```
du
```

The du (the name stands for *disk usage*) command reports the number of disk blocks used by a directory, the files it contains, and all the directories and files below it.

find

The find command searches a directory and all its subdirectories for files and directories that match a description specified on the command line. For example, you can search a tree for all files larger than one megabyte, not modified in the last week, that are readable by all users.

Lots more

Directory trees are an essential part of the file system. Unix includes many commands for working with trees. See how many you can find.

4.2.5   Almost No Limits to Tree Structure

Directories can contain many files and many subdirectories. The internal structure of the system imposes no limit on the depth of a directory tree. On the other hand, it is possible to create directories so deep they exceed the capacity of many of the commands that operate on trees.

Warning If you want to try the following experiment, do so on your own machine. The system administrator at school or work will not be amused if you try it there.

The simple shell script (see Chapter 8)

```
while true
do
    mkdir deep-well
    cd deep-well
done
```

creates a linked list of directories very deep, even if you press Ctrl-C after running it for just a second or two. What does the du utility do with this tunnel? How about find and ls -R?

On many versions of Unix, trying rm -r deep-well will not work. How can you remove this deep directory structure?

4.2.6   Summary of the Unix File System

In this section, we looked at the Unix file system from the user's viewpoint. The disk appears as a tree structure of directories extending deep and wide. Unix includes many programs for working with the objects of this structure. All files on a Unix system reside in this structure.

How does it all work? What is a directory? How does a file know which directory it is in? What does it mean for you, a human, to change from one directory to another? How does pwd figure out where you are?

4.3   INTERNAL STRUCTURE OF THE UNIX FILE SYSTEM

A disk is really a stack of magnetic platters. A few levels of abstraction convert the stack of platters into the file system we explored in the previous section.

4.3.1   Abstraction Zero: From Platters to Partitions

A disk can store a lot of data. Just as a country may be divided into states or counties, a disk may be divided into *partitions* to create separate regions within a larger entity. We shall treat each partition as a separate disk.

4.3.2   Abstraction One: From Platters to an Array of Blocks

A disk is a stack of magnetic platters. The surface of each platter is organized into concentric circles called tracks. Each of those tracks is divided into sectors, just as a suburban street is divided into housing lots. Each of these sectors stores some number of bytes, 512 for example. The sector is the basic unit of storage on the disk, and modern disks contain lots of them. Figure 4.3 shows how numbers are assigned to disk blocks:

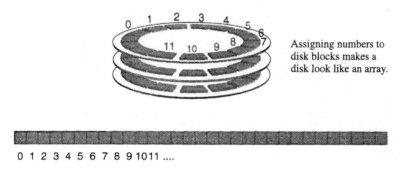

Assigning numbers to disk blocks makes a disk look like an array.

0 1 2 3 4 5 6 7 8 9 1011 ....

FIGURE 4.3
Assigning numbers to disk blocks.

Now for the important idea: numbering the disk blocks. Assign sequential numbers to the disk block by devising a system that counts every block on the disk. You could number all the blocks platter by platter working downward, or you could number all the blocks track by track working inward. Just as a mail carrier devises a sequence that includes every house on every street, software that stores data on the disk assigns a number to every block on every track on the disk.

A numbering system for disk sectors lets us treat a disk as an array of blocks.

4.3.3   Abstraction Two: From an Array of Blocks to Three Regions

A file system stores files. Specifically, a file system stores file contents, file properties (owner, date, etc.), and directories that hold those files. Where in this homogeneous sequence of blocks are the contents, properties, and directories?

Unix uses a simple method. Divide the array of blocks into three sections, as shown in Figure 4.4:

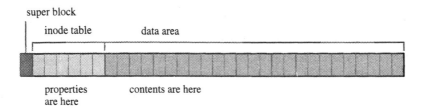

FIGURE 4.4

The three regions of a file system.

One section, called the *data area*, holds the contents of files. Another section, called the *inode table*, holds the properties of files. And the third section, called the *superblock*, holds information about the file system itself. This three-part structure imposed on a numbered sequence of blocks is called a *file system*.

The Superblock   The first block in the file system is called the superblock. This block contains information about the organization of the file system itself. For example, the superblock records the size of each area. The superblock also holds information about the location of unused data blocks. The exact contents and structure of the superblock depend on the version of Unix. Check the manual and header files to see what your superblock contains.

The Inode Table   The next part of the file system is called the *inode table*. Each file has a set of properties, such as size, user ID of the owner, and time of last modification. Those properties are recorded in a struct called an *inode*. All inodes are the same size, and the inode table is simply an array of those structs. Every file stored in the file system has one inode in the table. If you have root access, you can open the partition as a file and read and print an inode table. The technique is similar to reading and printing the utmp file.

This is important: Each inode is identified by its position in the inode table. For example, inode 2 is the third struct in the inode table of the file system.

The Data Area   The third part of the file system is the data area. The contents of files are kept in this section. All blocks on the disk are the same size. If a file contains more bytes than fit into one block, the contents of the file are stored in as many blocks as are needed. A large file could easily be spread over thousands of separate disk blocks. How does this system keep track of all those separate blocks?

4.3.4   The File System in Practice: Creating a File

The idea of one region for file contents and one region for file properties seems simple enough, but how does that work in practice? What happens when you create a new file? Consider the simple command

```
$ who > userlist
```

When the command is completed, there is a new file in the file system containing the output of the who command. How does this happen?

The file has contents, and the file has properties. The kernel has to store the contents of the file in the data area, the properties of the file in an inode, and the name in a directory. Figure 4.5 shows an example of creating a file requiring three blocks of storage:

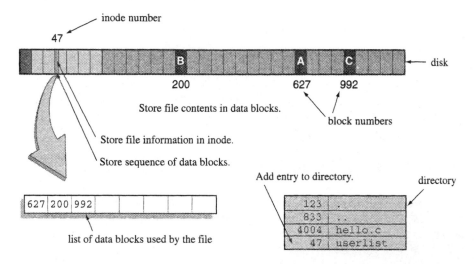

FIGURE 4.5

Internal structure of a file.

Creating a new file involves the following four main operations:

Store Properties

The file has properties. The kernel locates a free inode. Here, the kernel gets inode number 47. The kernel records information about the file in this inode.

Store Data

The file has contents; this new file requires three disk blocks of storage. The kernel locates three disk blocks from its list of free blocks. Here, it finds blocks 627, 200, and 992. The first chunk of bytes is copied from kernel buffers into block 627, the next chunk of bytes is copied into block 200, and the last chunk is copied into block 992.

Record Allocation

The contents of this file are in blocks 627, 200, and 992, in that order. The kernel records that sequence of block numbers in the disk allocation section of the inode. The disk allocation section is an array of block numbers. These three numbers are stored in the first three locations.

Add Filename to Directory

Our new file is called userlist. How does Unix record that new file in the current directory? The solution is simple. The kernel adds the entry (47, userlist) to the directory.

This association between the name of the file and the inode number is the link that connects the name of a file to the properties and contents of a file. This fact deserves its own section.

4.3.5   The File System in Practice: How Directories Work

A directory is a special kind of file that contains a list of names of files. The internal structure of a directory varies among versions of Unix, but the abstract model is always the same—a table of inode numbers and filenames:

i-num	filename
2342	.
43989	..
3421	hello.c
533870	myls.c

Looking Inside a Directory

You can see the contents of a directory with the command `ls -1ia` (the first option is the digit *one*):

```
$ ls -1ia demodir
 177865 .
 529193 ..
 588277 a
 200520 c
 204491 y
$
```

This output is a list of filenames and their corresponding inode numbers. For instance, the filename y refers to inode number 204491. The current directory, the item called ".", has inode number 177865. That means that the information about the size, owner, group, and so on about the current directory is stored in struct number 177865 in the inode table.

The -i and -1 (*one*, not *el*) options to `ls` may be new to you. The -i option tells `ls` to include the inode number in the listing, and -1 asks for one-column output. Try this on your own version of demodir to see what inode numbers you get.

Multiple Links to the Same File

You can use `ls -i` to find inode numbers for any files on the system. For example, you can look at the inode numbers of the items in the root directory of your system:

```
$ ls -ia /
      2 .          28673 etc          11 lost+found  438292 shlib
      2 ..        311297 home       4097 mnt          40961 tmp
      3 auto        8832 home2    108545 opt          18433 usr
  26625 bin        24646 initrd        1 proc         10241 var
 403457 boot       24579 install   24681 root          183 xfer.log
 225281 dev       161797 lib      233473 sbin           183 transfers
```

This listing contains two important examples. First, at the end of the rightmost column are files called xfer.log and transfers. Both these files have inode number 183. Therefore, both filenames refer to the same inode. The inode really *is* the file; the inode contains the properties and list of data blocks for the file. Therefore, xfer.log and transfers are two names for the same file. It is sort of like two listings in the telephone book with the same telephone number; both refer to the same house.[1]

The other important example in this listing of the root directory is dot and dotdot at the top left. Here, both those items have inode number 2, so it appears that "." and ".." refer to the same directory. How can the current directory be the same as the parent directory?[2] When the Unix command mkfs creates a file system, mkfs sets the parent of the root directory to point to itself.

4.3.6   The File System in Practice: How cat Works

We saw what happens internally when you write to a new file, as in who > userlist. What happens when you read from a file? For example, how does this command work?

```
$ cat userlist
```

We can follow the pointers back from the directory to the data:

Search the Directory for the Filename

Filenames are stored in directories. The kernel searches the directory for the entry containing the string userlist. The entry matching userlist contains inode number 47.

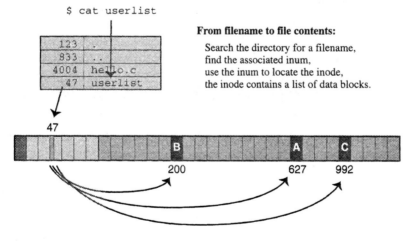

From filename to file contents:

Search the directory for a filename,
find the associated inum,
use the inum to locate the inode,
the inode contains a list of data blocks.

FIGURE 4.6

From filename to disk blocks.

---

[1]The telephone directory analogy is not exact, because two different people may live at that house. See the concept of *port* in the network programming chapter.

[2]Hear *I'm My Own Grandpa*, 1947, by Latham & Jaffe for a discussion of a related topic.

Locate and Read Inode 47

The kernel locates inode 47 in the inode region of the file system. Locating an inode requires a simple calculation; all inodes are the same size and each disk block contains a fixed number of inodes. The inode may already be in a buffer in the kernel. The inode contains a list of data blocks.

Go to the Data Blocks, One by One

The kernel now knows which data blocks, in which order, contain the contents of the file. As cat repeatedly calls read, the kernel steps through the data blocks, copying bytes from the disk to the kernel buffers and back to the array in user space.

All commands that read from files, cat, cp, more, who, and thousands more, pass a filename to open to gain access to the contents of the file. Every call to open looks in the directory for the filename, then uses the inode number in the directory to get the properties of the file and to locate contents of the file.

Now consider what happens when you attempt to open a file to which you do not have read or write permission. The kernel uses the filename to find the inode number, then uses the inode number to locate the inode. There, the kernel finds the permission bits and the user ID of the owner of the file. If your user ID, the user ID for the file, and the permission bits do not allow access, open returns -1 and sets errno to EPERM.

Using the picture of directories, inodes, and data blocks, you should be able to make sense of many other file operations. By examining the source code to some version of Unix, you can see how close your answers are.

4.3.7 Inodes and Big Files

How does the Unix file system keep track of large files? The explanation in the previous section is incomplete. In brief, the problem is

fact 1	A large file requires many disk blocks.
fact 2	The inode stores the disk block allocation list.
problem	How can a fixed-sized inode store a long allocation list?
Solution	Store most of the allocation list in data blocks, and leave pointers to those blocks in the inode.

Consider the situation depicted in Figure 4.7 below. The file requires fourteen data blocks to hold its contents. Therefore, the allocation list contains fourteen block numbers. Sad to say, the inode for the file has an allocation array with only thirteen spots. Sounds grim. How can a list of 14 block numbers fit into 13 spots? It is easy. Put the first 10 numbers of the allocation list in the inode, and put the last 4 block numbers in a data block. It's sort of like putting some inventory on the shelf and putting the overflow inventory in the warehouse.

Here are the details. The inode contains an array with space for 13 block numbers. The first 10 spots in the array are like 'shelf space'—the block numbers in those 10 spots are numbers of blocks that contain actual file data. If the allocation list has more than 10 elements, the extra block numbers are stored, not in the inode, but instead, in a

Recording data block allocation for a file with fourteen blocks of data:

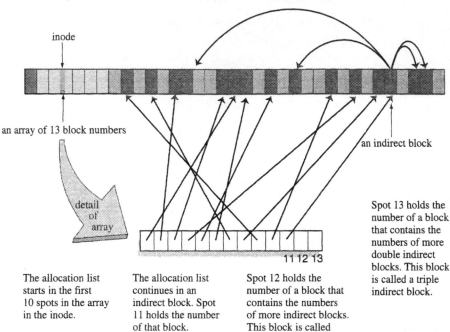

inode

an array of 13 block numbers

detail of array

an indirect block

11 12 13

The allocation list starts in the first 10 spots in the array in the inode.

The allocation list continues in an indirect block. Spot 11 holds the number of that block.

Spot 12 holds the number of a block that contains the numbers of more indirect blocks. This block is called a double indirect block.

Spot 13 holds the number of a block that contains the numbers of more double indirect blocks. This block is called a triple indirect block.

FIGURE 4.7

Block allocation list continues in data region.

data block. The number of the data block that holds the extra numbers is stored in the 11th spot in the inode—like a bookstore putting on the shelf a note saying, "excess inventory in warehouse, shelf 3."

Note that this file actually uses 15 data blocks. Fourteen contain the contents of the file, and 1 block contains the part of the allocation list that did not fit in the inode. This overflow block is called an *indirect block*.

What happens when the indirect block fills?   As more bytes are added to the file, the kernel allocates more data blocks, therefore the allocation list gets longer and requires more storage. Sooner or later, the allocation list overflows the indirect block, so the kernel promptly starts a second overflow box. What does the kernel do with the block number of the second overflow block? Should the kernel put the number of the second indirect block into spot 12 in the inode? It could, but that would mean that the file could only have three overflow blocks. Instead of putting the block number of the second overflow block in the inode, the kernel actually starts a block to store the list of these additional indirect blocks. Spot 12 in the inode holds the block number, not of the second overflow block, but instead the block number of the block that stores the block numbers of the second, third, fourth, and subsequent overflow blocks. This block is called a *double indirect block*.

What happens when the double indirect block fills? When the double indirect block fills, the kernel starts a new double indirect block. The kernel does not put the number of this new double indirect block into the inode array. Instead, the kernel creates a *triple indirect block* to hold the numbers of the new double indirect block and all the future double indirect blocks this file may need. It is the block number of this triple indirect block that is recorded in the last spot in the inode array.

What happens when the triple indirect block fills? The file has reached its limit. If you want to use really big files, you can set up a file system with larger disk blocks. When you create the file system, you specify not only the size of the inode table and the data area, you can also specify the size of a disk block. A disk block does not have to be the same size as the sector on the disk surface. Often a disk block consists of several disk sectors.

It sounds like large files involve a lot of overhead. This disk allocation system is quick and efficient for small files. As a file grows, the kernel uses more and more disk space to hold the larger allocation list. Seeking to a particular spot in the file can require fetching several indirect blocks just to get the number of the data block.

4.3.8 Variations on the Unix File System

The previous sections described the structure of the Unix file system. Different versions of Unix use various versions of this model. The simplicity of this classic approach suffers from some important weaknesses. For example, the superblock is a single point of failure. If that block is damaged, information about the entire structure of the file system is lost. Newer versions of Unix store backup copies of the superblock in the file system.

Fragmentation is another problem. As files are created and deleted, free blocks begin to spread across the disk. One solution is to create little file systems within the file system called *cylinder groups*.

This classic model is not obsolete. Files are still stored in blocks in the data area, file properties are still stored in inodes in the inode table, the inode contains the disk allocation list; and directories are simply lists of names and inode numbers. We can now return to the small directory tree we built and explored at the beginning of the chapter. With our understanding of the internal structure of the file system, we can look at the directories and files with a sort of X-ray vision.

4.4 UNDERSTANDING DIRECTORIES

Now that we know the internal structure of a Unix file system, we can see what is really going on in our `demodir` tree, and we can understand how the various directory commands work.

4.4.1 Understanding Directory Structure

Users see the file system as a collection of directories and subdirectories. Each directory can contain files, and each directory can have subdirectories. Each subdirectory has a parent directory. This tree of directories and files is often drawn as a collection of boxes connected by lines. In what sense is a file *in a directory*? What does it mean in technical terms to say "d1 is a subdirectory of c"? What do the lines on those drawings represent?

Internally, a directory is a file that contains a list of pairs: filename and inode number. Nothing more. Users see a list of filenames, while Unix sees a list of named pointers:

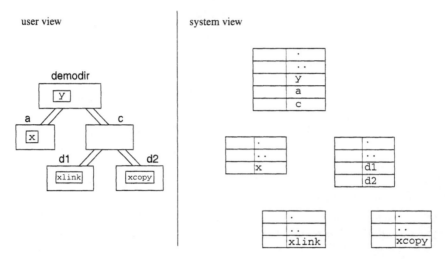

FIGURE 4.8

Two views of a directory tree.

How can we translate from one diagram to the other? By filling in the inode numbers, we can see exactly how the directory tree is held together. Use ls -iaR to list inode numbers for all files recursively down a tree.

```
$ ls -iaR demodir
 865 .     193 ..    277 a     520 c     491 y

demodir/a:
 277 .     865 ..    402 x

demodir/c:
 520 .     865 ..    651 d1    247 d2

demodir/c/d1:
 651 .     520 ..    402 xlink

demodir/c/d2:
 247 .     520 ..    680 xcopy
$
```

Figure 4.9 is the diagram with most of the inode numbers filled in:

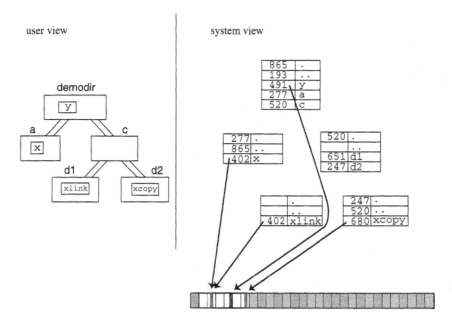

FIGURE 4.9

Filenames and pointers to files.

The Real Meaning of "A file is in a directory."

People say that files are in directories, but we now know that files are entries in the inode table with contents stored in the data region. In what sense is a file in a directory? For instance, the user view above shows file y contained in directory demodir. In

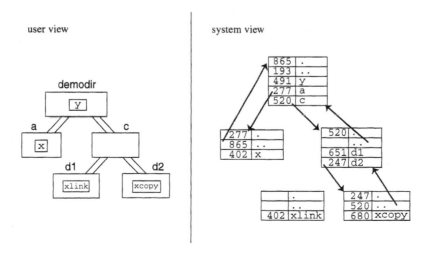

FIGURE 4.10

Directory names and pointers to directories.

the system view, we see the directory contains an entry with filename y and inode number 491.

Similarly, "file x is in directory a" means there is a link to inode 402 in the directory called a, and the filename attached to that link is x. Notice, also—and **this is important**—that the directory marked d1 at the lower left contains a link to inode 402, and that link is called xlink. These two links to inode 402, the one called demodir/a/x and the one called demodir/c/d1/xlink refer to the same file.

In short, directories contain references to files. Each of these references is called a *link*. The contents of the file are in data blocks, the properties of the file are recorded in a struct in the inode table, and the inode number and a name are stored in a directory. This same principle explains what it means for a directory to contain a subdirectory.

The Real Meaning of "A directory contains a subdirectory"

The user view shows that the directory called a is a subdirectory of the demodir directory. How does that work internally? Again, it means that demodir contains a link to the inode for that subdirectory. The top table in the system view contains a link called a to inode 277. How do we know 277 is the inode number for the directory at the left? Every directory has an inode, and the kernel installs in every directory an entry for its own inode; that entry is called ".". In the little box on the left, *dot* refers to inode 277, so the directory on the left *is* inode 277.

Look at the diagram, and note how the directory with inode number 520 is contained in demodir, where it is listed under the name c. Similarly, inode 247, another directory, is a subdirectory of 520, who knows it by the name d2.

The Real Meaning of "A directory has a parent directory."

Look at directory d2 in the user view. Its parent directory is marked c. This, again, is implemented as a simple link to an inode. Directory c is inode 520. Directory d2 contains an entry called "..". The inode number for that entry is 520. Dotdot is the reserved name for the *parent directory*. Thus, inode 520 is the parent of inode 247.

Fill in the Blanks, Connect the Dots

If you understood the preceding sections, you should be able to fill in the missing inode numbers in Figure 4.10. If you are not sure what goes in those blanks, examine the output of ls shown above and review the preceding section.

Multiple Links, Link Counts

In demodir, inode 402 has two links. One is called x in directory a, and the other is called xlink in directory d1. One may ask, which one is the original file and which is the link to it? In the Unix directory structure, these two links have the same status; they are called *hard links* to the file. The file is an inode and a bunch of data blocks; a link is a reference to an inode. You may create as many links to a file as you like.

The kernel records the number of links to a file. In the case of inode 402, that number is at least 2. There may be other links to inode 402 in other parts of the file system. The *link count* is stored in the inode. The link count is one of the members of the `struct stat` information returned by the `stat` system call.

Filenames

In the Unix file system, files do not have names. Links have names. Files have inode numbers. This fact will come in handy later.

4.4.2 Commands and System Calls for Directory Trees

The internal structure of the Unix file system is simple; it is a big linked data structure. The nodes are called inodes, the sets of pointers are called directories, and leaf nodes are called files. We manage this tree with standard Unix commands such as `mkdir`, `rmdir`, `mv`, `ln`, and `rm`. How do these commands work? In particular, what system calls do they use?

mkdir

The `mkdir` command creates new directories. It accepts one or more directory names on the command line. The `mkdir` command uses the `mkdir` system call:

mkdir		
PURPOSE	Create a directory	
INCLUDE	`#include <sys/stat.h>` `#include <sys/types.h>`	
USAGE	`int result = mkdir(char *pathname, mode_t mode)`	
ARGS	pathname	name of new directory
	mode	mask for permission bits
RETURNS	-1	if error
	0	if success

`mkdir` creates and links a new directory node to the file system tree. That is, `mkdir` creates the inode for the directory; allocates a disk block for its contents; installs in the directory the two entries, . and .., with inode numbers set to the correct values; and adds a link to that node to its parent directory.

rmdir

The `rmdir` command deletes a directory. It accepts one or more directory names on the command line. The `rmdir` command uses the `rmdir` system call:

---

rmdir

PURPOSE	Delete a directory. The directory must be empty.
INCLUDE	#include <unistd.h>
USAGE	int result = rmdir(const char *path);
ARGS	path name of directory
RETURNS	-1 if error
	0 if success

---

rmdir removes a directory node from a directory tree. The directory must be empty. That is, apart from the entries for dot and for dotdot, the directory may not contain any files or subdirectories. The link to the directory is removed from its parent directory. If the directory itself is not in use by another process, the inode and data blocks are freed.

rm

The rm command removes entries from a directory. rm accepts one or more filenames on the command line. The rm command uses the unlink system call:

---

unlink

PURPOSE	Remove a directory entry
INCLUDE	#include <unistd.h>
USAGE	int result = unlink(const char *path);
ARGS	path name of directory entry to remove
RETURNS	-1 if error
	0 if success

---

unlink deletes a directory entry. It decrements the link count for the corresponding inode. If the link count for the inode becomes zero, the data blocks and inode are freed. If there are other links to the inode, the data blocks and inode are otherwise untouched. unlink may not be used to unlink directories.

ln

The ln command creates a link to a file. ln uses the link system call:

link	
PURPOSE	Make a new link to a file
INCLUDE	#include <unistd.h>
USAGE	int result = link(const char *orig, const char *new);
ARGS	orig name of original link new name of new link
RETURNS	-1 if error 0 if success

link makes a new link to an inode. The new link contains the inode number of the original link and has the name specified. If there is already a link with the new name, link will fail. Nobody is allowed to use link to make new links to directories.

mv

The mv command changes the name or location of a file or directory. mv is the most flexible of the directory commands described in this section. We shall look at some of the internal details later. In many cases, though, mv just uses the rename system call:

rename	
PURPOSE	Rename or move a link
INCLUDE	#include <unistd.h>
USAGE	int result = rename(const char *from, const char *to);
ARGS	from name of original link to name of new link
RETURNS	-1 if error 0 if success

rename changes the name or location of a file or directory. For example, the call rename("y","y.old") changes the name of the file, while rename("y","c/d2/y.old") changes the name and the location of the file. rename can be used for directories as well as for files, but there are some restrictions on moving directories. For instance, you may not move a directory into one of its subdirectories. Sketch the outcome of rename("demodir/c","demodir/d2/c") to see what havoc would result. Unlike link, rename deletes an existing file or empty directory with the *to* name.

How rename Works, Why rename Exists

How does rename move a file to another directory? Files are not really in directories, links to files are in directories. Therefore, rename moves the link from one directory to another. Internally, renaming y to c/d2/y.old looks like Figure 4.11:

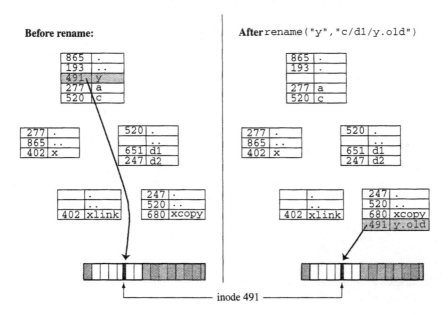

FIGURE 4.11

Moving a file to a new directory.

Before, a link to inode 491 called y, is in demodir. *After*, a link to inode 491 called y.old, is in c/d2, and the original link is gone. How does the kernel move the link?

In the Linux kernel, the basic logic of rename is

```
copy original link to new name and/or location
delete original link
```

Unix provides system calls link and unlink to perform these two operations. Therefore, the request rename("x","z"); works like this:

```
if ( link("x","z") != -1 )
     unlink("x");
```

In fact, in the *Olden Days*®, there was no rename system call, so the mv command used link and unlink. Adding rename to the kernel solves two problems. First, rename makes it possible to rename or relocate directories safely. In those old days, regular users were not allowed to link or unlink directories, so they had no way to rename directories.

Another advantage of rename is support for non-Unix file systems. Within Unix, renaming a file or directory consists of changing a link, but other systems may not work the same way. Adding a general method called rename to the kernel hides the details of implementation, allowing the same code to operate on all sorts of file systems.

cd

cd changes the current directory of a process. cd affects the process, not the directory. A user might say, "I changed into the /tmp directory and found a lot of my scratch files," the same way someone may say, "I went into the attic and found a lot of my old books." cd uses the chdir system call:

chdir	
PURPOSE	Change current directory of calling process
INCLUDE	#include <unistd.h>
USAGE	int result = chdir(const char *path);
ARGS	path path to new directory
RETURNS	-1 if error
	0 if success

Each running program on Unix has a current directory. The chdir system call changes the current directory of the process. The process is now "in that directory." Internally, the process keeps a variable that stores the inode number of the current directory. When you "change into a new directory," you just change the value of that variable.

An Important Exercise   How cd .. works Using the demodir example, imagine you are *in* the directory called c. What is the inode number of your current directory? You now type cd d1. What is the inode number of your current directory now? How does the kernel get that number? If you then type cd ../.., what is the inode number of your current directory? What steps does the kernel use to get that number?

If you understood how to do that Important Exercise, you understand how the pwd command works.

4.5   WRITING pwd

The pwd command prints the path to the current directory. For example, if you are down at the bottom of the sample tree in demodir/c/d2 and type pwd, you might see

```
$ pwd
/home/yourname/experiments/demodir/c/d2
```

Where is that long path stored? It is not stored in the current directory. The current directory calls itself "." and has an inode number. The directory is just a node in a set of linked nodes. How does pwd know the directory is called d2, and how does it know the parent of d2 is called c, and how does it know the parent of c is called demodir, and so forth?

4.5.1   How pwd Works

The answer, like the answer to almost all the questions in this chapter, is simple: Follow the links and read the directories. pwd actually climbs up the tree, directory by directory, noting at each step the inode number for dot, and then looking through the parent directory for the name assigned to that inode number, until it reaches the top of the tree. For example, consider Figure 4.12:

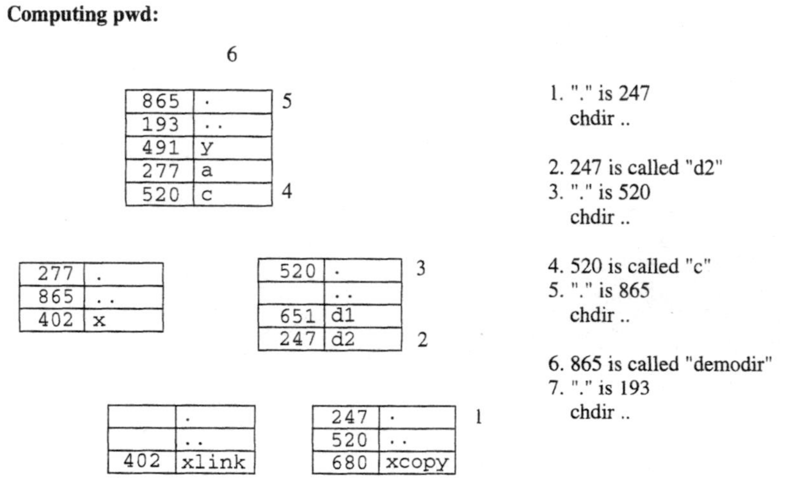

Computing pwd:

```
                        6

            865  .        5          1. "." is 247
            193  ..                     chdir ..
            491  y
            277  a               2. 247 is called "d2"
            520  c        4      3. "." is 520
                                    chdir ..

   277  .              520  .   3   4. 520 is called "c"
   865  ..                  ..      5. "." is 865
   402  x              651  d1         chdir ..
                       247  d2   2
                                   6. 865 is called "demodir"
                                   7. "." is 193
        .              247  .   1      chdir ..
        ..             520  ..
   402  xlink          680  xcopy
```

FIGURE 4.12

Computing the current path.

Our ascent starts in the current directory, the one at the lower right. In that directory, the name of our location is "." and has inode number 247. We now chdir up to the parent directory where we look for the entry with inode number 247. In the parent, inode 247 is called d2. Therefore, the last component in the path is d2. What is the name of the parent directory? Within the parent, its name is ".", and it has inode number 520. By chdiring into *its* parent, we can see that inode 520 is listed as c. Therefore the last two parts of the path are c/d2. The algorithm is a repetition of these three steps:

1. Note the inode number for ".", call it n (use stat)
2. chdir ..   (use chdir)
3. Find the name for the link with inode n (use opendir,readdir,closedir)
   Repeat (until you reach the top of the tree).

That sounds simple enough, but there are only two questions:

Question 1: How do we know when we reach the top of the tree?   In the root directory of a Unix file system, "." and ".." point to the same inode. Programmers often mark ends of linked structures with a NULL next pointer. The designers of Unix could have made ".." null in the root, but decided instead to have it loop back to itself. What is the advantage of that design? Thus, our version of pwd repeats until it gets to a directory in which inode numbers for "." and ".." are equal.

Question 2: How do we print the directory names in the correct order?   We could write a loop and build up a string of directory names with strcat or sprintf. We avoid string management with a recursive program that winds its way up to the top of the tree and prints the directory names, one by one, as it unwinds.

4.5.2   A Version of pwd

```
/* spwd.c: a simplified version of pwd
 *
 *       starts in current directory and recursively
 *       climbs up to root of filesystem, prints top part
 *       then prints current part
 *
 *       uses readdir() to get info about each thing
 *
 *       bug: prints an empty string if run from "/"
 **/
#include        <stdio.h>
#include        <sys/types.h>
#include        <sys/stat.h>
#include        <dirent.h>
ino_t    get_inode(char *);
void     printpathto(ino_t);
void     inum_to_name(ino_t , char *, int );

int main()
{
        printpathto( get_inode( "." ) );        /* print path to here  */
        putchar('\n');                          /* then add newline    */
        return 0;
}

void printpathto( ino_t this_inode )
/*
 *       prints path leading down to an object with this inode
 *       kindof recursive
 */
{
        ino_t    my_inode ;
        char     its_name[BUFSIZ];

        if ( get_inode("..") != this_inode )
```

```
            {
                    chdir( ".." );                          /* up one dir   */
                    inum_to_name(this_inode,its_name,BUFSIZ);/* get its name*/
                    my_inode = get_inode( "." );            /* print head   */
                    printpathto( my_inode );                /* recursively  */
                    printf("/%s", its_name );               /* now print    */
                                                            /* name of this */
            }
    }
    void inum_to_name(ino_t inode_to_find , char *namebuf, int buflen)
    /*
     *      looks through current directory for a file with this inode
     *      number and copies its name into namebuf
     */
    {
            DIR             *dir_ptr;               /* the directory */
            struct dirent   *direntp;               /* each entry    */
            dir_ptr = opendir( "." );
            if ( dir_ptr == NULL ){
                    perror( "." );
                    exit(1);
            }
            /*
             * search directory for a file with specified inum
             */
            while ( ( direntp = readdir( dir_ptr ) ) != NULL )
                    if ( direntp->d_ino == inode_to_find )
                    {
                            strncpy( namebuf, direntp->d_name, buflen);
                            namebuf[buflen-1] = '\0';   /* just in case */
                            closedir( dir_ptr );
                            return;
                    }
            fprintf(stderr, "error looking for inum %d\n", inode_to_find);
            exit(1);
    }
    ino_t get_inode( char *fname )
    /*
     *      returns inode number of the file
     */
    {
            struct stat info;
            if ( stat( fname , &info ) == -1 ){
                    fprintf(stderr, "Cannot stat ");
                    perror(fname);
                    exit(1);
            }
            return info.st_ino;
    }
```

Does It Work?   Here is actual output from the program:

```
$ /bin/pwd
/home/bruce/experiments/demodir/c/d2
$ spwd
/bruce/experiments/demodir/c/d2
$
```

Pretty close. The real version of pwd prints the path all the way to the root of the tree, but this version stops before it gets to the top of the tree. What is the problem? Is it an off-by-one coding error? No. The program actually works perfectly. It stops when it reaches the root of the file system. The root of this file system, though, is not the root of the entire tree on this computer.

Unix allows one to organize disk storage into a tree of trees. Each disk, or each partition on a disk, contains a directory tree. These separate trees are linked together into a single, almost seamlessly joined, tree. This version of pwd bumped into one of the seams.

4.6   MULTIPLE FILE SYSTEMS: A TREE OF TREES

What if a Unix system has two disks or partitions? We have seen how, using a few simple abstractions, we can organize a single partition into a tree of directories. If you have two partitions, do you have two separate trees?

What do other systems do? Some operating systems assign drive letters or volume names to each disk or partition and make the letter or name part of the full path to a file. At the other extreme, some systems assign block numbers across all disks to create a virtual single disk.

Unix takes a third approach. Each partition has its own file system tree. When there is more than one file system on a computer, Unix provides a way to graft these trees into one larger tree. Figure 4.13 shows the principle:

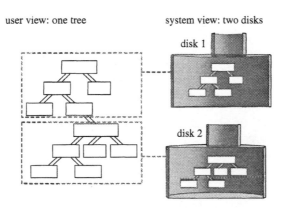

FIGURE 4.13

Tree grafting.

The user sees a seamless tree of directories. In reality there are two trees, one on disk 1 and one on disk 2. Each tree has a root directory. One file system is designated the *root filesystem*; the top of this tree really is the root of the entire tree. The other file system is attached to some subdirectory of the root file system. Internally, the kernel associates a pointer to the other file system with a directory on the root file system.

4.6.1   Mount Points

Unix uses the phrase *to mount a file system* in the sense of *to mount a butterfly* or to *mount a picture*—that is, to pin it to some existing support. The root directory of the subtree is pinned onto a directory on the root file system. The directory to which the subtree is attached is called the *mount point* for that second system.

The mount·command lists currently mounted file systems and their mount points:

```
$ mount
/dev/hda1 on / type ext2 (rw)
/dev/hda6 on /home type ext2 (rw)
none on /proc type proc (rw)
none on /dev/pts type devpts (rw,mode=0620)
$
```

The first line of output reports that partition 1 on /dev/hda (the first IDE drive) is mounted at the root of the tree. This partition is the root file system. The second line of output says the file system on /dev/hda6 is attached to the root file system at the /home directory. Thus, when a user chdirs from / to /home, she crosses from one file system to another. When our pwd winds its way up the tree, it stops at /home because it has reached the top of its file system.

E Pluribus Unix

Unix allows different types of file systems to be mounted on the root file system. For example, a CD-ROM containing an ISO9660 file system can be mounted on a Unix machine, and the files and directories on the disk will become part of the tree. A disk containing a Macintosh file system can be mounted if the kernel contains subroutines that know how to work with the Macintosh file system structure. Even file systems on other computers can be mounted using network connections.

4.6.2   Duplicate Inode Numbers and Cross-Device Links

Merging different file systems into one tree has many advantages. There is one small wrinkle, though. Under Unix, every file in a file system has an inode number. Just as two different streets may have a house with number 402, two different disks may have files with inode number 402. Several directories may contain filenames associated with inode 402. How does the kernel know which inode number 402 to use?

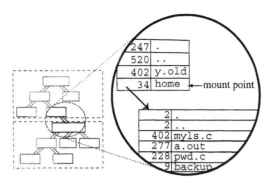

FIGURE 4.14

Inode numbers and file systems.

Look carefully at this close-up photo of two directories, one in the root file system, one in the mounted file system. Each directory contains a link to inode 402. myls.c and y.old appear to be links to the same inode, but where is that inode? The file system on disk 1 has an inode 402, and the file system on disk 2 has a different inode 402. These links do not refer to the same file at all.

This example shows a problem introduced by creating trees of trees. Suddenly, an inode number no longer identifies a file uniquely. As we just saw, the same inode number, 402, appears in two different directories but refers to two different files. It looks like those are links to the same file, but they are not.

How can I make links to the same file from different file systems?   You can't. A file exists as a set of data blocks and an inode on a disk. The link in the directory points to that inode. What would happen if a link on one disk pointed to an inode on another disk? If the other disk were unmounted, the file would be gone. Even worse, if a different disk were mounted with a different file called inode 402, say, then the contents of the file would be completely different. There are many other troubling scenarios you can think up.

Do the `link` and `rename` system calls know about this?   Yes. `link` refuses to create *cross-device links* and `rename` refuses to transfer an inode number across file systems. Read the manual pages to learn what error code they return.

4.6.3   Symbolic Links: Panacea or Pasta City?

Hard links are the pointers that connect directories into a tree; hard links are the pointers that link filenames to the files themselves.

Hard links cannot point to inodes in other file systems, and not even root can make hard links to directories. Good reasons exist, though, to point to directories or to files on other file systems. To meet those needs, Unix supports another kind of link: the *symbolic link*. A symbolic link refers to a file by name, not by inode number. The following is a comparison:

```
$ who > whoson
$ ln whoson ulist
$ ls -li whoson ulist
  377 -rw-r--r--   2 bruce    users    235 Jul 16 09:42 ulist
```

```
    377 -rw-r--r--    2 bruce    users    235 Jul 16 09:42 whoson
$ ln -s whoson users
$ ls -li whoson ulist users
    377 -rw-r--r--    2 bruce    users    235 Jul 16 09:42 ulist
    289 lrwxrwxrwx    1 bruce    users      6 Jul 16 09:43 users -> whoson
    377 -rw-r--r--    2 bruce    users    235 Jul 16 09:42 whoson
```

The files whoson and ulist are links to the same file. Both have inode number 377, and both have the same file size, modification time, and number of links. The hard link ulist was created with the ln command.

On the other hand, the command ln -s makes a symbolic link to the file whoson and calls that new link users. ls -li shows users has inode 289. The letter l in the file-type spot says that users is a symbolic link. The link count, modification time, and file size differ from those of the original file. This file, users, is not the original file whoson, but it behaves like the original file when programs read from or write to it. For example,

```
$ wc -l whoson users
      5 whoson
      5 users
     10 total
$ diff whoson users
$
```

The commands wc and diff read the files, counting lines and comparing contents, respectively. In those cases, the kernel uses the name to find the original file. On the other hand, calls to stat return information about the link, not about the original file.[3]

Symbolic links may span file systems because they do not store the inode of the original file. Symbolic links may also point to directories, because they are different from, and can be distinguished from, the real links that hold the file system together.

Symbolic links suffer from the problems we mentioned in discussing cross-device links. If the file system containing the original file is removed, or the original file gets a new name, or if a different file with that name is installed, the symbolic link will point to nothing, nothing, and something different, respectively. Symbolic links to directories can point to parent directories, thereby creating loops in the directory tree. Symbolic links can turn your file system into spaghetti. The kernel knows these are only symbolic links, not real links, and can check them for lost references and infinite loops.

System Calls for Symbolic Links

The symlink system call creates a symbolic link. The readlink system call obtains the name of the original file. lstat obtains information about the original file. Read the manual pages on unlink, link to see what they do with symbolic links.

---

[3]The lstat system call dereferences the link.

SUMMARY

MAIN IDEAS

- Unix organizes disk storage into file systems. A file system is a collection of files and directories. A directory is a list of names and pointers. Each entry in a directory points to a file or directory. A directory contains entries that point to its parent directory and to its subdirectories.
- A Unix file system contains three main parts: a superblock, an inode table, and a data region. File contents are stored in data blocks. File attributes are stored in an inode. The position of the inode in the table is called the inode number of the file. The inode number is the unique identifier of a file.
- The same inode number may appear in several directories with various names. Each entry is a called a hard link to a file. A symbolic link is a link that refers to a file by name instead of by inode number.
- Several file systems can be connected into one tree. The kernel operation that connects a directory of one file system to the root of another file system is called *mounting*.
- Unix includes system calls that allow a programmer to create and remove directories, duplicate pointers, move pointers, change the names associated to pointers, and attach and detach other file systems.

VISUAL SUMMARY

A directory entry is a filename and an inode number. The inode number points to a struct on the disk. That struct contains the file information and the data block allocation.

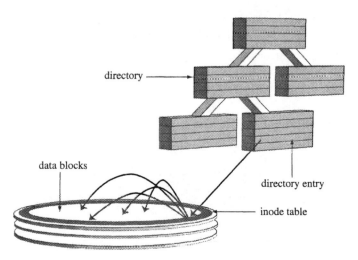

FIGURE 4.15

Inodes, data blocks, directories, pointers.

WHAT'S NEXT?

Files are only one source of data. Programs also process data from devices like terminals, cameras, and scanners. How do Unix programs read data from and send data to devices?

EXPLORATIONS

4.1   pwd prints the path to the current directory in the file system. In some sense, that directory is your location in the tree. That directory is actually a collection of bytes stored somewhere on a disk with a location that can be specified by head, track, sector, and byte, or by cylinder, head, sector, and byte. Is there a way to translate current working directory to these hardware locations?

4.2   Investigate one of the hard disks on a system you use. Find out how many partitions it has, and for each partition determine the number of inodes and the number of data blocks.

4.3   Not only does Unix use this disk-as-array abstraction internally to create file systems, it also makes that abstraction available to anyone with suitable access permissions. You need to have root access for this project.

The /dev directory contains files that allow you to read the bytes stored in the blocks on the disk just as though those bytes were the contents of a file. On Linux systems with an IDE drive, you will see files called /dev/hda, /dev/hdb, /dev/hdc, /dev/hdd. These device files are not regular data files like /etc/passwd, or /var/adm/utmp. These device files provide access to raw data on the disk, and you can use cat, more, cp, and any other file command to read the contents of the disk. Like the utmp file the disk has a clear structure. One way to examine the contents of the disk block by block is the command od -c /dev/hda | more. As you page through the output of that command, you are reading the contents of the disk as though it were one continuous sequence of disk blocks. Each partition is represented by one of these special files. For example, the first partition on /dev/hda is called /dev/hda1.

Explore your /dev directory to determine which of the special files in the directory correspond to the hard drives, floppy drives, CD-ROM drives, or other disk devices on the system.

4.4   The text stated the kernel had to locate a free inode and free disk blocks when it created a new file. How does the kernel know which blocks are free? How does the kernel know which inodes are free? What method does the file system on your machine use to keep track of unused blocks and inodes?

4.5   Unix can read and mount disks containing non-Unix file systems, such as PC-DOS and Macintosh disks. Internally, these systems do not have inodes. Nonetheless, when you use the mount command to connect one of these disks to a Unix system, the command ls -i lists inodes.

Examine the Linux source code to determine where these numbers come from. Why does Linux add them?

4.6   The text explained allocation lists by describing inodes that contain ten direct blocks, one indirect block, one double indirect block and one triple indirect block. Some versions of Unix use different numbers.

(a)   What is the format of an inode allocation list on the system you use? The header files should contain the details.

(b)   What is the size of a data block on your system?

(c) On your system, what is the largest file that uses no indirect blocks?

(d) On your system, what is the largest file that uses no double indirect blocks? How many blocks does that largest file really use?

4.7 *Link counts for directories* A file may have multiple links. The link count for the file records the number of links. What about directories? In your own version of the demodir tree, use ls -l to find the link counts for each of the directories. Compare these link counts to the arrows on the diagram. Explain what the link count for a directory means. Why does every directory have a link count of at least 2?

4.8 *Links to directories* Nobody is allowed to use link to make new links to directories. In the *Olden Days*®, the superuser was allowed to make hard links to directories. In the demodir example, draw in user view and in system view the effect of the system call link("demodir/c","demodir/d2/e"). Then, explain what the command ls -iaR demodir would do.

4.9 *Hidden Subtrees* When you attach one file system to another with the mount command, the mount point must be a directory on the original file system. For example, you might attach the file system on /dev/hda4 to the directory called /home2. Explore these two questions: (a) What happens if the mount point, in this case home2, does not exist? (b) What happens if the mount point exists and contains files and subdirectories?

4.10 The rmdir command will not delete a directory that contains files or subdirectories. Why is that good?

On the other hand, you *can* remove a directory that contains a user. Try the following and amaze your friends: make a new directory with any name you like, change into that directory, then open another shell window and remove that new directory. Close the second shell window and type the command /bin/pwd. Explain what is going on.

4.11 What does the term *cylinder* mean on a hard disk? What is it about the physical construction of a hard disk that makes the cylinder concept important to efficient use of the disk?

Search the Web for the term *cylinder group*. Explain the connection between this idea and the model of the file system presented in the text.

4.12 *Running out of space* Most people are familiar with the idea of running out of space on a disk. A Unix file system has a region for inodes and a region for data, so it is possible to run out of inodes even if free space is available in the data area. When you install a new disk for Unix, you need to divide the disk into the inode table and the data area. Every file on that file system requires one inode. The larger the inode table, the less space is left for file contents.

Say you are about to set up a new hard drive. The mkfs command makes a new file system and lets you specify the size of the inode table. Read the manual page on this command. Why would you want to ask for a lot of inodes? Why would you want to ask for fewer than normal?

4.13 The stat system call is passed the name of a file and a pointer to a struct and fills the struct with information about the file. Explain, using the directory, inode, and data model, how stat works. Where does it find the data it copies into the stat structure?

PROGRAMMING EXERCISES

4.14 Write a single Unix command line that builds the entire demodir tree of directories.

4.15 The Unix mkdir command accepts a -p option. Write a version of mkdir that supports that option.

4.16   The mv command is more than just a wrapper around the rename system call. Write a version of mv that accepts two arguments. The first argument must be the name of a file, and the second argument may be the name of a file or the name of a directory. If the destination is the name of a directory, then mv moves the file into that directory. Otherwise mv renames the file if possible.

4.17   The text presents a version of rename written using link and unlink. That code fragment checks the return value from link but does not check the return value from unlink. Expand that code to handle errors from unlink correctly.

4.18   Read the manuals and header files to learn about the structure of the superblock on your system. Write a program that opens a file system, reads the superblock, and displays some of the settings in a clear readable format. This exercise is similar to the programs we wrote to display the contents of utmp records and of stat structures.

4.19   The explanation of creating a new file lists four main operations. All four operations must be completed successfully for the file to be added to the file system correctly. What would happen if the computer lost power somewhere in this sequence? For example, what would happen if the data were stored in the data area but an inode had not been allocated?

   (a)   Select an order for these four main operations. Explain your choice.
   (b)   Now suppose that a system is built using your answer to part (a). What if the system were to crash between two of the steps in your procedure? For example, if your procedure has four steps, there are three interstep points. For a crash at each of those points in the code, explain what file system inconsistencies would occur.
   (c)   Read about the Unix command fsck. How similar is your answer to part (b) to the list of things fsck looks for?

4.20   In Chapter 3, we wrote a version of ls -l. Revise that program so it prints out the inode number in addition to the other information. Where does your new version of ls find the inode number?

PROJECTS

Based on the material in this chapter, you can learn about and write versions of the following Unix programs:

    find, du, ls -R, mount, dump

# CHAPTER 5

Connection Control
Studying stty

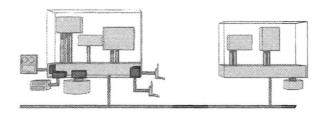

OBJECTIVES

Ideas and Skills

- Similarities between files and devices
- Differences between files and devices
- Attributes of connections
- Race conditions and atomic operations
- Controlling device drivers
- Streams

System Calls and Functions

- fcntl, ioctl
- tcsetattr, tcgetattr

Commands

- stty
- write

5.1   PROGRAMMING FOR DEVICES

We have spent several chapters looking at programs that work with files and directories. A computer also has other sources of data: peripheral devices like modems, printers, scanners, mice, speakers, cameras, and terminals. In this chapter, we study similarities and differences between files and devices, and we see how to use those ideas to manage connections to devices.

The project for the chapter is to write a version of the `stty` command. `stty` lets users examine and modify the settings that control the connection to the keyboard and screen.

5.2   DEVICES ARE JUST LIKE FILES

Many people think a file is a bunch of data stored on a disk, but Unix takes a more abstract approach. First, consider the facts about files: files contain data, files have properties, and files are identified by names in directories. You can read bytes from a file, and you can write bytes to a file. Now, notice that these same facts and operations apply to devices.

Consider a sound card connected to a microphone and speaker. You speak into the microphone, the sound card translates signals from your voice into a stream of data, and a program can read that stream of data. When a program writes a stream of data to the card, sound comes out of the speakers. To a program, a sound card is a source of data and a destination for data.

A terminal, with keyboard and display, also behaves like a file. Keystrokes that you type can be read by a program as input data, and characters that a process writes to the terminal are displayed on the screen.

To Unix, sound cards, terminals, mice, and disk files are the same sort of object. In a Unix system, every device is treated as a file. Every device has a filename, an inode number, an owner, a set of permission bits, and a last-modified time. The works. Everything you know about working with files automatically applies to terminals and all other devices.

5.2.1   Devices Have Filenames

Every device (terminal, printer, mouse, disk, etc.) attached to a Unix machine is represented by a filename. By tradition, files that represent devices are in the `/dev` directory, but you can create device files in any directory. Explore the `/dev` directory on various Unix machines. Here is a partial listing on the machine I am using now:

```
$ ls -C /dev | head -5
XOR         fd1u720   loop1   ptyqf   sda7   stderr   ttysd
agpgart     fd1u800   lp0     ptyr0   sda8   stdin    ttyse
apm_bios    fd1u820   lp1     ptyr1   sda9   stdout   ttysf
arcd        fd1u830   lp2     ptyr2   sdb    tape     ttyt0
dsp         flash0    mcd     ptyr3   sdb1   tcp      ttyt1
```

This listing shows several sorts of devices. The `lp*` files in the third column are printers. The `fd*` files in the second column are the floppy-disk drives. The `sd*` files are partitions on SCSI devices, and /dev/tape is the device file for the backup tape drive. The tty* files in the last column are terminals. Programs get user keystrokes by reading those files and send data to terminal screens by writing to those files.

The dsp file is a connection to a sound card. A process plays a sound file by writeing bytes to that device file. A process may open /dev/mouse to read mouse clicks and changes in position.

5.2.2   Devices and System Calls

Not only do devices have filenames, devices also support all file-related system calls: open, read, write, lseek, close, and stat.

For example, code to read from a magnetic tape could look like this:

```
int fd;
fd = open("/dev/tape", O_RDONLY);    /* connect to tape drive   */
lseek(fd, (long) 4096, SEEK_SET);    /* fast forward 4096 bytes */
n = read(fd, buf, buflen);           /* read data from tape     */
close(fd);                           /* disconnect              */
```

The same system calls you use for disk files work for devices. In fact, Unix provides no other means to communicate with devices.

Some Devices Do Not Support All File Operations

When you move the mouse and click the buttons, the mouse sends bytes to the system, where a process can read them. What would it mean to write to that device? Sending data to a mouse will not make it move or make its buttons click. The /dev/mouse file does not support the write system call. Of course, someone could build a mouse containing a motor and then write an enhanced mouse driver that would accept as well as generate mouse events.

Terminals support read and write, but they do not support lseek. Why is that?

5.2.3   Example: Terminals Are Just Like Files

Much user input to Unix comes from terminals. The files ttysd, ttyse, etc., in the sample listing represent terminals. A terminal is anything that behaves like the classic keyboard and display unit, including an actual 1970s printing terminal, a keyboard and CRT attached to a serial port, or a PC with a modem and terminal emulation software dialed up over a phone line. A telnet or ssh window logged in over the Internet behaves like a terminal. The essential components of a terminal are a source of character input from the user and a display unit for output to the user. The display unit could even generate braille or speech.

The command tty tells you the name of the file that represents your terminal. Let us experiment with terminal files:

```
$ tty
/dev/pts/2
$ cp /etc/motd /dev/pts/2
Today is Monday, we are running low on disk space.  Please delete files.
  - your sysadmin
```

```
$ who > /dev/pts/2
bruce    pts/2    Jul 17 23:35 (ice.northpole.org)
bruce    pts/3    Jul 18 02:03 (snow.northpole.org)
$ ls -li /dev/pts/2
      4 crw--w--w-  1 bruce    tty      136,  2 Jul 18 03:25 /dev/pts/2
```

tty says my terminal is attached to the file called /dev/pts/2, that is, the filename is 2 in the pts subdirectory of /dev. We can use any file commands and operations with that file: cp, output redirection with >, mv, ln, rm, cat, or ls.

The cp command reads from the regular file /etc/motd and writes into the device /dev/pts/2 causing those contents to appear on the screen. Writing into a device file sends bytes to the device. The next line in the example shows that sending the output of who, with the > redirection operator, into /dev/pts/2 also displays data on the screen as characters.[1]

5.2.4 Properties of Device Files

Device files have most of the properties disk files have. The output of ls above shows that /dev/pts/2 has inode 4, permission bits rw--w--w-, 1 link, owner bruce and group tty, and last modified date of Jul 18 at 03:25. The file type is "c," indicating that this file is really a device that transfers data character by character. The permission bits look a little weird, and the expression 136, 2 appears where the file size usually goes. What happened to the file size?

Device Files and File Size   Regular disk files contain bytes; the number of bytes in a disk file is the size of the file. A device file is a connection, not a container. Keyboards and mice do not store a specific number of keystrokes or clicks. The inode of a device file stores, not a file size and storage list, but a pointer to a subroutine in the kernel. A subroutine in the kernel that gets data into and out of a device is called a *device driver*.

In our /dev/pts/2 example, the code that moves data into and out of our terminal is subroutine number 136 in a table of device-processing code. That subroutine accepts an integer argument. In the case of /dev/pts/2, the argument is the number 2. These two numbers, 136 and 2, are called the *major number* and *minor number* of the device. The major number specifies which subroutine handles the actual device, and the minor number is passed to that subroutine.

Device Files and Permission Bits   Every file has bits that specify read, write, and execute permission for the file. What do permission bits mean when the file is really a device? Writing data into the file sends data to the device, so write permission means being allowed to send bytes to the device. In the current example, the owner of the file and members of group tty are allowed to write to the terminal, but only the owner of the file is allowed to read from the terminal. Reading from a device file, like reading from a regular file, gets data from the file. Input from a terminal consists of user keystrokes. If users other than the owner of the file have permission to read

---

[1]Or as braille or as sound.

/dev/pts/2, other people can read characters typed at that keyboard. Reading keystrokes from another person's terminal can cause trouble.

On the other hand, writing characters to another person's terminal is the purpose of the Unix write command.

5.2.5 Writing `write`

Back in the *Olden Days*®, before instant messaging and chat rooms, Unix users chatted with friends at other terminals with the write command:

```
$ man 1 write
WRITE(1)              Linux Programmer's Manual              WRITE(1)

NAME
        write - send a message to another user

SYNOPSIS
        write user [ttyname]

DESCRIPTION
        Write allows you to communicate with other users by copy-
        ing lines from your terminal to theirs.

        When you run the write command, the user you  are  writing
        to gets a message of the form:

             Message  from yourname@yourhost on yourtty at hh:mm
             ...

        Any further lines you enter will be copied to  the  speci-
        fied user's  terminal.  If the other user wants to reply,
        they must run write as well.

        When you are done, type an end-of-file or interrupt  char-
        acter.  The other user will see the message EOF indicating
        that the conversation is over.
```

The following simple version of write does not send the "Message from ..." introduction and requires the filename for the terminal (the *ttyname*), not the username of the other person:

```
/* write0.c
 *
 *      purpose: send messages to another terminal
 *       method: open the other terminal for output then
 *               copy from stdin to that terminal
 *        shows: a terminal is just a file supporting regular i/o
 *        usage: write0 ttyname
 */

#include        <stdio.h>
#include        <fcntl.h>

main( int ac, char *av[] )
```

```
{
        int     fd;
        char    buf[BUFSIZ];

        /* check args */
        if ( ac != 2 ){
                fprintf(stderr,"usage: write0 ttyname\n");
                exit(1);
        }

        /* open devices */
        fd = open( av[1], O_WRONLY );
        if ( fd == -1 ){
                perror(av[1]); exit(1);
        }

        /* loop until EOF on input */
        while( fgets(buf, BUFSIZ, stdin) != NULL )
                if ( write(fd, buf, strlen(buf)) == -1 )
                        break;
        close( fd );
}
```

Examine this code carefully to find the special features required to connect your keyboard to the screen of another user. There are none. This simple write program copies lines from one file to another. This sample program and the examples in the previous section show that terminals, like all devices attached to a Unix machine, can be treated exactly like disk files.

5.2.6 Device Files and Inodes

How do these device files work? How does the Unix file system of inodes and data blocks support this idea of device files? Figure 5.1 shows the connections:

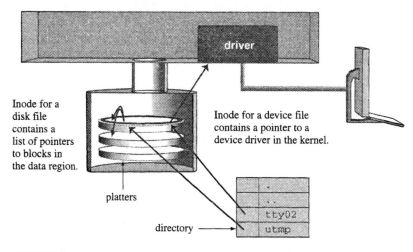

Inode for a disk file contains a list of pointers to blocks in the data region.

Inode for a device file contains a pointer to a device driver in the kernel.

driver

platters

directory

FIGURE 5.1

Inode points to data blocks or to driver code.

A directory is a list of filenames and inode numbers. Nothing in a directory tells you which names represent disk files and which names represent devices. The distinction between types of files appears at the inode level.

Each inode number points to a struct in the inode table. An inode can be a disk-file inode or a device-file inode. The type of the inode is recorded in the type portion of the st_mode member of struct stat.

A disk-file inode contains pointers to the blocks on the disk holding data. A device-file inode contains a pointer into a table of kernel subroutines. That *major number* tells where to find the code that gets data from the device.

Consider, for example, how read works. The kernel finds the inode for the file descriptor. The inode tells the kernel the type of the file. If the file is a disk file, the kernel gets data by consulting the block allocation list. If the file is a device file, the kernel reads data by calling the read part of the driver code for that device. The other operations—open, write, lseek, and close—follow similar logic.

5.3   DEVICES ARE NOT LIKE FILES

Disk files and device files look similar on the surface. Both have filenames and properties. The open system call creates a connection to files and to devices. But a connection to a disk file is different from a connection to a terminal. This picture shows a process with two file descriptors, one a connection to a disk file and the other a connection to a user at a terminal:

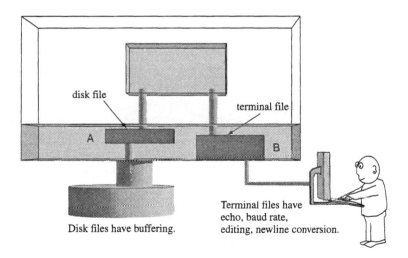

disk file

terminal file

A

B

Disk files have buffering.

Terminal files have echo, baud rate, editing, newline conversion.

FIGURE 5.2

A process with two file descriptors.

We already know something about the internals of these connections. A connection to a disk file usually involves kernel buffers. Bytes flowing from a process to the disk are accumulated into and transferred later from buffers in kernel memory. Buffering is an attribute of the connection to the disk. Connections to terminals are different; processes want data sent to terminals to be delivered pretty quickly.

A connection to a terminal or modem also has attributes. A serial connection has a baud rate, parity, and number of stop bits. Characters you type usually appear on the screen, but sometimes, for example when you type your password, the characters do not *echo* back to you. Echoing of characters is not part of the keyboard and is not something the program does; echoing is an attribute of the connection. Connections to disk files do not have these attributes.

5.3.1   Connection Attributes and Control

Unix makes files and devices look similar where they are similar and makes them look different where they differ. A connection to a disk file differs from a connection to a modem. We look at the attributes of connections:

1. What attributes can a connection have?
2. How can you examine the current attributes?
3. How can you change the current attributes?

We next look at two examples: connections to disk files and connections to terminals.

5.4   ATTRIBUTES OF DISK CONNECTIONS

The open system call creates a connection between a process and a disk file. That connection has several attributes. We look in detail at two of those attributes and then mention some of the other ones.

5.4.1   Attribute 1: Buffering

The next diagram depicts a file descriptor as two channels connected by a processing unit. That processing unit is kernel code that does buffering and other processing tasks. Inside that box are control variables that determine which processing steps the file descriptor performs. The picture looks like this:

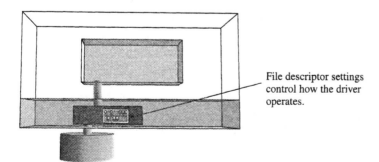

File descriptor settings control how the driver operates.

FIGURE 5.3

A processing unit in a data stream.

You modify the action of the file descriptor by changing those control variables. For example, you turn off disk buffering with a simple, three-step procedure:

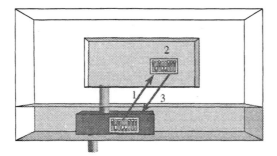

To change driver settings:
1. Get settings,
2. modify them
3. send them back.

FIGURE 5.4

Modifying the operation of a file descriptor.

First, make a system call to copy the control variables from the file descriptor into your process. Second, modify your copy of the control variables. Finally, send the revised values back to the kernel. The new settings are installed in the processing code, and the kernel processes data according to the new settings. Here is code that follows those three steps:

```
#include  <fcntl.h>
int s;                               // settings
s = fcntl(fd, F_GETFL);              // get flags
s |= O_SYNC;                         // set SYNC bit
result = fcntl(fd, F_SETFL, s);      // set flags
if ( result == -1 )                  // if error
    perror("setting SYNC");          //    report
```

Attributes of a file descriptor are coded as bits in an integer. The fcntl system call lets you control a file descriptor by reading and writing that integer:

fcntl	
PURPOSE	Control file descriptors
INCLUDE	#include <fcntl.h> #include <unistd.h> #include <sys/types.h>

USAGE	int result = fcntl(int fd, int cmd);
	int result = fcntl(int fd, int cmd, long arg);
	int result = fcntl(int fd, int cmd, struct flock *lockp);

ARGS	fd the file descriptor to control cmd the operation to perform arg arguments to the operation lock lock information
RETURNS	-1 if error other depends on operation

`fcntl` performs operation *cmd* on the open file specified by *fd. arg* represents an argument used by the operation *cmd*. In the sample code, the `F_GETFL` operation gets the current set of bits (also known as *flags*). The variable s stores this *flagset*. The *bitwise or* operator turns on the `O_SYNC` bit. That bit tells the kernel that calls to `write` should return only when the bytes are written to the actual hardware rather than the default action of returning when the bytes are copied to a kernel buffer.

Finally, we send the revised settings back to the kernel. We specify the `F_SETFL` operation as the second argument and pass the revised settings as the third argument. This three-step procedure—read the current settings from the kernel into a variable, change those settings, and then send those settings back to the kernel—is the standard technique for reading and modifying the attributes of data connections in Unix.

Setting `O_SYNC` eliminates all the efficiency kernel buffering provides. You need a good reason to turn off buffering.

5.4.2   Attribute 2: Auto-Append Mode

Another attribute of a file descriptor is the *auto-append mode*. Auto append is useful for files written to by several processes at the same time.

Why Auto Append is Useful

Consider the `wtmp` logfile. `wtmp` stores a history of all logins and logouts. When a user logs in, the `login` program adds a record to the end of `wtmp`. When a user logs out, the system adds a log-out record to the end of `wtmp`, sort of a diary the system keeps. As with diaries humans keep, each entry should be added at the end.

Can't you just use `lseek` to add to the end?   Consider the following logic for `login`:

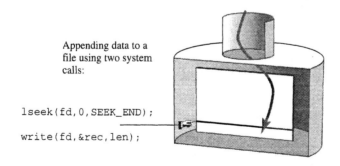

Appending data to a file using two system calls:

`lseek(fd,0,SEEK_END);`

`write(fd,&rec,len);`

FIGURE 5.5

Appending with `lseek` and `write`.

`lseek` sets the current position to the end of the file, and *then* `write` adds the login record. What could go wrong here?

What If Two People Log In at the Same Time?   Consider Figure 5.6, which shows time progressing down the page:

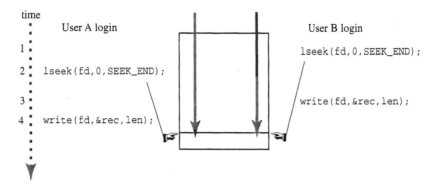

FIGURE 5.6

Interleaved lseek and write = chaos.

The wtmp file is shown in the middle, time's arrow is on the left, and four time increments are shown. The code for the login for user A is shown on the left, and the code for the login for user B is shown on the right. OK so far? The important facts are that Unix is a time-sharing system and that this procedure requires two separate steps, lseek and write.

Now, watch this in slow motion:

time **1**—B's login process seeks to end of file

time **2**—B's time slice is up, A's login process seeks to end of file

time **3**—A's time slice is up, B's login process writes record

time **4**—B's time slice is up, A's login process writes record

Thus, the record of B's login is lost, overwritten with the record written by A's login process.

This situation is called a *race condition*. The net effect on the file shared by these two processes depends on how the two processes are scheduled. With a slight change in timing, the login record for A might have been lost, or neither would have been lost.

How Can this Race Condition Be Avoided?   There are lots of ways to avoid race conditions. Race conditions are a critical problem for system programming, and we shall return to the topic several times. For this particular case, the kernel provides a simple solution: auto-append mode. When the O_APPEND bit is set for a file descriptor, each call to write automatically includes an lseek to the end of file.

This code fragment enables auto append and then calls write:

```
#include  <fcntl.h>

int s;                        // settings
s = fcntl(fd, F_GETFL);       // get flags
s |= O_APPEND;                // set APPEND bit
result = fcntl(fd, F_SETFL, s);  // set flags
```

```
if ( result == -1 )                  // if error
   perror("setting APPEND");         //    report
else
   write(fd, &rec, 1);               // write record at end
```

Atomic Operations   The important term *race condition* is related to the important term *atomic operation*. Calls to `lseek` and `write` are separate system calls; the kernel is free to interrupt the process between the two operations. When `O_APPEND` is set, the kernel combines `lseek` and `write` into an *atomic operation*. The two are joined into one indivisible unit.

5.4.3   Controlling File Descriptors with `open`

`O_SYNC` and `O_APPEND` are two attributes of a file descriptor; there are several more. We discuss other settings in later chapters. The manual page for `fcntl` lists all the options and operations supported on your system.

`fcntl` is not the only way to set file-descriptor attributes. Often you know what settings you want when you open the file. The `open` system call lets you specify file descriptor attribute bits as part of its second argument. For example, the call

```
fd = open(WTMP_FILE, O_WRONLY|O_APPEND|O_SYNC);
```

opens the `wtmp` file for writing with `O_APPEND` and `O_SYNC` bits turned on. The second argument to `open` is more than a selection of read, write, or read/write.

For example, you can ask `open` to create a file by including the `O_CREAT` flag. The following two calls are equivalent:

```
fd = creat(filename, permission_bits);
fd = open(filename, O_CREAT|O_TRUNC|O_WRONLY, permission_bits);
```

Why does `creat` exist when `open` can do the job? In the *Olden Days*®, `open` only opened files and `creat` created new ones. Later, `open` was modified to support more flags, including the create option.

Other Flags `open` Supports

`O_CREAT`   Create the file if it does not exist. See `O_EXCL`.

`O_TRUNC`   If the file exists, truncate the file to length zero.

`O_EXCL`   The `O_EXCL` flag is intended to prevent two processes from creating the same file. If the named file exists and `O_CREAT` is also set, return -1.

The combination of `O_CREAT` and `O_EXCL` is supposed to eliminate the following race condition: What if two processes try to create the same file at the same time? For example, what if two processes wanted to write to `wtmp` but had to create the file if it did not exist? A program could see if the file exists by first calling `stat` and then calling `creat` if the file does not exist. Problems arise if the process is interrupted between `stat` and `creat`. The `O_EXCL`/`O_CREAT` combination joins those two calls into an atomic operation. Although well intentioned, the combination does not work in some important cases. A reliable alternative is to use link. An exercise provides an example.

5.4.4 Summary of Disk Connections

The kernel transfers data between disks and processes. The code in the kernel that performs these transfers has many options. A program can use the open and fcntl system calls to control the inner workings of these data transfers.

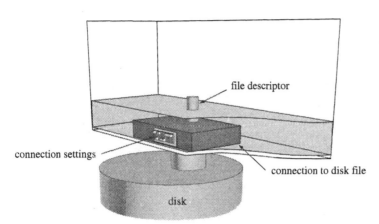

FIGURE 5.7

Connections to files have settings.

5.5 ATTRIBUTES OF TERMINAL CONNECTIONS

The open system call creates a connection between a process and a terminal. We now look in detail at some of the attributes of a connection to a terminal.

5.5.1 Terminal I/O Is Not as Simple as It Appears

A connection between a terminal and a process looks simple. Using getchar and putchar, you transfer bytes between device and process. The data-stream abstraction makes it look as though the keyboard and screen plug right into the process:

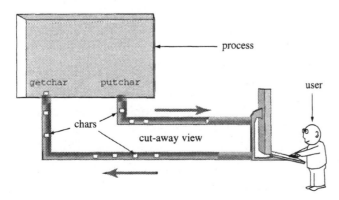

FIGURE 5.8

The illusion of a simple, direct connection.

A simple experiment shows this model is incomplete. Consider this program:

```
/*  listchars.c
 *        purpose: list individually all the chars seen on input
 *         output: char and ascii code, one pair per line
 *          input: stdin, until the letter Q
 *          notes: useful to show that buffering/editing exists
 */

#include          <stdio.h>

main()
{
        int      c, n = 0;

        while( ( c = getchar()) != 'Q' )
                printf("char %3d is %c code %d\n", n++, c, c );
}
```

The program processes characters one by one, reading a character and then printing a count, the character itself, and its internal code. Compile and run this program. A sample run looks like the following:

```
$ ./listchars
hello
char    0 is h code 104
char    1 is e code 101
char    2 is l code 108
char    3 is l code 108
char    4 is o code 111
char    5 is
 code 10
Q
$
```

What is going on? If character codes flowed directly from keyboard to `getchar`, we would see a response after each character. Instead, we press the five letters in the word *hello* and then the Enter key. Only then does the program process these characters. Input appears buffered. Like data flowing to the disk, bytes flowing from a terminal are stored somewhere along the way.

`listchars` shows something else. The Enter or Return key usually sends ASCII code 13, the *carriage return* character. Output of `listchars` shows that ASCII code 13 is replaced, en route, by character code 10, the number for *line feed* or *newline*.

A third sort of processing affects program output. `listchars` sends a newline (\n) at the end of each string. The newline code tells the cursor to move down one line, it does not tell the cursor to return to the left margin. Code 13 (carriage return) tells the cursor to return to the left margin.[2]

---

[2]Ask your grandparents to tell you about pushing the shiny handle on the left side of a typewriter carriage to return it and the paper to the left margin.

Running `listchars` shows that there must be a processing layer somewhere in the middle of the file descriptor. Figure 5.9 shows some of the effects of this layer.

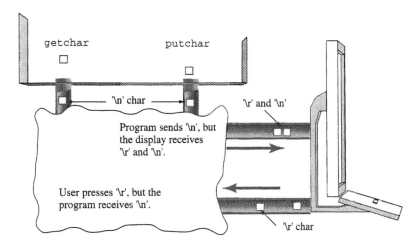

FIGURE 5.9

Kernel processes terminal data.

This example shows three sorts of processing:

1. The process receives no data until user presses Return
2. User presses Return (ASCII 13), process sees newline (ASCII 10)
3. Process sends newline, terminal receives Return-Newline pair

Connections to terminals contain a complex set of properties and processing steps.

5.5.2   The Terminal Driver

A connection between a terminal and a process looks as shown in Figure 5.10.

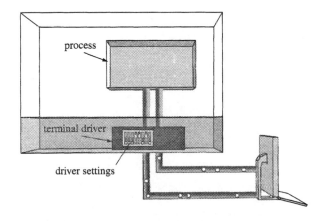

FIGURE 5.10

The terminal driver is part of the kernel.

The collection of kernel subroutines that process data flowing between a process and the external device is called the *terminal driver* or the *tty driver*.[3] The driver contains many settings that control its operation. A process may read, modify, and reset those driver control flags.

5.5.3   The `stty` Command

The `stty` command lets users read and change settings in the driver for a terminal.

*Using **stty** to Display Driver Settings*   Output of `stty` looks like the following:

```
$ stty
speed 9600 baud; line = 0;
$ stty -all
speed 9600 baud; rows 15; columns 80; line = 0;
intr = ^C; quit = ^\; erase = ^?; kill = ^U; eof = ^D; eol = <undef>;
eol2 = <undef>; start = ^Q; stop = ^S; susp = ^Z; rprnt = ^R; werase = ^W;
lnext = ^V; flush = ^O; min = 1; time = 0;
-parenb -parodd cs8 -hupcl -cstopb cread -clocal -crtscts
-ignbrk brkint ignpar -parmrk -inpck -istrip -inlcr -igncr icrnl ixon -
ixoff
-iuclc -ixany imaxbel
opost -olcuc -ocrnl onlcr -onocr -onlret -ofill -ofdel nl0 cr0 tab0 bs0
vt0 ff0
isig icanon iexten echo echoe echok -echonl -noflsh -xcase -tostop -
echoprt
echoctl echoke
```

The default listing is brief. The `-all` option lists many more settings. Some settings are variables with values, and some are boolean. For example, the baud rate and the number of screen rows and columns have numerical values. Items such as `intr`, `quit`, and `eof` have character values. Finally, settings such as `icrnl`, `-olcuc`, and `onlcr` are values that are on or off.

What do these all mean? `icrnl` is the abbreviation for *Input: convert Carriage Return to NewLine*, which is exactly what our earlier example showed the driver does. The abbreviation `onlcr` stands for *Output: add to NewLine a Carriage Return*. The minus sign in front of an attribute indicates the operation is turned off. For example, `-olcuc` means to disable the action for *Output: convert LowerCase to UpperCase*. Many early terminals only printed uppercase letters, so converting output to uppercase was more useful then.

*Using **stty** to Change Driver Settings*   Here are some samples of using `stty` to change driver settings:

```
$ stty erase X        # make 'X' the erase key
$ stty -echo          # type invisibly
$ stty erase @ echo   # multiple requests
```

---

[3]*tty* refers to the original printing terminals manufactured by the Teletype Corporation.

In the first example, we use `stty` to change the key you press to correct a typing error. The backspace or delete key is the typical setting, but you can make any character the erase key.[4] In the second example, we turn off keystroke echoing. When you type a password at login, keystrokes are not printed back to your screen. At other times, keystrokes are echoed back to your screen. Turning off this echoing means you can type and not see what you are typing. In the third example, we use `stty` to change several settings at once. We change the erase character to the '@' sign and turn echo mode back on.

How does `stty` work? Can we write `stty`?

5.5.4   Programming the Terminal Driver: The Settings

The tty driver contains dozens of operations it can perform on data passing through it. These operations are grouped into four categories:

input   what the driver does with characters coming from the terminal

output   what the driver does with characters going to the terminal

control   how characters are represented—number of bits, parity, stop bits, etc.

local   what the driver does while characters are inside the driver

Input processing includes converting lowercase to uppercase, stripping off the high bit, and converting carriage returns to newlines. Output processing includes replacing tab characters by sequences of spaces, converting newlines to carriage returns, and converting lowercase letters to uppercase. Control settings include even parity, odd parity, and the number of stop bits. Local processing includes echoing keystrokes back to the user and buffering input until the user presses Return.

In addition to on–off settings, the driver keeps a list of keystrokes with special meanings. For example, users may press the backspace key to erase a character. The terminal driver watches for and handles that *erase key*. The terminal driver watches for several other *control characters*.

The manual page for `stty` lists most of the settings and control characters.

5.5.5   Programming the Terminal Driver: The Functions

Changing settings in the terminal driver works like changing settings of disk file connections:

(a) Get the attributes from the driver.
(b) Modify any attributes you need to change.
(c) Send those revised attributes back to the driver.

For example, the following code turns on keystroke echoing for a connection:

---

[4] Some Unix shells handle this function, taking the job away from the driver and adding fancier features than the driver provides.

```
#include  <termios.h>
struct termios attribs;            /* struct to hold attributes  */
tcgetattr(fd, &settings);          /* get attribs from driver    */
settings.c_lflag |= ECHO ;         /* turn on ECHO bit in flagset */
tcsetattr(fd, TCSANOW, &settings); /* send attribs back to driver */
```

The general procedure is depicted in Figure 5.11:

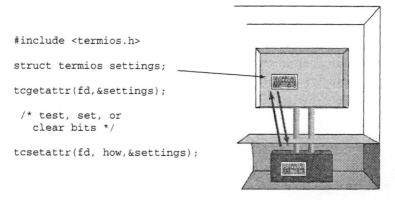

FIGURE 5.11

Controlling the terminal driver with `tcgetattr` and `tcsetattr`.

The library functions `tcgetattr` and `tcsetattr` provide access to the terminal driver. Both functions transfer settings in a `struct termios`. Here are the details:

tcgetattr	
PURPOSE	Read attributes from tty driver
INCLUDE	`#include <termios.h>` `#include <unistd.h>`
USAGE	`int result = tcgetattr(int fd, struct termios *info);`
ARGS	`fd` file descriptor connected to a terminal `info` pointer to a struct termios
RETURNS	`-1` if error `0` if success

`tcgetattr` copies current settings from the terminal driver associated to the open file *fd* into the struct pointed to by *info*.

---

tcsetattr

PURPOSE	Set attributes in tty driver

INCLUDE	`#include <termios.h>`
	`#include <unistd.h>`

USAGE	`int result = tcsetattr(int fd, int when, struct termios *info);`

ARGS	fd	file descriptor connected to a terminal
	when	when to change the settings
	info	pointer to a struct termios

RETURNS	-1	if error
	0	if success

`tcsetattr` copies driver settings from the struct pointed to by *info* to the terminal driver associated to the open file *fd*. The *when* argument tells `tcsetattr` when to update the driver settings. The values allowed for *when* are as follows:

TCSANOW

Update driver settings immediately.

TCSADRAIN

Wait until all output already queued in the driver has been transmitted to the terminal. Then update the driver.

TCSAFLUSH

Wait until all output already queued in the driver has been transmitted. Next, flush all queued input data. Then make the changes.

5.5.6 Programming the Terminal Driver: The Bits

The `struct termios` data type contains several flagsets and an array of control characters. All versions of Unix include the following members:

```
struct termios
  {
    tcflag_t c_iflag;              /* input mode flags */
    tcflag_t c_oflag;              /* output mode flags */
    tcflag_t c_cflag;              /* control mode flags */
    tcflag_t c_lflag;              /* local mode flags */
    cc_t     c_cc[NCCS];           /* control characters */
    speed_t  c_ispeed;             /* input speed */
    speed_t  c_ospeed;             /* output speed */
  };
```

Baud rates for data flowing in and out of the driver are stored in the `c_ispeed` and `c_ospeed` members.

The individual bits in each flagset are shown in Figure 5.12:

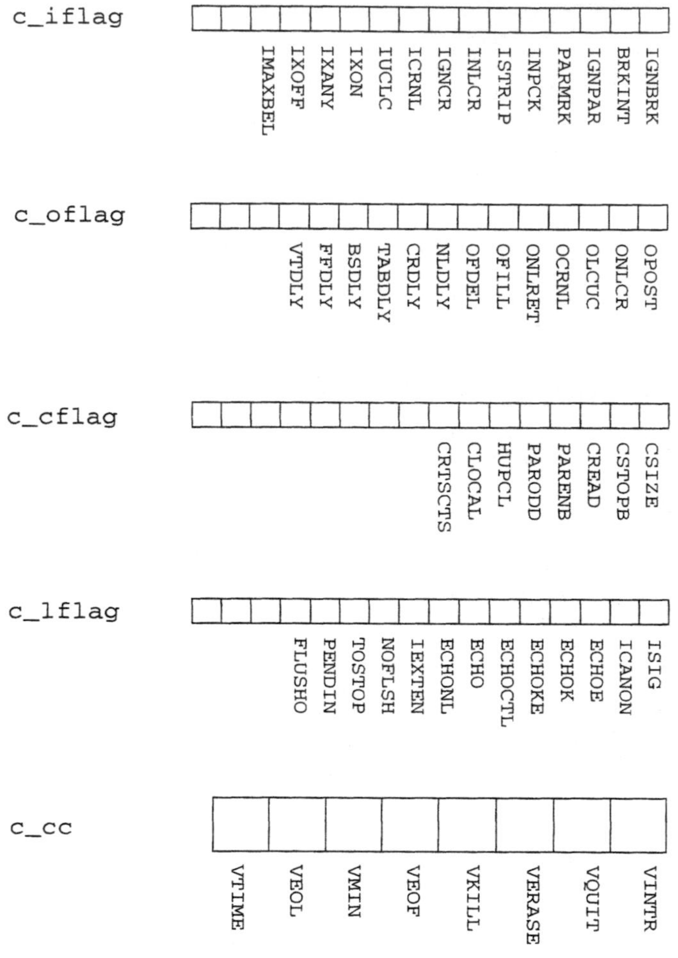

`c_iflag`

IMAXBEL IXOFF IXANY IXON IUCLC ICRNL IGNCR INLCR ISTRIP INPCK PARMRK PARMRK IGNPAR BRKINT IGNBRK

`c_oflag`

VTDLY FFDLY BSDLY TABDLY CRDLY NLDLY OFDEL OFILL ONLRET OCRNL OLCUC ONLCR ONOCR OPOST

`c_cflag`

CRTSCTS CLOCAL HUPCL PARODD PARENB CREAD CSTOPB CSIZE

`c_lflag`

FLUSHO PENDIN TOSTOP NOFLSH IEXTEN ECHONL ECHO ECHOCTL ECHOKE ECHOK ECHOE ICANON ISIG

`c_cc`

VTIME VEOL VMIN VEOF VKILL VERASE VQUIT VINTR

FIGURE 5.12

Bits and chars in termios members.

The first four members depicted are flagsets. Each flagset contains bits for operations in that group. For instance, the `c_iflag` member contains a bit for the value INLCR. The `c_cflag` member contains a bit for odd parity, that mask is called PARODD. All these masks are defined in `termios.h`. When you read the current attributes from the driver into a `struct termios`, all the values in this struct are available to be examined and modified.

The `c_cc` member is the array of *control characters*. Keystrokes that perform various control functions are stored in this array. Each position in the array is defined by a constant in `termios.h`. For example, the assignment `attribs.c_cc[VERASE]='\b'` tells the driver to treat the backspace key as the erase character.

Programming the Terminal Driver: Bit Operations

Now that we know how to get the settings from the driver and how to store the settings back to the driver, we look at the techniques for modifying driver attributes.

Each attribute is a bit in one of the flagsets. Masks for the attributes are defined in termios.h. To test an attribute, you mask the flagset with the mask for that bit. To enable the attribute, you turn on the bit; to disable the attribute, you turn off the bit. The following table is illustrative:

Action	Code
test a bit	`if( flagest & MASK ) . . .`
set a bit	`flagset | = MASK`
clear a bit	`flagset &= ~MASK`

5.5.7 Programming the Terminal Driver: Sample Programs

Example: echostate.c – show state of echo bit

Our first sample program tells us whether the terminal is set to echo characters. We read the settings, test a bit, and report the result:

```
/* echostate.c
 *   reports current state of echo bit in tty driver for fd 0
 *   shows how to read attributes from driver and test a bit
 */

#include       <stdio.h>
#include       <termios.h>

main()
{
        struct termios info;
        int rv;

        rv = tcgetattr( 0, &info );     /* read values from driver    */

        if ( rv == -1 ){
                perror( "tcgetattr");
                exit(1);
        }
        if ( info.c_lflag & ECHO )
                printf(" echo is on , since its bit is 1\n");
        else
                printf(" echo if OFF, since its bit is 0\n");
}
```

This program reads the terminal attributes for file descriptor 0. Zero is the file descriptor for standard input, the file descriptor usually attached to the keyboard. Here is a sample compilation and run of the program:

```
$ cc echostate.c -o echostate
$ ./echostate
 echo is on , since its bit is 1
$ stty -echo
$ ./echostatr: not found
$ echo is OFF, since its bit is 0
```

The example shows that the command `stty -echo` disables keystroke echoing in the driver. The user types two more commands after that, but they do not show on the screen. On the other hand, output in response to those two lines does appear.

Example: `setecho.c` – change state of echo bit

Our second sample program turns keyboard echo on or off. If the command-line argument begins with "y", the echo flag for the terminal is turned on. Otherwise, echo is turned off. The program is as follows:

```c
/* setecho.c
 *    usage:   setecho [y|n]
 *    shows:   how to read, change, reset tty attributes
 */

#include        <stdio.h>
#include        <termios.h>

#define  oops(s,x) { perror(s); exit(x); }

main(int ac, char *av[])
{
        struct termios info;

        if ( ac == 1 )
                exit(0);

        if ( tcgetattr(0,&info) == -1 )            /* get attribs  */
                oops("tcgettattr", 1);

        if ( av[1][0] == 'y' )
                info.c_lflag |= ECHO ;             /* turn on bit  */
        else
                info.c_lflag &= ~ECHO ;            /* turn off bit */

        if ( tcsetattr(0,TCSANOW,&info) == -1 ) /* set attribs   */
                oops("tcsetattr",2);
}
```

We test and run our two programs and regular `stty`:

```
$ echostate; setecho n ; echostate ; stty echo
 echo is on, since its bit is 1
 echo is OFF, since its bit is 0
$ stty -echo ; echostate ; setecho y ; setecho n
 echo is OFF, since its bit is 0
```

On the first command line, we used `setecho` to turn off echoing. Then we used `stty` to turn echoing back on. The driver and driver settings are stored in the kernel, not in the process. One process can change settings in the driver, and a different process can read or change the settings.

Example: `showtty.c` – display many driver attributes

We can repeat the techniques in `setecho.c` and `echostate.c` to build a complete version of `stty`. The `tty` driver contains three sorts of settings: special characters, numerical values, and bits. `showtty` contains functions to display each of these types of data. The following is the code:

```c
/* showtty.c
 *        displays some current tty settings
 */

#include      <stdio.h>
#include      <termios.h>

main()
{
        struct  termios ttyinfo;          /* this struct holds tty info */

        if ( tcgetattr( 0 , &ttyinfo ) == -1 ){   /* get info */
                perror( "cannot get params about stdin");
                exit(1);
        }

                                          /* show info */
        showbaud ( cfgetospeed( &ttyinfo ) );     /* get + show baud rate */
        printf("The erase character is ascii %d, Ctrl-%c\n",
                    ttyinfo.c_cc[VERASE], ttyinfo.c_cc[VERASE]-1+'A');
        printf("The line kill character is ascii %d, Ctrl-%c\n",
                    ttyinfo.c_cc[VKILL], ttyinfo.c_cc[VKILL]-1+'A');

        show_some_flags( &ttyinfo );              /* show misc. flags    */
}

showbaud( int thespeed )
/*
 *        prints the speed in english
 */
{
        printf("the baud rate is ");
        switch ( thespeed ){
                case B300:      printf("300\n");          break;
                case B600:      printf("600\n");          break;
                case B1200:     printf("1200\n");         break;
                case B1800:     printf("1800\n");         break;
                case B2400:     printf("2400\n");         break;
                case B4800:     printf("4800\n");         break;
                case B9600:     printf("9600\n");         break;
```

```
                    default:          printf("Fast\n");        break;
            }
    }

    struct flaginfo { int    fl_value; char   *fl_name; };

    struct flaginfo input_flags[] = {
                    IGNBRK  ,         "Ignore break condition",
                    BRKINT  ,         "Signal interrupt on break",
                    IGNPAR  ,         "Ignore chars with parity errors",
                    PARMRK  ,         "Mark parity errors",
                    INPCK   ,         "Enable input parity check",
                    ISTRIP  ,         "Strip character",
                    INLCR   ,         "Map NL to CR on input",
                    IGNCR   ,         "Ignore CR",
                    ICRNL   ,         "Map CR to NL on input",
                    IXON    ,         "Enable start/stop output control",
                /* _IXANY  ,        "enable any char to restart output",    */
                    IXOFF   ,         "Enable start/stop input control",
                    0       ,         NULL };

    struct flaginfo local_flags[] = {
                    ISIG    ,         "Enable signals",
                    ICANON  ,         "Canonical input (erase and kill)",
                /* _XCASE          ,   "Canonical upper/lower appearance", */
                    ECHO    ,         "Enable echo",
                    ECHOE   ,         "Echo ERASE as BS-SPACE-BS",
                    ECHOK   ,         "Echo KILL by starting new line",
                    0       ,         NULL };

    show_some_flags( struct termios *ttyp )
    /*
     *      show the values of two of the flag sets_: c_iflag and c_lflag
     *      adding c_oflag and c_cflag is pretty routine - just add new
     *      tables above and a bit more code below.
     */
    {
            show_flagset( ttyp->c_iflag, input_flags );
            show_flagset( ttyp->c_lflag, local_flags );
    }

    show_flagset( int thevalue, struct flaginfo thebitnames[] )
    /*
     * check each bit pattern and display descriptive title
     */
    {
            int     i;

            for ( i=0; thebitnames[i].fl_value ; i++ ) {
                    printf( "  %s is ", thebitnames[i].fl_name);
                    if ( thevalue & thebitnames[i].fl_value )
```

```
                              printf("ON\n");
                    else
                              printf("OFF\n");
              }
       }
```

`showtty` prints the current state, with explanatory text, of about sixteen attributes in the driver. Our program uses a table of structs to simplify the code. A single function `show_flagset` is passed an integer and a set of driver flags. `show_flagset` loops through all the bits testing and displaying the status of each in turn. What would be required to add the other flagsets to this program? What would be required to turn this program into a complete version of `stty`?

5.5.8   Summary of Terminal Connections

A terminal is a device human beings use to communicate with Unix processes. A terminal has a keyboard from which a process reads characters and a display to which a process sends characters. A terminal is a device, so it appears as a special file in the directory tree, usually in the /dev directory.

The transfer and processing of data between the terminal and a process is handled by the terminal driver, a part of the kernel. That kernel code provides buffering, editing, and data conversion. Programs may examine and modify the settings of that driver by calling `tcgetattr` and `tcsetattr`.

5.6   PROGRAMMING OTHER DEVICES: `ioctl`

A connection to a disk file has one set of attributes, and a connection to a terminal has a different set of attributes. What about connections to other types of devices?

Consider CD recorders. Rewritable CDs can be erased; CDs can be recorded at different speeds. Scanners have their own sort of settings, such as scanning resolution and color depth. Other types of devices have other types of settings. How does a programmer examine and control settings for a device?

Every device file supports the `ioctl` system call:

ioctl		
PURPOSE	Control a Device	
INCLUDE	# include <sys/ioctl.h>	
USAGE	int result = ioctl (int fd, int operation [, arg..])	
ARGS	fd	file descriptor connected to device
	operation	operation to perform
	arg...	any args required for the operation
RETURNS	-1	if error
	other	depends on device

The `ioctl` system call provides access to the attributes and operations of the device driver connected to *fd*. Each type of device has its own set of properties and `ioctl` operations.

A video terminal screen, for example, has a size measured in rows and columns or in pixels. The code

```
#include <sys/ioctl.h>

void print_screen_dimensions()
{
    struct winsize wbuf;

    if ( ioctl(0, TIOCGWINSZ, &wbuf) != -1 ){
        printf("%d rows x %d cols\n", wbuf.ws_row, wbuf.ws_col);
        printf("%d wide x %d tall\n", wbuf.ws_xpixel, wbuf.ws_ypixel);
    }
}
```

prints the dimensions of the screen. The symbol TIOCGWINSZ is the function code, and the address of wbuf is the argument to that device-control function.

Reading the header file is a good place to learn about the types of devices and their functions. Manual pages for devices also include lists of properties and functions. The Linux manual page for st(4), for example, describes details of using `ioctl` to control a SCSI tape drive.

5.7 UP IN THE SKY! IT'S A FILE, IT'S A DEVICE, IT'S A STREAM!

Unix thinks of a file as any source or destination for data. The basic system calls apply equally to disk files and to device files; differences appear in the operation of the connections. A file descriptor to a disk file contains code for buffering and appending. A file descriptor to a terminal contains code for editing, echoing, character conversion, and other operations.

We described each processing step as an attribute of a connection, but we could instead say a connection is simply a combination of processing steps. System V Unix, the variety of Unix developed at AT&T during the 1980s, developed a model for data flow based on the idea of a sequence of processing steps, like a car wash. First your car gets sprayed with soapy water. Then the big brushes scrub the dirt. Next, the high-pressure hoses drive the soap scum and dirt off the surface, the undercarriage rust inhibitor is applied, the hot wax is sprayed on, and the hubcap chrome polish is applied. Then the soft cloth and hot air buff up the surface, and you are done.

Of course, each stage is really a separate module the owner of the car wash purchased from the car wash parts company and installed at some step in the sequence. Furthermore, you can arrange to disable any particular step. (No hot wax, please!)

That is a rough idea of the STREAMS model of data flow and connection attributes. An elegant part of the streams model is the modularity of the processing. If you are not satisfied with having a terminal driver that only supports boring operations like converting lowercase to uppercase or vice versa, you can devise and install a module to convert digits into Roman numerals. That's right, you write a processing module to

perform the Arabic digit to Roman numeral conversion. You write it to the STREAMS module specifications and then use special system calls to install that module right between the hubcap polish and the soft cloth buffing. When your car reaches the other end, every digit on the dashboard has been replaced by a Roman numeral.

Consult your manual for *streamio* to learn more about this solution to the question of managing properties of connections. STREAMS are used in some versions of Unix to implement network services.

SUMMARY

MAIN IDEAS

- The kernel transfers data between processes and things in the outside world. Things in the outside world include disk files, terminals, and peripheral devices (such as printers, tape drives, sound cards, and mice). Connections to disk files and connections to devices have similarities and differences.
- Disk files and device files have names, properties, and permission bits. Standard file system calls, open, read, write, close, and lseek, may be used for any file or device. File permission bits control access to devices the same way they control access to disk files.
- Connections to disk files differ from connections to device files in the way they process and transfer data. Kernel code that manages connections to a device is called a device driver. Processes can read and change settings in a device driver by using fcntl and ioctl.
- Connections to terminals are so important that special functions tcgetattr and tcsetattr are provided for controlling terminal drivers.
- The Unix command stty gives the user access to the tcgetattr and tcsetattr functions.

VISUAL SUMMARY

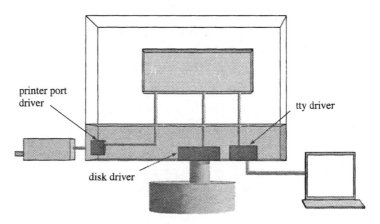

printer port driver

tty driver

disk driver

FIGURE 5.13

File descriptors, connections, and drivers.

A process uses `read` and `write` to move data into and out of file descriptors. File descriptors can connect to disk files, terminals, and peripheral devices. A file descriptor leads to a device driver, a device driver has settings.

WHAT'S NEXT?

Reading data from disks is pretty easy, but reading input from people can be tricky, because people are so unpredictable. Programs designed to read from people can use features of the terminal driver to control the connection. In the next chapter, we look in detail at some programming topics for user programs.

EXPLORATIONS

5.1   On a Linux machine, it is easy to read the output of the mouse. You need to be in text mode to do this. At the shell, make sure the program called gpm is not running; type gpm -k. Then, type `cat /dev/mouse`. Now move the mouse and click the buttons. The `cat` command is reading data from the device file. The bytes read from that file are the clicks and motion messages generated by the mouse.

5.2   What does the execute bit mean for a device file? Study the `biff` command to see an imaginative use for this bit.

5.3   *Directory operations and device files* We discussed how file input/output operations work for device files. What about directory operations like `ln`, `mv`, and `rm`, etc? Using Figure 5.1, explain how each of these three commands affects directories, inodes, and drivers.

5.4   `rm` *and special files* The `rm` command and the underlying `unlink` system call delete a link to an inode. If the number of links for that inode drops to zero, the kernel frees the disk blocks and the inode. A device inode does not have an allocation list, and it has no data blocks. Instead, an inode for a device file contains a pointer to the device-driver subroutine in the kernel. If you delete the filename for a device and the kernel frees the inode, the driver is still in the kernel. How can you create a new file to connect to that device? (Hint: Read about `mknod`.)

5.5   Consider the race condition involved in appending to a file. The discussion in the text describes one of several possible scheduling sequences. How many possible scheduling sequences are there for those two operations for those two processes? What is the outcome of each of those sequences?

5.6   Examine the Linux kernel code to see where the O_APPEND bit is checked. How is the automatic seek implemented?

5.7   *How rename works* The `rename` system call is an atomic operation. What steps are combined in that single call? Search the kernel code of some flavor of Unix to see all the race conditions and possible conflicts the kernel handles. The comments in the Linux kernel code are pretty chatty and amusing.

5.8   The standard library function `fopen` supports opening a file in append mode. For example, `fopen("data","a")`. On your system does the append mode enable O_APPEND, or does it simply `lseek` to the end of the file after it opens the file? Find the source code to `fopen`, or experiment by writing a program that opens the same file twice in append mode and then writes to the two streams alternately.

5.9   *Checking echostate of other devices* The sample program `echostate.c` reports the status of the echo bit in the driver for file descriptor 0. Use the redirection operator < to attach standard input to other files or devices. Try these experiments:

```
echostate < /dev/tty
echostate < /dev/lp
echostate < /etc/passwd
echostate < `tty`
```

Explain the output produced by each of these commands.

5.10 *Changing attributes of other terminals* The setecho program changes the echo bit in the driver attached to standard input. If you attach standard input to a different terminal, you can change the echo bit for that terminal.

Try this experiment:

(a) Log in twice to the same machine (or open two windows on one).

(b) Type tty in each window to find the names of the device files for those two windows. Say one is connected to /dev/ttyp1 and the other window is connected to /dev/ttyp2.

(c) At ttyp1, type **setecho n < /dev/ttyp2**

(d) In the ttyp2 window, type the command **echostate**

(e) Now, in ttyp1, type **echostate < /dev/ttyp2**

(f) Explain what happened.

(g) Try the same thing with the regular stty command.

You may find this extremely helpful someday.

5.11 *Device files and terminal control* The examples in the text use the value 0 for the file descriptor in the calls to tcgetattr and tcsetattr. That first argument is the file descriptor and may be any value that refers to a connection to a terminal device.

File descriptor 1 refers to standard output. Modify echostate and setecho to use file descriptor 1 instead of 0. How does that change affect the operation of the programs? Often standard input and standard output refer to the terminal. Explain what happens with echostate >> echostate.log. Are there advantages to using file descriptor 0?

5.12 If you want to set up a system to accept incoming ppp connections, you have to install a modem and configure the serial port. The terminal driver for the serial port has to be configured to work with the modem. Read about the file called /etc/gettydefs and /etc/inittab to learn how Unix defines terminal settings for logins on serial lines.

5.13 Some versions of Unix support three versions of O_SYNC: data blocks only, inodes only, and both. Why would you want to ensure writes of one and not the other? What are the names of the flags that control each of these three sorts?

5.14 What do the read and write permission bits on a terminal special file control? Use tty to determine the name of your terminal, then use chmod 000 /dev/yourtty to make your terminal unreadable even to yourself. What happens? Why?

5.15 Look through the /dev directory on your system, and find files that do not support read, files that do not support write, and files that do not support lseek.

5.16 Use ls -l in /dev to find the major and minor numbers of various devices. What pattern do you see? What devices share the same major number? What do those devices have in common, how do they differ?

5.17 Name the four groups of tty driver settings, explain the purpose of each group, and name two bits in each group.

5.18 A program uses tcsetattr to turn off echo mode for the current terminal. When that program exits, the terminal stays in no-echo mode. On the other hand, when a program opens a file and uses `fcntl` to set the descriptor to `O_APPEND` mode, the next program that opens that file does not get auto-append mode. Explain this apparent inconsistency.

5.19 A connection to a terminal is a regular file descriptor. Can you use `fcntl` to set the `O_APPEND` attribute for a connection to a file descriptor? What does auto append mean for devices?

5.20 What is the difference between `ioctl` and `fcntl`?

5.21 The `/dev` directory contains the files `/dev/null` and `/dev/zero`. These files are not really connections to devices, but they do not represent disk files either. What do these files do, and why are they useful? Can you find other files in `/dev` that are virtual devices like these two?

PROGRAMMING EXERCISES

5.22 Enhance the simple version of `write` presented in the chapter. The version in the text requires the user to type the name of the device file, and that version does not print the identifying greeting. Write a new version that accepts a username as argument and prints on the screen of that user your request to communicate. See what the regular version of `write` prints.

Your program has to handle special cases. The person you want to chat with might not be logged on. On the other hand, the person you want to chat with might be logged on at several terminals.

5.23 Users who do not want to be bothered by people trying to `write` to them can use the `mesg` command. Read about `mesg`, experiment with the program to see how it works, then write a version of this program.

5.24 *Using link() for locking* A common race condition involves two processes trying to update the same file at the same time. For example, when you change your password on some systems, the `passwd` program rewrites the file `/etc/passwd`. What if two users changed their password at the same time?

One technique that prevents simultaneous access to a file is to exploit an important feature of the `link` system call. Consider this code:

```
/*
 * tries to make a link called /etc/passwd.LCK
 * returns 0 if ok, 1 if already locked, 2 if other problem
 */
int lock_passwd()
{
        int rv = 0;                         /* default return value */

        if ( link("/etc/passwd", "/etc/passwd.LCK") == -1 )
                rv = ( errno == EEXISTS ? 1 : 2 );
        return rv;
}
```

(a) If two processes execute this code at the same instant, only one will succeed. What is it about the `link` system call that makes it a useful way to lock files?

(b) Write a short program that uses this technique to append a line of text to a file. Your program should attempt to make the link. If the link succeeds, the program can open the file, append the line, then delete the link. If the link fails, your program should use `sleep(1)` to wait a second then try again. Make sure your program does not wait forever.

(c) Write the `unlock_passwd` function that undoes `lock_passwd`.

(d) The example shown allows processes to lock an existing file, but how can a program use `link` to prevent two processes from both `creating` the same file?

(e) Study the command `vipw`. Does `vipw` use links for locks?

5.25 *Links and locks, Part II* The previous problem showed how to use links to lock files. File locks must be removed when the program that set the lock finishes modifying the file. If the program does not release a lock, other programs will wait forever. What if the program has a bug and crashes or is killed by the user pressing Ctrl-C before it has a chance to release the lock?

One technique is for the program that holds the lock to modify the file every *n* seconds. The program can use `utime` to do that. Programs that are waiting for the lock can check the modification time to see if the lock is still "warm." If the lock has not been modified in the agreed-upon interval, other programs are free to delete the link then try to create the link again.

Write a new version of the `lock_passwd` function that takes as an argument a number of seconds. This new version will implement the logic described in the previous paragraph.

5.26 What is the effect on performance if you turn off buffering? Write a program that writes a large disk file in small pieces, say a 2-megabyte file in 16-byte chunks. Try this with `O_SYNC` on and with `O_SYNC` off. Adjust the file size and the chunk size to see how they affect the results.

5.27 The text includes code to turn off disk buffering for a file descriptor. Write a function that turns buffering back on.

5.28 Write a program called `uppercase.c` that toggles the `OLCUC` bit in the terminal driver and reports the current resulting state of that bit.

5.29 *ioctl and window size* The output of `stty -a` includes the number of rows and columns for the terminal window. These values do not come from `tcgetattr`, they come from `ioctl`. Use this system call to modify the version of `more` from Chapter 1 so that it uses the size of the terminal screen instead of the fixed value of 24.

PROJECTS

Based on the material in this chapter, you can learn about and write versions of the following Unix programs:

`write, stty, passwd, wall, biff, mt` (magtape control program, may not be on your system)

CHAPTER 6

Programming for Humans
Terminal Control and Signals

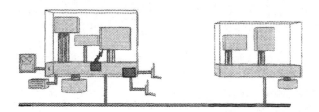

OBJECTIVES

Ideas and Skills

- Software tools vs. user programs
- Reading and changing settings of the terminal driver
- Modes of the terminal driver
- Nonblocking input
- Timeouts on user input
- Introduction to signals: How Ctrl-C works

System Calls

- fcntl
- signal

6.1 SOFTWARE TOOLS VS. DEVICE-SPECIFIC PROGRAMS

On a Unix system, devices look a lot like disk files, but devices are not the same as disk files. We saw in Chapter 5 that programs can open, close, read, write, and lseek devices, but we also saw that devices have drivers, and those drivers can contain many device-specific controls and attributes. What do programs think about this duality?

Software Tools: Read `stdin` or Files, Write to `stdout`

Programs that see no difference between disk files and devices are called software tools. Unix systems have hundreds of software tools, including who, ls, sort, uniq, grep, tr, and du. Software tools are based on the model shown in Figure 6.1:

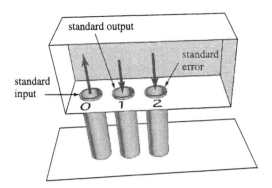

Fact: Most processes automatically have the first three file descriptors open. They do not need to call open() to make these connections.

FIGURE 6.1

The three standard file descriptors.

A software tool reads bytes from standard input, does some processing, then writes a resulting stream of bytes to standard output. A tool sends error messages, again simply streams of bytes, to standard error. These file descriptors could be connected to files, terminals, mice, photocells, printers, and pipes; tools make no assumptions about sources and destinations of data they process. Many of these programs also read from files named on the command line.

Input and output for these programs can be easily attached to all sorts of connections:

```
$ sort > outputfile
$ sort x > /dev/lp
$ who | tr '[a-z]' '[A-Z]'
```

Device-Specific Programs: Control Device for Particular Application

Other programs, though, are written to interact with specific devices. Examples include programs to control scanners, record compact disks, operate tape drives, and take digital photographs. In this chapter, we explore the ideas and techniques of writing device-specific programs by looking at the most common type of device-specific programs, programs that interact with terminals, designed to be used by human beings. We refer to these terminal-oriented programs as *user programs*.

User Programs: A Common Type of Device-Specific Program

Examples of user programs are vi, emacs, pine, more, lynx, hangman, robots, and many of the games from the University of California at Berkeley.[1] These programs adjust settings in the terminal driver to control how keystrokes are handled and output is

---

[1]The source code for these may be found on the Web. Look for bsdgames.

processed. The driver has lots of settings, but common concerns of user programs include

(a) immediate response to keys

(b) limited input set

(c) timeout on input

(d) resistance to Ctrl-C

We shall learn about these topics by writing a program that implements all these features.

6.2   MODES OF THE TERMINAL DRIVER

We first discussed the terminal driver in the previous chapter. We now explore the driver in more detail by experimenting with a short translation program:[2]

```
/* rotate.c : map a->b, b->c, .. z->a
 *    purpose: useful for showing tty modes
 */

#include   <stdio.h>
#include   <ctype.h>
int main()
{
    int c;
    while ( ( c=getchar() ) != EOF ){
        if ( c == 'z' )
            c = 'a';
        else if (islower(c))
            c++;
        putchar(c);
    }
}
```

6.2.1   Canonical Mode: Buffering and Editing

Run the program using the default settings: (<- is backspace):

```
$ cc rotate.c -o rotate
$ ./rotate
abx<-cd
bcde
efgCtrl-C
$
```

---

[2]You can do this with `tr`, but the GNU version of `tr` buffers its input, making it useless for this pedagogical example.

Figure 6.2 shows the terminal, the kernel, the `rotate` program, and the data streams:

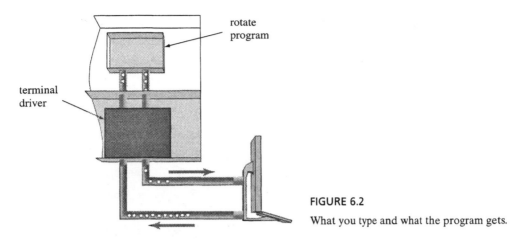

FIGURE 6.2

What you type and what the program gets.

Our experiments reveal the following features of standard input processing:

(a) The "x" key is never seen by the program; backspace erases it.
(b) Characters appears on the screen as you type them, but
(c) The program does not receive any input until you press the Enter key.
(d) The Ctrl-C key discards input and stops the program.

The `rotate` program does none of these operations. Buffering, echoing, editing, and control key processing are all done by the terminal driver. Figure 6.3 shows these operations as layers in the driver:

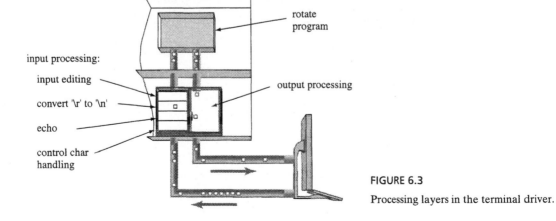

FIGURE 6.3

Processing layers in the terminal driver.

Buffering and editing comprise *canonical processing.* When these features are enabled, the terminal connection is said to be in *canonical mode.*

6.2.2 Noncanonical Processing

Now, try this experiment (the input is again *abx<-cd*, then *efg Ctrl-C*):

```
$ stty -icanon ; ./rotate
abbcxy^?cdde
effgh
$ stty icanon
```

The command `stty -icanon` turns off *canonical mode* processing in the driver. The printed page does not give the full flavor of noncanonical mode but shows how input processing has changed.

In particular, *noncanonical mode* has no buffering. When you press the letter "a", the driver skips the buffering layer and delivers the character to `rotate`, which prints back the letter "b". Unbuffered user input can be a nuisance. When the user tries to erase a character, the driver cannot do anything about it; the character is already in user space.

For a final experiment, try this command, and again type "*abx<-cd*" and then "*efg*" *Ctrl-C*:

```
$ stty -icanon -echo ; ./rotate
bcy^?de
fgh
$ stty icanon echo    (Note: You won't see this. Why?)
```

In this example, we turn off canonical mode and also turn off echo mode. The driver no longer prints back the characters as we type them. Output comes only from the program. When you exit the program, the driver is still in no-echo, noncanonical mode and remains in that mode until a program changes the settings. The shell prints a prompt and waits for your next command line. Some shells reset the driver, some do not. If your shell does not reset the driver, you will continue in no-echo, noncanonical mode.

6.2.3 Summary of Terminal Modes

If you have not yet tried the examples at a terminal, do so now. These examples show that the terminal driver operates in different modes. When you design a user program for Unix, you need decide which terminal mode matches the application.

canonical mode

Canonical mode, also called *cooked mode*, is the mode users expect. The driver stores incoming characters in a buffer and only sends those buffered characters to the program when the driver receives the Enter key.[3] Buffering data lets the driver perform basic editing functions such as deleting a character, word, or the entire line. These functions are invoked when the user presses the *erase key*, the *word-erase key*, or the *kill*

---

[3]Or the currently defined EOF key, usually Ctrl-D.

key respectively. The specific keystrokes assigned to these three functions are settings in the driver and may be changed with the `stty` command or `tcsetattr` system call.

noncanonical mode pka *crmode*

When buffering, and thus editing functions, is turned off, the connection is said to be in *noncanonical mode*. The terminal driver still does specific character processing such as handling Ctrl-C and translating between newline and carriage return. But the editing keystrokes for *erase, word-erase*, and *kill* have no special meaning so are treated as regular data.

   If you write a program that uses noncanonical mode and you want users to be able to edit their input, you need to write editing functions in your program.

non-anything mode pka *raw mode*

Each processing step is controlled by a separate bit. For example, the `ISIG` bit controls if the interrupt key, usually Ctrl-C, has the usual effect of killing a program. A program is free to turn off all processing steps.

   When all processing is turned off, the driver passes input directly to the program. In this case, the driver is said to be in *raw mode*. In the *Olden Days*®, when the terminal driver was simpler, there was a specific mode called raw mode. The `stty` command supports *raw* as a command-line option, and the manual page for `stty` tells what raw mode means.

   The terminal driver is a complex set of routines in the kernel. As we study and experiment with it, though, the various components and their roles become more clearly defined. Figure 6.4 shows the major parts:

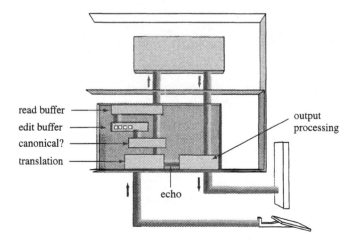

read buffer
edit buffer
canonical?
translation

output
processing

echo

FIGURE 6.4

Major components of the terminal driver.

These modes were invented because they are useful. To understand the practical value of these modes, we develop a user program that uses various driver modes.

6.3 WRITING A USER PROGRAM: `play_again.c`

Many user applications, such as automated teller machines and video games, ask users *yes/no* questions. The following shell script is the main loop for a bank machine:

```
#!/bin/sh
#
# atm.sh - a wrapper for two programs
#
while true
do
     do_a_transaction      # run a program
     if play_again         # run our program
     then
          continue         # if "y" loop back
     fi
     break                 # if "n" break
done
```

In typical Unix style, this bank machine is built as a shell script that combines separate components. The first component, a program called do_a_transaction, does the work of the ATM. The second component, play_again, obtains a yes or no answer from the user. We shall write that second program. This component architecture allows us to snap in new versions of play_again easily.

The logic of play_again.c is simple:

> prompt user with question
> accept input
> if "y", return 0
> if "n", return 1

Example: `play_again0.c` – does the job

```
/* play_again0.c
 *      purpose: ask if user wants another transaction
 *       method: ask a question, wait for yes/no answer
 *      returns: 0=>yes, 1=>no
 *       better: eliminate need to press return
 */
#include           <stdio.h>
#include           <termios.h>

#define QUESTION        "Do you want another transaction"
int get_response( char * );

int main()
{
        int       response;

        response = get_response(QUESTION);      /* get some answer      */
```

```
                return response;
        }
        int get_response(char *question)
        /*
         * purpose: ask a question and wait for a y/n answer
         *  method: use getchar and ignore non y/n answers
         * returns: 0=>yes, 1=>no
         */
        {
                printf("%s (y/n)?", question);
                while(1){
                        switch( getchar() ){
                                case 'y':
                                case 'Y': return 0;
                                case 'n':
                                case 'N':
                                case EOF: return 1;
                        }
                }
        }
```

This program prints a question and then loops, reading user input until the user types "y" or "n" or "Y" or "N". play_again0 has two problems, both caused by running in canonical mode. First, the user has to press the Enter key before play_again0 can act on input. Second, the program receives and processes an entire line of data when the user presses Enter. Therefore, play_again0 reads the input

```
$ play_again0
Do you want another transaction (y/n)? sure thing!
```

as a negative response. Our first improvement is to turn off canonical input so the program receives and processes characters as the user types them.

Example: `play_again1.c` – immediate response

```
/* play_again1.c
 *      purpose: ask if user wants another transaction
 *       method: set tty into char-by-char mode, read char, return result
 *      returns:  0=>yes, 1=>no
 *       better: do no echo inappropriate input
 */
#include         <stdio.h>
#include         <termios.h>

#define QUESTION        "Do you want another transaction"

main()
{
        int     response;
```

```
        tty_mode(0);                          /* save tty mode       */
        set_crmode();                         /* set chr-by-chr mode */
        response = get_response(QUESTION);    /* get some answer     */
        tty_mode(1);                          /* restore tty mode    */
         return response;
}
int get_response(char *question)
/*
 * purpose: ask a question and wait for a y/n answer
 *  method: use getchar and complain about non y/n answers
 * returns: 0=>yes, 1=>no
 */
{
        int input;
        printf("%s (y/n)?", question);
        while(1){
                switch( input = getchar() ){
                        case 'y':
                        case 'Y': return 0;
                        case 'n':
                        case 'N':
                        case EOF: return 1;
                        default:
                                printf("\ncannot understand %c, ", input);
                                printf("Please type y or no\n");
                }
        }
}

set_crmode()
/*
 * purpose: put file descriptor 0 (i.e. stdin) into chr-by-chr mode
 *  method: use bits in termios
 */
{
        struct  termios ttystate;

        tcgetattr( 0, &ttystate);                /* read curr. setting   */
        ttystate.c_lflag        &= ~ICANON;      /* no buffering         */
        ttystate.c_cc[VMIN]     = 1;             /* get 1 char at a time */
        tcsetattr( 0 , TCSANOW, &ttystate);      /* install settings     */
}

/* how == 0 => save current mode,  how == 1 => restore mode */
tty_mode(int how)
{
        static struct termios original_mode;
        if ( how == 0 )
                tcgetattr(0, &original_mode);
        else
                return tcsetattr(0, TCSANOW, &original_mode);
}
```

`play_again1` first puts the terminal in character-by-character mode, then calls the function to print a prompt and get a response, and finally restores the terminal to its previous mode. Notice we do not set the terminal driver to canonical mode at the end. Instead, we copy the original settings into a struct called `original_mode` and later restore those settings.

Putting the terminal into character input mode involves two parts. We turn off the ICANON bit and also assign the value 1 to the VMIN element in the control character array. The VMIN value tells the driver how many characters at a time we are reading. We want to read characters one by one, so we set this value to 1. If we wanted to read characters three at time,[4] we would set that value to 3.

We compile and run this program, typing *sure* as a response:

```
$ make play_again1
cc      play_again1.c   -o play_again1
$ ./play_again1
Do you want another transaction (y/n)?s
cannot understand s, Please type y or no
u
cannot understand u, Please type y or no
r
cannot understand r, Please type y or no
e
cannot understand e, Please type y or no
y$
```

As intended, `play_again1` receives and processes characters as they are typed without waiting for the Enter key. But complaining about every character is annoying. A cleaner design is to turn off echo mode and just discard characters until we get acceptable input.

Example: `play_again2.c` – ignore illegal keys

```
/* play_again2.c
 *        purpose: ask if user wants another transaction
 *         method: set tty into char-by-char mode and no-echo mode
 *                 read char, return result
 *        returns: 0=>yes, 1=>no
 *         better: timeout if user walks away
 *
 */
#include        <stdio.h>
#include        <termios.h>

#define QUESTION        "Do you want another transaction"

main()
```

---

[4] I actually used this to handle function keys. On many keyboards, function keys send multicharacter sequences, such as escape-[-1-1-~ . When my program read the escape character (ASCII 27) it was expecting three or four characters all in a row.

```
{
        int     response;

        tty_mode(0);                                /* save mode */
        set_cr_noecho_mode();                       /* set -icanon, -echo   */
        response = get_response(QUESTION);          /* get some answer       */
        tty_mode(1);                                /* restore tty state     */
        return response;
}

int get_response(char *question)
/*
 * purpose: ask a question and wait for a y/n answer
 *  method: use getchar and ignore non y/n answers
 * returns: 0=>yes, 1=>no
 */
{
        printf("%s (y/n)?", question);
        while(1){
                switch( getchar() ){
                        case 'y':
                        case 'Y': return 0;
                        case 'n':
                        case 'N':
                        case EOF: return 1;
                }
        }
}
set_cr_noecho_mode()
/*
 * purpose: put file descriptor 0 into chr-by-chr mode and noecho mode
 *  method: use bits in termios
 */
{
        struct  termios ttystate;

        tcgetattr( 0, &ttystate);                   /* read curr. setting   */
        ttystate.c_lflag       &= ~ICANON;          /* no buffering         */
        ttystate.c_lflag       &= ~ECHO;            /* no echo either       */
        ttystate.c_cc[VMIN]    =   1;               /* get 1 char at a time */
        tcsetattr( 0 , TCSANOW, &ttystate);         /* install settings     */
}

/* how == 0 => save current mode,   how == 1 => restore mode */
tty_mode(int how)
{
        static struct termios original_mode;
        if ( how == 0 )
                tcgetattr(0, &original_mode);
        else
                return tcsetattr(0, TCSANOW, &original_mode);
}
```

This program differs from the previous version in two ways. The function that sets the terminal driver mode turns off the echo bit. Note that the restore function does not have to turn it back on explicitly. The other change is that the get_response function no longer reports errors for illegal input. It just ignores them.

Compile and try this program. If you type *sure* to it, nothing shows up. Only when you press *y* or *n* does the program return.

play_again2 does exactly what we intended, but it needs one more feature. What if this program were used at a real ATM and a customer wandered away without pressing *y* or *n*. The next customer could press *y* and have access to the account of the customer who walked away. User programs are more secure when they include a timeout feature.

6.3.1   Nonblocking Input: `play_again3.c`

The next version of our program includes a timeout feature. We create this timeout feature by telling the terminal driver not to wait for input. If we find no input, we sleep a few seconds then look again for input. After three tries, we give up.

Blocking vs. Nonblocking Input

When you call getchar or read to read data from a file descriptor, the call usually waits for input. In the play_again examples, our call to getchar causes the program to wait until the user types a character. The program is *blocked*, the way a car is blocked at a railroad crossing from further motion, until some characters become available or the end of file is detected. How do we turn off input blocking?

Blocking is a property of any open file, not only connections to terminals. Programs can use fcntl or open to enable *nonblocking input* for a file descriptor. play_again3 uses fcntl to turn on the O_NDELAY[5] flag for the file descriptor.

We turn off blocking on a file descriptor and call read. Now what? If input is available, read gets it and returns the number of characters it got. If no characters are available, read returns 0, just as it does at end of file. read returns -1 if there is an error.

Internally, nonblocking operation is pretty simple. Each file has a space to hold available unread data, shown in Figure 6.4 as the top storage box inside the driver. If the file descriptor has the O_NDELAY bit set and that space is empty, the read call returns 0. If you grep the Linux source code for O_NDELAY you can find the implementation details.

Example: `play_again3.c` – use nonblocking mode for timeouts

```
/* play_again3.c
 *      purpose: ask if user wants another transaction
 *       method: set tty into chr-by-chr, no-echo mode
 *               set tty into no-delay mode
 *               read char, return result
 *      returns: 0=>yes, 1=>no, 2=>timeout
 *       better: reset terminal mode on Interrupt
 */
#include        <stdio.h>
#include        <termios.h>
```

---

[5]You can also use the O_NONBLOCK bit, check your manual.

```
#include          <fcntl.h>
#include          <string.h>

#define ASK          "Do you want another transaction"
#define TRIES      3                              /* max tries */
#define SLEEPTIME  2                              /* time per try */
#define BEEP         putchar('\a')                /* alert user */

main()
{
        int     response;

        tty_mode(0);                             /* save current mode   */
        set_cr_noecho_mode();                    /* set -icanon, -echo  */
        set_nodelay_mode();                      /* noinput => EOF      */
        response = get_response(ASK, TRIES);     /* get some answer     */
        tty_mode(1);                             /* restore orig mode   */
        return response;
}
get_response( char *question , int maxtries)
/*
 * purpose: ask a question and wait for a y/n answer or maxtries
 *   method: use getchar and complain about non-y/n input
 * returns: 0=>yes, 1=>no, 2=>timeout
 */
{
        int     input;

        printf("%s (y/n)?", question);            /* ask             */
        fflush(stdout);                           /* force output */
        while ( 1 ){
                sleep(SLEEPTIME);                 /* wait a bit    */
                input = tolower(get_ok_char());   /* get next chr */
                if ( input == 'y' )
                        return 0;
                if ( input == 'n' )
                        return 1;
                if ( maxtries-- == 0 )            /* outatime?    */
                        return 2;                 /* sayso        */
                BEEP;
        }
}

/*
 *  skip over non-legal chars and return y,Y,n,N or EOF
 */
get_ok_char()
{
        int c;
        while( ( c = getchar() ) != EOF && strchr("yYnN",c) == NULL )
                ;
        return c;
}
```

```
set_cr_noecho_mode()
/*
 * purpose: put file descriptor 0 into chr-by-chr mode and noecho mode
 *  method: use bits in termios
 */
{
        struct  termios ttystate;

        tcgetattr( 0, &ttystate);               /* read curr. setting  */
        ttystate.c_lflag        &= ~ICANON;     /* no buffering        */
        ttystate.c_lflag        &= ~ECHO;       /* no echo either      */
        ttystate.c_cc[VMIN]     = 1;            /* get 1 char at a time */
        tcsetattr( 0 , TCSANOW, &ttystate);     /* install settings    */
}
set_nodelay_mode()
/*
 * purpose: put file descriptor 0 into no-delay mode
 *  method: use fcntl to set bits
 *   notes: tcsetattr() will do something similar, but it is complicated
 */
{
        int     termflags;
        termflags = fcntl(0, F_GETFL);          /* read curr. settings */
        termflags |= O_NDELAY;                  /* flip on nodelay bit */
        fcntl(0, F_SETFL, termflags);           /* and install 'em     */
}
/* how == 0 => save current mode,  how == 1 => restore mode */
/* this version handles termios and fcntl flags            */

tty_mode(int how)
{
        static struct termios original_mode;
        static int              original_flags;
        if ( how == 0 ){
                tcgetattr(0, &original_mode);
                original_flags = fcntl(0, F_GETFL);
        }
        else {
                tcsetattr(0, TCSANOW, &original_mode);
                fcntl( 0, F_SETFL, original_flags);
        }
}
```

The new features in this version of the program are the use of `fcntl` to turn on and off nonblocking mode and the use of `sleep` and the `maxtries` counter in `get_response`.

Small Problems with `play_again3`

`play_again3` is not ideal. Running in nonblocking mode, the program sleeps for two seconds before calling `getchar` to give the user a chance to type something. If the user types within one second, the program does not get the character until two seconds pass. Users may get confused.

Can we make the program respond faster? We could reduce the sleep time between calling getchar and compensate by increasing the number of iterations.

Second, notice the call to fflush after printing the prompt. Without that line, the prompt does not appear until the program calls getchar. Here is why. Not only does the terminal driver buffer input on a line-by-line basis, the driver also line-buffers output. The driver buffers output until it receives a newline or until the program tries to read from the terminal. In this example, by postponing calling for input to give the user a chance to read the prompt, we need to add the fflush call.

Other Methods to Implement Timeouts

Unix provides better ways to implement timeouts on user input. The VTIME element in the c_cc[] array in the driver moves the timeout to the terminal driver. An exercise provides details. The select system call includes a timeout parameter. We discuss select in a later chapter.

A Big Problem with play_again3

play_again3 ignores letters it does not want, identifies and processes legal input, and exits if no legal input arrives during the specified interval. What happens if the user presses Ctrl-C ? Here is a sample run:

```
$ make play_again3
cc      play_again3.c   -o play_again3
$ ./play_again3
Do you want another transaction (y/n)?  press Ctrl-C now
$ logout
Connection to host closed.
bash$
```

When we pressed Ctrl-C to kill the play_again program, we killed the program and also killed the entire login session. How did that happen? Here are the steps: play_again3 has three parts—initialization, get user input, and restore settings—as indicated in Figure 6.5:

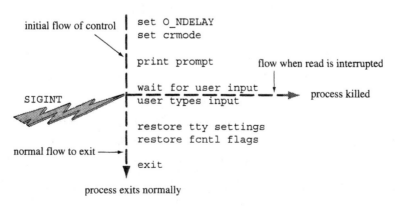

FIGURE 6.5

Ctrl-C kills a program. It leaves terminal unrestored.

The initialization part sets the terminal for nonblocking input. The program then enters the main loop to prompt, sleep, and read input. We then killed the program in the middle by pressing Ctrl-C. What is the state of the terminal driver?

The program quits at once and does not execute the code to reset the driver. The terminal is still in nonblocking mode when the shell returns to print its prompt and get a command line from the user. The shell calls read to get the command line, but read, operating in nonblocking mode, returns 0 immediately. In summary, the program left the file descriptor and underlying driver with the wrong attributes. Our next project is to learn how to protect our program from Ctrl-C.

When I Tried It, I Didn't Get Logged Out!

Many Unix shells include editing features, such as full use of arrow keys to scroll through the list of previous commands. These shells run in raw mode with exactly the settings they need to provide these features. Shells such as bash and tcsh reset terminal attributes as soon as your program exits or dies.

6.4   SIGNALS

The Ctrl-C key interrupts the currently running program. This interruption is produced by a kernel mechanism called a *signal*. Signals are a simple, powerful idea. We explore the basic ideas of signals and learn how to use them to solve our play_again3 problem. In the next chapter, we look at signals in much more depth.

6.4.1   What Does Ctrl-C Do?

You press the Ctrl-C key and a program dies. How does a single keystroke cause the death of a process? The terminal driver plays a role here; Figure 6.6 shows the chain of events:

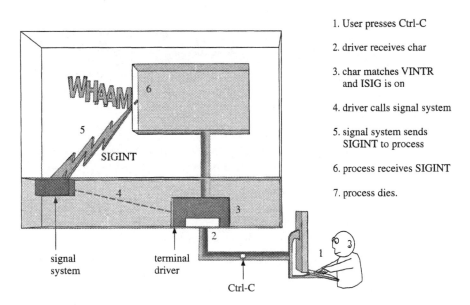

1. User presses Ctrl-C
2. driver receives char
3. char matches VINTR and ISIG is on
4. driver calls signal system
5. signal system sends SIGINT to process
6. process receives SIGINT
7. process dies.

FIGURE 6.6
How Ctrl-C works.

The key does not have to be Ctrl-C, you can use `stty` (or `tcsetattr`) to replace the current VINTR control char with another keystroke.

6.4.2   What Is a Signal?

Pressing Ctrl-C generates a signal, but what is a signal? A signal is a one-word message. A green light is a signal, a stop sign is a signal, and an umpire's gesture is a signal. These items and events do not contain messages; they are messages: *go, stop*, and *out!* When you press the Ctrl-C key, you ask the kernel to send the *interrupt signal* to the currently running process. Each signal has a numerical code. The *interrupt* signal usually is code number 2.[6]

Where Do Signals Come From?   Signals come from the kernel, but requests for signals come from three sources as illustrated in Figure 6.7:

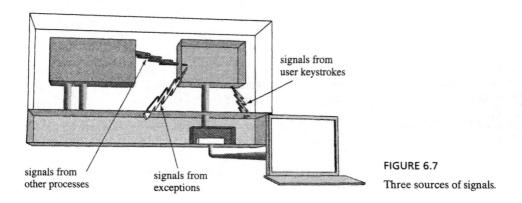

signals from
user keystrokes

signals from
other processes

signals from
exceptions

FIGURE 6.7
Three sources of signals.

users   A user can press Ctrl-C, Ctrl-\, or any other key assigned in the terminal driver to a signal control character.

kernel   The kernel sends a signal to a process when the process does something wrong, such as a segmentation violation, a floating point exception, or an illegal machine-language command. The kernel also uses signals to notify a process of certain events.

processes   A process may send a signal to another process by using the `kill` system call. Sending a signal is one way a process can communicate with other processes.

Signals caused by something a process does, such as dividing by zero, are called *synchronous signals*. Signals caused by events outside the process, such as a user pressing the interrupt key, are called *asynchronous signals*.

---

[6]And if it were to change, a *lot* of shell scripts will break.

Where Can I Find a List of Signals?   Signal numbers and their symbolic names often appear in `/usr/include/signal.h`. Here is a sample section of that file:

```
#define SIGHUP    1   /* hangup, generated when terminal disconnects */
#define SIGINT    2   /* interrupt, generated from terminal special char */
#define SIGQUIT   3   /* (*) quit, generated from terminal special char */
#define SIGILL    4   /* (*) illegal instruction (not reset when caught)*/
#define SIGTRAP   5   /* (*) trace trap (not reset when caught) */
#define SIGABRT   6   /* (*) abort process */
#define SIGEMT    7   /* (*) EMT instruction */
#define SIGFPE    8   /* (*) floating point exception */
#define SIGKILL   9   /* kill (cannot be caught or ignored) */
#define SIGBUS    10  /* (*) bus error (specification exception) */
#define SIGSEGV   11  /* (*) segmentation violation */
#define SIGSYS    12  /* (*) bad argument to system call */
#define SIGPIPE   13  /* write on a pipe with no one to read it */
#define SIGALRM   14  /* alarm clock timeout */
#define SIGTERM   15  /* software termination signal */
```

For example, the *interrupt signal* is called SIGINT, the *quit* signal is called SIGQUIT, and the segmentation violation signal is SIGSEGV. Each version of Unix has a manual page that includes more information. Under Linux, see the `signal(7)` manpage.

What Do Signals Do?   It depends. Many signals cause processes to die. One second a process is running, the next instant it is gone, vanished from memory, all file descriptors closed, removed from the process table. We used SIGINT to kill a process. But a process can protect itself.

6.4.3   What Can a Process Do about a Signal?

A process does not have to die when it receives SIGINT. A process can tell the kernel, by using the `signal` system call, how it wants to respond to a signal. A process has three choices:

accept the default action (usually death)

The manual page lists the default action for each signal. The default action for SIGINT is death. A process does not have to use `signal` to accept the default, but a process can restore the default action with

```
signal(SIGINT, SIG_DFL);
```

ignore the signal

A process can don a signal proof vest. A program tells the kernel it wants to ignore SIGINT with this call:

```
signal(SIGINT, SIG_IGN);
```

call a function

This third choice is the most powerful of the three. Consider the `play_again3` example. When the user presses Ctrl-C, the program, as it is now, exits at once without calling the function to restore driver settings. The program would be better if, upon receiving `SIGINT`, it called a function to restore settings and then `exit`.

The third option of the `signal` call allows exactly this sort of response. A program can tell the kernel which function to call if the signal arrives. The function called on arrival of a signal is called a *signal handler*. To install a signal handler, a program calls

```
signal( signum, functionname );
```

---

signal	
PURPOSE	Simple signal handling
INCLUDE	#include <signal.h>
USAGE	result = signal (int signum, void (*action)(int))
ARGS	signum the signal to respond to action how to respond
RETURNS	-1 if error prevaction if success

The `signal` call installs a new signal handler for the signal with number *signum*. The *action* may be the name of a function or either of these two special values:

SIG_IGN   ignore the signal

SIG_DFL   reset signal to its default action

`signal` returns the previous handler. The value is a pointer to a function.

6.4.4   Examples of Signal Handling

Example 1: Catching a Signal

```
/* sigdemo1.c - shows how a signal handler works.
 *             - run this and press Ctrl-C a few times
 */

#include        <stdio.h>
#include        <signal.h>

main()
{
        void    f(int);                 /* declare the handler  */
        int     i;
```

```
            signal( SIGINT, f );            /* install the handler  */
            for(i=0; i<5; i++ ){            /* do something else     */
                    printf("hello\n");
                    sleep(1);
            }
    }

    void f(int signum)                      /* this function is called */
    {
            printf("OUCH!\n");
    }
```

The main function consists of two parts, a call to signal and a loop. sigdemo1.c calls signal to install the function f to handle SIGINT. If the process receives SIGINT, the kernel causes the program to call the function f. The program jumps to that function, executes the code there, and then returns to where it was in the program, just like any subroutine call.

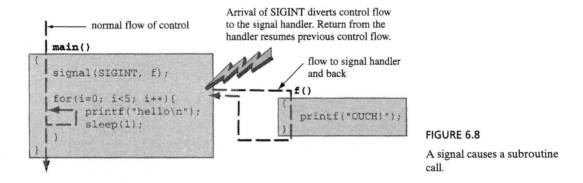

FIGURE 6.8

A signal causes a subroutine call.

Figure 6.8 shows two independent flows of control: the normal path into main, around the loop, and back from main, and the signal-induced path into f and back.

Here is the program in action:

```
$ ./sigdemo1
hello
hello       press Ctrl-C now
OUCH!
hello       press Ctrl-C now
OUCH!
hello
hello
$
```

Compile and try this yourself. There is no explicit call to f in the program. The receipt of the signal invokes that function.

Example 2: Ignoring a Signal

```
/* sigdemo2.c - shows how to ignore a signal
 *              - press Ctrl-\ to kill this one
 */

#include        <stdio.h>
#include        <signal.h>

main()
{
        signal( SIGINT, SIG_IGN );

        printf("you can't stop me!\n");
        while( 1 )
        {
                sleep(1);
                printf("haha\n");
        }

}
```

sigdemo2.c uses signal to arrange to ignore the interrupt signal. The user can press Ctrl-C hundreds of times and have no effect on the process.

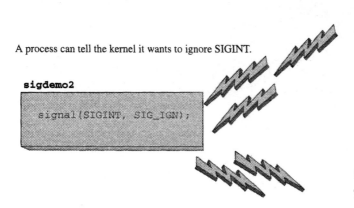

A process can tell the kernel it wants to ignore SIGINT.

sigdemo2

signal(SIGINT, SIG_IGN);

FIGURE 6.9

The effect of signal(SIGINT, SIG_IGN).

Here is the program in action:

```
$ ./sigdemo2
you can't stop me!
haha
haha
haha          press Ctrl-C now
haha          press Ctrl-C nowpress Ctrl-C now
haha
haha
haha          press ^\ now
Quit
$
```

The Ctrl-\ key sends a different signal, the *quit* signal, and this program has not made arrangements to ignore or catch SIGQUIT.

6.5   PREPARED FOR SIGNALS: `play_again4.c`

We now know how to modify play_again3.c to handle signals, but we have to make a design decision. Do we ignore signals and require the user to type a yes or no answer? Do we catch keyboard signals and exit as if the user typed *no*, or do we exit and return a value to indicate the program was killed?

The following version catches SIGINT, resets the driver, and returns the *no* code:

```
/* play_again4.c
 *        purpose: ask if user wants another transaction
 *         method: set tty into chr-by-chr, no-echo mode
 *                 set tty into no-delay mode
 *                 read char, return result
 *                 resets terminal modes on SIGINT, ignores SIGQUIT
 *        returns: 0=>yes, 1=>no, 2=>timeout
 *         better: reset terminal mode on Interrupt
 */
#include        <stdio.h>
#include        <termios.h>
#include        <fcntl.h>
#include        <string.h>
#include        <signal.h>

#define ASK             "Do you want another transaction"
#define TRIES       3                               /* max tries */
#define SLEEPTIME   2                               /* time per try */
#define BEEP        putchar('\a')                   /* alert user */

main()
{
        int     response;
        void    ctrl_c_handler(int);

        tty_mode(0);                            /* save current mode    */
        set_cr_noecho_mode();                   /* set -icanon, -echo   */
        set_nodelay_mode();                     /* noinput => EOF       */
        signal( SIGINT, ctrl_c_handler );       /* handle INT           */
        signal( SIGQUIT, SIG_IGN );             /* ignore QUIT signals  */
        response = get_response(ASK, TRIES);    /* get some answer      */
        tty_mode(1);                            /* reset orig mode      */
        return response;
}
get_response( char *question , int maxtries)
/*
 * purpose: ask a question and wait for a y/n answer or timeout
 *  method: use getchar and complain about non-y/n input
 * returns: 0=>yes, 1=>no
 */
```

```
{
        int     input;

        printf("%s (y/n)?", question);                  /* ask          */
        fflush(stdout);                                 /* force output */
        while ( 1 ){
                sleep(SLEEPTIME);                       /* wait a bit   */
                input = tolower(get_ok_char());         /* get next chr */
                if ( input == 'y' )
                        return 0;
                if ( input == 'n' )
                        return 1;
                if ( maxtries-- == 0 )                  /* outatime?    */
                        return 2;                       /* sayso        */
                BEEP;
        }
}

/*
 *  skip over non-legal chars and return y,Y,n,N or EOF
 */
get_ok_char()
{
        int c;
        while( ( c = getchar() ) != EOF && strchr("yYnN",c) == NULL )
                ;
        return c;
}
set_cr_noecho_mode()
/*
 * purpose: put file descriptor 0 into chr-by-chr mode and noecho mode
 *   method: use bits in termios
 */
{
        struct  termios ttystate;

        tcgetattr( 0, &ttystate);               /* read curr. setting   */
        ttystate.c_lflag        &= ~ICANON;     /* no buffering         */
        ttystate.c_lflag        &= ~ECHO;       /* no echo either       */
        ttystate.c_cc[VMIN]     = 1;            /* get 1 char at a time */
        tcsetattr( 0 , TCSANOW, &ttystate);     /* install settings     */
}

set_nodelay_mode()
/*
 * purpose: put file descriptor 0 into no-delay mode
 *   method: use fcntl to set bits
 *    notes: tcsetattr() will do something similar, but it is complicated
 */
{
        int     termflags;

        termflags = fcntl(0, F_GETFL);          /* read curr. settings  */
```

```
            termflags |= O_NDELAY;                    /* flip on nodelay bit  */
            fcntl(0, F_SETFL, termflags);             /* and install 'em      */
    }

    /* how == 0 => save current mode,  how == 1 => restore mode */
    /* this version handles termios and fcntl flags            */

    tty_mode(int how)
    {
            static struct termios original_mode;
            static int          original_flags;
            static int          stored = 0;

            if ( how == 0 ){
                    tcgetattr(0, &original_mode);
                    original_flags = fcntl(0, F_GETFL);
                    stored = 1;
            }
            else if ( stored ) {
                    tcsetattr(0, TCSANOW, &original_mode);
                    fcntl( 0, F_SETFL, original_flags);
            }
    }

    void ctrl_c_handler(int signum)
    /*
     * purpose: called if SIGINT is detected
     *  action: reset tty and scram
     */
    {
            tty_mode(1);
            exit(1);
    }
```

The other designs are left as an exercise.

6.6 PROCESSES ARE MORTAL

A program uses signal to tell the kernel it wants to ignore a signal. What if someone writes a program that sets SIG_IGN for all signals, then executes an endless loop?

Luckily for system administrators (and programmers) Unix makes it impossible for a program to be immortal. There are two signals that cannot be ignored or caught. Read the manual or the list of signals in the header file to see which signals always get through.

6.7 PROGRAMMING FOR DEVICES

We looked at three aspects of writing a program that controls the terminal. First we studied attributes of the driver and how to control connections. Then we looked at the particular needs of the application and adjusted the driver to meet those needs. Finally, we learned to handle signals—a form of interruption.

These three aspects apply to all devices. Consider a sound card or disk drive. The device has various settings controlled by the device driver; you need to learn about the settings. Also, the program has to perform in certain ways; you adjust the driver to meet those needs. Finally, many device drivers generate signals to announce errors or certain events. A disk drive may send a signal when it finishes copying a block of data from the disk to memory; the program must be able to respond to these signals.

SUMMARY

MAIN IDEAS

- Some programs process data from specific devices. These device-specific programs have to control the connection to the device. The most common device on Unix systems is the terminal.
- A terminal driver has many settings. A collection of settings is called a mode of the terminal driver. Programs for users often set the mode of the terminal driver.
- Keys users press fall into three categories, and the terminal driver handles those keys differently. Most keys represent *regular data* and are moved through the driver to the program. Some keys invoke *editing functions* in the driver itself. If you press the erase key, the driver removes the previous character from its line buffer and sends codes to the terminal screen to remove the character from the display. Finally, some keys invoke *process control functions*. The Ctrl-C key tells the driver to invoke a function somewhere else in the kernel, the function to send a signal to a process. The terminal driver supports keys for several process control functions, all implemented by sending signals to the process.
- A signal is a short message sent from the kernel to a process. Users, other processes, and the kernel itself may request a signal. A process tells the kernel how it wants to respond when it receives a signal.

WHAT'S NEXT?

A Unix machine receives data from lots of terminals and other devices all the time. Users generate terminal data at unpredictable times, and the kernel has to process those keystrokes. A Unix machine also has to run several programs. How does the kernel keep several things going at once and also respond to multiple, unpredictable interruptions? We explore this question by writing a video game.

EXPLORATIONS

6.1 Many Unix software tools read input from files named on the command line. The tr command does not. What is the purpose of tr? Can you think of a reason why it does not accept filenames on the command line? Are there other Unix tools that read input only from standard input and not from named files? Most Unix commands are stored in the directories called /bin, /usr/bin and /usr/local/bin.

6.2 *Nonblocking on other files* O_NDELAY is an attribute of any file descriptor, not an attribute only of the terminal driver. That means the attribute can be applied to disk files as well as device files.

What does nonblocking mean for a disk file? What does nonblocking mean for devices other than terminal files?

PROGRAMMING EXERCISES

6.3 *Some-delay mode* File descriptors may be in blocked mode or in no-delay (a.k.a. non-blocking) mode. The terminal driver provides finer control; it allows you to set a timeout period for input. The element at position VTIME in the array of control characters, c_cc[] in the struct termios for the driver, sets the timeout period in tenths of seconds. Thus, assigning s.c_cc[VTIME] = 20 sets the timeout for the driver to two seconds.

Recode play_again3.c so it uses the timeout feature in the driver rather putting the file descriptor into nonblocking mode.

6.4 *Handling signals in play_again*
   (a) Modify play_again3.c to ignore keyboard signals and only respond to yes or no input.
   (b) Modify play_again3.c so, upon receiving a keyboard signal, it resets the terminal attributes and exits with a value of 2.

6.5 Modify the rotate.c program so it changes the tty modes itself. The revised program should turn off canonical mode and turn off echo. It should then read characters and print out the next letter in the alphabet. When the user presses the letter "Q," the program should restore the tty settings and exit.

Your program should ignore keyboard signals or handle them by resetting the driver before exiting.

6.6 Writing a line editor. One problem with writing a program that runs in noncanonical mode is the lack of input editing. Modify your revised version of rotate.c to support character and line editing. In particular, when the program receives a backspace or delete character, it erases the previous character from the screen. To erase a character, your program has to print out a backspace character, a space character, and then a backspace character.

Also modify the program to handle the line-kill character the way the terminal driver does. That is, it erases from the screen all the characters typed on the current line.

What would you need to do to implement the word-erase function of the driver?

6.7 Modify the sigdemo1.c program so it counts the number of times the user presses Ctrl-C. The revised program will print the message OUCH!, then OUCH!!, where the number of exclamation points equals the number of times the handler has been called.

In addition to printing an increasing number of exclamation points, the program should accept an integer as a command-line argument. After the user presses Ctrl-C that many times, the program should exit.

6.8 *Are you sure?* Modify the sigdemo1.c program so that it asks if the user really meant to kill the program. A sample run should look like the following:

```
hello
hello
    Interrupted!  OK to quit (y/n)? n
hello
hello
    Interrupted!  OK to quit (y/n)? y
$
```

What happens if the user presses Ctrl-C when the program is waiting for an answer to the *OK to quit (y/n)?* question? Write the code and see what happens.

6.9   A program can use `signal` to tell the kernel it wants to ignore certain signals, such as `SIGINT` and `SIGQUIT`. A different strategy is to prevent those signals from being generated in the first place. The terminal driver has a flag called `ISIG`. Read the manual pages to learn what that flag does. Then rewrite `sigdemo2.c` so it uses that flag.

What would your revised program do if it received a `SIGINT` from somewhere other than the keyboard? Learn about the `kill` command and use `kill` to send `SIGINT` to the version that turns off `ISIG`.

6.10   Interruptions are not always destructive. Imagine you are working on a project taking several days. You may get phone calls from your boss asking how the work is going. Those are interrupts designed to run a *status report* subroutine, not designed to kill the process. Write a C program that performs a time-consuming task. For example, write a program that finds prime numbers using a slow method. The program should keep track of the largest prime number it has found so far. Add to this program a handler function for `SIGINT` that prints out a brief report showing how many numbers it has checked and the largest prime it has found.

How could that idea be used in system programs?

6.11   *Return of* `more` In Chapter 1, we wrote a few versions of the Unix `more` utility. At that time, we did not know how to control the terminal driver. Enhance that program to run in no-echo, noncanonical mode and to respond to interrupt and kill signals correctly.

6.12   *Signals and windows* A user can generate signals not only by pressing certain keys, but also by changing the size of the terminal window. Each time the window changes size, the process is sent `SIGWINCH`. By default, processes ignore `SIGWINCH`. Write a program that fills the terminal screen by printing as many letter "A"s as positions on the screen. For example, if the window has ten rows and twenty columns, the program should print the letter "A", two hundred times. When the window is resized, the program should then fill the screen with the letter "B". The next time, use "C", and so forth. When the user presses the letter "Q," the screen clears and the program exits. When the user presses any other key, the screen starts over with the letter "A".

# CHAPTER 7

Event-Driven Programming Writing a Video Game

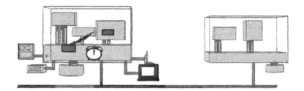

OBJECTIVES

Ideas and Skills

- Programs driven by asynchronous events
- The curses library: purpose and use
- Alarms and interval timers
- Reliable signal handling
- Reentrant code, critical sections
- Asynchronous input

System Calls and Functions

- `alarm`, `setitimer`, `getitimer`
- `kill`, `pause`
- `sigaction`, `sigprocmask`
- `fcntl`, `aio_read`

7.1   VIDEO GAMES AND OPERATING SYSTEMS

Dennis Ritchie and Ken Thompson at Bell Labs wanted to play a video game called *Space Travel*, so they created Unix. Ritchie writes:

> *Also during 1969, Thompson developed the game of Space Travel. First writ-*
> *ten on Multics, then transliterated into Fortran for GECOS (the operating sys-*
> *tem for the GE, later Honeywell, 635), it was nothing less than a simulation of*

the movement of the major bodies of the Solar System, with the player guiding a ship here and there, observing the scenery, and attempting to land on the various planets and moons. The GECOS version was unsatisfactory in two important respects: first, the display of the state of the game was jerky and hard to control because one had to type commands at it, and second, a game cost about $75 for CPU time on the big computer. It did not take long, therefore, for Thompson to find a little-used PDP-7 computer with an excellent display processor; the whole system was used as a Graphic-II terminal. He and I rewrote Space Travel to run on this machine. The undertaking was more ambitious than it might seem; because we disdained all existing software, we had to write a floating-point arithmetic package, the pointwise specification of the graphic characters for the display, and a debugging subsystem that continuously displayed the contents of typed-in locations in a corner of the screen. All this was written in assembly language for a cross-assembler that ran under GECOS and produced paper tapes to be carried to the PDP-7.

Space Travel, though it made a very attractive game, served mainly as an introduction to the clumsy technology of preparing programs for the PDP-7. Soon Thompson began implementing the paper file system (perhaps chalk file system would be more accurate) that had been designed earlier. A file system without a way to exercise it is a sterile proposition, so he proceeded to flesh it out with the other requirements for a working operating system, in particular the notion of processes. Then came a small set of user-level utilities: the means to copy, print, delete, and edit files, and of course a simple command interpreter (shell). Up to this time all the programs were written using GECOS and files were transferred to the PDP-7 on paper tape; but once an assembler was completed the system was able to support itself. Although it was not until well into 1970 that Brian Kernighan suggested the name "Unix," in a somewhat treacherous pun on "Multics," the operating system we know today was born.[1]

Video games and operating systems have a lot in common. In this chapter, we write a simple video game. Writing this game introduces us to more Unix services and some basic principles and techniques of operating-system design.

What a Video Game Does

Consider a space travel video game for two players. The program creates images of planets, asteroids, spaceships, and other objects, and keeps those images moving. Each object has a speed, position, direction, momentum, and other attributes. Objects interact; an asteroid may encounter a spaceship or another asteroid.

---

[1]*AT&T Bell Laboratories Technical Journal* 63 No. 6 Part 2, October 1984, pp. 1577–93.

The game also responds to user input. Players operate buttons, mice, and trackballs, generating input at unpredictable times, and the program must respond quickly. These input events affect attributes of objects in the game. By pressing a button, a user might increase the velocity and decrease the mass of a ship. Changes in a ship affect how it interacts with other objects.

How a Video Game Works

A video game combines several basic ideas and principles:

Space	The game has to draw images at specific locations on the computer screen. How does a program control a video display?
Time	Images move across the screen at different speeds. Changes in position happen at certain intervals. How does a program keep track of time and arrange to do things at specific times?
Interruptions	The program moves objects smoothly across the screen, but users can send input whenever they like. How does a program respond to interruptions?
Doing several things	The game has to keep several objects moving and also respond to interruptions at the same time. How can a program manage multiple activities and not get confused or make a mess of things?

Operating Systems Address Similar Questions

An operating system faces these same four problems. The kernel loads programs into memory space and keeps track of the location of each program. The kernel schedules programs to run for short intervals and also schedules certain internal tasks to be done at specific times. Users and other external devices send input at unpredictable times, and the kernel has to respond quickly. Doing several things at once can be tricky. How does the kernel keep data from becoming disordered and confused?[2]

Screen Management, Time, Signals, Sharing Resources

In this chapter, we study screen management, time, signals, and how to do several things at once safely. We shall write animated games for a character-based terminal in order to learn about these four fundamental topics.

Why Character-based Graphics?

Why not use more powerful X11 programming or Java graphics? There are lots of reasons. First, character-based games are like high-resolution graphics games, just with fatter pixels. The next reason is portability. Character-graphics games require only a terminal emulator and a connection, something available on every computer system. Third, less time on graphics means more time to spend on systems programming. If you prefer, though, the Web site has X windows versions of the sample programs.

---

[2]To read other papers concerning the analogy between Unix and space ships, search the Web for *DEC Wars* and *Unix Wars*.

7.2   THE PROJECT: WRITE SINGLE-PLAYER *pong*

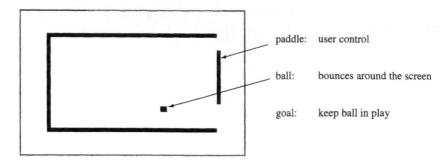

FIGURE 7.1

A single-player video game.

Let's get started. The main project for this chapter is a single-player version of the classic arcade and home-entertainment set game, *pong*. Figure 7.1 shows the three main elements: walls, ball, and paddle. The general outline of the program is as follows:

(a) Ball keeps moving at some speed.

(b) Ball bounces off walls and paddle.

(c) User presses keys to move paddle up and down.

Writing this game requires understanding how to manage the screen, time, and interruptions and how to do several things at once safely. We study each topic in turn.

7.3   SPACE PROGRAMMING: THE curses LIBRARY

The *curses library* is a set of functions that allow a programmer to set the position of the cursor and control the appearance of text on a terminal screen. The *curses library*, or simply *curses* as it is usually known, was originally developed in the *Olden Days*® at UCB. Most programs that control the terminal screen use curses. Once a simple set of functions, curses now includes many sophisticated features. We shall use a tiny fraction of these features.

7.3.1   Introduction to curses

Curses treats the terminal screen as a grid of character cells, each identified by a (*row, column*) coordinate pair. The origin of the coordinate system is the upper left corner of the screen. Row numbers increase downward, and column numbers increase rightward. Figure 7.2 shows the curses screen.

Curses includes functions to move the cursor to any cell on the screen, add characters to and erase characters from the screen, set visual attributes of characters, such

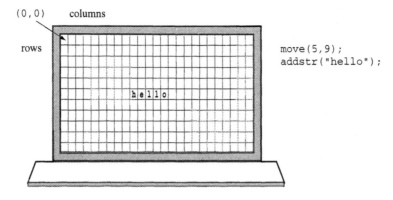

FIGURE 7.2

Curses views the screen as a grid.

as color and brightness, and create and control windows and other regions of text. The manual pages describe all curses functions. We shall use nine of them:

Basic Curses Functions	
initscr()	Initializes the curses library and the tty
endwin()	Turns off curses and resets the tty
refresh()	Makes screen look the way you want
move(r,c)	Moves cursor to screen position (r,c)
addstr(s)	Draws string s on the screen at current position
addch(c)	Draws char c on the screen at current position
clear()	Clears the screen
standout()	Turns on **standout** mode (usually reverse video)
standend()	Turns off **standout** mode

Curses Example 1: hello1.c

This first program shows the basic logic of a curses program:

```
/* hello1.c
 *      purpose  show the minimal calls needed to use curses
 *      outline  initialize, draw stuff, wait for input, quit
 */

#include        <stdio.h>
#include        <curses.h>

main()
{
        initscr() ;             /* turn on curses      */

                                /* send requests       */
        clear();                        /* clear screen */
```

```
        move(10,20);                            /* row10,col20  */
        addstr("Hello, world");                 /* add a string */
        move(LINES-1,0);                         /* move to LL   */

        refresh();                /* update the screen    */
        getch();                  /* wait for user input  */

        endwin();                 /* turn off curses      */
    }
```

Compiling and running the program is easy:

```
$ cc hello1.c -lcurses -o hello1
$ ./hello1
```

The output screen is shown in Figure 7.3. The program works on any terminal connection from any computer system to any Unix machine.

FIGURE 7.3

Our first curses-based program.

Curses Example 2: `hello2.c`

Combining curses functions with loops, variables, and other functions produces more complex displays. Predict the output of this second example:

```
/* hello2.c
 *       purpose  show how to use curses functions with a loop
 *       outline  initialize, draw stuff, wrap up
 */

#include        <stdio.h>
#include        <curses.h>

main()
{
        int     i;

        initscr();                          /* turn on curses       */
           clear();                         /* draw some stuff      */
             for(i=0; i<LINES; i++ ){             /* in a loop      */
```

```
            move( i, i+i );
            if ( i%2 == 1 )
                    standout();
            addstr("Hello, world");
            if ( i%2 == 1 )
                    standend();
        }
        refresh();                  /* update the screen   */
        getch();                    /* wait for user input */
    endwin();                       /* reset the tty etc   */
}
```

Compile and run it. Was your prediction correct?

7.3.2   Curses Internals: Virtual and Real Screens

What does the refresh function do? Experiment; comment out that line, recompile and run the program. Nothing will appear on the screen.

Curses is designed to update your text screen without clogging the communication line. Curses minimizes data flow by working with *virtual screens*. (See Figure 7.4.)

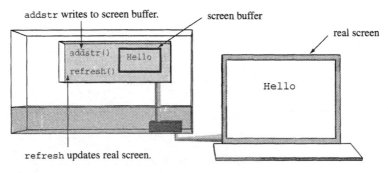

FIGURE 7.4

Curses keeps a copy of the real screen.

The real screen is the array of characters in front of your eyes. Curses keeps two internal versions of the screen. One internal screen is a copy of the real screen. A second internal screen is a workspace, recording changes to the screen. Each function, move, addstr, etc., modifies the characters on the workspace screen. Most functions in the curses library affect only this workspace screen, like disk buffering.

The refresh function compares the workspace screen to the copy of the real screen. refresh then sends out through the terminal driver the characters and screen-control codes needed to make the real screen match the working screen. For example, if the real screen shows the name *Smith, James* at the upper left corner, and you then use addstr to put *Smith, Jane* at the same position, the call to refresh might only replace the *m* and *s* in *James* with *n* and a space. The technique of transmitting changes instead of images is used in streaming video.

7.4   TIME PROGRAMMING: `sleep`

To write a video game, we have to put images at specific places at specific times. We use curses to put images at specific places. We now add time to our programs. For a first step, we use the system `sleep` function.

Animation example 1: `hello3.c`

```
/* hello3.c
 *        purpose  using refresh and sleep for animated effects
 *        outline  initialize, draw stuff, wrap up
 */
#include          <stdio.h>
#include          <curses.h>

main()
{
        int     i;

        initscr();
            clear();
            for(i=0; i<LINES; i++ ){
                move( i, i+i );
                if ( i%2 == 1 )
                        standout();
                addstr("Hello, world");
                if ( i%2 == 1 )
                        standend();
                sleep(1);
                refresh();
            }
            endwin();
}
```

When you compile and run this program, you should see the hello messages cascading down the screen, one line per second, alternately displayed in reverse video then normal video. Why do we need to call `refresh` each time in the loop? What would happen if we moved that function call after the loop?

Animation example 2: `hello4.c`

```
/* hello4.c
 *        purpose show how to use erase, time, and draw for animation
 */
#include          <stdio.h>
#include          <curses.h>
```

```
main()
{
        int     i;

        initscr();
            clear();
            for(i=0; i<LINES; i++ ){
                move( i, i+i );
                if ( i%2 == 1 )
                        standout();
                addstr("Hello, world");
                if ( i%2 == 1 )
                        standend();
                refresh();
                sleep(1);
                move(i,i+i);                         /* move back   */
                addstr("            ");              /* erase line  */
            }
            endwin();
}
```

hello4 creates an illusion of motion. The message proceeds slowly downward along a diagonal. Our secret is to draw the message at one location, sleep for a second, then draw a string of spaces over the message to erase it, then advance the position. Notice that by calling refresh after the two requests, we ensure that the old message vanishes and the new message appears in one pass. Figure 7.5 is a "snapshot" of the screen.

FIGURE 7.5

A message drifts slowly down the screen.

The next example bounces a message back and forth across the screen.

Animation example 3: `hello5.c`

```
/* hello5.c
 *      purpose  bounce a message back and forth across the screen
 *      compile  cc hello5.c -lcurses -o hello5
 */
#include        <curses.h>
```

```c
#define LEFTEDGE        10
#define RIGHTEDGE       30
#define ROW             10

main()
{
        char    message[] = "Hello";
        char    blank[]   = "        ";
        int     dir = +1;
        int     pos = LEFTEDGE ;

        initscr();
          clear();
          while(1){
                move(ROW,pos);
                addstr( message );              /* draw string      */
                move(LINES-1,COLS-1);           /* park the cursor  */
                refresh();                      /* show string      */
                sleep(1);
                move(ROW,pos);                  /* erase string     */
                addstr( blank );
                pos += dir;                     /* advance position */
                if ( pos >= RIGHTEDGE )         /* check for bounce */
                        dir = -1;
                if ( pos <= LEFTEDGE )
                        dir = +1;
        }
}
```

The variable `dir` controls the velocity of the message. When `dir` is +1, the message moves one column to the right each second, and when `dir` is −1, the message moves one column to the left each second. Change the sign of `dir` to change the direction of motion. Figure 7.6 is a "snapshot" of the screen at a particular instant:

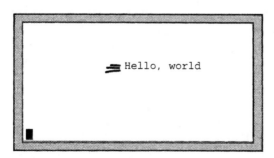

FIGURE 7.6

A message bounces back and forth.

How Are We Doing?

How close are we now to knowing enough to write a decent action video game? We know how to draw strings anywhere on the screen, and we know how to create animation by introducing delays between drawings, erasings, and redrawings. Our programs are nice, but

(a) One-second delays are too long; we need better control of time.

(b) We need to add user input.

These two problems lead us to new topics: programming with time and advanced signals. After many pages, we shall return to the game.

7.5　PROGRAMMING WITH TIME I: ALARMS

Programs can use time in many ways. A program can introduce a delay in the flow of a program. The past three samples use `sleep` to add a delay. Another use of time is to schedule an action in the future, the way you set an egg timer then do other things until the timer sounds. Unix provides `alarm` for that purpose.

7.5.1　Adding a Delay: `sleep`

To add a delay to a program, use the `sleep` function:

```
sleep(n)
```

`sleep(n)` suspends the current process for *n* seconds or until an unignored signal arrives.

7.5.2　How sleep() Works: Using Alarms in Unix

The `sleep` function works just the way you sleep for a specified amount of time:

(a) Set an alarm for the number of seconds you want to sleep.

(b) Pause until the alarm goes off.

Figure 7.7 shows the basic idea. Each process in the system has a private alarm clock. This alarm clock, like a kitchen timer, can be set to ring after a number of seconds

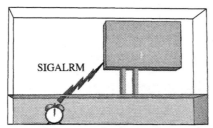

SIGALRM

Every process has its own timer.

How the sleep function works:

```
signal(SIGALRM,handler);

alarm(n);

pause();
```

FIGURE 7.7

A process sets an alarm then suspends execution.

passes. When time is up, the clock sends a signal, SIGALRM, to the process. Unless the process has installed a handler for SIGALRM, the signal kills the process. Thus, the sleep function consists of these three steps:

1. Install a handler for SIGALRM.
2. Call alarm(num_seconds).
3. Call pause.

The pause system call suspends the process until a signal arrives, any signal, not just SIGALRM. We combine these ideas to write the following code:

```
/* sleep1.c
 *      purpose show how sleep works
 *      usage   sleep1
 *      outline sets handler, sets alarm, pauses, then returns
 */
#include        <stdio.h>
#include        <signal.h>
// #define      SHHHH

main()
{
        void    wakeup(int);

        printf("about to sleep for 4 seconds\n");
        signal(SIGALRM, wakeup);                /* catch it     */
        alarm(4);                               /* set clock    */
        pause();                                /* freeze here  */
        printf("Morning so soon?\n");           /* back to work */
}

void wakeup(int signum)
{
#ifndef SHHHH
        printf("Alarm received from kernel\n");
#endif
}
```

We call signal to install a handler function for SIGALRM, then call alarm to set a timer for four seconds, and finally call pause to wait for the alarm to ring.

The purpose of pause is to suspend the process until a signal is handled. After four seconds pass on the alarm timer, the kernel sends SIGALRM to the process, causing control to jump from the pause line to the signal handler. The code in the signal handler is executed, and then control returns. After the signal is handled, pause returns, and the process proceeds. Figure 7.8 summarizes the action of pause.

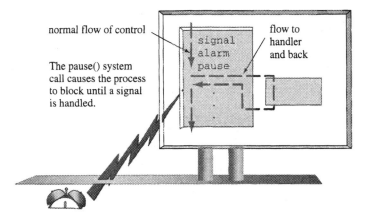

normal flow of control

flow to
handler
and back

The pause() system
call causes the process
to block until a signal
is handled.

FIGURE 7.8

Flow of execution into handler.

Here are the details regarding both `alarm` and `pause`:

alarm	
PURPOSE	Set an alarm timer for delivery of a signal
INCLUDE	#include <unistd.h>
USAGE	unsigned old = alarm(unsigned seconds)
ARGS	seconds how long to wait
RETURNS	-1 if error old time left on timer

`alarm` sets the alarm timer of the calling process to expire in *seconds* seconds. When that time passes, the kernel sends SIGALRM to the process. If the timer had already been set, `alarm` returns the number of seconds remaining. (Note: the call `alarm(0)` turns off the alarm.)

pause	
PURPOSE	Wait for signal
INCLUDE	#include <unistd.h>
USAGE	result = pause()
ARGS	no args
RETURNS	-1 always

pause suspends the calling process until a signal is received. If the calling process is terminated by the signal, pause does not return. If the calling process catches the signal with a handler, pause returns when control returns from the handler. In this case, errno is set to EINTR.

7.5.3 Scheduling a Future Action

The other way to use time is to schedule an action for some future time and do something else in the meantime. Scheduling an action in the future is easy, set the timer by calling alarm and then proceed to do something else. When the timer reaches zero, the signal will be sent, and the handler will be invoked.

7.6 PROGRAMMING WITH TIME II: INTERVAL TIMERS

sleep and alarm have been in Unix since early times. They provide a resolution of one second, too coarse for many applications. A more powerful and comprehensive timer system was added later. This new system, using a concept called an *interval timer*, has higher resolution and not one, but three separate timers for each process. And that's not all. Each of those timers has two settings: a single alarm setting *and* a repeating timer. alarm and sleep are still supported, though, and are perfectly adequate for many applications. The idea is depicted in Figure 7.9.

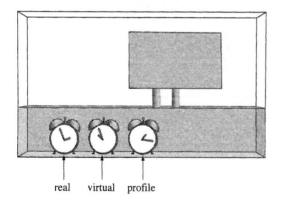

Every process has three timers.

Each timer has two settings: the time until the first alarm and the interval between repeating alarms.

real   virtual   profile

FIGURE 7.9

Each process has three timers.

We can use this new system to add delays and schedule events.

7.6.1 Adding a Finer Delay: `usleep`

To add a finer delay to a program, use usleep:

```
usleep(n)
```

usleep(n) suspends the current process for *n* microseconds or until an unignored signal arrives.

7.6.2   Three Kinds of Timers: Real, Process, Profile

Processes can measure three kinds of time. Consider a program that finishes 30 seconds after it starts running. On a time-sharing system, the program is not running all that time; other programs are taking turns using the processor. Figure 7.10 is a graph showing what might happen during those 30 seconds:

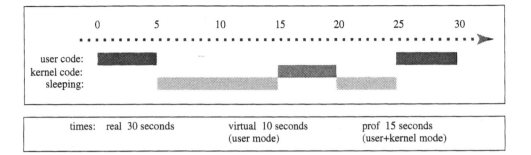

FIGURE 7.10

Where does the time go?

The graph shows that from time 0 to time 5, the process ran in user mode; then it went to sleep from time 5 until time 15, then it changed into kernel mode until time 20, then went back to sleep, and so on. Of those 30 seconds from start to finish, the program used 10 seconds of user time and 5 seconds of system time. This diagram shows three types of time: real, user, and user+system. The kernel provides timers to measure each of these types. The names of those three timers are as follows:

ITIMER_REAL

This timer ticks in real time, that is, the time measured on your wristwatch regardless of how much CPU time the process uses in user mode or kernel mode. When this timer expires, it sends SIGALRM.

ITIMER_VIRTUAL

This timer, like a clock during a football game, only ticks when the process runs in user mode. Thirty seconds on the virtual timer takes longer than thirty seconds in real time. The virtual timer sends SIGVTALRM when it expires.

ITIMER_PROF

This timer counts down when the process is running in user mode and also when the kernel is running system calls made by this process. When this timer expires, it sends SIGPROF.

7.6.3 Two Kinds of Intervals: Initial and Repeating

A doctor hands you some pills and tells you, "take the first one an hour from now, and then take one every four hours." You need to set a timer to go off in one hour, and then each time it goes off, you need to reset it for four hours. Each interval timer has settings for these two numbers: an initial value and a repeating interval. In the struct used by the interval timer, the initial interval is called it_value, and the repeating amount is called it_interval. If you do not want the repeating feature, set it_interval to zero. To turn off both timers, set it_value to zero.

7.6.4 Programming with the Interval Timers

Programming with alarm is easy; you just pass alarm a number of seconds. Programming an interval timer is more complicated; you have to choose a type of time, and then you have to decide on an initial interval and a repeating interval. Furthermore, you have to set values in a struct itimerval. For example, to use an interval timer to remind you to take pills on the schedule described in the preceding paragraph, set the it_value member to 1 hour, set the it_interval member to 4 hours, and then pass that structure to the timer by calling setitimer. To read timer settings, use getitimer. The concept is depicted in Figure 7.11.

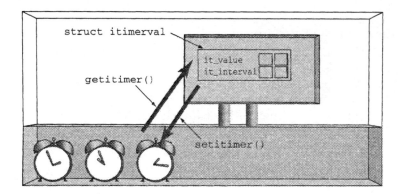

FIGURE 7.11

Reading and writing timer settings.

Interval Timer Example: ticker_demo.c

The following program, ticker_demo.c, demonstrates use of an interval timer:

```
/* ticker_demo.c
 *      demonstrates use of interval timer to generate regular
 *      signals, which are in turn caught and used to count down
 */

#include         <stdio.h>
#include         <sys/time.h>
#include         <signal.h>
```

```
int main()
{
        void    countdown(int);

        signal(SIGALRM, countdown);
        if ( set_ticker(500) == -1 )
                perror("set_ticker");
        else
                while( 1 )
                        pause();
        return 0;
}

void countdown(int signum)
{
        static int num = 10;
        printf("%d ..", num--);
        fflush(stdout);
        if ( num < 0 ){
                printf("DONE!\n");
                exit(0);
        }
}

/* [from set_ticker.c]
 * set_ticker( number_of_milliseconds )
 *      arranges for interval timer to issue SIGALRM's at regular intervals
 *      returns -1 on error, 0 for ok
 *      arg in milliseconds, converted into whole seconds and microseconds
 *      note: set_ticker(0) turns off ticker
 */

int set_ticker( int n_msecs )
{
        struct itimerval new_timeset;
        long    n_sec, n_usecs;

        n_sec = n_msecs / 1000 ;                       /* int part    */
        n_usecs = ( n_msecs % 1000 ) * 1000L ;    /* remainder   */

        new_timeset.it_interval.tv_sec  = n_sec;   /* set reload */
        new_timeset.it_interval.tv_usec = n_usecs; /* new ticker value */
        new_timeset.it_value.tv_sec     = n_sec  ; /* store this       */
        new_timeset.it_value.tv_usec    = n_usecs; /* and this         */

        return setitimer(ITIMER_REAL, &new_timeset, NULL);
}
```

Trace the flow of control in `ticker_demo.c`. First, we use `signal` to install the function called `countdown` to handle SIGALRM, then we pass a number of milliseconds to `set_ticker`.

set_ticker sets the interval timer by loading the initial interval and the repeating interval. Each of those intervals is stored as two values: a number of seconds and a number of microseconds, just like the integer part and fractional part of a real number. The timer is now ticking, and control returns to main.

Back at main, ticker_demo.c enters an infinite loop calling pause. After each 500 millisecond interval, control jumps to the function called countdown. The countdown function decrements a static variable, prints a message, and usually returns to its caller. When the variable num reaches zero, countdown calls exit.

Of course, main does not have to call pause. The main program could do something more interesting and would still jump to countdown at each timer tick.

Details of Data Structures Interval timer settings are passed in a struct itimerval. These structs contain the initial interval and the repeating interval, both values stored in a struct timeval:

```
struct itimerval
{
    struct timeval it_value;       /* time to next timer expiration */
    struct timeval it_interval;    /* reload it_value with this     */
};
struct timeval {
    time_t       tv_sec;      /* seconds */
    suseconds_t  tv_usec;     /* and microseconds */
};
```

The details of a struct timeval vary from one version of Unix to another. Check the manual page and header files for your system.

Figure 7.12 shows the structs within structs, and Figure 7.13 shows how to load the struct so that the first alarm arrives in 60.5 seconds and then every 240.25 seconds thereafter:

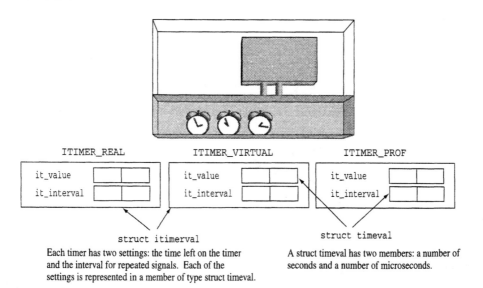

Each timer has two settings: the time left on the timer and the interval for repeated signals. Each of the settings is represented in a member of type struct timeval.

A struct timeval has two members: a number of seconds and a number of microseconds.

FIGURE 7.12

Inside the interval timers.

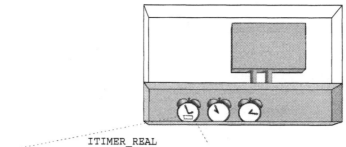

ITIMER_REAL

it_value	60	500000
it_interval	240	250000
	tv_sec	tv_usec

This example sets the real time interval timer to send a signal in 60.5 seconds and then to send signals every 240.25 seconds.

FIGURE 7.13

Seconds and microseconds.

System Call Summaries

getitimer, setitimer
PURPOSE Get or set value of interval timer
INCLUDE #include <sys/time.h>
USAGE result = getitimer(int which, struct itimerval *val); result = setitimer(int which, const struct itimerval *newval, struct itimerval *oldval);
ARGS which   timer being read or set val   pointer to current settings newval pointer to settings to be installed oldval pointer to settings being replaced
RETURNS -1   on error 0   on success

getitimer reads the current settings for the specified timer into the struct pointed to by *val*. setitimer sets the timer to the settings pointed to by *newval*. If the *oldval* pointer is not null, the previous settings for that timer are copied into the struct pointed to by *oldval*.

The value of *which* specifies the timer to be read or updated. The codes for the timers are ITIMER_REAL, ITIMER_VIRTUAL, and ITIMER_PROF.

7.6.5   How Many Clocks Does the Computer Have?

How can every process on the system have three separate clocks? Some systems run hundreds of processes at once. Are there hundreds of separate clocks in the computer? No, a system needs only one clock to set the tempo. Like the steady ticking of one metronome counting time for a string quartet or the regular swinging of one pendulum driving several hands in a grandfather clock, the pulsing of one hardware clock is the only timer a computer needs. With only one clock, how can one process set a private timer for 5 seconds while another one sets a private timer for 12 seconds?

How, on the grandfather clock, does the hour hand move at one rate, the minute hand at another, the second hand at a third, and the phase of the moon indicator at yet a fourth? The answer to all these questions is the same. Each player, process, and gear sets its own counter, and the operating system decrements all counters at each clock tick. A worked example can clarify the idea.

A Concrete Example   Consider two processes, process A and process B. Process A sets its real timer to go off in 5 seconds, and process B sets its real timer to go off in 12 seconds. To keep the numbers simpler, imagine the system clock beats at 100 beats per second. When process A sets its timer, the kernel sets a counter equal to 500 for that process. When process B sets its timer, the kernel sets a counter equal to 1200 for that process. OK so far? Look at Figure 7.14.

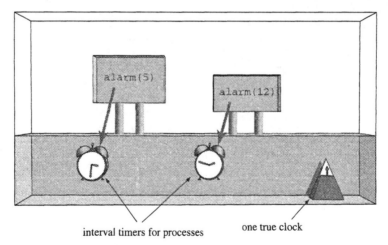

interval timers for processes   one true clock

Each process sets its private timer by calling `alarm`. The kernel updates all process timers at each signal from its clock.

FIGURE 7.14

Two timers, one clock.

At each pulse from the system clock, the kernel runs through the set of all interval timers, decrementing each counter by one. When the counter for process A reaches zero, which it does after 500 clock ticks, the kernel sends SIGALRM to process A. If process A has set the `it_interval` value for that timer, the kernel copies that value into the `it_value` counter, otherwise the kernel turns off the timer.

Sometime later, the kernel decrements the counter for process B for the 1200th time, bringing that value to zero and causing the kernel to send a signal to process B. If B has set the reload value for the timer, the kernel reloads `it_value` and goes down the line to the next timer.

This simple mechanism allows each process to set its own alarm clock, a timer that counts down even when the process is sleeping.

How do the other two timers work? They do not count down steadily, but only when the process is in certain states. The Linux source code shows clearly how these timers work.

7.6.6 Summary of Timers

A Unix program uses timers to suspend execution and to schedule future actions. A timer is a mechanism in the kernel that sends a signal to the process after a specified interval. The `alarm` system call arranges to send `SIGALRM` to the process after a specified number of seconds of real time. The `setitimer` system call controls timers with high resolution and the ability to send signals at regular intervals.

We now know how to manage time in our programs. The video-game project requires another skill: managing interruptions.

7.7   SIGNAL HANDLING I: USING `signal`

Our game has to handle interruptions. The game may be in the middle of moving an image when a user presses a key. Or the game may be in the middle of responding to user input when a timer sends a signal. If the game supports two players, the program might be in the middle of responding to one player when the other player presses a key.

Handling interruptions is an essential part of an operating system and of system programs. Unix refers to software interruptions as *signals*. We now look in detail at the topic of *signal handling*. First, we review the original Unix model for handling signals, then we examine the problems with that model, and finally we study the POSIX model for handling signals.

7.7.1 Old-Style Signal Handling

The kernel sends signals to a process in response to a variety of events, including certain user keystrokes, illegal process behavior, and elapsed timers. Chapter 6 introduced the original model of signal handling. A process calls `signal` to select one of three responses to a signal:

(a) default action (usually termination), for example, `signal(SIGALRM, SIG_DFL)`

(b) ignore the signal, for example, `signal(SIGALRM, SIG_IGN)`

(c) invoke a function, for example, `signal(SIGALRM, handler)`

7.7.2 Handling Multiple Signals

The original signal model works fine if only one signal arrives. What happens when multiple signals arrive? For the *termination* and *ignore* responses, the outcome is clear. For the *invoke a function* response, the answer is neither clear nor consistent.

The Mousetrap Problem

A signal handler is like a mousetrap. A signal shows up expecting to do damage, and *snap!* The mouse or signal is caught and rendered ineffective.

In the *Olden Days*®, signal catchers were like mousetraps in another respect: you had to reset them after each catch. For example, a SIGINT handler might look like the following:

```
void handler(int s)
{
    /* process is vulnerable here */

    signal(SIGINT, handler);    /* reset handler */
    ...                         /* do work here  */
}
```

Even if you are really quick about it, there is a time, between the springing and resetting of the handler, when another mouse could get by. This window of vulnerability made the original signal handling *unreliable*. Oddly, some use the term *unreliable signals*, which makes as much sense as referring to unreliable mice.

Planning for a Better System

The mousetrap problem is only one weakness of the original signal system. To understand the complexity of the topic, consider these real-world examples.

Multiple Signals for a Human

The real world is full of signals, that is, unpredictable interruptions. Imagine you are working in your office. The telephone might ring, someone might knock on the door, or the fire alarm might sound. Each of these events is an interruption you can ignore or handle. Handling a telephone call means putting aside for the moment your current work, answering the phone, speaking to the caller, hanging up, then returning to the work you put aside. Handling a door knock signal works similarly.

What happens if a visitor arrives while you are executing the telephone call handler? You could put aside the telephone call for the moment, putting the call on hold, and then go answer the door, speak with the person there, and return to the telephone call. Later, when you finish handling the telephone call, you return to your work on the desk. In this case, we say the second signal interrupted the handling of the first signal.

Next, what happens if a second person comes to the door when you are speaking to the first visitor? Often, the first person blocks access to the door, so the second person waits until you are done handling the first visitor. When you finish handling the first visitor, the second visitor can knock. In this case, we say the second visitor was *blocked* until the handling of the first visitor was completed.

Also, what if a visitor interrupts you when you are listening to someone on the telephone? When you return from the door, do you pick up right where you left off, or do you tell the person that you lost track of what the two of you were talking about?

Finally, and your life may depend on understanding this example, what would happen if the phone rang or someone knocked on your door while you were handling an interruption from the fire alarm? For a signal as critical as the fire alarm, you would probably want to *block other signals*, such as phone and door, while you were handling the fire-alarm signal. And there are times when you want to block signals even when you are not handling a signal.

Multiple Signals for a Process

Life for your processes is not much different from life for you. Imagine a process working in its little virtual cubicle somewhere in computer memory. (See Figure 7.15.) A user might press Ctrl-C generating SIGINT, press Ctrl-\ generating SIGQUIT, or a timer might expire sending SIGALRM. All these signals could arrive, like phone calls and people knocking on your door, at the same time. How, under Unix, does a process respond to multiple signals?

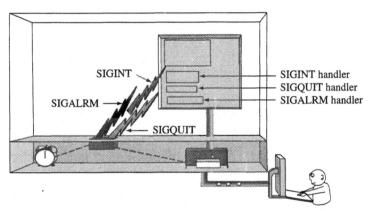

FIGURE 7.15

A process receiving multiple signals.

1. Is the handler disabled after each use? (Mousetrap model)
2. What happens if a SIGY arrives while the process is in the SIGX handler?
3. What happens if a second SIGX arrives while the process is still in the SIGX handler? Or a third SIGX?
4. What happens if a signal arrives while the program is blocking on input in `getchar` or `read`?

Different versions of Unix answered these questions in different ways. Writing programs to work with all the variations was difficult.

7.7.3 Testing Multiple Signals

How does your system answer these question? Compile and run `sigdemo3.c` to learn how processes on your system respond to combinations of signals:

```
/* sigdemo3.c
 *      purpose:   show answers to signal questions
 *      question1: does the handler stay in effect after a signal arrives?
 *      question2: what if a signalX arrives while handling signalX?
 *      question3: what if a signalX arrives while handling signalY?
```

```
   *          question4: what happens to read() when a signal arrives?
   */

   #include           <stdio.h>
   #include           <signal.h>

   #define INPUTLEN          100

   main(int ac, char *av[])
   {
           void      inthandler(int);
           void      quithandler(int);
           char      input[INPUTLEN];
           int       nchars;

           signal( SIGINT,  inthandler );         /* set handler */
           signal( SIGQUIT, quithandler );        /* set handler */

           do {
                   printf("\nType a message\n");
                   nchars = read(0, input, (INPUTLEN-1));
                   if ( nchars == -1 )
                           perror("read returned an error");
                   else {
                           input[nchars] = '\0';
                           printf("You typed: %s", input);
                   }
           }
           while( strncmp( input , "quit" , 4 ) != 0 );
   }

   void inthandler(int s)
   {
           printf(" Received signal %d .. waiting\n", s );
           sleep(2);
           printf("  Leaving inthandler \n");
   }

   void quithandler(int s)
   {
           printf(" Received signal %d .. waiting\n", s );
           sleep(3);
           printf("  Leaving quithandler \n");
   }
```

Try various mixtures of regular input and the two signal-generating keys Ctrl-C and
Ctrl-\. In particular, test the following combinations, trying various delays between
keys and tracing the flow of control through the functions shown in Figure 7.16.

(a) ^C^C^C^C

(b) ^\^C^\^C

(c) hello^C *Return*

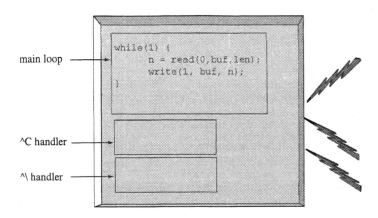

main loop

```
while(1) {
    n = read(0,buf,len);
    write(1, buf, n);
}
```

^C handler

^\ handler

FIGURE 7.16

Trace control flow through these functions.

(d) hello *Return* ^C
(e) ^\^\hello^C

Results of these experiments show how your system handles combinations of signals:

1. **Unreliable signals (mousetrap)**

   If two SIGINTs kill the process, you have unreliable signals: handlers must be reset each time. If multiple SIGINTs do not kill the process, handlers stay in effect after being invoked. With modern signal handling, you can have either action.

2. **SIGY interrupts SIGX handler (phone then door)**

   When you pressed Ctrl-C then Ctrl-\ you should have seen the program first jump to `inthandler`, then to `quithandler`, then back to `inthandler`, then back to the main loop. What does your experiment show?

3. **SIGX interrupts SIGX handler (door twice)**

   This situation is like two people coming to your door. Consider the three ways this situation *could* be handled:

   1. Recursively, call the same handler.[3]
   2. Ignore the second signal, like a phone without call waiting.
   3. Block the second signal until done handling the first.

   The original signal-handling systems used method 1, allow recursive calls. A safer choice is method 3. Like the second person at the door, the second signal is blocked, not ignored, until the handler finishes processing the first instance of the signal. Does your system block the second instance of a signal, does it recursively call the handler? Does your system queue multiple signals?

---

[3]This is involuntary recursion because the handler does not call itself, but the effects are like regular recursion.

4. Interrupted System Calls (door while listening)

This one happens a lot. Programs often receive signals while waiting for input. In the test program above, the main loop blocks waiting to read from the keyboard. When you press the interrupt or quit key, the program jumps to a signal handler. When the handler finishes, the program returns to main, supposedly resuming where it left off. Is that true? What if you type "hel" then press Ctrl-C then type "lo" and press Enter? Does the program see the complete string "hello", or does it see just the "lo"? Does the program restart read or does it return from read with errno set to EINTR?

This question, *restart or return*, was decided one way by AT&T (return −1 with errno set to EINTR, the classic model) and the other way by UCB (restart automatically).

7.7.4 More Signal Weaknesses

The original signal system has two other weaknesses.

You Do Not Know Why the Signal Was Sent

A signal handler is a function that is called when a particular signal arrives. The kernel passes the signal number to the handler. In sigdemo3.c the function inthandler is called with the value SIGINT. Receiving the signal number as an argument allows one function to handle several signals. For example, in sigdemo3.c, we could replace the two handlers with one handler that uses the argument to decide what message to print.

The original model tells the handler which signal invoked it, but does not tell the handler *why* the signal was generated. For example, a *floating-point exception* can be generated for several types of arithmetic errors, such as dividing by zero, integer overflow, and floating-point underflow. A handler needs to know about the cause of the problem.

You Cannot Safely Block Other Signals while in a Handler

When you respond to a fire alarm, you usually ignore signals from the telephone. Say we want our program to ignore SIGQUIT when it responds to SIGINT. Using classic signals, we would modify the inthandler to look like the following:

```
void inthandler(int s)
{
    int rv ;
    void (*prev_qhandler)();                 /* holds prev handler */

    prev_qhandler = signal(SIGQUIT, SIG_IGN); /* ignore QUIT's */
    ...
    signal( SIGQUIT, prev_qhandler );        /* restore handler */
}
```

That is, we disable the quit handler as we enter the interrupt handler and reenable it on the way out. Two problems arise with this solution. First, there is a window of vulnerability between the call to inthandler and the call to signal. We really want the call to inthandler and the ignoring of SIGQUIT to happen at the same time.

Second, we do not want to ignore SIGQUIT, we just want to block it until the fire alarm is over. We are happy to get back to SIGQUIT when the critical event is done.

7.8 SIGNAL HANDLING II: `sigaction`

Different groups over the years developed different solutions to the questions and problems with the original signal model. We shall study only the POSIX model and set of system calls. The classic signal system call is still supported and is appropriate for some applications.

7.8.1 Handling Signals: `sigaction`

sigaction is the POSIX replacement for signal. The arguments even work similarly. You specify which signal to handle and how you want to handle that signal. If you like, you can find out the previous settings for that signal.

```
int sigaction( signalnumber, action, prevaction )
```

The summary is as follows:

	sigaction
PURPOSE	Specify handling for a signal
INCLUDE	#include <signal.h>

USAGE	res = sigaction(int signum,
	        const struct sigaction *action,
	            struct sigaction *prevaction);

ARGS	signum signal to handle action pointer to struct describing action prevaction pointer to struct to receive old action
RETURNS	-1 on error 0 on success

The first argument, *signum*, is the signal you want to handle, the second argument, *action*, points to a struct that describes how to react to the signal, and the third argument, *prevaction*, if not null, points to a struct to receive the old handling settings. The call returns 0 if the new action has been installed and −1 if not.

Customized Signal Handling: `struct sigaction`

In the old days, your choice of signal handling was simple: SIG_DFL, SIG_IGN, or *function*. You still have that choice, but it is just one part of a struct sigaction that defines how to handle a signal. The following is the complete structure:

```
struct sigaction {
  /* use only one of these two */
```

```
    void     (*sa_handler)();      /* SIG_DFL, SIG_IGN, or function   */
    void (*sa_sigaction)(int, siginfo_t *, void *);   /* NEW handler  */

    sigset_t sa_mask;              /* signals to block while handling */
    int      sa_flags;             /* enable various behaviors        */
}
```

sa_handler *xor* sa_sigaction

First, you decide between the old-style signal-handling choice and the new more powerful version. If one of the old choices—SIG_DFL, SIG_IGN, or *function*—is sufficient, you set sa_handler to one of those three values. Of course, if you specify an old style signal handler, you are only told the signal number. If instead you set sa_sigaction to the name of a handler, that handler will be called with the signal number and also information about the cause and context of the problem. The difference between the two style handlers may be summarized as follows:

Using an old-style handler
```
struct sigaction action;
action.sa_handler = handler_old;
```

Using a new-style handler
```
struct sigaction action;
action.sa_sigaction = handler_new;
```

How do you tell the kernel you are using the new-style handler? Easy, you set the SA_SIGINFO bit in sa_flags.

sa_flags

Next, you decide how you want your handler to respond to the four questions of the previous section. The sa_flags member is a set of bits that controls how the handler answers those four questions. Check your manual for the full list and complete details. This is a partial list:

Flag	Meaning
SA_RESETHAND	Reset the handler when invoked. This enables mousetrap mode.
SA_NODEFER	Turn off automatic blocking of a signal while it is being handled. This allows recursive calls to a signal handler.
SA_RESTART	Restart, rather than return, system calls on slow devices and similar system calls. This enables BSD mode.
SA_SIGINFO	Use the value in sa_sigaction for the handler function. If this bit is not set, use the value in sa_handler. If the sa_sigaction value is used, that handler function is passed not only the signal number, but also pointers to structs containing information about why and how the signal was generated.

sa_mask

Finally, you decide if you want to block any other signals while in the handler. Bits in
sa_mask specify which signals to block. Using sa_mask, you can block phone calls and
visitors while you run down the fire escape. This value sa_mask contains a set of signals
to block. Blocking signals is an important technique for preventing data corruption. We
examine this topic in detail in the next section.

Example: Using `sigaction`

The following program demonstrates the use of sigaction (note how the program
blocks SIGQUIT while handing SIGINT):

```
/* sigactdemo.c
 *               purpose: shows use of sigaction()
 *               feature: blocks ^\ while handling ^C
 *                        does not reset ^C handler, so two kill
 */

#include        <stdio.h>
#include        <signal.h>
#define INPUTLEN        100

main()
{
        struct sigaction newhandler;            /* new settings       */
        sigset_t          blocked;              /* set of blocked sigs */
        void              inthandler();         /* the handler        */
        char              x[INPUTLEN];

        /* load these two members first */
        newhandler.sa_handler = inthandler;     /* handler function   */
        newhandler.sa_flags = SA_RESETHAND | SA_RESTART; /* options   */

        /* then build the list of blocked signals */
        sigemptyset(&blocked);                  /* clear all bits     */
        sigaddset(&blocked, SIGQUIT);           /* add SIGQUIT to list */
        newhandler.sa_mask = blocked;           /* store blockmask    */

        if ( sigaction(SIGINT, &newhandler, NULL) == -1 )
                perror("sigaction");
        else
                while( 1 ){
                        fgets(x, INPUTLEN, stdin);
                        printf("input: %s", x);
                }
}

void inthandler(int s)
{
        printf("Called with signal %d\n", s);
        sleep(s);
        printf("done handling signal %d\n", s);
}
```

Try this program. If you press Ctrl-C then Ctrl-\ in rapid succession, the quit signal will be blocked until the handler for the interrupt signal completes. Make sure you see what that means in practice. If you press two Ctrl-C's, the program will be killed by the second one. If you prefer to catch all Ctrl-C's, omit the SA_RESETHAND mask from sa_flags.

7.8.2   Summary of Signals

A process can be interrupted by signals from various sources. Signals can arrive in any order and at any time. signal provides a simple, incompletely defined method for handling signals. The POSIX interface, sigaction, provides a comprehensive, clearly defined method for controlling how a process responds to combinations of signals.

We now know how to manage time and interruptions in our programs. Our video game requires one last skill: preventing confusion.

7.9   PROTECTING DATA FROM CORRUPTION

When you have too many things going on at once, do you ever get confused and make mistakes? If the doorbell rings when you are looking for a stamp, you might end up mailing a letter without postage. Programs are the same way. They're in the middle of something, get called away, get confused, and mess things up.

We examine a real-world example of how interruptions can cause data errors. Then we examine programming ideas and techniques to prevent trouble.

7.9.1   Examples of Data Corruption

We continue the story about your office with the interrupting telephone calls and knocks on the door. The people knocking at your office door are there to add their names and addresses to a list. Each person must add exactly three lines to the bottom of the list: name, street, then city, state, and zip. Consider the following two problems:

First, a visitor is in the process of adding information to the list when someone calls on the telephone asking for the names and addresses on the list. If you pick up the list and read the contents to the caller, you will deliver incomplete data. You can prevent this type of error by blocking telephone calls while handling visitors.

Next, consider a different kind of problem. One visitor has just finished adding one line of data to the list when a second SIGKNOCK arrives. If you allow recursive signal handling, you suspend the first visitor and admit the second person, who writes three lines of information at the bottom of the list then leaves. The first person resumes at the end of the list, adding the street and then city, state, and zip. The list now contains bad data; one record is in the middle of another record. You can prevent this type of error by handling visitors sequentially rather than recursively.

These two examples demonstrate the idea of an operation that should not be interrupted by some other operations. A data structure, the list in this case, is in the process of being modified. Until the change is complete, other functions should not read or change the data structure. Of course, it is safe to handle the fire-alarm signal, because that handler does not read or change the list.

7.9.2   Critical Sections

A section of code that modifies a data structure is called a *critical section* if interruptions to that section of code can produce incomplete or damaged data. When you program with signals, you must determine which parts of your code are critical sections and arrange to protect those sections. Critical sections are not always in signal handlers; many are in the regular flow of a program. The simplest way to protect critical sections is to block or ignore signals that call handlers that use or change the data.

7.9.3   Blocking Signals: `sigprocmask` and `sigsetops`

You can block signals at the signal-handler level and at the process level.

Blocking Signals in a Signal Handler

To block signals while handling a signal, set the `sa_mask` member of the `struct sigaction` you pass to `sigaction` when you install the handler. `sa_mask` is of type `sigset_t`, a set of signals. We shall explain these sets shortly.

Blocking Signals for a Process

A process has, at all times, a set of signals it is blocking. Not ignoring, but blocking. That set of signals is called the *signal mask*. To modify that set of blocked signals, use `sigprocmask`. `sigprocmask` takes a set of signals and, in an atomic operation, uses that set to change the current set of blocked signals:

sigprocmask	
PURPOSE	Modify current signal mask
INCLUDE	`#include <signal.h>`

USAGE	`int res = sigprocmask( int how,`
	`            const sigset_t *sigs,`
	`            sigset_t *prev);`

ARGS	`how` how to modify the signal mask `sigs` pointer to list of signals to use `prev` pointer to list of previous signal mask (or NULL)
RETURNS	`-1` on error `0` on success

`sigprocmask` modifies the current signal mask by adding to, removing from, or replacing it with the signals in *sigs* as specified by a *how* value of `SIG_BLOCK`, `SIG_UNBLOCK`, and `SIG_SET`, respectively. If *prev* is not null, the previous signal mask is copied to *prev*.

Building Signal Sets with `sigsetops`

A `sigset_t` is an abstract set of signals that has methods for adding and removing signals. The basic facts are as follows:

`sigemptyset(sigset_t *setp)`

>   Clear all signals from the list pointed to by *setp*.

`sigfillset(sigset_t *setp)`

>   Add all signals to the list pointed to by *setp*.

`sigaddset(sigset_t *setp, int signum)`

>   Add *signum* to the set pointed to by *setp*.

`sigdelset(sigset_t *setp, int signum)`

>   Remove *signum* from the set pointed to by *setp*.

>   The manual page for `sigsetops` includes all the details.

Example: Temporarily Blocking User Signals

A program can block `SIGINT` and `SIGQUIT` temporarily with the following code:

```
sigset_t   sigs, prevsigs;                  /* define two signal sets */
sigemptyset( &sigs );                       /* turn off all bits      */
sigaddset( &sigs, SIGINT );                 /* turn on SIGINT bit     */
sigaddset( &sigs, SIGQUIT );                /* turn on SIGQUIT bit    */
sigprocmask( SIG_BLOCK, &sigs, &prevsigs);  /* add that to proc mask  */
// .. modify data structure here ..
sigprocmask( SIG_SET, &prevsigs, NULL);     /* restore previous mask  */
```

Notice how, as we did when changing settings of a tty driver or a file descriptor, we store the previous settings and then use that value to reset the signal mask. It is good manners to leave a program resource just as you found it unless your job is to change it.

7.9.4   Reentrant Code: Dangers of Recursion

The example of one visitor interrupting another visitor and inserting a name and address in the middle of another record introduces another concept related to data corruption: *reentrant function*.

A signal handler, or any function for that matter, that can be called when it is already active and not cause any problems is said to be *reentrant*.

`sigaction` allows you turn on recursive handling by setting the `SA_NODEFER` flag and to turn on blocking by clearing the flag. How do you choose?

If the handler is not reentrant, you must use blocking. But if you block signals, you can lose signals. Signals do not stack up like little *while you were out* phone notes. Those signals may be significant; is it safe to miss some?

Losing signals or scrambling data? Which is worse? Is there a way to avoid these problems? When you design programs that use signals, you must keep these questions in mind. Signal-handling bugs show up intermittently, usually when the system is very busy and accurate performance counts. Debugging them requires understanding how signal handlers work and where they can get into trouble.

7.9.5 Critical Sections in Video Games

A ball moves around a screen at a regular speed, bouncing off walls and a paddle. A user presses keys to move the paddle up and down. Producing regular motion of a ball is a job for an interval timer. User input to move a paddle sounds like unpredictable events, like signals. Are there times when we need to block user input? Are there critical sections in the game when the paddle should not move? Before we apply all this new knowledge to our video-game project, we look at one more source of signals: other processes.

7.10   `kill`: SENDING SIGNALS FROM A PROCESS

Signals arise from interval timers, from the terminal driver, from the kernel, and from processes. A process sends a signal to another process by using the `kill` system call:

`kill`	
PURPOSE	Send a signal to a process
INCLUDE	`#include <sys/types.h>` `#include <signal.h>`
USAGE	`int kill(pid_t pid, int sig)`
ARGS	`pid` process id of target `sig` signal to throw
RETURNS	`-1` on error `0` on success

`kill` sends a signal to a process. The process sending the signal must have the same user ID as the target process, or the sending process must be owned by the superuser. A process may send signals to itself.

A process can send any signal to another process, including signals that usually come from the keyboard, from interval timers, or from the kernel. For example, a process can send a SIGSEGV to another process as though the receiving process had attempted an illegal memory reference.

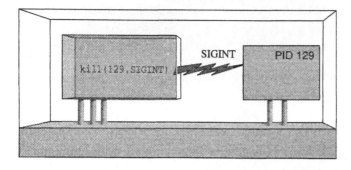

FIGURE 7.17

A process uses kill() to send a signal.

The Unix command kill uses the kill system call. (See Figure 7.17.)

Implications for Interprocess Communication

The receiving process may set signal handlers for almost any signal. Consider our example program that prints OUCH! when it receives SIGINT. What would happen if another program sent SIGINT to the OUCH! program? The OUCH! program would catch the signal, jump to the handler, and print OUCH!. (See Figure 7.18.)

Take this idea farther. If the first program set an interval timer that called a handler that sends SIGINT to the OUCH! program, thereby invoking the handler in that program, then a timer for one process could control a function in another process. In fact, a team of processes could toss a signal around the way soccer players pass a ball around a field.

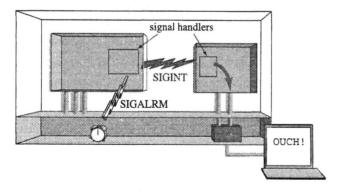

FIGURE 7.18

Complex use of signals.

Signals Designed for IPC: SIGUSR1, SIGUSR2

Unix includes two signals you can use for custom applications. The signals SIGUSR1 and SIGUSR2 have no predefined role. You can use these signals without having to use a signal that already has a specific meaning.

We look at techniques for *interprocess communication* in later chapters. The `kill` and `sigaction` combination offers a lot of intriguing programming possibilities.

7.11 USING TIMERS AND SIGNALS: VIDEO GAMES

We now return to the video-game project. The game has two main elements: animation and user input. The animation has to continue smoothly, and the user input has to modify the motion. This next program, `bounce1d.c`, lets the user bounce a message back and forth across the screen.

7.11.1 `bounce1d.c` : Controlled Animation on a Line

First, consider what `bounce1d` looks like and does. The display looks like that shown in Figure 7.19. `bounce1d.c` moves a single word smoothly across the screen. When the user presses the space bar, though, the message reverses direction. The letters "s" and "f" make the message move slower and faster, respectively. The "Q" key quits the game.

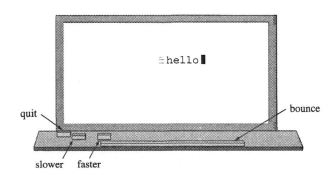

FIGURE 7.19

`bounce1d` in action: user-controlled animation.

How can we build this program? We know how to do animation. Draw a string at one location, wait a few milliseconds, then undraw the string and redraw the string one cell to the left or right. We want the undrawing and redrawing to happen at regular intervals, so we use an interval timer to invoke a signal handler.

Two variables hold the direction and speed of motion. A direction variable, set to +1 or to −1, makes the message move to the left or to the right. A delay variable sets the interval between timer ticks. A longer delay between ticks produces slower motion, a shorter delay between ticks produces faster motion.

Now we add user control of direction and speed to the program. We read keystrokes and modify the direction and speed variables in response to user input. The logic for the program is depicted in Figure 7.20. `bounce1d` contains two important ideas: *state variables* and *event handling*. The variables for position, direction, and delay define the state of the animation. User input and timer ticks are events that modify these state variables. Each timer tick calls code to change the position, and each user keystroke calls code to change the direction variable or speed variable. Here is the code:

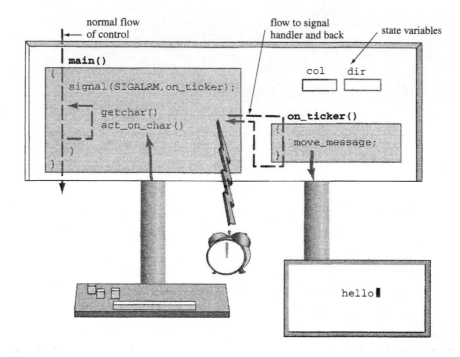

normal flow
of control

flow to signal
handler and back

state variables

```
main()
{
    signal(SIGALRM,on_ticker);

        getchar()
        act_on_char()

    )
}
```

col   dir

```
on_ticker()
{
    move_message;
}
```

hello█

FIGURE 7.20

User input changes values. Values control action.

```
/* bounce1d.c
 *      purpose animation with user controlled speed and direction
 *      note    the handler does the animation
 *              the main program reads keyboard input
 *      compile cc bounce1d.c set_ticker.c -lcurses -o bounce1d
 */
#include        <stdio.h>
#include        <curses.h>
#include        <signal.h>

/* some global settings main and the handler use */

#define MESSAGE "hello"
#define BLANK   "     "

int     row;    /* current row           */
int     col;    /* current column        */
int     dir;    /* where we are going    */

int main()
{
        int     delay;          /* bigger => slower      */
```

```
        int     ndelay;             /* new delay             */
        int     c;                  /* user input            */
        void    move_msg(int);      /* handler for timer     */

        initscr();
        crmode();
        noecho();
        clear();

        row   = 10;                 /* start here            */
        col   = 0;
        dir   = 1;                  /* add 1 to row number   */
        delay = 200;                /* 200ms = 0.2 seconds   */

        move(row,col);              /* get into position     */
        addstr(MESSAGE);            /* draw message          */
        signal(SIGALRM, move_msg );
        set_ticker( delay );

        while(1)
        {
                ndelay = 0;
                c = getch();
                if ( c == 'Q' ) break;
                if ( c == ' ' ) dir = -dir;
                if ( c == 'f' && delay > 2 ) ndelay = delay/2;
                if ( c == 's' ) ndelay = delay * 2 ;
                if ( ndelay > 0 )
                        set_ticker( delay = ndelay );
        }
        endwin();
        return 0;
}

void move_msg(int signum)
{
        signal(SIGALRM, move_msg);         /* reset, just in case   */
        move( row, col );
        addstr( BLANK );
        col += dir;                        /* move to new column    */
        move( row, col );                  /* then set cursor       */
        addstr( MESSAGE );                 /* redo message          */
        refresh();                         /* and show it           */
        /*
         * now handle borders
         */
        if ( dir == -1 && col <= 0 )
                dir = 1;
        else if ( dir == 1 && col+strlen(MESSAGE) >= COLS )
                dir = -1;
}
```

Recurse or Block: A Real Example

When we examined data corruption in signal handlers, we mentioned reentrant functions. bounce1d presents a real example to think about. Initially the signal handler, move_msg, is called five times a second. Pressing the "f" key speeds up the animation by reducing the interval on the timer. If we press "f" enough times, the interval between signals might be shorter than the time it takes to execute the handler. What happens if the next alarm signal arrives while the handler is busy undrawing and redrawing the message and modifying the position variable?

This analysis is left as an exercise. We use the signal interface in this code, so the call will recurse or block depending on your system.

What Next?

How do we convert bounce1d into a ping-pong game? First, we can replace the string "hello" with the letter "O" to represent a ball. Second, we need to make the ball move up and down as well as left and right. Adding up and down motion requires more state variables. We already have col and row to hold the position of the ball and dir to hold the horizontal direction. What new variables do we need to add vertical motion?

7.11.2 bounce2d.c: Animation in Two Dimensions

The next program, bounce2d.c, produces animation in two dimensions and allows the user to control the horizontal and vertical speeds. Figure 7.21 is illustrative.

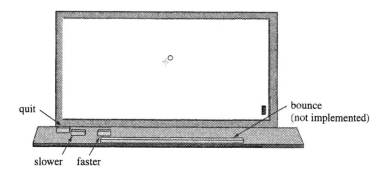

FIGURE 7.21

Animation in two directions.

bounce2d uses the same three-part design of bounce1d:

Timer Driven

The interval timer is set to send a steady stream of SIGALRMs to the process. On each signal, the ball can move ahead.

Keyboard Blocked

The program blocks on keyboard input and receives and acts on characters as they are typed.

State Variables

The position and speed of the ball are stored as variables. User input modifies the variables that represent the speed. The timer handler uses the speed and position to know where and when to draw the ball.

This outline sounds just like bounce1d, but there is one new, important question:

How Does the Ball Move along a Diagonal?

Creating diagonal motion is a new problem. In the one-dimensional program, each timer tick caused the image to move one screen position. That was simple: one tick, one cell, but motion in two dimensions is not so simple. Consider the path shown in Figure 7.22. This path consists of moving up one row for every three columns. One technique is to move the image from **A** to **B** on each timer tick. Depending on the ratio of the two sides of the triangle, though, the jump might be large. For example, a line with slope $\frac{3}{4}$ produces diagonal jumps of five units.

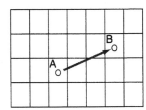

Question: How to move 'O' from cell A to cell B smoothly?

FIGURE 7.22

A path with a slope of $\frac{1}{3}$.

Moving an image one cell at a time looks better. With a slope of $\frac{1}{3}$, an object moving cell by cell follows a path like that shown in Figure 7.23. Note that the image takes three horizontal steps then one vertical step. Horizontal steps need to occur three times as often as vertical steps.

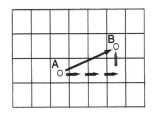

To approximate diagonal motion:

move right every two timer ticks, and move up every six timer ticks.

This technique requires two counters, one to count timer ticks for horizontal motion and one to count timer ticks for vertical motion.

FIGURE 7.23

Moving one cell at a time looks better.

This Sounds like Two Timers Exactly. Consider one timer ticking. After each 2 ticks, the program moves the image one unit to the right. After each 6 ticks, the program moves the image one unit upward. The ball would follow the same path if the intervals were 10 ticks and 30 ticks, but the motion would be slower.

A program only has one real-time interval ticker, so we need to build two timers of our own and use the interval timer to count down each of our timers. We use the logic presented in Figure 7.23 to drive our two-dimensional animation.

The Code

To produce motion in two directions at once, we create two counters to serve as timers. Each of those counters has two parts, a value and an interval, just like the two parts in system interval timers. The value represents the number of *ticks to go* before the next redraw, and the interval is the number of *ticks to move*—that is, the interval between each redraw. These two members use the abbreviations ttg and ttm. The code is as follows:

```
/*  bounce2d 1.0
 *       bounce a character (default is 'o') around the screen
 *       defined by some parameters
 *
 *       user input:     s slow down x component, S: slow y component
 *                       f speed up x component,  F: speed y component
 *                       Q quit
 *
 *       blocks on read, but timer tick sends SIGALRM caught by ball_move
 *       build:   cc bounce2d.c set_ticker.c -lcurses -o bounce2d
 */

#include         <curses.h>
#include         <signal.h>
#include         "bounce.h"

struct ppball the_ball ;

/** the main loop **/

void set_up();
void wrap_up();

int main()
{
        int     c;

        set_up();

        while ( ( c = getchar()) != 'Q' ){
                if ( c == 'f' )       the_ball.x_ttm--;
                else if ( c == 's' ) the_ball.x_ttm++;
                else if ( c == 'F' ) the_ball.y_ttm--;
                else if ( c == 'S' ) the_ball.y_ttm++;
```

```
        }
        wrap_up();
}

void set_up()
/*
 *      init structure and other stuff
 */
{
        void    ball_move(int);

        the_ball.y_pos = Y_INIT;
        the_ball.x_pos = X_INIT;
        the_ball.y_ttg = the_ball.y_ttm = Y_TTM ;
        the_ball.x_ttg = the_ball.x_ttm = X_TTM ;
        the_ball.y_dir = 1  ;
        the_ball.x_dir = 1  ;
        the_ball.symbol = DFL_SYMBOL ;
        initscr();
        noecho();
        crmode();

        signal( SIGINT , SIG_IGN );
        mvaddch( the_ball.y_pos, the_ball.x_pos, the_ball.symbol  );
        refresh();

        signal( SIGALRM, ball_move );
        set_ticker( 1000 / TICKS_PER_SEC );  /* send millisecs per tick */
}

void wrap_up()
{
        set_ticker( 0 );
        endwin();                       /* put back to normal    */
}

void ball_move(int signum)
{
        int     y_cur, x_cur, moved;

        signal( SIGALRM , SIG_IGN );                    /* dont get caught now  */
        y_cur = the_ball.y_pos ;                        /* old spot             */
        x_cur = the_ball.x_pos ;
        moved = 0 ;

        if ( the_ball.y_ttm > 0 && the_ball.y_ttg-- == 1 ){
                the_ball.y_pos += the_ball.y_dir ;      /* move */
                the_ball.y_ttg = the_ball.y_ttm ;       /* reset*/
                moved = 1;
        }
```

```
            if ( the_ball.x_ttm > 0 && the_ball.x_ttg-- == 1 ){
                    the_ball.x_pos += the_ball.x_dir ;       /* move */
                    the_ball.x_ttg = the_ball.x_ttm  ;       /* reset*/
                    moved = 1;
            }

            if ( moved ){
                    mvaddch( y_cur, x_cur, BLANK );
                    mvaddch( y_cur, x_cur, BLANK );
                    mvaddch( the_ball.y_pos, the_ball.x_pos, the_ball.symbol );
                    bounce_or_lose( &the_ball );
                    move(LINES-1,COLS-1);
                    refresh();
            }
            signal( SIGALRM, ball_move);              /* for unreliable systems */
    }

    int bounce_or_lose(struct ppball *bp)
    {
            int     return_val = 0 ;

            if ( bp->y_pos == TOP_ROW ){
                    bp->y_dir = 1 ;
                    return_val = 1 ;
            } else if ( bp->y_pos == BOT_ROW ){
                    bp->y_dir = -1 ;
                    return_val = 1;
            }
            if ( bp->x_pos == LEFT_EDGE ){
                    bp->x_dir = 1 ;
                    return_val = 1 ;
            } else if ( bp->x_pos == RIGHT_EDGE ){
                    bp->x_dir = -1;
                    return_val = 1;
            }
            return return_val;
    }
```

The following is the header file:

```
    /* bounce.h                      */

    /* some settings for the game    */

    #define BLANK            ' '
    #define DFL_SYMBOL       'o'
    #define TOP_ROW          5
    #define BOT_ROW          20
    #define LEFT_EDGE        10
    #define RIGHT_EDGE       70
```

```
#define X_INIT        10       /* starting col    */
#define Y_INIT        10       /* starting row    */
#define TICKS_PER_SEC 50       /* affects speed   */

#define X_TTM         5
#define Y_TTM         8

/** the ping pong ball **/

struct ppball {
              int      y_pos, x_pos,
                       y_ttm, x_ttm,
                       y_ttg, x_ttg,
                       y_dir, x_dir;
              char     symbol ;
        } ;
```

7.11.3   Now for the Complete Game

The rest of the work is left as an exercise for the reader. You need to add a paddle, logic to serve the ball, logic to bounce the ball off the paddle, and logic to determine if the ball goes out of play.

We have examined in detail all the ideas you need to complete the project. Think carefully about the problems of reentrant code. Where might the same code be called at the same time? Do you want to block or recurse on the timer handler?

7.12   SIGNALS ON INPUT: ASYNCHRONOUS I/O

The animations and games in this chapter wait for two types of events: timer ticks and keyboard input. We set a handler to manage animation on timer ticks, and we block on keyboard input with getch. Instead of blocking, could we be notified of user input with a signal, just as we are notified when the timer expires?

Yes. Programs can ask the kernel to send a signal when input arrives, like asking the letter carrier to ring the doorbell when the mail arrives. Instead of sitting in the front hall staring at the mailbox for hours, you can do other things or sleep and receive a signal as soon as input is available.

Unix includes two systems for *asynchronous input*. One method sends a signal when input is ready to read, and the other system sends a signal when input has been read. The first method, setting the O_ASYNC bit for a file descriptor, came from UCB. The other method, calling aio_read, is part of the POSIX standard. We demonstrate both methods. First, we look at the idea.

7.12.1   Bouncing with Asynchronous I/O

The new design of the bounce program is illustrated in Figure 7.24. We expect two kinds of signals, SIGIO and SIGALRM, so we create two handlers. The SIGIO handler reads and acts on keystrokes. The SIGALRM handler drives the animation and checks for bounces. To keep the program simple, we remove speed control.

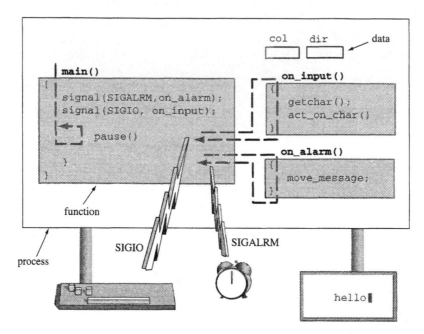

FIGURE 7.24

Keyboard and timer both send signals.

7.12.2 Method 1: Using O_ASYNC

Using O_ASYNC requires four changes to the bounce program. First, create and install a handler that is called when keyboard input is available. Second, use the F_SETOWN command of fcntl to tell the kernel to send input notification signals to our process. Other processes may have connections to the keyboard, and we do not want those processes sent the signal. Third, turn on input signals by calling fcntl to set the O_ASYNC attribute in file descriptor 0. Finally, execute a simple loop calling pause to wait for signals from the timer or from the keyboard. When a character arrives from the keyboard, the kernel sends SIGIO to the process. The handler for SIGIO uses the standard curses function getch to read the character. When the timer interval expires, the kernel sends SIGALRM, which we handle as before. Here is the source code:

```
/* bounce_async.c
 *        purpose animation with user control, using O_ASYNC on fd
 *        note    set_ticker() sends SIGALRM, handler does animation
 *                keyboard sends SIGIO, main only calls pause()
 *        compile cc bounce_async.c set_ticker.c -lcurses -o bounce_async
 */
#include        <stdio.h>
#include        <curses.h>
#include        <signal.h>
#include        <fcntl.h>

/* The state of the game */
```

```c
#define MESSAGE "hello"
#define BLANK   "     "

int     row   = 10;      /* current row          */
int     col   = 0;       /* current column       */
int     dir   = 1;       /* where we are going   */
int     delay = 200;     /* how long to wait     */
int     done  = 0;

main()
{
        void    on_alarm(int);  /* handler for alarm    */
        void    on_input(int);  /* handler for keybd    */
        void    enable_kbd_signals();

        initscr();              /* set up screen */
        crmode();
        noecho();
        clear();

        signal(SIGIO, on_input);            /* install a handler       */
        enable_kbd_signals();               /* turn on kbd signals     */
        signal(SIGALRM, on_alarm);          /* install alarm handler   */
        set_ticker(delay);                  /* start ticking           */

        move(row,col);                      /* get into position       */
        addstr( MESSAGE );                  /* draw initial image      */

        while( !done )                      /* the main loop */
                pause();
        endwin();
}
void on_input(int signum)
{
        int     c = getch();                /* grab the char */

        if ( c == 'Q' || c == EOF )
                done = 1;
        else if ( c == ' ' )
                dir = -dir;
}

void on_alarm(int signum)
{
        signal(SIGALRM, on_alarm);          /* reset, just in case  */
        mvaddstr( row, col, BLANK );        /* note mvaddstr()      */
        col += dir;                         /* move to new column   */
        mvaddstr( row, col, MESSAGE );      /* redo message         */
        refresh();                          /* and show it          */

        /*
         * now handle borders
         */
        if ( dir == -1 && col <= 0 )
                dir = 1;
```

```
            else if ( dir == 1 && col+strlen(MESSAGE) >= COLS )
                    dir = -1;
    }
    /*
     * install a handler, tell kernel who to notify on input, enable signals
     */
    void enable_kbd_signals()
    {
            int   fd_flags;

            fcntl(0, F_SETOWN, getpid());
            fd_flags = fcntl(0, F_GETFL);
            fcntl(0, F_SETFL, (fd_flags|O_ASYNC));
    }
```

7.12.3   Method 2: Using `aio_read`

Using `aio_read` is more complicated, but more flexible, than setting `O_ASYNC` in the file descriptor. We make four changes to the bounce program. First, we install `on_input`, the handler we want called when input is read.

Second, we set values in a `struct kbcbuf` to describe what input to wait for and what signal to send when that input is read. In our simple application, we say we want one character from file descriptor 0, and we want to receive `SIGIO` when that character is read. We could specify any signal, even `SIGARLM` or `SIGINT`.

Third, we place a read request by passing that struct to `aio_read`. Unlike a call to regular `read`, `aio_read` does not block the process. Instead, `aio_read` will send a signal when it completes.

Our program is now free to do anything it likes. In this simple case, we just call `pause` to wait for a signal. When a user types a character, `aio_read` sends `SIGIO` to the process, invoking the handler.

Finally, we write the handler to get the input character, by calling `aio_return`, and then process that character.

```
    /* bounce_aio.c
     *      purpose animation with user control, using aio_read() etc
     *      note    set_ticker() sends SIGALRM, handler does animation
     *              keyboard sends SIGIO, main only calls pause()
     *      compile cc bounce_aio.c set_ticker.c -lrt  -lcurses -o bounce_aio
     */
    #include         <stdio.h>
    #include         <curses.h>
    #include         <signal.h>
    #include         <aio.h>

    /* The state of the game                        */

    #define MESSAGE "hello"
    #define BLANK    "       "

    int     row   = 10;     /* current row          */
```

```
int     col   = 0;      /* current column      */
int     dir   = 1;      /* where we are going  */
int     delay = 200;    /* how long to wait    */
int     done  = 0;

struct aiocb kbcbuf;    /* an aio control buf  */

main()
{
        void    on_alarm(int);  /* handler for alarm   */
        void    on_input(int);  /* handler for keybd   */
        void    setup_aio_buffer();

        initscr();              /* set up screen */
        crmode();
        noecho();
        clear();

        signal(SIGIO, on_input);            /* install a handler      */
        setup_aio_buffer();                 /* initialize aio ctrl buff */
        aio_read(&kbcbuf);                  /* place a read request   */

        signal(SIGALRM, on_alarm);          /* install alarm handler  */
        set_ticker(delay);                  /* start ticking          */

        mvaddstr( row, col, MESSAGE );      /* draw initial image     */

        while( !done )                      /* the main loop */
                pause();
        endwin();
}
/*
 * handler called when aio_read() has stuff to read
 *   First check for any error codes, and if ok, then get the return code
 */
void on_input()
{
        int  c;
        char *cp = (char *) kbcbuf.aio_buf;     /* cast to char * */

        /* check for errors */
        if ( aio_error(&kbcbuf) != 0 )
                perror("reading failed");
        else
                /* get number of chars read */
                if ( aio_return(&kbcbuf) == 1 )
                {
                        c = *cp;
                        if ( c == 'Q' || c == EOF )
                                done = 1;
                        else if ( c == ' ' )
                                dir = -dir;
                }
        /* place a new request */
```

```
                      aio_read(&kbcbuf);
        }

        void on_alarm()
        {
                signal(SIGALRM, on_alarm);      /* reset, just in case  */
                mvaddstr( row, col, BLANK );    /* clear old string     */
                col += dir;                     /* move to new column   */
                mvaddstr( row, col, MESSAGE );  /* draw new string      */
                refresh();                      /* and show it          */
                /*
                 * now handle borders
                 */
                if ( dir == -1 && col <= 0 )
                        dir = 1;
                else if ( dir == 1 && col+strlen(MESSAGE) >= COLS )
                        dir = -1;
        }
        /*
         * set members of struct.
         *    First specify args like those for read(fd, buf, num)  and offset
         *    Then  specify what to do (send signal) and what signal (SIGIO)
         */
        void setup_aio_buffer()
        {
                static char input[1];                   /* 1 char of input */

                /* describe what to read */
                kbcbuf.aio_fildes    = 0;               /* standard intput */
                kbcbuf.aio_buf       = input;           /* buffer          */
                kbcbuf.aio_nbytes    = 1;               /* number to read  */
                kbcbuf.aio_offset    = 0;               /* offset in file  */

                /* describe what to do when read is ready */
                kbcbuf.aio_sigevent.sigev_notify = SIGEV_SIGNAL;
                kbcbuf.aio_sigevent.sigev_signo  = SIGIO;  /* send sIGIO   */
        }
```

7.12.4 Do We Need Asynchronous Reads for Bounce?

No. The bounce programs works fine blocking on user input and moving in response to interval timer ticks. The advantage of asynchronous reads is that the program does not have to block on input and can instead spend its time doing something else.

A fancier game could, for example, play music, generate sound effects, compute a complex background image, even do some public service. Increasingly, computers are invited to contribute spare time to help with large number-crunching projects in mathematics, astronomy, and medicine.

The bounce program could spend its free time computing *pi* to an arbitrary number of decimal places and use asynchronous input to be notified when the user presses a key. We would change the loop in main as follows:

```
Before                  After
while( !done )          compute_pi();
  pause();             endwin();
endwin();
```

The revised program calls the function that computes *pi*. When a character arrives, the program jumps to the handler, processes input, then resumes the calculation. When a timer tick arrives, the program jumps to that handler, processes the timer tick, then resumes the calculation.

The program needs to handle the "Q" key in a new way. How would you modify the program to handle that?

7.12.5 Asynchronous Input, Video Games, and Operating Systems

We started this chapter by comparing a video game to an operating system. Our bounce program does not need asynchronous input, but an operating system does. The kernel runs programs and cannot waste processor time waiting for user input. The kernel sets handlers that are called when the keyboard, serial lines, or network cards detect input. The kernel jumps from running a program to the handler, processes the input, then goes back to running the program. In critical sections, the kernel blocks signals.

The kernel uses the hardware version of asynchronous input, and processes use a software version. What is the connection between these two versions? The video game is running. Suddenly, the user presses a key sending an electrical signal to the keyboard port. The keyboard port generates a real, hardware signal that causes control to jump from the middle of the video game into the device driver for the keyboard.

Device-driver code in the kernel reads the character from the wire, passes the character through the processing steps in the terminal driver. If the file descriptor attached to that driver is set for asynchronous input, the kernel then sends a Unix signal to the process. When the process resumes, control passes to the signal handler within the process.

SUMMARY

MAIN IDEAS

- Some programs follow a simple flow of control. Some programs respond to outside events. A video game responds to time and to user input. An operating system also responds to time and to input from external devices.
- The curses library is a set of functions that programs can call to manage the appearance of a text screen.
- A process schedules events by setting timers. Each process has three separate timers. A timer "rings" by sending a signal. Each timer can be set to ring once or to ring at regular intervals.
- Handling a single signal is easy. Handling multiple signals, sometimes at once, is complicated. A process can decide to ignore signals or block signals and can tell the kernel which signals to block or ignore at which times.

- Some functions perform complex operations that should not be interrupted. A program can protect these critical sections by careful use of signal masks.

WHAT'S NEXT?

In this chapter, we saw how a video game does several things at once by receiving and handling signals. Unix runs several programs at once. How do processes run? Where do processes come from? Next, we shift our attention from basic operating-system questions and principles to specific details of how to create and coordinate Unix processes.

EXPLORATIONS

7.1 pause waits for any signal to arrive, including signals generated from the keyboard, such as SIGINT.

    (a) Run sleep1 and press Ctrl-C. What happens? Why?

    (b) Modify sleep1 to handle SIGINT.

    (c) Now run the program and press Ctrl-C. What happens? Why?

7.2 *Slow Devices* The read system can be interrupted in some cases. A user may, for example, press Ctrl-C when the program is reading keyboard input. On the other hand, when a program calls read to get data from the disk, pressing Ctrl-C does not interrupt the system call.

Read the manual or search the Web to learn about the term *slow device*. Which calls to read can be interrupted and which cannot be? Why?

7.3 *sigprocmask vs. ISIG* Another way to make sure a critical section of code is not interrupted by a keyboard signal is to turn off ISIG in the tty driver. How does that solution differ from adding those signals to the signal mask?

7.4 Devise a reentrant system for the people adding their names and addresses to the list in your office. Can you translate that system into an algorithm for adding three lines of data to the end of a text file at each invocation of a handler? See the section in Chapter 5 on auto-append mode and the exercise about file locking with link.

7.5 Discuss the effect on bounce1d.c if the timer interval is shorter than the time it takes to execute move_msg. What happens to the variable pos? What happens to the screen? Answer these questions for recursing and for blocking. Is there a way to prevent data corruption and not lose signals?

7.6 *Interrupted System Calls* On some versions of Unix, calls to getch are interrupted when timer ticks are handled. On these systems getch returns EOF at each timer tick. What effect does that have on the program? Is this a problem? Can it be changed?

7.7 *Blocking and recursing with async io* The versions of bounce that use asynchronous input have two signal handlers. What will happen if a SIGIO arrives when the program is in the SIGALRM handler? What about the opposite situation? Can these two handlers interfere with each other? Do you need to block signals when handling signals here? What about recursive calls? Will there be a problem if a new character arrives when the program is handling SIGIO?

List all possible combinations, and list problems that may arise.

PROGRAMMING EXERCISES

7.8 *Blinking Text* Some Web browsers support the blinking-text feature and the theater-marquee text feature. Modify hello1.c to display a blinking message. If the user supplies a message on the command line, your program should display that message, otherwise the program should display the default message. Use the sleep function to pause the program between printing the message and then erasing it.

7.9 *Theater Marquee/Ticker Tape* Write a program that uses curses to create a theater-marquee display to show the contents of a file. A marquee (or ticker-tape display) is a horizontal region that displays text, scrolling horizontally, character by character across the screen. Your program should accept on the command line a filename and a length, position, and speed for the display.

7.10 Modify hello5.c replacing the call to sleep with a call to usleep. Select an interval that gives smooth, but not too fast, action.

Modify the program so the message slows down as it approaches the left and right extremes of its path and speeds up as it returns to the middle of the screen. See how closely you can approximate the simple harmonic motion typical of a pendulum or mass on a spring.

Imagine the right side of the screen is a planet and the message is falling from space to the surface. Modify the program so the falling simulates the acceleration of gravity. For extra credit, when the message hits the planet, simulate a crash landing with the words splintering into separate letters.

7.11 The ticker_demo.c program exits from the signal handler. Could the program exit from main rather than from the signal handler? Add a global variable to the program called done. Then make two more changes to the program so that it returns from main. What are the advantages and disadvantages of the original approach and this new approach?

7.12 *Argument to signal handler* Modify sigdemo3.c by combining the two signal handlers into one signal handler that checks its argument to determine which signal invoked the handler. How does this change affect the way the program behaves on your system?

7.13 *Autologout* Do you ever connect to a remote machine and forget to log out? It would be helpful to have a program running in the background that would, after a specified amount of time, send the SIGKILL signal to your log-in shell.

(a) Write a program timeout.c that accepts as command-line arguments a process ID number and a number of seconds. The program sleeps for that many seconds, then sends SIGKILL to the specified process ID. You can run it from your log-in shell with the command timeout $$ 3600 &. The symbol $$ represents the process ID of the shell.

(b) The problem with timeout.c is that it logs you out even if you are still working an hour later. Change the program so it only logs you out if there has been no input or output to your tty for ten minutes. (Hint: the modification time of /dev/ttyxx represents the last time data were read from or written to that device. Change the program so it accepts as an argument the name of the tty.)

7.14 For this exercise, you will write a user-level simulation of the situation depicted in figure 7.14 showing how one real clock can drive two different timers.

First, write a program called ouch.c based on sigdemo1.c, the OUCH program in Chapter 6. The ouch.c program will accept on the command line two arguments, a message the signal handler prints and the number of times the signal handler must be called before it prints the message. For example,

```
$ ouch hello 10 &
```

will run in the background a program that prints the message "hello" every tenth time it receives SIGINT.

Then write a metronome program called metronome.c that accepts a list of process ID numbers on the command line. This program should use an interval timer to generate SIGALRM every second. The handler for that signal should use the kill system call to send SIGINT to all the processes specified on the command line. For example,

```
$ metronome 1 3456 7777 2345
```

will send SIGINT to processes 3456, 7777, and 2345 every second.

Start in the background three instances of ouch, each with a different message and a different interval. Note the process ID numbers of those three processes. Then run the metronome program, passing as arguments the number 1 and those three processes' ID numbers.

7.15 *Blocking on usleep(), handling input* In bounce1d.c, the main loop blocked on getch, and the program handled animation in a signal handler. Reverse the roles of user input and animation by writing a new version of bounce1d.c based on hello5.c. In this new version, the main loop should block on usleep, and the program should handle user input in a signal handler.

7.16 *Reaction-Time Tester* Write a program that measures how quickly a user can respond. The program waits for a random interval of time and then prints a single digit on the screen. The user has to type that digit as quickly as possible. The program records how long it takes the user to respond. Your program should perform 10 such tests and report the minimum, maximum, and average response time. (Hint: Read the manual page for gettimeofday.)

7.17 Finish the pong game started in the text. Add scoring, multiple players, bumpers, and anything else you think would make it fun to play and write.

PROJECTS

Based on the material in this chapter, you can learn about and write versions of the following Unix programs:

snake, worms

# CHAPTER 8

Processes and Programs Studying `sh`

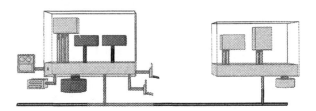

OBJECTIVES

Ideas and Skills

- What a Unix shell does
- The Unix model of a process
- How to run a program
- How to create a process
- How parent and child processes communicate

System Calls and Functions

- `fork`
- `exec`
- `wait`
- `exit`

Commands

- `sh`
- `ps`

8.1 PROCESSES = PROGRAMS IN ACTION

How does Unix run programs? It looks easy enough; you log in, your shell prints a prompt, you type a command and press Enter. Soon, a program runs. When the program finishes, your shell prints a new prompt. How does that work? What is the shell? What does a shell do? What does the kernel do? What *is* a program, and what does it mean to *run* a program?

A program is a sequence of machine-language instructions stored in a file, usually produced by compiling source code into binary code. Running a program means loading that list of machine-language instructions into memory and then having the processor (the CPU) execute the instructions, one by one.

In Unix terminology, an *executable program* is a list of machine-language instructions and data, and a *process* is the memory space and settings with which the program runs. Figure 8.1 shows programs and processes.

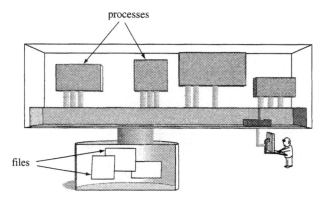

processes

files

FIGURE 8.1

Processes are programs in action.

Data and programs are stored in files on the disk; programs run in processes. In these next few chapters, we explore the concept of a *process*. We begin by experimenting with the commands ps and sh and by writing our own version of a Unix shell.

8.2   LEARNING ABOUT PROCESSES WITH ps

Processes live in *user space*, the portion of computer memory that holds running programs and their data. (See Figure 8.2.) We can explore the contents of user space with the ps (short for *process status*) command, which lists current processes:

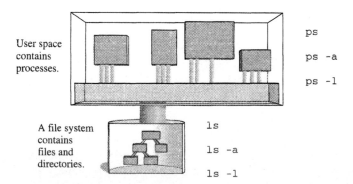

User space
contains
processes.

ps

ps -a

ps -l

A file system
contains
files and
directories.

ls

ls -a

ls -l

FIGURE 8.2

The ps command lists current processes.

```
$ ps
  PID TTY          TIME CMD
 1755 pts/1    00:00:17 bash
 1981 pts/1    00:00:00 ps
```

I am running two processes: bash (a shell) and the ps command. Each process has a unique identifying number, called a *process ID*, commonly called a PID. Each of these processes is connected to a terminal, in this case /dev/pts/1, and each has an elapsed time. Note the elapsed time for ps is so brief it is listed as zero seconds.

ps supports many options. ps, like ls, supports a -*a* option:

```
$ ps -a
  PID TTY          TIME CMD
 1779 pts/0    00:00:13 gv
 1780 pts/0    00:00:07 gs
 1781 pts/0    00:00:01 vi
 2013 pts/2    00:00:23 xpaint
 2017 pts/2    00:00:02 mail
 2018 pts/1    00:00:00 ps
```

The -a option lists more processes, including ones being run by other uses and at other terminals. The output from -a does not include the shells, though. ps also includes a −*l* option to print longer, more informative lines:

```
$ ps -la
  F S   UID   PID  PPID  C PRI  NI ADDR   SZ WCHAN  TTY          TIME CMD
000 S   504  1779  1731  0  69   0    - 1086 do_sel pts/0    00:00:13 gv
000 S   504  1780  1779  0  69   0    - 2309 do_sel pts/0    00:00:07 gs
000 S   504  1781  1731  0  72   0    - 1320 do_sel pts/0    00:00:01 vi
000 S   519  2013  1993  0  69  19    - 1300 do_sel pts/2    00:00:23 xpain
000 S   519  2017  1993  0  69   0    -  363 read_c pts/2    00:00:02 mail
000 R   500  2023  1755  0  79   0    -  750 -      pts/1    00:00:00 ps
```

The column marked S shows the status of each process. The process for ps is running, indicated by the letter R, and the rest of the processes in the list are sleeping, indicated by the letter S. Each process belongs to a user; a user ID (UID) is listed for each process. Each process has a PID, and we also see that each process has *parent process ID* (PPID).

Columns marked PRI and NI contain priority and *niceness* levels of the process. The kernel uses these values to decide when to run processes. A process may increase its niceness level, like a person in a checkout lane allowing other customers to move ahead in line. The superuser is allowed to decrease the niceness level, sort of like pushing to the head of the checkout line.

A process has a *size*, shown in the SZ column. This number represents the amount of memory the process is using. This example shows that the mail program is using much less memory than the xpaint program, which has to allocate lots of memory to store images. The size of a process may change as it runs. A program that allocates memory when it runs can get larger.

The WCHAN column shows why a process is sleeping. All the processes in this example are waiting for input; the entries *read_c* and *do_sel* refer to addresses in the kernel. The ADDR and F values are no longer used, but appear in the output for compatibility with programs that expect to see them. The -ly option produces the modern set of values.

Command-line options for ps vary widely from one version of Unix to another. The -a and -l options mentioned in the previous paragraph might not work on your system, or they may work differently. Read your local manual pages. The examples shown here are from a version called procps 2.0.6. and show only some of the variety of information ps displays.

The ps command is versatile. The -fa options produce the following output:

```
$ ps -fa
UID         PID  PPID  C STIME TTY          TIME CMD
betsy      1779  1731  0 19:53 pts/0     00:00:01 gv dinner.ps
betsy      1780  1779  0 19:53 pts/0     00:00:07 gs -dNOPLATFONTS
betsy      1781  1731  0 19:54 pts/0     00:00:02 vi dinner
yuriko     2013  1993  0 20:15 pts/2     00:00:00 xpaint
yuriko     2017  1993  0 20:16 pts/2     00:00:00 mail bruce
bruce      2401  1755  0 20:36 pts/1     00:00:00 ps -af
```

The -f format is easier to read. The username is displayed instead of the UID number; the complete command line is listed in the CMD column.

8.2.1   System Processes

In addition to processes run by users, you will find processes Unix runs to perform system tasks:

```
$ ps -ax|head -25
PID TTY        STAT    TIME COMMAND
   1 ?         S       0:05 init
   2 ?         SW      3:54 [kflushd]
   3 ?         SW      0:38 [kupdate]
   4 ?         SW      0:00 [kpiod]
   5 ?         SW      2:13 [kswapd]
  35 ?         SW      0:00 [uhci-control]
  36 ?         SW      0:00 [khubd]
 420 ?         S       0:25 syslogd
 423 ?         S       0:36 klogd -k /boot/System.map-2.2.14
 437 ?         SW      0:00 [inetd]
 449 ?         S       0:02 amd -F /etc/am.d/conf
 461 ?         SW      0:00 [rpciod]
 466 ?         S       0:00 cron
 471 ?         S       0:00 atd
 476 ?         S       0:00 sendmail: accepting connections on port 25
 484 ?         SW      0:00 [rpc.rstatd]
 500 ?         S       0:46 sshd
 504 ?         SW      0:00 [calserver]
 506 ?         SW      0:00 [keyserver]
 512 ?         SW      0:00 [portsentry]
 514 ?         SW      0:00 [portsentry]
 561 tty1      SW      0:00 [getty]
 562 tty2      SW      0:00 [getty]
```

```
563 tty3      SW      0:00 [getty]
$ ps -ax| wc -1
     82
```

The above sample shows the first 24 of the 82 processes running now on the system. Some are system processes. Many of these system processes do not have a terminal; they are started when the system starts up and are not typed by a user at a command line. What do all these system processes do?

The first few processes on the list manage different parts of memory, including kernel buffers and virtual memory pages. Other processes on this list manage system logfiles (klogd, syslogd), schedule batch jobs (cron, atd), watch for potential intruders (portsentry), and allow regular users to log in (sshd, getty). You can learn a lot about your Unix system by reading the output of ps -ax and the manual pages. Running ps is like gazing through a microscope into a drop of pond water; you can see the number and diversity of processes living in your computer.

8.2.2 Process Management and File Management

Our explorations using ps show that processes have many attributes. Each process belongs to a user ID, has a size, a starting time, an elapsed running time, a priority, and niceness. Some processes have a terminal, many do not. Where are these properties stored? We asked the same question about files. The kernel manages processes in memory and files on the disk. How similar are these activities?

Files contain data, processes contain executable code. Files have attributes, processes have attributes. The kernel creates and destroys files. The same is true for processes. The kernel stores several processes in memory just as it stores several files on the disk, and the kernel has to allocate space and keep track of which processes use which blocks of memory. How similar is memory management to disk management?

8.2.3 Computer Memory and Computer Programs

The idea of a process is abstract, but it represents something very concrete: a bunch of bytes in memory. Figure 8.3 shows three models of computer memory.

Memory can be viewed as an expanse of space containing the kernel and processes.

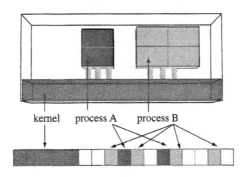

kernel   process A   process B

Many systems view memory as an array of "pages" and split processes into several pages.

The array of pages may be stored physically in solid state chips.

FIGURE 8.3

Three models of computer memory.

Memory in a Unix system is divided into kernel space and user space. Processes live in user space. Memory, though, is a sequence of bytes, just a big array. If your machine has 64 megabytes of memory, the array consists of about 67 million *memory locations*. Some of those memory locations contain the machine-language instructions and data that constitute the kernel.

Some of those memory locations contain the machine-language instructions and data that comprise processes. A process does not have to occupy a single chunk of memory. Processes are usually divided into smaller chunks, just as disk files are divided into disk blocks. And, just as a file has an allocation list of disk blocks, a process has a structure to hold the allocation list of *memory pages*. Therefore, diagrams that show each process as a compact box inside of user space are abstractions.

Diagrams depicting memory as a continuous array of bytes are abstractions, too. Memory these days is usually a collection of chips on little circuit boards.

Creating a process is similar to creating a disk file. The kernel has to find some free pages of memory to hold the machine-language codes and data bytes for the program. The kernel sets up some data structures to store memory allocation information and the attributes of the process.

The magical part of the operating system is that, in the same way the file system structure converts a sequence of sectors on a stack of spinning platters into something that appears as a tree of neatly ordered directories, the process system structure converts a sequence of storage bits on bunches of silicon chips into something that appears as a society of processes—thriving, interacting, cooperating, being born, doing their jobs, and dying. Like an ant farm.

To understand processes, we shall study and write a Unix shell, a program that manages processes and runs programs.

8.3   THE SHELL: A TOOL FOR PROCESS AND PROGRAM CONTROL

A shell is a program that manages processes and runs programs. There are many shells available for Unix, just as there are many programming languages, all with different styles and strengths. All popular shells provide three main functions:

(a) Shells run programs.

(b) Shells manage input and output.

(c) Shells can be programmed.

Consider this sequence of shell commands:

```
$ grep lp /etc/passwd
lp:x:4:7:lp:/var/spool/lpd:
$ TZ=PST8PDT ; export TZ ; date ; TZ=EST5EDT
Sat Jul 28 02:10:05 PDT 2001
$ date
Sat Jul 28 05:10:14 EDT 2001
$ ls -l /etc > etc.listing
$ NAME=lp
$ if grep $NAME /etc/passwd
```

```
> then
>   echo hello | mail $NAME
> fi
lp:x:4:7:lp:/var/spool/lpd:
$
```

Running Programs

The commands grep, date, ls, echo, and mail are just regular programs written in C, compiled to machine language. The shell loads those programs into memory and runs them. Most people think of a shell as a program launcher.

Managing Input and Output

The shell does more than simply run programs. Using >, <, and |, the symbols for *input/output redirection*, a user tells the shell to attach the input and output of processes to disk files or to other processes.

Programming

The shell is also a programming language with variables and flow control (*if, while*, etc.). In the previous example, we see two uses of variables. First, the TZ variable is set to a string that represents the time-zone on the west coast of the U.S. That value is used by the date command when it prints the current date and time.

Later in the example, we see an *if..then* statement. The variable NAME is set to the string "lp". The value of that variable, $NAME, is used in the grep command, and the result of the command is tested by *if*. If the command succeeds in its search for the string "lp" in the file /etc/passwd, the shell executes the command echo hello | mail $NAME; otherwise control skips to the next command.

In this chapter, we look at how the shell runs programs. In later chapters, we shall look at variables and control flow in the shell and at input and output redirection.

8.4   HOW THE SHELL RUNS PROGRAMS

The shell prints a prompt, you type a command, the shell runs the command, and then the shell prints a prompt—over and over again. What is happening behind the scenes?

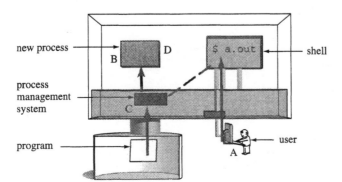

FIGURE 8.4

A user asks a shell to run a program.

A shell follows these steps, which describe the main loop of the shell (see Figure 8.4):

A. The user types a.out.

B. The shell creates a new process to run the program.

C. The shell loads the program from the disk into the process.

D. The program runs in its process until it is done.

8.4.1   The Main Loop of a Shell

The shell consists of the following loop:

```
while ( ! end_of_input )
    get command
    execute command
    wait for command to finish
```

Consider this typical interaction with the shell:

```
$ ls
Chap.bak   Story08.tr   chap08.ps      chap08.tr   outline.08
Makefile   chap08       chap08.short   code        pix
$ ps
  PID TTY          TIME CMD
29182 pts/5     00:00:00 bash
29183 pts/5     00:00:00 ps
$
```

We represent the sequence of events with the time line shown in Figure 8.5. In the figure, time moves from left to right. The shell is represented by the box marked "sh"; it begins at the left side of the picture and moves rightward as time passes. The shell reads the string "ls" from the user. The shell creates a new process, then runs the ls program in that process, and waits for the process to finish.

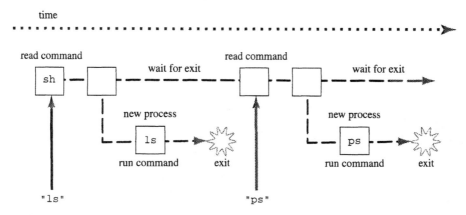

FIGURE 8.5

A time line of the main loop of the shell.

The shell then reads a new line of input, creates a new process, runs the program in that process, and waits for that process to exit.

When the shell detects end of input, it exits.

To write a shell, we need to learn how to

1. Run a program
2. Create a process
3. Wait for exit()

When we know those three skills, we can put them together and write our own shell.

8.4.2 Question 1: How Does a Program Run a Program?

Answer: The program calls execvp.

Figure 8.6 shows how a program runs a program. For example, to run ls -la, a program calls execvp("ls", arglist) where arglist is an array of the command-line strings. The kernel loads the program into memory from the disk. The command-line arguments ls and -la are passed to the program, and the program runs. In short,

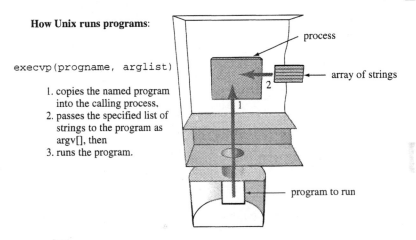

How Unix runs programs:

execvp(progname, arglist)

1. copies the named program into the calling process,
2. passes the specified list of strings to the program as argv[], then
3. runs the program.

process

array of strings

program to run

FIGURE 8.6

execvp copies into memory and runs a program.

1. Program calls execvp
2. Kernel loads program from disk into the process
3. Kernel copies arglist into the process
4. Kernel calls main(argc, argv)

Here is a complete program that runs ls -l:

```
/* exec1.c - shows how easy it is for a program to run a program
 */

main()
{
        char    *arglist[3];
```

```
        arglist[0] = "ls";
        arglist[1] = "-l";
        arglist[2] = 0 ;
        printf("* * * About to exec ls -l\n");
        execvp( "ls" , arglist );
        printf("* * * ls is done. bye\n");
    }
```

execvp takes two arguments: the name of the program to run and an array of command-line arguments for that program. The array of command-line arguments appears as argv[] when the program runs. Notice we set the first string to the name of the program. Notice also that the array must have a null pointer as the last element.

We compile and run the program:

```
$ cc exec1.c -o exec1
$ ./exec1
* * * About to exec ls -l
total 28
drwxr-x---    2 bruce     users        1024 Jul 14 21:02 a
drwxr-x---    3 bruce     users        1024 Jul 16 03:16 c
-rw-r--r--    1 bruce     users           0 Jul 14 21:03 y
$
```

Where is the Second Message?   Look at the code again. The program announces it is about to exec the ls program, execs ls, and then announces when exec finishes. Where is the second message?

A program runs in a process—a chunk of memory and supporting kernel data structures. Thus, execvp loads the program from the disk into a process so it can run, but into which process? Here is the weird part: The kernel loads the new program into the current process, *replacing* the code and data of that process.

execvp is *Like a Brain Transplant*   "I'd like to solve this problem using the brain of Albert Einstein, and after that I'm going to do the twist," one might wish. One way to do that is to remove your brain and put the brain of Albert Einstein into your head. The thoughts and analytic skills inside your head are now those of Albert Einstein. The plan to do the twist[1] though, vanished with your original brain.

The exec system call[2] clears out the machine-language code of the current program from the current process, then, in the now empty process, puts the code of the program named in the exec call, and then runs that new program. exec changes the memory allocation of the process to fit the space requirements of the new program. The process is the same, the contents are new.

---

[1] and all other items on your to-do list
[2] execvp is one of a family of related functions all of which use the system call execve. They collectively are called exec.

Summary of Execvp()

execvp	
PURPOSE	Execute a file, with PATH searching
INCLUDE	#include <unistd.h>
USAGE	result = execvp(const char *file, const char *argv[])
ARGS	file name of file to execute argv array of strings
RETURNS	-1 if error

execvp loads the program specified by *file* into the current process and attempts to execute it. execvp passes to the program the list of strings in the NULL-terminated array *argv*. execvp searches for *file* in the directories specified in the PATH environment variable.

execvp does not return if it succeeds. The current program is removed from the process, the new program executes in the current process.

Example 2: A Prompting Shell   We now know enough to write a first version of a shell. We know how to run a program and pass it command-line arguments. This first shell prompts the user for a program name and arguments and then runs the program. We call this program psh1.c, which stands for a *prompting shell*:

```
/*      prompting shell version 1
 *              Prompts for the command and its arguments.
 *              Builds the argument vector for the call to execvp.
 *              Uses execvp(), and never returns.
 */

#include        <stdio.h>
#include        <signal.h>
#include        <string.h>

#define MAXARGS         20                      /* cmdline args */
#define ARGLEN          100                     /* token length */

int main()
{
        char    *arglist[MAXARGS+1];            /* an array of ptrs    */
        int     numargs;                        /* index into array    */
        char    argbuf[ARGLEN];                 /* read stuff here     */
        char    *makestring();                  /* malloc etc          */
        numargs = 0;
        while ( numargs < MAXARGS )
```

```
            {
                    printf("Arg[%d]? ", numargs);
                    if ( fgets(argbuf, ARGLEN, stdin) && *argbuf != '\n' )
                            arglist[numargs++] = makestring(argbuf);
                    else
                    {
                            if ( numargs > 0 ){              /* any args?   */
                                    arglist[numargs]=NULL;   /* close list  */
                                    execute( arglist );      /* do it       */
                                    numargs = 0;             /* and reset   */
                            }
                    }
            }
            return 0;
    }

    int execute( char *arglist[] )
    /*
     *      use execvp to do it
     */
    {
            execvp(arglist[0], arglist);                /* do it */
            perror("execvp failed");
            exit(1);
    }

    char * makestring( char *buf )
    /*
     * trim off newline and create storage for the string
     */
    {
            char    *cp, *malloc();

            buf[strlen(buf)-1] = '\0';                  /* trim newline */
            cp = malloc( strlen(buf)+1 );               /* get memory   */
            if ( cp == NULL ){                          /* or die       */
                    fprintf(stderr,"no memory\n");
                    exit(1);
            }
            strcpy(cp, buf);                            /* copy chars   */
            return cp;                                  /* return ptr   */
    }
```

psh1.c is our first draft of a Unix shell. psh1 asks for each string separately, first the program name then each argument in turn. The code consists of two steps: (1) Build the arglist, string by string, and add NULL to the end; (2) pass the string arglist[0] and the array arglist to execvp. (See Figure 8.7.)

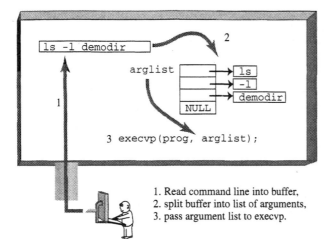

1. Read command line into buffer,
2. split buffer into list of arguments,
3. pass argument list to execvp.

FIGURE 8.7

Building an arglist from one string.

We compile and run the program:

```
$ cc psh1.c -o psh1
$ ./psh1
Arg[0]? ls
Arg[1]? -1
Arg[2]? demodir
Arg[3]?
total 2
drwxr-x---    2 bruce     users          1024 Jul 14 21:02 a
drwxr-x---    3 bruce     users          1024 Jul 16 03:16 c
-rw-r--r--    1 bruce     users             0 Jul 14 21:03 y
$
```

How'd It Go? The program works OK, but as we expected, execvp replaces the code of the shell with the code of the command, then exits, preventing our shell from looping back to accept another command. A user must run the shell again to run another command.

How can a shell run a command and still be around to run another command? A solution is to create a new process and have that new process execute the program.

8.4.3 Question 2: How Do We Get a New Process?

Answer: A process calls fork to replicate itself.

Usage: fork();   /* takes no arguments */

Explanation of fork

Let us continue with the problem of thinking with Einstein's brain. As we saw earlier, transplanting Einstein's brain into your head puts Einstein's thoughts into your head, but precludes any more of your thoughts being in your head.

One solution is to duplicate yourself with some sort of three-dimensional photocopier that identifies every atom in your body and assembles an exact atom-for-atom replica. Once you have created that replica, put Einstein's brain into *its* head. That replica can now solve that tricky problem using Einstein's brain, and you can continue with your own plans and thoughts. At one stage in your life, there is one of you, then after you press the big green button on the replicator, there are two of you. This split in your being is like a fork in the road. At first there is one road, and now there are two, just like that.

Before fork:

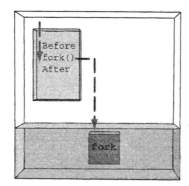

After fork:

parent process   child process

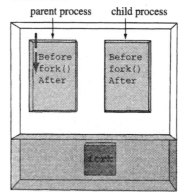

The new process contains the same code and data as the parent process.

FIGURE 8.8

fork() makes a copy of a process.

That is exactly what the fork system call does. Figure 8.8 shows the system before and after the call to fork. The process contains the program and a current location in the program. The process then calls fork. Control passes into the fork code inside the kernel. The kernel does this:

(a) Allocates a new chunk of memory and kernel data structures
(b) Copies the original process into the new process
(c) Adds the new process to the set of running processes
(d) Returns control back to *both* processes

After you press the *Go* button on the replicator, there are two of you, both physically identical, both in the middle of the same thought, but each a separate being able to go your (its?) own way. Similarly, after a process calls fork, there are two if it, both digitally identical, both in the middle of the same code, but each a separate process able to go its (her?) own way. Let us look at some sample programs.

Example: forkdemo1.c—Creating a New Process

forkdemo1.c contains two print statements, one before fork is called and one after fork is called:

```
/*  forkdemo1.c
 *      shows how fork creates two processes, distinguishable
 *      by the different return values from fork()
 */

#include        <stdio.h>
main()
{
        int     ret_from_fork, mypid;

        mypid = getpid();                               /* who am i?        */
        printf("Before: my pid is %d\n", mypid);   /* tell the world   */

        ret_from_fork = fork();

        sleep(1);
        printf("After: my pid is %d, fork() said %d\n",
                        getpid(), ret_from_fork);
}
```

If this were a normal program, you would see two lines of output, one for each print statement. When it runs, though, we see

```
$ cc forkdemo1.c -o forkdemo1
$ ./forkdemo1
Before: my pid is 4170
After: my pid is 4170, fork() said 4171
$ After: my pid is 4171, fork() said 0
```

We see three lines of output, one Before: message and two After: messages. Process 4170 prints a Before: message, and it prints an After: message—nothing odd there. The other After: message is printed by process 4171. Notice that 4171 did *not* print a Before: message. Why not? The close-up picture of user space presented in Figure 8.9 shows what is happening before and after 4170 calls fork.

Before fork:

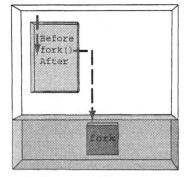

One flow of control enters the
fork kernel code.

After fork:

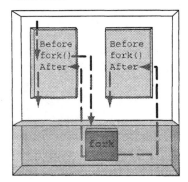

Two flows of control return from
fork kernel code.

FIGURE 8.9

The child executes the code after fork().

The kernel creates process 4171 by replicating process 4170, copying the code and the *current line* in the code into the new process. The *current line* is indicated in the figure by the arrow head moving down through the code. The new process, 4171, begins executing right as fork returns, not at the beginning. Therefore, 4171, picking up in the middle of the game, does not print a Before: message.

Example: `forkdemo2.c`—Children Creating Processes

The child process begins its life, not at the start of main but at the return from fork. Predict how many lines of output this program will produce:

```
/* forkdemo2.c - shows how child processes pick up at the return
 *               from fork() and can execute any code they like,
 *               even fork().  Predict number of lines of output.
 */

main()
{
        printf("my pid is %d\n", getpid() );
        fork();
        fork();
        fork();
        printf("my pid is %d\n", getpid() );
}
```

Compile and run it now to test your prediction. How'd it go?

Example: `forkdemo3.c`—Distinguishing Parent from Child

In forkdemo1.c, we saw process 4170 call fork and create a child process with PID 4171. Both processes ran the same code at the same line with all the same data and process attributes. How can a process determine if it is the parent process or if it is the child process?

The two processes are not identical. The output from forkdemo1.c shows that fork returns different values to the different processes. In the child process, fork returns a value of 0, and in the parent process, fork returns a value of 4171. Checking the return value from fork is the easiest way for a process to determine if it is the child or the parent.

Our next example, forkdemo3.c, shows how a single program uses the return value from fork to print different messages:

```
/*  forkdemo3.c - shows how the return value from fork()
 *                allows a process to determine whether
 *                it is a child or process
 */

#include         <stdio.h>

main()
{
        int      fork_rv;
```

```
        printf("Before: my pid is %d\n", getpid());

        fork_rv = fork();                /* create new process   */

        if ( fork_rv == -1 )             /* check for error      */
                perror("fork");

        else if ( fork_rv == 0 )
                printf("I am the child.  my pid=%d\n", getpid());
        else
                printf("I am the parent. my child is %d\n", fork_rv);
}
```

Here is a sample run:

```
$ ./forkdemo3
Before: my pid is 5931
I am the parent. my child is 5932
I am the child.  my pid=5932
$
```

Summary of fork

fork	
PURPOSE	Create a process
INCLUDE	#include <unistd.h>
USAGE	pid_t result = fork(void)
ARGS	none
RETURNS	-1 if error 0 to child process pid pid of child to parent process

The fork system call is exactly what we need to solve the one-command-only problem in our shell. Using fork, we can create a new process, and we can distinguish the new process from the original process. The new process can then call execvp to run whatever program the user requests.

We now understand two of the three skills needed to build a shell. We know how to create a new process (fork), and we know how to run a program (execvp). The last part is telling the parent to wait until the child process finishes executing the command.

8.4.4 Question 3: How Does the Parent Wait for the Child to exit?

Answer: A process calls wait to wait for a child to finish.

Usage: pid = wait(&status);

Explanation of wait()

The wait system call does two things. First, wait pauses the calling process until a child process finishes running. Second, wait retrieves the value the child process had passed to exit.

Figure 8.10 shows how wait works. Note that time flows from left to right in the figure. The parent process begins at the left and calls fork. The kernel constructs a child process, depicted here as another little box, and starts it running concurrently with its parent. The parent calls wait. The kernel suspends that process until the child finishes running. The parent is paused for the stretch of the diagram marked wait.

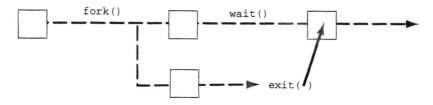

FIGURE 8.10

wait pauses the parent until the child finishes.

Sooner or later, the child process finishes its tasks and calls exit(n), passing as an argument a number between 0 and 255.

When the child calls exit, the kernel wakes up the parent and delivers the value the child passed to exit. This notification and transfer of the exit value is represented by the arrow leading from the parentheses in exit to the parent process. Thus, wait performs two operations: notification and communication.

Example: waitdemo1.c—Notification

waitdemo1.c shows how the call to exit in a child process triggers a return from wait in its parent:

```
/* waitdemo1.c - shows how parent pauses until child finishes
 */

#include         <stdio.h>

#define DELAY    2

main()
{
        int  newpid;
        void child_code(), parent_code();
```

```
            printf("before: mypid is %d\n", getpid());

            if ( (newpid = fork()) == -1 )
                    perror("fork");
            else if ( newpid == 0 )
                    child_code(DELAY);
            else
                    parent_code(newpid);
}
/*
 * new process takes a nap and then exits
 */
void child_code(int delay)
{
            printf("child %d here. will sleep for %d seconds\n", getpid(),
               delay);
            sleep(delay);
            printf("child done. about to exit\n");
            exit(17);
}
/*
 * parent waits for child then prints a message
 */
void parent_code(int childpid)
{
            int wait_rv;                /* return value from wait() */
            wait_rv = wait(NULL);
            printf("done waiting for %d. Wait returned: %d\n", childpid,
               wait_rv);
}
```

In action, waitdemo1.c looks like this:

```
$ ./waitdemo1
before: mypid is 10328
child 10329 here. will sleep for 2 seconds
child done. about to exit
done waiting for 10329. Wait returned: 10329
```

Run this program and adjust the time to see that the parent always waits until the child calls exit. Figure 8.11 shows flow of control and transfer of data between two processes. In the parent, control flow starts at the top and then blocks at wait. In the child, control flow starts in the middle of main, continues to the child_code function, and ends with the call to exit. The call to exit by the child is like a signal that wakes up the parent.

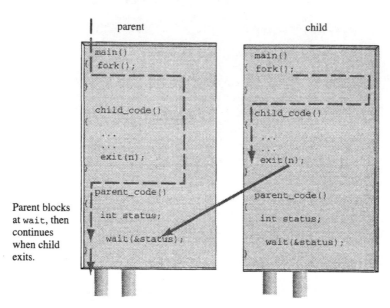

FIGURE 8.11

Control flow and communication with `wait()`.

Conclusions from `waitdemo1.c`   This program shows two important facts about `wait`:

1. `wait` *blocks the calling program until a child finishes*

   In this sample run, the parent process is blocked until the child process calls `exit`. This fact allows two processes to synchronize their actions. A parent process might `fork` a child process to do some work, such as sorting a file. The parent has to wait until that task is completed before processing the file. The pair of system calls `exit` and `wait` is one method processes may use to synchronize these tasks.

2. `wait` *returns the PID of the finishing process*

   In this sample run, the return value from `wait` is the PID of the child that called `exit`. As we saw in `forkdemo2.c`, a process can create several child processes. Consider a program that consolidates data from two different remote databases. The program could `fork` two processes, one to connect to and extract data from one database, and the other process to retrieve data from the other database. The extract from the first database may require one sort of postprocessing, while the extract from the second database may not require any postprocessing.

   The return value from `wait` tells the parent which task finished, so it can continue with the processing effectively.

Example: `waitdemo2.c`—communication

One purpose of `wait` is to notify a parent *that* a child process finished running. The other purpose of `wait` is to tell the parent *how* a child process finished.

Success, Failure, and Death   A process ends in one of three ways. First, a process can succeed at its task. The Unix convention is that successful programs call `exit(0)` or return 0 from `main`.

Second, a program can fail at its task. For example, a program might exit early if it runs out of memory. The Unix convention is that programs that encounter errors call exit with a nonzero value. The programmer assigns various exit values for various sorts of errors and documents these codes in the manual page.

Finally, a program might be killed by a *signal*. (See Chapters 6 and 7.) The signal could arise from the keyboard, from an interval timer, from the kernel, or from another process. Usually, a signal that is neither ignored nor caught kills the process.

wait returns to the parent the PID of the child process that finished. How does the parent know if the child succeeded, failed, or died?

The answer is in the argument to wait. The parent calls wait with the address of an integer variable, and the kernel stores in that integer the termination status of the child. If the child calls exit, the kernel puts the exit value into the integer. If the child is killed, the kernel puts the signal number into the integer. The integer consists of three regions—eight bits for exit value, seven bits for signal number, and one bit to indicate a core dump. Figure 8.12 illustrates the three parts of the child's status value.

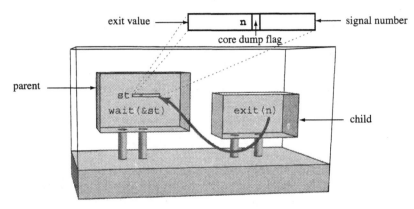

FIGURE 8.12

The child status value has three parts.

Our next example, waitdemo2.c, based on waitdemo1.c, displays the status of the finished child:

```
/* waitdemo2.c - shows how parent gets child status
 */

#include          <stdio.h>

#define DELAY   5

main()
{
        int  newpid;
        void child_code(), parent_code();

        printf("before: mypid is %d\n", getpid());

        if ( (newpid = fork()) == -1 )
                perror("fork");
        else if ( newpid == 0 )
                child_code(DELAY);
```

```
                    else
                            parent_code(newpid);
        }
        /*
         * new process takes a nap and then exits
         */
        void child_code(int delay)
        {
                printf("child %d here. will sleep for %d seconds\n", getpid(),
                    delay);
                sleep(delay);
                printf("child done. about to exit\n");
                exit(17);
        }
        /*
         * parent waits for child then prints a message
         */
        void parent_code(int childpid)
        {
                int wait_rv;                /* return value from wait() */
                int child_status;
                int high_8, low_7, bit_7;

                wait_rv = wait(&child_status);
                printf("done waiting for %d. Wait returned: %d\n", childpid,
                    wait_rv);

                high_8 = child_status >> 8;     /* 1111 1111 0000 0000 */
                low_7  = child_status & 0x7F;   /* 0000 0000 0111 1111 */
                bit_7  = child_status & 0x80;   /* 0000 0000 1000 0000 */
                printf("status: exit=%d, sig=%d, core=%d\n", high_8, low_7,
                    bit_7);
        }
```

First, we allow waitdemo2 to exit normally. The exit status is copied from child to parent:

```
$ ./waitdemo2
before: mypid is 10855
child 10856 here. will sleep for 5 seconds
child done. about to exit
done waiting for 10856. Wait returned: 10856
status: exit=17, sig=0, core=0
$
```

Next, we run waitdemo2 in the background and use kill (see Chapter 7) to send SIGTERM to the child:

```
$ ./waitdemo2 &
$ before: mypid is 10857
child 10858 here. will sleep for 5 seconds
kill 10858
$ done waiting for 10858. Wait returned: 10858
status: exit=0, sig=15, core=0
```

Summary of wait()

	wait
PURPOSE	Wait for process termination
INCLUDE	#include <sys/types.h> #include <sys/wait.h>
USAGE	pid_t result = wait(int *statusptr)
ARGS	statusptr child result
RETURNS	-1 if error, pid of terminated process
SEE ALSO	waitpid(2), wait3(2)

The wait system call suspends the calling process until termination status is available for one of its child processes. Termination status is either an exit value or a signal number. If one of its children has already exited or been killed, return is immediate. wait returns the PID of the terminated process. If *statusptr* is not NULL, wait copies into the integer pointed to by *statusptr* the exit status or signal number. These values may be examined using macros in <sys/wait.h>.

wait returns −1 if the calling process has no children and no uncollected termination-status values.

8.4.5   Summary: How the Shell Runs Programs

This section began with the question, "How does the shell run programs?" We now have the answer: The shell uses fork to create a new process. The shell then uses exec to run, in the new process, the program the user requests. Finally, the shell uses wait to wait until the new process finishes running the command. The wait system call also obtains from the kernel the exit status or signal number that tells how the child process terminated.

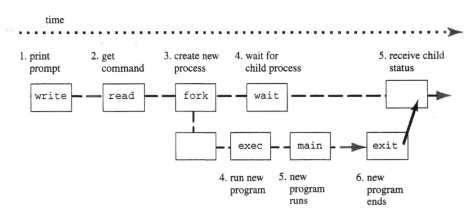

FIGURE 8.13

Shell loop with fork(), exec(), and wait().

Every Unix shell uses the model shown in Figure 8.13. We now combine these three system calls to write a real shell.

8.5   WRITING A SHELL: psh2.c

Figure 8.14 is a simplified flowchart of the operation of a Unix shell. Our next shell, psh2.c, incorporates the logic shown in the diagram:

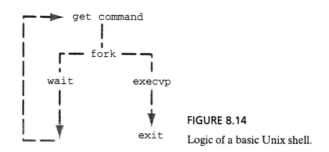

FIGURE 8.14

Logic of a basic Unix shell.

```
/**    prompting shell version 2
 **
 **                Solves the 'one-shot' problem of version 1
 **                    Uses execvp(), but fork()s first so that the
 **                    shell waits around to perform another command
 **                New problem: shell catches signals.  Run vi, press ^c.
 **/

#include        <stdio.h>
#include        <signal.h>

#define MAXARGS         20                              /* cmdline args */
#define ARGLEN          100                             /* token length */

main()
{
        char    *arglist[MAXARGS+1];         /* an array of ptrs   */
        int     numargs;                     /* index into array   */
        char    argbuf[ARGLEN];              /* read stuff here    */
        char    *makestring();               /* malloc etc         */

        numargs = 0;
        while ( numargs < MAXARGS )
        {
                printf("Arg[%d]? ", numargs);
                if ( fgets(argbuf, ARGLEN, stdin) && *argbuf != '\n' )
                        arglist[numargs++] = makestring(argbuf);
                else
                {
                        if ( numargs > 0 ){             /* any args?    */
                                arglist[numargs]=NULL;   /* close list   */
```

```
                        execute( arglist );        /* do it         */
                        numargs = 0;               /* and reset     */
                    }
                }
            }
            return 0;
    }
    execute( char *arglist[] )
    /*
     *      use fork and execvp and wait to do it
     */
    {
            int     pid, exitstatus;                 /* of child      */

            pid = fork();                            /* make new process */
            switch( pid ){
                    case -1:
                            perror("fork failed");
                            exit(1);
                    case 0:
                            execvp(arglist[0], arglist);        /* do it */
                            perror("execvp failed");
                            exit(1);
                    default:
                            while( wait(&exitstatus) != pid )
                                    ;
                            printf("child exited with status %d,%d\n",
                                        exitstatus>>8, exitstatus&0377);
            }
    }
    char *makestring( char *buf )
    /*
     * trim off newline and create storage for the string
     */
    {
            char    *cp, *malloc();

            buf[strlen(buf)-1] = '\0';               /* trim newline */
            cp = malloc( strlen(buf)+1 );            /* get memory    */
            if ( cp == NULL ){                       /* or die        */
                    fprintf(stderr,"no memory\n");
                    exit(1);
            }
            strcpy(cp, buf);                         /* copy chars    */
            return cp;                               /* return ptr    */
    }
```

We test psh2 to see if our changes to execute solve the one-command-only problem:

```
$ ./psh2
Arg[0]? ls
```

```
Arg[1]? -1
Arg[2]? demodir
Arg[3]?
total 2
drwxr-x---  2 bruce    users       1024 Jul 14 21:02 a
drwxr-x---  3 bruce    users       1024 Jul 16 03:16 c
-rw-r--r--  1 bruce    users          0 Jul 14 21:03 y
child exited with status 0,0
Arg[0]? ps
Arg[1]?
  PID TTY          TIME CMD
11616 pts/4     00:00:00 bash
11648 pts/4     00:00:00 psh2
11664 pts/4     00:00:00 ps
child exited with status 0,0
Arg[0]? psh1   Look! We can run psh1
Arg[1]?
Arg[0]? ps     This is the prompt from psh1!
Arg[1]?
  PID TTY          TIME CMD
11616 pts/4     00:00:00 bash
11648 pts/4     00:00:00 psh2
11683 pts/4     00:00:00 ps
child exited with status 0,0
Arg[0]? grep
Arg[1]? fred
Arg[2]? /etc/passwd
Arg[3]?
child exited with status 1,0
Arg[0]? press ^D here a few times
Arg[0]? Arg[0]? Arg[0]? exit
Arg[1]?
execvp failed: No such file or directory
child exited with status 1,0
Arg[0]? press ^C here
$
```

How'd We Do?

`psh2.c` works well. This new shell accepts a program name and a list of arguments, runs the command, reports the result, and loops back to accept and execute another program. `psh2.c` lacks the polish of regular shells, but it is a solid start.

Here are two improvements for the next release:

(a) Allow the user to quit by pressing Ctrl-D or by typing "exit".

(b) Allow the user to type all the arguments on one line.

We add these features to the version we work on in the next chapter. In that version, we add variables and some control flow to the shell, making the program into more of a programming language.

First, though, we need to correct a serious problem in psh2.c.

8.5.1 Signals and **psh2.c**

As we saw in our test drive, the only way out of psh2 is to press Ctrl-C. What happens if we press Ctrl-C when psh2 is waiting for the child process to finish? For example,

```
$ ./psh2
Arg[0]? tr
Arg[1]? [a-z]
Arg[2]? [A-Z]
Arg[3]?
hello
HELLO
now to press
NOW TO PRESS
Ctrl-Cpress ^C here
$
```

The child process ends, but our prompting shell does, too. The SIGINT generated by pressing Ctrl-C appears to have killed the process running tr and also the process running psh2. What happened?

Keyboard signals go to ALL attached processes The programs psh2 and tr are both connected to our terminal. (See Figure 8.15.) When you press the interrupt key, the tty driver tells the kernel to send SIGINT to *all* processes controlled by that terminal. tr dies. Our program, psh2 also dies even though it is waiting for its child process to terminate.

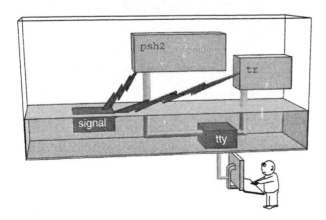

FIGURE 8.15

Keyboard signals go to all attached processes.

How can we prevent our shell from being killed when the user presses the interrupt or quit keys? This change is left as an exercise.

8.6   REFLECTION: PROGRAMMING WITH PROCESSES

We wanted to understand Unix processes, so we played with the ps command and learned how a shell uses fork, exec, exit, and wait to control processes and run programs.

Before we move on to the next chapter and ideas about adding variables and loops to our shell, consider this similarity between functions and processes.

execvp/exit are like call/return

call/return

A C program consists of lots of functions. One function can call another function and pass it a list of arguments. The called function performs some operations and returns a value. Each function has its own local variables, and the various functions communicate through this call/return system.

The model of functions with private data communicating by passing lists of arguments and returning values is the basis of structured programming. Unix encourages you to extend this model from functions within a program to the programs themselves. The model may be depicted as shown in Figure 8.16.

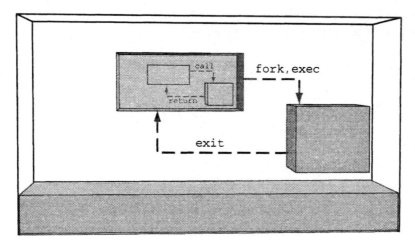

FIGURE 8.16

Calling functions and calling programs.

exec/exit

A C *program* can fork/exec another *program* and pass it a list of arguments. The called program performs some operations and can return a value using exit(n). The calling process can receive the exit value by using wait(&result). The exit value from the subprogram appears in bits 8–15 of the result.

The stack of calls is almost unlimited. A called function can call other functions, a fork/exec'd program can fork/exec other programs. Unix is designed to make creating new processes quick and easy. The fork/exec and exit/wait method for calling a program and returning a value is not just for shells. Unix applications are often designed as a set of programs running subprograms instead of as one big program containing lots of functions.

Arguments passed by exec must be strings. Limiting interprocess arguments to strings forces all communication with subprograms to use text as the data type for program arguments. In turn, this requirement of a text-based interface between programs enforces, almost by accident, cross-platform interoperability. The consequences have been dramatic.

Global variables and fork/exec

Global variables are bad, violating principles of encapsulation, leading to surprising side effects[3] and unmaintainable code. Sometimes the alternative is worse. How do you manage a bunch of values everyone needs access to without cluttering up argument lists, especially when you have to pass them down a few levels.

Unix provides a method of creating global values. The *environment* is a collection of string variables passed by value to child processes. Immune from side effects, the environment is a useful complement to the fork/exec, exit/wait mechanism. In the next chapter, we shall see how it works and how to use it.

8.7   EXTRA ABOUT EXIT AND EXEC

The main topics of this chapter are processes, fork, execvp, and wait, but we need to look at a few details about exit and exec.

8.7.1   Death of a Process: **exit** and **_exit**

A process can stop running by calling exit, sort of the opposite of fork. fork creates a process, and exit deletes a process. Well, almost.

exit flushes all streams, calls functions that have been registered with atexit and on_exit, and performs any other functions associated with exit for the current system, then calls the system call _exit. The system call _exit is the kernel operation that deallocates all the memory assigned to the process, closes all files the process has open, and frees all data structures the kernel needs to maintain a running process.

What happens to the argument passed to exit by the child process? That value, representing the last words of the process, is stored in the kernel until the parent of the process retrieves the value with the wait system call. If the parent is not currently waiting, the exit value remains in the kernel until the parent calls wait to be notified of the termination of the child, and receive its last words.

A process that has died but still has an uncollected exit value is called a *zombie* process. Many modern versions of ps list these processes as *defunct*.

---

[3]Some people say global variables cause warts.

Summary of `_exit()`

	_exit
PURPOSE	Terminate the current process
INCLUDE	`#include <unistd.h>` `#include <stdlib.h>`
USAGE	`void _exit(int status)`
ARGS	status return value
RETURNS	nothing
SEE ALSO	`atexit(3)`, `exit(3)`, `on_exit(3)`

The `_exit` system call terminates the current process and performs all required clean-up operations. These operations vary from one version of Unix to another, but all include the following:

(a) Close all file descriptors and directory descriptors

(b) Change the parent PID of all its children to the PID of *init*

(c) Notify the parent if it is running `wait` or `waitpid`

(d) Send the parent `SIGCHLD`

If a process exits before its children do, the children continue to run. They do not become orphans, instead, they are made children of the *init* process, sort of like wards of the state. Notice also that even if the parent has not called `wait`, the kernel notifies the parent of the event by sending `SIGCHLD`. The default action for `SIGCHLD`, though, is to be ignored. If you want your program to respond to this signal, you need to set a handler.

8.7.2   The `exec` Family

We used `execvp` in our shell and in our sample programs to show how a process can run programs. `execvp` is not a system call; it is a library function that uses the system call `execve` to invoke the kernel services. The *e* in `execve` stands for *environment*, so we defer discussion of that until the next chapter.

Other useful functions call `execve`. The following are some other members of the family:

```
execlp(file,argv0,argv1, ..., NULL)
```

`execlp` does not use an array of arguments as does `execvp`. Instead, the arguments to be passed to `main` as `argv[]`, are simply included as arguments to `execlp`. For example,

```
execlp("ls", "ls", "-a", "demodir", NULL);
```

runs the program ls with the specified arguments. execlp is useful when you know in advance the command and arguments you want to run. It is not useful in the shell, because you do not know how many arguments there will be until the user types a command line.

```
execl(fullpath, argv0, argv1, ..., NULL )
```

The *p* in execlp and execvp stands for *path*. These two functions search for the program specified as the first argument by looking in all directories listed in the environment variable called PATH. If you know the exact location of the file, you can specify the full path of the file as the first argument in execl. For example,

```
execl("/bin/ls", "ls", "-a", "demodir", NULL);
```

runs the program /bin/ls with the specified arguments. Specifying the location of the program is faster than using execlp, which has to search for the file in several directories. Specifying the exact location is also safer using than execlp. If the PATH variable contains the wrong list of directories, you may run the wrong version of the program.

```
execv(fullpath, arglist)
```

execv is just like execvp except it does not search for the file in the search PATH. The first argument has to be the exact path to the program to run. Using execv or execl with an explicit path to the program is more secure than relying on a safe list of directories in PATH, which can be more easily altered by malicious users.

SUMMARY

MAIN IDEAS

- Unix runs a program by loading the executable code into a process and running that code. A process is memory space and other system resources required to run a program.
- Each running program runs in its own process. A process has a unique process ID number, an owner, a size, and other properties.
- The fork system call creates a new process by making an almost exact replica of the calling process. The new process is called a child process.
- A program loads and executes a new program in the current process by calling a function in the exec family.
- A program can wait for a child process to terminate by calling wait
- A calling program can pass a list of strings to main in the new program. The new program can send back a small character value by calling exit.
- A Unix shell runs programs by calling fork, exec, and wait .

WHAT'S NEXT

The shell runs programs, but the shell also is a programming language. Next, we look at shell scripts and how to modify our shell to support scripts, control logic, and variables.

EXPLORATIONS

8.1 *parent vs. child* The return value from fork allows a process to determine if it is the parent or child process. What other technique can a process use?

8.2 Predict the output of this program:

```
main()
{
        int     n;

        for(n = 0; n<10 ; n++ )
        {
                printf("my pid = %d, n = %d\n", getpid(), n);
                sleep(1);
                if ( fork() != 0 )        /* what if these two    */
                        exit(0);          /* lines were removed?  */
        }
}
```

How would the output change if the two lines with comments were removed?

8.3 psh2.c uses a fixed-size array to hold the argument list. How would you modify the program so there is no limit on the number of arguments the user can enter for a command? Is this change necessary? That is, does Unix impose a limit on the number or length of arguments exec will accept?

8.4 fork *and file descriptors* Consider this code:

```
main()
{
        int     fd;
        int     pid;
        char    msg1[] = "Testing 1 2 3 ..\n";
        char    msg2[] = "Hello, hello\n";

        if ( (fd = creat("testfile", 0644)) == -1 )
                return 0;
        if ( write(fd, msg1, strlen(msg1)) == -1 )
                return 0;

        if ( (pid = fork())  == -1 )
                return 0;
        if ( write(fd, msg2, strlen(msg2)) == -1 )
                return 0;
        close(fd);
        return 1;
}
```

Test this program. After the call to fork, both processes have a file descriptor set to the same current position in the output file. How many messages appear in the file? What does the number of lines tell you about file descriptors and connections to files?

8.5 fork *and standard I/O* Consider this code:

```
#include <stdio.h>

main()
```

```
{
        FILE *fp;
        int   pid;
        char  msg1[] = "Testing 1 2 3 ..\n";
        char  msg2[] = "Hello, hello\n";
        if ( (fp = fopen("testfile2", "w")) == NULL )
                return 0;
        fprintf(fp, "%s", msg1);

        if ( (pid = fork())  == -1 )
                return 0;
        fprintf(fp, "%s", msg2);
        fclose(fp);
        return 1;
}
```

Test this program. How many messages appear in the file? Explain the results. Compare this program to the output of forkdemo1.c in the text.

8.6 *Background processing* Compile and run this program:

```
main()
{
        int   i;

        if ( fork() != 0 )
                exit(0);
        for ( i=1 ; i<=10 ; i++ ){
                printf("still here..\n");
                sleep(i);
        }
        return 0;
}
```

Explain what this program does and how it works. Unix shells allow users to run programs *in the background*. How is this program similar to a background process?

8.7 *Errors with* exec If exec fails in the child process, the program calls exit. Calling exit seems extreme. Why not just return from the function with an error code ?

PROGRAMMING EXERCISES

8.8 *Waiting for two children* Expand the code in waitdemo1.c so that the parent creates two children and then waits until both children exit.

Expand your solution further so the program accepts an integer as a command-line argument. The program then creates that number of child processes and assigns each child a random number of seconds to sleep. Finally, the parent process reports as each child exits.

8.9 *Using* SIGCHLD Write a program to help learn about using SIGCHLD. Modify waitdemo2.c to set a handler for SIGCHLD and then execute a loop that prints "waiting" once a second. When its child exits, the parent should print a message, report the exit status of the child, and exit.

8.10 *Multiple* SIGCHLDs Write a program that takes as an argument an integer and then creates that many child processes. All the children sleep for five seconds, then exit. The parent process sets a signal handler for SIGCHLD then enters a loop printing a message once a second. The handler calls wait and prints out the process ID of the child and increments a counter. When the counter reaches the original number of children, the program exits. Test this program for various numbers of children. The program is likely to miss some children as the number gets larger. Can you explain why it misses some signals? Is there a solution?

8.11 Modify psh2.c to exit when the user types the command "exit" or when the program sees end of file.

8.12 *Signals and shells* Standard Unix shells do not die when the user sends the interrupt or quit signal when the child is running. How does a standard Unix shell respond to these signals when reading a command line? Modify psh2.c to behave like a regular shell.

# CHAPTER 9

A Programmable Shell Shell Variables and the Environment

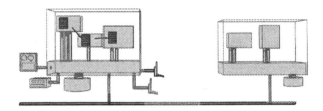

OBJECTIVES

Ideas and Skills

- A Unix shell is a programming language
- What is a shell script? How does a shell process a script?
- How do shell control structures work? `exit(0)` = success
- Shell variables: why and how
- What is the environment? How does it work?

System Calls and Functions

- `exit`
- `getenv`

Commands

- `env`

9.1   SHELL PROGRAMMING

A Unix shell runs programs *and* is itself a programming language. Shell programs, called *shell scripts*, are an essential part of Unix; the Unix boot procedure and many administrative programs use shell scripts. In this chapter, we begin by exploring the programming features of the shell, then we add some of those features to the shell we wrote in the last chapter. In particular, we add an *if..then* control structure, local variables, and global variables.

9.2   SHELL SCRIPTS: WHAT AND WHY?

A Unix shell is an interpreter for a programming language. This interpreter interprets commands from the keyboard and also interprets sequences of commands stored in *shell scripts*.

9.2.1   A Shell Script Is a Batch of Commands

A shell script is a file that contains a batch of commands. Running a script means executing each command in the file. You can use a shell script to perform several commands with a single request. Here is an example:

```
# this is called script0
# it runs some commands
ls
echo the current date/time is
date
echo my name is
whoami
```

The first two lines are comments; the shell ignores lines that start with the # character. The rest of this script consists of commands. The shell executes the commands one by one until end of file or until the shell finds an `exit` command.

Running a Shell Script   You can run a shell script by passing its name as an argument to the shell:

```
$ sh script0
script0  script1  script2  script3
the current date/time is
Sun Jul 29 23:29:49 EDT 2001
my name is
bruce
$
```

Or you can set the executable attribute of the file and simply type the name of the script:

```
$ chmod +x script0
$ script0
script0  script1  script2  script3
```

```
the current date/time is
Sun Jul 29 23:31:23 EDT 2001
my name is
bruce
$
```

You only need to use chmod once for a script. The execute bit remains set until you change it. This second method, marking the file as executable and invoking the script by name, is the easier way. Marking a script as executable makes the script a command, just like any system command or program you write.

Which Shell Are We Using? We are studying and writing scripts that use the syntax of the original Unix shell, sh, called the *Bourne Shell*, named for the person who wrote it. Many shells have been written over the years, each with different features or syntax. The tiny subset of syntax we shall study is common to several shells, including sh, bash, and ksh.

Programming Features of sh: Variables, I/O, and If..Then

Shell scripts are real programs. Notice the features in script2:

```
#!/bin/sh
# script2: a real program with variables, input,
#          and control flow

BOOK=$HOME/phonebook.data
echo find what name in phonebook
read NAME
if grep $NAME $BOOK > /tmp/pb.tmp
then
        echo Entries for $NAME
        cat /tmp/pb.tmp
else
        echo No entries for $NAME
fi
rm /tmp/pb.tmp
```

Here is script2 in action:

```
$ ./script2
find what name in phonebook
dave
Entries for dave
dave    432-6546
$ ./script2
find what name in phonebook
fran
No entries for fran
$ cat $HOME/phonebook.data
ann     222-3456
```

```
bob      323-2222
carla    123-4567
dave     432-6546
eloise   567-9876
$
```

More than a batch of commands, this script also includes the following:

variables

The shell has variables. In `script2`, we set variables called BOOK and NAME, and we use them later in the script. Use the $ prefix to retrieve the value stored in a variable. Variables do not have to be upper case, I just use that convention.

user input

The `read` command tells the shell to read strings from standard input. You can use `read` to make scripts interactive and also to get values from files or pipes.

control

This example shows the *if..then..else..fi* control structure of the shell. Other shell control structures include *while, case,* and *for.*

environment

This script uses a variable called HOME. HOME contains the path to your home directory. HOME is set by the `login` program and is available to all descendants of your log-in shell. HOME is one of several *environment variables* that allow users to record personalized settings that affect the behavior of various programs. For example, the TZ variable records the current time zone. Setting TZ to `"EST5EDT"`, for example, tells programs that use `ctime`, such as `date` and `ls -l`, to display times for U.S. eastern time. We look at the role and structure of the environment later in the chapter.

Improving Our Shell

In the last chapter, we wrote a shell that uses `fork`, `execvp`, and `wait` to create processes and run commands. In this chapter, we make several improvements to our shell. First, we add command-line parsing, so that the user can type the command and all the arguments on a single line. Next, we add an *if..then* structure to the shell, and finally we add local and environment variables.

9.3   smsh1—COMMAND-LINE PARSING

The first improvement to our shell is to add command-line parsing. This version is called `smsh1.c`. The user may now type a single line, such as

```
find /home -name core -mtime +3 -print
```

and the program splits that command line into an array of strings, ready to be passed to `execvp`. The program logic of `smsh1.c` is shown in Figure 9.1. Improvements from psh2.c include splitting the command line into arguments; ignoring SIGINT and SIGQUIT in the shell, but restoring their default action in the child; and allowing the user to exit by pressing the end-of-file indicator, Ctrl-D.

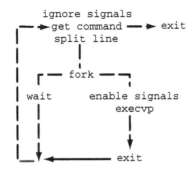

FIGURE 9.1

A shell with signals, exit, and parsing.

The main function of the shell is

```c
int main()
{
        char    *cmdline, *prompt, **arglist;
        int     result;
        void    setup();

        prompt = DFL_PROMPT ;
        setup();

        while ( (cmdline = next_cmd(prompt, stdin)) != NULL ){
                if ( (arglist = splitline(cmdline)) != NULL  ){
                        result = execute(arglist);
                        freelist(arglist);
                }
                free(cmdline);
        }
        return 0;
}
```

These three functions do the work:

next_cmd

next_cmd reads the next command from an input stream. It calls malloc to accept command lines of any length. It returns NULL at end of file.

splitline

splitline splits a string into an array of words and returns that array. It calls malloc to accept command lines with any number of arguments. The array is terminated with a NULL pointer.

execute

execute uses fork, execvp, and wait to run the command. execute returns the termination status of the command.

smsh1 is built from three files: smsh1.c, splitline.c, and execute.c. We compile them and test smsh1:

```
$ cc smsh1.c splitline.c execute.c -o smsh1
$ ./smsh1
> ps -f
UID          PID  PPID  C STIME TTY           TIME CMD
bruce      23203 23199  0 Jul29 pts/4     00:00:00 bash
bruce      25383 23203  0 08:23 pts/4     00:00:00 ./smsh1
bruce      25385 25383  0 08:23 pts/4     00:00:00 ps -f
> press Ctrl-D here
$
```

Notice how ps -f is a child of ./smsh1, which is a child process of bash. Here is the code to smsh1.c:

```
/**  smsh1.c   small-shell version 1
 **            first really useful version after prompting shell
 **            this one parses the command line into strings
 **            uses fork, exec, wait, and ignores signals
 **/

#include       <stdio.h>
#include       <stdlib.h>
#include       <unistd.h>
#include       <signal.h>
#include       "smsh.h"

#define DFL_PROMPT      "> "

int main()
{
        char    *cmdline, *prompt, **arglist;
        int     result;
        void    setup();

        prompt = DFL_PROMPT ;
        setup();

        while ( (cmdline = next_cmd(prompt, stdin)) != NULL ){
                if ( (arglist = splitline(cmdline)) != NULL  ){
                        result = execute(arglist);
                        freelist(arglist);
                }
                free(cmdline);
        }
        return 0;
}
```

```
void setup()
/*
 * purpose: initialize shell
 * returns: nothing. calls fatal() if trouble
 */
{
        signal(SIGINT,  SIG_IGN);
        signal(SIGQUIT, SIG_IGN);
}

void fatal(char *s1, char *s2, int n)
{
        fprintf(stderr,"Error: %s,%s\n", s1, s2);
        exit(n);
}
```

Here is the code to execute.c:

```
/* execute.c - code used by small shell to execute commands */

#include         <stdio.h>
#include         <stdlib.h>
#include         <unistd.h>
#include         <signal.h>
#include         <sys/wait.h>

int execute(char *argv[])
/*
 * purpose: run a program passing it arguments
 * returns: status returned via wait, or -1 on error
 *  errors: -1 on fork() or wait() errors
 */
{
        int     pid ;
        int     child_info = -1;

        if ( argv[0] == NULL )             /* nothing succeeds     */
                return 0;

        if ( (pid = fork())  == -1 )
                perror("fork");
        else if ( pid == 0 ){
                signal(SIGINT, SIG_DFL);
                signal(SIGQUIT, SIG_DFL);
                execvp(argv[0], argv);
                perror("cannot execute command");
                exit(1);
        }
        else {
                if ( wait(&child_info) == -1 )
                        perror("wait");
        }
        return child_info;
}
```

Here is the code to `splitline.c`:

```c
/* splitline.c - commmand reading and parsing functions for smsh
 *
 *      char *next_cmd(char *prompt, FILE *fp) - get next command
 *      char **splitline(char *str);            - parse a string
 */

#include         <stdio.h>
#include         <stdlib.h>
#include         <string.h>
#include         "smsh.h"

char * next_cmd(char *prompt, FILE *fp)
/*
 * purpose: read next command line from fp
 * returns: dynamically allocated string holding command line
 *  errors: NULL at EOF (not really an error)
 *          calls fatal from emalloc()
 *   notes: allocates space in BUFSIZ chunks.
 */
{
        char    *buf ;                          /* the buffer       */
        int     bufspace = 0;                   /* total size       */
        int     pos = 0;                        /* current position */
        int     c;                              /* input char       */

        printf("%s", prompt);                           /* prompt user   */
        while( ( c = getc(fp)) != EOF ) {
                /* need space? */
                if( pos+1 >= bufspace ){                /* 1 for \0      */
                        if ( bufspace == 0 )            /* y: 1st time   */
                                buf = emalloc(BUFSIZ);
                        else                            /* or expand     */
                                buf = erealloc(buf,bufspace+BUFSIZ);
                        bufspace += BUFSIZ;             /* update size   */
                }

                /* end of command? */
                if ( c == '\n' )
                        break;

                /* no, add to buffer */
                buf[pos++] = c;
        }
        if ( c == EOF && pos == 0 )             /* EOF and no input  */
                return NULL;                    /* say so            */
        buf[pos] = '\0';
        return buf;
}

/**
```

```
**      splitline ( parse a line into an array of strings )
**/
#define is_delim(x) ((x)==' '||(x)=='\t')
char ** splitline(char *line)
/*
 * purpose: split a line into array of white-space separated tokens
 * returns: a NULL-terminated array of pointers to copies of the tokens
 *          or NULL if line if no tokens on the line
 *  action: traverse the array, locate strings, make copies
 *    note: strtok() could work, but we may want to add quotes later
 */
{
        char    *newstr();
        char    **args ;
        int     spots = 0;                      /* spots in table      */
        int     bufspace = 0;                   /* bytes in table      */
        int     argnum = 0;                     /* slots used          */
        char    *cp = line;                     /* pos in string       */
        char    *start;
        int     len;

        if ( line == NULL )                     /* handle special case */
                return NULL;

        args    = emalloc(BUFSIZ);              /* initialize array    */
        bufspace = BUFSIZ;
        spots   = BUFSIZ/sizeof(char *);

        while( *cp != '\0' )

        {
                while ( is_delim(*cp) )         /* skip leading spaces */
                        cp++;
                if ( *cp == '\0' )              /* quit at end-o-string */
                        break;

                /* make sure the array has room (+1 for NULL) */
                if ( argnum+1 >= spots ){
                        args = erealloc(args,bufspace+BUFSIZ);
                        bufspace += BUFSIZ;
                        spots += (BUFSIZ/sizeof(char *));
                }

                /* mark start, then find end of word */
                start = cp;
                len   = 1;
                while (*++cp != '\0' && !(is_delim(*cp)) )
                        len++;
                args[argnum++] = newstr(start, len);
        }
        args[argnum] = NULL;
        return args;
}
```

```
/*
 * purpose: constructor for strings
 * returns: a string, never NULL
 */
char *newstr(char *s, int l)
{
        char *rv = emalloc(l+1);

        rv[l] = '\0';
        strncpy(rv, s, l);
        return rv;
}

void
freelist(char **list)
/*
 * purpose: free the list returned by splitline
 * returns: nothing
 *   action: free all strings in list and then free the list
 */
{
        char    **cp = list;
        while( *cp )
                free(*cp++);
        free(list);
}

void * emalloc(size_t n)
{
        void *rv ;
        if ( (rv = malloc(n)) == NULL )
                fatal("out of memory","",1);
        return rv;
}
void * erealloc(void *p, size_t n)
{
        void *rv;
        if ( (rv = realloc(p,n)) == NULL )
                fatal("realloc() failed","",1);
        return rv;
}
```

Here is the code to smsh.h:

```
#define YES     1
#define NO      0

char    *next_cmd();
char    **splitline(char *);
void    freelist(char **);
void    *emalloc(size_t);
```

```
void    *erealloc(void *, size_t);
int     execute(char **);
void    fatal(char *, char *, int );
```

9.3.1   Notes on smsh1

smsh1 is much easier to use than psh2. Additional conveniences to consider are as follows:

Multiple commands on a line

The regular shell allows the user to separate commands with semicolons, allowing the user to type several commands on one line:

```
ls demodir; ps -f ; date
```

Background processing

The regular shell allows a user to run a process *in the background* by ending the command with an ampersand (&), as in

```
find /home -name core -print &
```

Running a process in the background means you start it, the prompt returns at once, and the process continues to run while you use the shell to run other commands. This one sounds tricky, but the principle behind it is surprisingly simple. Study the flowchart to see how to get your prompt back without waiting for the command to terminate. The idea is simple and elegant, but you need to plan to handle signals and avoid zombies. Sounds like an adventure movie.

An exit command

The regular shell allows the user to type exit to quit from the shell. The exit command accepts an integer argument, as in exit 3. In this case, the numerical value of the argument is passed as an argument to the exit function.

9.4   CONTROL FLOW IN THE SHELL: WHY AND HOW

Our second improvement to our shell is to add the *if..then* control structure.

9.4.1   What if Does

The shell provides an *if* control structure. Say you plan to back up your disk every Friday. Consider the following example:

```
if date | grep Fri
then
   echo time for backup.  Insert tape and press enter
   read x
   tar cvf /dev/tape /home
fi
```

The *if* structure in the shell works like *if* in other languages: a condition is tested, and if the result of that test is positive, a block of code is executed. In the shell, the *condition* is a command, and a *positive result* means the command succeeded.

In the example, the command is date | grep Fri, which searches for the string "Fri" in the output of date. The grep program either succeeds in its search for that string or it fails. How can a program indicate success?

exit(0) for Success The grep program calls exit(0) to indicate success. All Unix programs follow the convention that an exit value of 0 signifies success. For example, the diff command compares two text files. diff returns 0 if it finds no differences, its idea of success. File- and directory-management programs such as mv, cp, and rm, return 0 if they successfully, respectively, rename, copy, and remove files. The *if..then* logic in shell scripts is based on the assumption that an exit status of zero means success.

if supports else An *if* control structure can include an *else* block, as in

```
ls
who
if diff file1 file1.bak
then
      echo no differences found, removing backup
      rm file1.bak
else
      echo backup differs, making it read-only
      chmod -w file1.bak
fi
date
```

The *else* block may, like the *then* block, contain any number of commands, including other *if..then* control structures.

The *if* control structure has yet another feature. *if* accepts a block of commands between *if* and *then*. The exit value from the last command in the block determines the success of the condition.

9.4.2 How *if* Works

The *if* control structure works as follows:

(a) The shell runs the command that follows the word *if*.
(b) The shell checks the exit status of the command.
(c) An exit status of 0 means *success*, nonzero means *failure*.
(d) The shell executes commands after the *then* line if success.
(e) The shell executes commands after the *else* line if failure.
(f) The keyword *fi* marks the end of the *if* block.

9.4.3   Adding *if* to `smsh`

We now know what the *if* control structure does, and we know how it works. How do we add an *if* structure to our shell?

We know how to run a command—we call `execute`. We know how to check an exit status from a program—that comes from `wait`. We can store the result from the command after *if* in some variable. We then need to keep track of whether we are reading commands in a *then* block or in an *else* block. We also need to make sure we see *then* on the line after *if*.

Adding a New Layer: `process`

Our original model is too simple. The flowchart for `smsh1` contains a direct path from `splitline` to `fork`; every command is passed to `exec`. In the new version, some lines are not passed to `exec`: lines that begin with *if*, *then*, or *fi*, and commands in the *then* part when the condition fails. Adding the *if* syntax makes command processing more complicated, so we write a wrapper function called `process` to contain the complexity. A revised flowchart is shown in Figure 9.2.

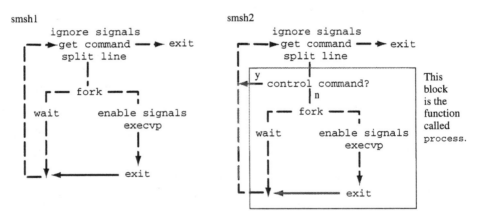

FIGURE 9.2

Adding flow control commands to `smsh`.

What `process` Does

`process` manages the control flow of a script by watching for keywords like *if*, *then*, and *fi* and calling `fork` and `exec` only when appropriate. `process` must record the result of condition commands so it can decide how to handle *then* and *else* blocks.

How Does `process` Work? Regions of Code, States of Execution

`process` views the script as a sequence of different regions. One region is the *then* block, another region is the *else* block, a third region is the part completely outside the *if* structure. The shell treats commands in different regions in different ways, as is exemplified in Figure 9.3.

Consider the region outside the *if* structures. We shall call that the *neutral* region. There, the shell simply reads, parses, and executes commands.

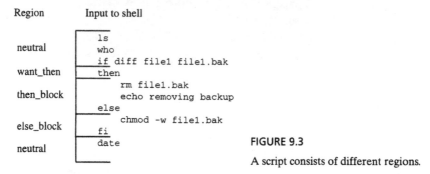

Region   Input to shell

neutral   ls
                  who
                  if diff file1 file1.bak
want_then   then
                      rm file1.bak
then_block   echo removing backup
                  else
                      chmod -w file1.bak
else_block   fi
                  date
neutral

FIGURE 9.3

A script consists of different regions.

The next region is the region between the *if* line and the *then* line. In that region, the shell executes a command then records the exit status of the command. Another region extends from the *then* line to the *else* or *fi* line. The last region begins at the *else* line and ends at the *fi* line. After *fi*, we are back in the neutral region.

The shell must keep track of the current region, and it also has to keep track of the success or failure of the command executed when it shifted into the WANT_THEN region.

Different regions require different types of processing. The program is said to be in a particular *state* when processing input in a certain way. process calls three functions that manage these state variables:

is_control_command

is_control_command is a boolean-valued function that tells process if the command is part of the shell programming language or if the command is something to execute.

do_control_command

do_control_command handles the keywords *if*, *then*, and *fi*. Each word is a boundary between two states. This function updates the state variable and performs any appropriate operations.

ok_to_execute

ok_to_execute checks the current state and the result of the condition command and returns a boolean value to indicate if the current command should be executed.

9.4.4   smsh2.c: The Revised Code

smsh2.c is based on smsh1.c. main has only one change—the call to execute has been replaced by a call to process:

```
/** smsh2.c - small-shell version 2
 **              small shell that supports command line parsing
 **              and if..then..else.fi logic (by calling process())
 **/
#include          <stdio.h>
#include          <stdlib.h>
```

```
#include        <unistd.h>
#include        <signal.h>
#include        <sys/wait.h>
#include        "smsh.h"

#define DFL_PROMPT      "> "

int main()
{
        char    *cmdline, *prompt, **arglist;
        int     result, process(char **);
        void    setup();

        prompt = DFL_PROMPT ;
        setup();

        while ( (cmdline = next_cmd(prompt, stdin)) != NULL ){
                if ( (arglist = splitline(cmdline)) != NULL  ){
                        result = process(arglist);
                        freelist(arglist);
                }
                free(cmdline);
        }
        return 0;
}

void setup()
/*
 * purpose: initialize shell
 * returns: nothing. calls fatal() if trouble
 */
{
        signal(SIGINT,  SIG_IGN);
        signal(SIGQUIT, SIG_IGN);
}
void fatal(char *s1, char *s2, int n)
{
        fprintf(stderr,"Error: %s,%s\n", s1, s2);
        exit(n);
}
```

The other changes are in two new files, process.c and controlflow.c:

```
/* process.c
 * command processing layer
 *
 * The process(char **arglist) function is called by the main loop
 * It sits in front of the execute() function.  This layer handles
 * two main classes of processing:
 *       a) built-in functions (e.g. exit(), set, =, read, .. )
 *       b) control structures (e.g. if, while, for)
 */
```

```
#include          <stdio.h>
#include          "smsh.h"

int is_control_command(char *);
int do_control_command(char **);
int ok_to_execute();

int process(char **args)
/*
 * purpose: process user command
 * returns: result of processing command
 * details: if a built-in then call appropriate function, if not execute()
 *   errors: arise from subroutines, handled there
 */
{
        int               rv = 0;

        if ( args[0] == NULL )
                rv = 0;
        else if ( is_control_command(args[0]) )
                rv = do_control_command(args);
        else if ( ok_to_execute() )
                rv = execute(args);
        return rv;
}


/* controlflow.c
 *
 * "if" processing is done with two state variables
 *    if_state and if_result
 */
#include          <stdio.h>
#include          "smsh.h"

enum states   { NEUTRAL, WANT_THEN, THEN_BLOCK };
enum results  { SUCCESS, FAIL };

static int if_state  = NEUTRAL;
static int if_result = SUCCESS;
static int last_stat = 0;

int     syn_err(char *);

int ok_to_execute()
/*
 * purpose: determine the shell should execute a command
 * returns: 1 for yes, 0 for no
 * details: if in THEN_BLOCK and if_result was SUCCESS then yes
 *          if in THEN_BLOCK and if_result was FAIL    then no
 *          if in WANT_THEN  then syntax error (sh is different)
 */
{
        int    rv = 1;          /* default is positive */
```

```
            if ( if_state == WANT_THEN ){
                    syn_err("then expected");
                    rv = 0;
            }
            else if ( if_state == THEN_BLOCK && if_result == SUCCESS )
                    rv = 1;
            else if ( if_state == THEN_BLOCK && if_result == FAIL )
                    rv = 0;
            return rv;
}

int is_control_command(char *s)
/*
 * purpose: boolean to report if the command is a shell control command
 * returns: 0 or 1
 */
{
    return (strcmp(s,"if")==0 || strcmp(s,"then")==0 || strcmp(s,"fi")==0);
}

int do_control_command(char **args)
/*
 * purpose: Process "if", "then", "fi" - change state or detect error
 * returns: 0 if ok, -1 for syntax error
 */
{
        char    *cmd = args[0];
        int     rv = -1;

        if( strcmp(cmd,"if")==0 ){
                if ( if_state != NEUTRAL )
                        rv = syn_err("if unexpected");
                else {
                        last_stat = process(args+1);
                        if_result = (last_stat == 0 ? SUCCESS : FAIL );
                        if_state = WANT_THEN;
                        rv = 0;
                }
        }
        else if ( strcmp(cmd,"then")==0 ){
                if ( if_state != WANT_THEN )
                        rv = syn_err("then unexpected");
                else {
                        if_state = THEN_BLOCK;
                        rv = 0;
                }
        }
        else if ( strcmp(cmd,"fi")==0 ){
                if ( if_state != THEN_BLOCK )
                        rv = syn_err("fi unexpected");
```

```
                        else {
                                if_state = NEUTRAL;
                                rv = 0;
                        }
                }
                else
                        fatal("internal error processing:", cmd, 2);
                return rv;
        }

        int syn_err(char *msg)
        /* purpose: handles syntax errors in control structures
         * details: resets state to NEUTRAL
         * returns: -1 in interactive mode. Should call fatal in scripts
         */
        {
                if_state = NEUTRAL;
                fprintf(stderr,"syntax error: %s\n", msg);
                return -1;
        }
```

The code in controlflow.c does not handle the *else* part of the *if* control structure.
That is left as an exercise to the reader. We compile and test this version:

```
$ cc -o smsh2 smsh2.c splitline.c execute.c process.c controlflow.c
$ ./smsh2
> grep lp /etc/passwd
lp:x:4:7:lp:/var/spool/lpd:
> if grep lp /etc/passwd
lp:x:4:7:lp:/var/spool/lpd:
> then
>    echo ok
ok
> fi
> if grep pati /etc/passwd
> then
>    echo ok
> fi
> echo ok
ok
> then
syntax error: then unexpected
```

How'd We Do?

It looks OK. How does it compare to the regular shell?

```
$ if grep lp /etc/passwd
> then
>    echo ok
```

```
> fi
lp:x:4:7:lp:/var/spool/lpd:
ok
$
```

This shell handles the *if* structure in a different way from ours. The standard shell defers execution of the entire structure until the closing *fi*. How does that work? Why do that? The regular shell also supports nested *if* structures. Can our program be modified to handle nested *if*s?

9.5   SHELL VARIABLES: LOCAL AND GLOBAL

Like any programming language, a Unix shell has variables. You can assign values to variables, retrieve values from variables, and list variables, as in the following code:

```
$ age=7                          # assigning a value
$ echo $age                      # retrieving a value
7
$ echo age                       # the $ is required
age
$ echo $age+$age                 # purely string operations
7+7
$ read name                      # input from stdin
fido
$ echo hello, $name, how are you # can be interpolated
hello, fido, how are you
$ ls > $name.$age                # used as part of a command
$ food = muffins                 # no spaces in assignment
food: not found
$
```

The shell includes two types of variables: local variables and environment variables. We mentioned earlier in this chapter that variables like HOME and TZ let users pass personalized settings to programs. These environment variables behave somewhat like global variables; their values are accessible to all child processes of the shell. Later in the chapter, we shall study the details of the environment. For now, we only need to remember that there are two sorts of variables.

9.5.1   Using Shell Variables

The previous example demonstrates most operations with variables. They are as follows:

Operation	Syntax	Notes
assignment	var=value	no spaces
reference	$var	
delete	unset var	
stdin input	read var	also, read var1 var2 ..
list vars	set	
make global	export var	

Variable names are combinations of the characters A–Z, a–z, 0–9, and _. The first character may not be a digit. The names are case sensitive.

Variable values are strings. There are no numerical values. All variable operations are string operations.

Listing variables involves the set command, which lists all variables currently defined in the shell, as in the following code:

```
$ set
BASH=/bin/bash
BASH_VERSION=1.14.7(1)
DISPLAY=:0.0
EUID=500
HOME=/home2/bruce
HOSTTYPE=i386
IFS=

LANG=en
LANGUAGE=en
LD_LIBRARY_PATH=/usr/lib:/usr/local/lib
LOGNAME=bruce
OPTERR=1
OPTIND=1
OSTYPE=Linux
PATH=/bin:/usr/bin:/usr/X11R6/bin:/usr/local/bin:/home2/bruce/bin
PPID=30928
PS4=+
PWD=/home2/bruce/projs/ubook/src/ch09
SHELL=/bin/bash
SHLVL=2
TERM=xterm-color
UID=500
USER=bruce
_=/bin/vi
age=7
name=fido
```

This list includes many environment variables that were set when I logged in, plus the two local variables I added later.

9.5.2   A Storage System for Variables

To add variables to our shell, we need a place to store these names and values. This storage system must distinguish local variables from global variables. Here is an abstract model for a storage system:

Model

variable	value	global?
data	"phonebook.dat"	n
HOME	"/home2/fido"	y
TERM	"t1061"	y

Interface (Partial)

`VLstore(char *var, char *val)` adds/updates *var=val*

`VLlookup(char *var)` retrieves value for *var*

`VLlist` lists table to stdout

Implementation

We could implement this table with a linked list, a hash table, a tree—almost anything. For this first draft, we use an array of structs. Each variable is

```
struct var {
                char *str;              /* name=val string    */
                int  global;            /* a boolean          */
        };
static struct var tab[MAXVARS];
```

The picture is shown in Figure 9.4.

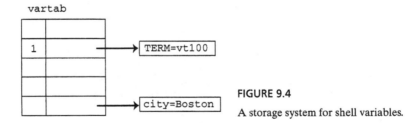

FIGURE 9.4

A storage system for shell variables.

9.5.3   Adding Variable Commands: Built-ins

We have a place to store variables, now we need to add the assign, list, and retrieve commands to our shell. That is, in our shell, users should be able to type

```
> TERM=xterm
> set
> echo $TERM
```

set is a command to our shell, not a program the shell runs, just as *if* and *then* are keywords the shell handles itself. To distinguish set from commands the shell runs with exec, we call set a *built-in* command.

Commands of the form varname=value tell the shell to add an entry to its table of variables. Assignment statements are also *built-in* commands.

Adding built-ins to our shell requires another change to the flowchart. Before we call fork and exec, we have to see if the command is built into the shell. (See Figure 9.5.)

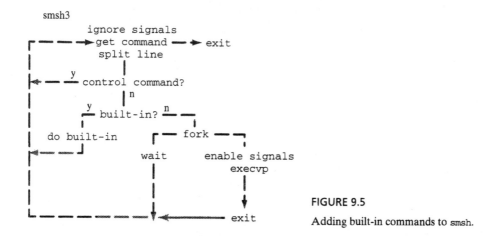

FIGURE 9.5

Adding built-in commands to smsh.

We revise the process function to check for built-ins before calling fork/exec:

```
            if ( args[0] == NULL )
                    rv = 0;
            else if ( is_control_command(args[0]) )
                    rv = do_control_command(args);
            else if ( ok_to_execute() ){
                if( !builtin_command(args, &rv) )
                        rv = execute(args);
        }
```

The new function, builtin_command, combines into one call operations of checking for and executing built-in commands. builtin_command returns a boolean value and modifies the status by reference.

The new code is in builtin.c:

```
/* builtin.c
 * contains the switch and the functions for builtin commands
 */

#include         <stdio.h>
#include         <string.h>
#include         <ctype.h>
#include         "smsh.h"
#include         "varlib.h"

int assign(char *);
int okname(char *);
```

```
int builtin_command(char **args, int *resultp)
/*
 * purpose: run a builtin command
 * returns: 1 if args[0] is built-in, 0 if not
 * details: test args[0] against all known built-ins.  Call functions
 */
{
        int rv = 0;

        if ( strcmp(args[0],"set") == 0 ){               /* 'set' command? */
                VLlist();
                *resultp = 0;
                rv = 1;
        }
        else if ( strchr(args[0], '=') != NULL ){   /* assignment cmd */
                *resultp = assign(args[0]);
                if ( *resultp != -1 )                /* x-y=123 not ok */
                        rv = 1;
        }
        else if ( strcmp(args[0], "export") == 0 ){
                if ( args[1] != NULL && okname(args[1]) )
                        *resultp = VLexport(args[1]);
                else
                        *resultp = 1;
                rv = 1;
        }
        return rv;
}

int assign(char *str)
/*
 * purpose: execute name=val AND ensure that name is legal
 * returns: -1 for illegal lval, or result of VLstore
 * warning: modifies the string, but retores it to normal
 */
{
        char    *cp;
        int     rv ;

        cp = strchr(str,'=');
        *cp = '\0';
        rv = ( okname(str) ? VLstore(str,cp+1) : -1 );
        *cp = '=';
        return rv;
}
int okname(char *str)
/*
 * purpose: determines if a string is a legal variable name
 * returns: 0 for no, 1 for yes
 */
{
        char    *cp;
```

```
for(cp = str; *cp; cp++ ){
        if ( (isdigit(*cp) && cp==str) || !(isalnum(*cp) || *cp=='_' ))
                return 0;
}
return ( cp != str );    /* no empty strings, either */
}
```

9.5.4   How'd We Do?

We compile and run our revised program:

```
$ cc -o smsh3 smsh2.c splitline.c execute.c process2.c \
controlflow.c builtin.c varlib.c
$ ./smsh3
> set
> day=monday
> temp=75
> TZ=CST6CDT
> x.y=z
cannot execute command: No such file or directory
> set
    day=monday
    temp=75
    TZ=CST6CDT
> date
Tue Jul 31 11:56:59 EDT 2001
> echo $temp, $day
$temp, $day
```

Works OK   Our shell now supports variables. We can assign values to variables, and we can list the variables. The program is even careful not to accept illegal variable names, treating such expressions as names of programs to execute.

But TZ is Not Passed to Date   Our sample run shows two things we need to work on. First, we set the TZ variable to the code for U.S. central time, but the date command reported the time for U.S. eastern time. We said earlier that the TZ variable is part of the environment and is passed from parent to child. How does that work? How can our shell put variables into the environment so the children will receive our values? Our next topic will be the *environment*.

And $temp, $day are Not Evaluated   Our test run also reveals that our shell does not evaluate variable references. That is, when our shell processes the command echo $temp, $day, it does not replace the variables with their values. Those variables are local to shell. The echo command does not know the values of those variables. The shell has to perform *variable substitution* before it runs external programs. We explore this question at the end of the chapter.

9.6 THE ENVIRONMENT: PERSONALIZED SETTINGS

People like to personalize their computers. Some people like scenic images on their screens, some prefer solid colors. Some like editing with emacs, while others prefer vi. Unix lets users store preferences in a set of variables called the *environment*. Each user has a unique home directory, username, file for incoming mail, terminal type, and favorite editor. Many customized settings are recorded in environment variables.

Some programs base their behavior on these settings. For example, running this script, script3, shows that date uses the value stored in TZ:

```
#!/bin/sh
# script3 - shows how an environment variable is passed to commands
# TZ is time zone, affect things like date, and ls -l
#
echo "The time in Boston is"
        TZ=EST5EDT
        export TZ              # add TZ to the environment
        date                   # date uses the value in TZ
echo "The time in Chicago is"
        TZ=CST6CDT
        date
echo "The time in LA is"
        TZ=PST8PDT
        date
```

The environment is not part of the shell, but the shell includes commands that let users read and change their environment. As usual, we first see what the environment does, then learn how it works, and finally add it to our own code.

9.6.1 Using the Environment

Listing Your Environment

The env command lists all the settings in your environment:

```
$ env
LOGNAME=bruce
LD_LIBRARY_PATH=/usr/lib:/usr/local/lib
TERM=xterm-color
HOSTTYPE=i386
PATH=/bin:/usr/bin:/usr/X11R6/bin:/usr/local/bin:/home2/bruce/bin
HOME=/home2/bruce
SHELL=/bin/bash
USER=bruce
LANGUAGE=en
DISPLAY=:0.0
LANG=en
_=/usr/bin/env
SHLVL=2
```

env is a regular program, not a shell built-in. The list of settings shown here contains values useful to many programs. For instance, the LANG variable is used by some programs that display information or messages. A Web browser can use LANG to set the language for button labels and menu options. DISPLAY tells X Windows where you want it to open windows. The TERM variable tells curses which set of screen control codes to use.

Updating the Environment

var=value

Revise a setting in your environment simply by assigning a new string to the variable. For example, if your Web browser supports French messages and menu choices, you can ask for them by setting LANG=fr.

export var

Use the export built-in in the shell to add a new variable to the environment. If *var* exists as a local variable, *var* is added to the environment. If *var* does not exist, the shell creates it. bash allows you to combine assignment and exporting: export var=value

Reading the Environment in C Programs

The standard C library includes the getenv function, as in

```
#include <stdlib.h>
main()
{
        char *cp = getenv("LANG");

        if ( cp != NULL && strcmp(cp, "fr") == 0 )
            printf("Bonjour\n");
        else
            printf("Hello\n");
}
```

9.6.2 What is the Environment? How it Works

The environment is simply an array of strings available to every program. (See Figure 9.6.) Each string in the array is of the form var=value. The address of the array is stored in the

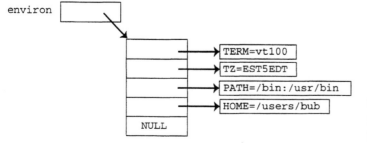

environ

TERM=vt100
TZ=EST5EDT
PATH=/bin:/usr/bin
HOME=/users/bub
NULL

FIGURE 9.6

The environment is an array of pointers to strings.

global variable called environ. There is nothing more to it. The environment *is* whatever array of strings the variable environ points to. To read the environment, read that array of strings. To change the environment, change the strings, change the pointers in the array, or set the global variable to point to a different array.

Sample Programs
showenv.c works just like the env command:

```
/*  showenv.c - shows how to read and print the environment
 */

extern char    **environ;    /* points to the array of strings */

main()
{
        int    i;

        for( i = 0 ; environ[i] ; i++ )
                printf("%s\n", environ[i] );
}
```

changeenv.c changes the environment and then runs env:

```
/* changeenv.c  - shows how to change the environment
 *               note: calls "env" to display its new settings
 */
#include        <stdio.h>

extern char ** environ;

main()
{
        char *table[3];

        table[0] = "TERM=vt100";                 /* fill the table */
        table[1] = "HOME=/on/the/range";
        table[2] = 0;

        environ = table;                         /* point to that table */

        execlp("env", "env", NULL);              /* exec a program      */
}
```

Here is a demonstration:

```
$ ./changeenv
TERM=vt100
HOME=/on/the/range
$
```

Look at this program carefully. We create a table of strings in one program, changeenv, and then call execlp to run a different program, env. That second program is able to read the table of strings. Somehow that array was copied from the data space of the first program to the data space of the second one.

But *exec* Wipes Out All Data!

When we discussed the exec system calls, we said they work like brain transplants, replacing all code and data of the calling program with the code and data of the new program. The array pointed to by environ is the single exception to that rule. When the kernel executes the execve system call, it copies the array and the strings into the data space of the new program. (See Figure 9.7.)

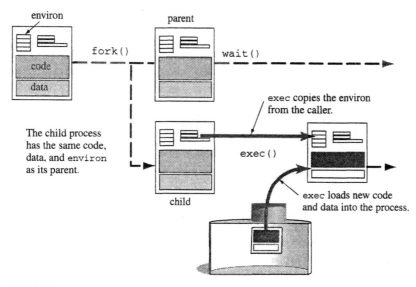

FIGURE 9.7

Strings in environ are copied by exec().

Let us trace this array from the parent process to the new program. fork copies the entire parent process, all its code and data, including the environment. exec removes all code and data from the process and inserts the code and data of the new program. The only values that are copied from the old program are the arguments passed to execvp and the strings stored in the environment.

Children Cannot Alter the Environment of Parents

Settings in the environment are copies of the strings in the parent. The child cannot modify the environment of the parent. Passing values in the environment is easy and convenient because the entire table is copied automatically when a process calls fork and exec.

9.6.3   Adding Environment Handling to smsh

We now change our shell to provide access to the environment. First, our shell will include environment variables in its list of variables. Second, users of our shell will be able to modify and add environment variables.

Access to Environment Variables

We know the structure of the environment, and we have a set of functions for adding variables to our list of variables. When our shell starts, we copy the environment values into our variable table. (See Figure 9.8.) Once the values are copied to our variable table, we can use the set command and the assignment operator to view and modify the settings.

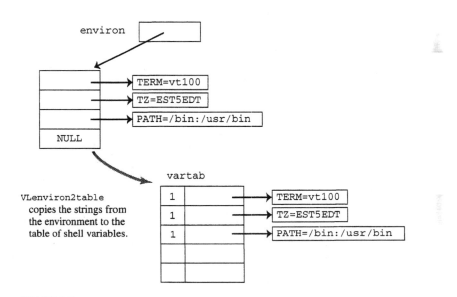

FIGURE 9.8

Copying values from the environment to vartab.

Changing the Environment

Our test run of smsh3 showed that the change to TZ was not passed to date. We now know how to change environment variables. The simplest way to change the environment is to build a whole new table that contains environment settings from our table of shell variables and set the global variable environ to point to this new table. (See Figure 9.9.) Now when we call exec, the kernel copies those settings to the new program. Notice that the original environment table, now unreferenced, still contains the original values.

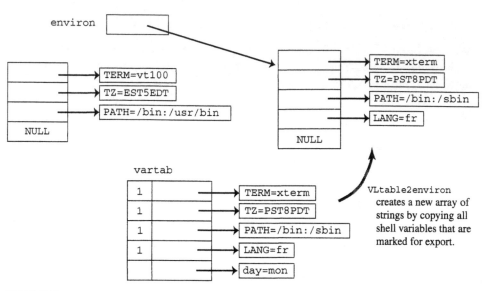

FIGURE 9.9

Copying values from `vartab` to a new environment.

Changes to smsh

We add two steps to the program flow, as shown in Figure 9.10. The steps are implemented by adding two lines to the code:

setup in smsh4.c

```
void setup()
/*
 * purpose: initialize shell
 * returns: nothing. calls fatal() if trouble
 */
{
        extern char **environ;
        VLenviron2table(environ);
        signal(SIGINT,  SIG_IGN);
        signal(SIGQUIT, SIG_IGN);
}
```

execute in execute2.c

```
        if ( (pid = fork())  == -1 )
                perror("fork");
        else if ( pid == 0 ){
                environ = VLtable2environ();   /* new line */
                signal(SIGINT, SIG_DFL);
                signal(SIGQUIT, SIG_DFL);
                execvp(argv[0], argv);
                perror("cannot execute command");
                exit(1);
```

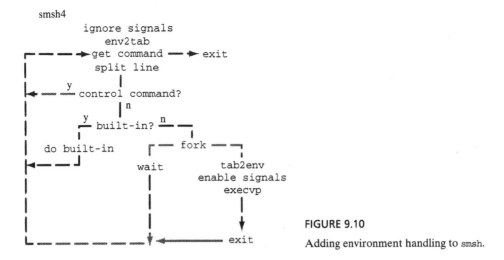

FIGURE 9.10

Adding environment handling to smsh.

Test the Changes

```
$ make smsh4
cc -o smsh4 smsh4.c splitline.c execute2.c process2.c controlflow.c \
        builtin.c varlib.c
$ ./smsh4
> date
Tue Jul 31 09:51:03 EDT 2001
> TZ=PST8PDT
> export TZ
> date
Tue Jul 31 06:51:30 PDT 2001
>
```

The user can modify and add to the set of environment variables, and the shell sends those new values to any programs it runs.

9.6.4   Code for `varlib.c`

```
/* varlib.c
 *
 * a simple storage system to store name=value pairs
 * with facility to mark items as part of the environment
 *
 * interface:
 *      VLstore( name, value )      returns 1 for 0k, 0 for no
 *      VLlookup( name )            returns string or NULL if not there
 *      VLlist()                    prints out current table
 *
 * environment-related functions
 *      VLexport( name )            adds name to list of env vars
```

```
 *       VLtable2environ()          copy from table to environ
 *       VLenviron2table()          copy from environ to table
 *
 * details:
 *       the table is stored as an array of structs that
 *       contain a flag for global and a single string of
 *       the form name=value.  This allows EZ addition to the
 *       environment.  It makes searching pretty easy, as
 *       long as you search for "name="
 *
 */

#include         <stdio.h>
#include         <stdlib.h>
#include         "varlib.h"
#include         <string.h>

#define MAXVARS 200              /* a linked list would be nicer */

struct var {
                char *str;             /* name=val string       */
                int  global;           /* a boolean             */
        };

static struct var tab[MAXVARS];                 /* the table    */

static char *new_string( char *, char *);       /* private methods      */
static struct var *find_item(char *, int);

int VLstore( char *name, char *val )
/*
 * traverse list, if found, replace it, else add at end
 * since there is no delete, a blank one is a free one
 * return 1 if trouble, 0 if ok (like a command)
 */
{
        struct var *itemp;
        char    *s;
        int     rv = 1;

        /* find spot to put it              and make new string */
          if ((itemp=find_item(name,1))!=NULL&&
          (s=new_string(name,val))!=NULL)
          {
                if ( itemp->str )                /* has a val?   */
                        free(itemp->str);        /* y: remove it */
                itemp->str = s;
                rv = 0;                          /* ok! */
          }
          return rv;
}

char * new_string( char *name, char *val )
/*
 * returns new string of form name=value or NULL on error
```

```
     */
     {
             char    *retval;

             retval = malloc( strlen(name) + strlen(val) + 2 );
             if ( retval != NULL )
                     sprintf(retval, "%s=%s", name, val );
             return retval;
     }
     char * VLlookup( char *name )
     /*
      * returns value of var or empty string if not there
      */
     {
             struct var *itemp;

             if ( (itemp = find_item(name,0)) != NULL )
                     return itemp->str + 1 + strlen(name);
             return "";
     }
     int VLexport( char *name )
     /*
      * marks a var for export, adds it if not there
      * returns 1 for no, 0 for ok
      */
     {
             struct var *itemp;
             int    rv = 1;

             if ( (itemp = find_item(name,0)) != NULL ){
                     itemp->global = 1;
                     rv = 0;
             }
             else if ( VLstore(name, "") == 1 )
                     rv = VLexport(name);
             return rv;
     }
     static struct var * find_item( char *name , int first_blank )
     /*
      * searches table for an item
      * returns ptr to struct or NULL if not found
      * OR if (first_blank) then ptr to first blank one
      */
     {
             int    i;
             int    len = strlen(name);
             char   *s;

             for( i = 0 ; i<MAXVARS && tab[i].str != NULL ; i++ )
             {
                     s = tab[i].str;
```

```
                        if ( strncmp(s,name,len) == 0 && s[len] == '=' ){
                                return &tab[i];
                        }
                }
                if ( i < MAXVARS && first_blank )
                        return &tab[i];
                return NULL;
        }

void VLlist()
/*
 * performs the shell's set command
 * Lists the contents of the variable table, marking each
 * exported variable with the symbol  '*'
 */
{
        int     i;
        for(i = 0 ; i<MAXVARS && tab[i].str != NULL ; i++ )
        {
                if ( tab[i].global )
                        printf("  * %s\n", tab[i].str);
                else
                        printf("    %s\n", tab[i].str);
        }
}

int VLenviron2table(char *env[])
/*
 * initialize the variable table by loading array of strings
 * return 1 for ok, 0 for not ok
 */
{
        int     i;
        char    *newstring;

        for(i = 0 ; env[i] != NULL ; i++ )
        {
                if ( i == MAXVARS )
                        return 0;
                newstring = malloc(1+strlen(env[i]));
                if ( newstring == NULL )
                        return 0;
                strcpy(newstring, env[i]);
                tab[i].str = newstring;
                tab[i].global = 1;
        }
        while( i < MAXVARS ){           /* I know we don't need this   */
                tab[i].str = NULL ;     /* static globals are nulled   */
                tab[i++].global = 0;    /* by default                  */
        }
```

```
                return 1;
        }

char ** VLtable2environ()
/*
 * build an array of pointers suitable for making a new environment
 * note, you need to free() this when done to avoid memory leaks
 */
{
        int     i,                      /* index                        */
                j,                      /* another index                */
                n = 0;                  /* counter                      */
        char    **envtab;               /* array of pointers            */

        /*
         * first, count the number of global variables
         */

        for( i = 0 ; i<MAXVARS && tab[i].str != NULL ; i++ )
                if ( tab[i].global == 1 )
                        n++;

        /* then, allocate space for that many variables */
        envtab = (char **) malloc( (n+1) * sizeof(char *) );
        if ( envtab == NULL )
                return NULL;

        /* then, load the array with pointers            */
        for(i = 0, j = 0 ; i<MAXVARS && tab[i].str != NULL ; i++ )
                if ( tab[i].global == 1 )
                        envtab[j++] = tab[i].str;
        envtab[j] = NULL;
        return envtab;

}
```

9.7   STATE-OF-THE-SHELL REPORT

In this chapter, we studied the Unix shell as a programming language and added three essential features: command line parsing, *if..then* logic, and variables. Our small shell is growing quickly. Here is a report card:

feature	supports	needs
commands	runs programs	
variables	=, set	read, $var substitution
if	if,then	else
environ	all	
exit		exit
cd		cd
>,<,|	none	all

Variable Substitution Adding variable substitution requires more study. Where in the flowchart does the shell replace $X with the value stored in *X*? Notice this behavior:

```
$ read x
who am i
$ $x
mori.xyz.com!nobody     tty1     Dec 31 13:56
$ grep $x /etc/passwd
grep: am: No such file or directory
grep: i: No such file or directory
$
```

What does this output tell us about the relationship between the parsing stage of the shell and the variable-substitution part of the shell? Are there advantages to this design? How can we add it to our program?

Input/Output Redirection The shell allows users to redirect input and output of a process to files and to other processes. How does that work? Can we add it to our shell? We study *I/O redirection* in the next chapter.

SUMMARY

MAIN IDEAS

- A Unix shell runs programs called shell scripts. A shell script can run programs, accept user input, use variables, and follow complex logic.
- The *if..then* logic in the shell depends on the convention that a program returns an exit value of 0 to indicate success. The shell uses `wait` to obtain the exit status from a program.
- The shell programming language includes variables. These variables store strings and may be used in any command. Shell variables are local to the script.
- Every program inherits a list of strings from the process that called it. The list of strings is called the *environment*. The environment is used to define global settings for the session and to set parameters for specific programs. The shell allows users to view and modify the environment.

WHAT'S NEXT?

We learn about input/output redirection.

EXPLORATIONS

9.1 *Built-in Dangers* Write a C program or shell script named `set` and try to execute that program from the shell. What happens? Write a C program or shell script named `no=dice` and try to execute it. What happens? Try the same thing with a program called `test`. Is there a way to run these programs?

9.2 *Nested ifs* Can the design used in `process.c` and `controlflow.c` be extended to support nested ifs. That is, can it handle input of the form

```
if cmd1
then
    if cmd2
    then
        cmd3
    else
        cmd4
    fi
else
    cmd5
fi
```

with any depth of nesting, not just the single level shown here? Do you need more state variables? Do you need to use a stack for state variables? If you are going to build a stack, does it make more sense to write a recursive solution?

9.3 The `varlib.c` functions to update the environment create a whole new environment array. Why not just use `realloc` to adjust the size of the original one?

PROGRAMMING EXERCISES

9.4 *Multiple commands* Modify `smsh1.c` to accept multiple commands on a line. The easy way to do this is to modify `next_cmd`. Beware of printing the prompt too often.

9.5 *exit 3* Modify `smsh1.c` to accept an `exit` command that takes an optional argument. Make sure your program rejects nonnumeric arguments (for example: `exit left`). How does this command fit into the flowchart? Do we need to add a new item in the logic?

9.6 *else* Modify `process.c` to support the *else* part of the *if* control structure.

9.7 The `ok_to_execute` function uses two variables to keep track of the current region and current state. You can replace the two variables with one variable that takes on more values. Consider this set of states:

```
NEUTRAL, IF_SUCCEEDED, IF_FAILED, SKIPPING_THEN, DOING_THEN,
SKIPPING_ELSE, DOING_ELSE
```

Revise `controlflow.c` to use this single-variation system.

9.8 *Background processes* Modify `smsh1.c` to accept the `&` command terminator to run a command in the background. You need to make another change to `next_cmd`.

9.9 The regular shell defers execution of the entire structure until the final *fi* is read. (Note: *fi* does not stand for *final*. It is *if* backwards.) A completely different solution is to read all the lines in the *if* structure into a data structure with three parts. The first part is the condition command, the next part is a list of commands for the *then* region, and the last part is a list of commands for the *else* region.

After reading the entire structure into memory, you can then execute the condition command and, based on that, execute the *then* list or the *else* list. Write a version of smsh that processes *if* using this method. Your solution should handle nested *if*s.

9.10 Add a *while* loop to your shell. For this addition, you need to read the body of the loop into a list. Beware of memory leaks.

9.11 A process has many attributes. One attribute of a process is the current directory for that process. The inventors of Unix wrote a program to call `chdir`, along with the other standard directory programs: `pwd`, `ls`, `mv`, etc. That program was discarded, and the feature was coded directly into the shell. What was wrong with the `chdir` utility? Add the `cd` command to your shell.

9.12 The shell supports special variables to represent system settings. For example, the variable `$$` stands for the process ID of the shell, and `$?` stands for the `exit` value of the last command. Add these variables to your program.

9.13 Standard Unix shells allow quoted command-line arguments. A command like `vi "My Book Report"` contains two command-line arguments. Add quoted arguments to your shell. Where in the logic of the shell are the quotes noted? Consider the command `rm "file1.c;2"`. If your shell recognizes the semicolon as a command separator, this expression should still parse as one command with two arguments.

9.14 *User-defined prompt* Most shells allow users to set the prompt by assigning a string to a specified variable. Add this feature to your shell. Decide on a shell variable to use for this purpose. `sh` and `bash` use `PS1`, while the `csh` family uses `prompt`.

# CHAPTER 10

I/O Redirection and Pipes

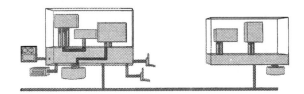

OBJECTIVES

Ideas and Skills

- I/O Redirection: What and why?
- Definitions of standard input, output, and error
- Redirecting standard I/O to files
- Using `fork` to redirect I/O for other programs
- Pipes
- Using `fork` with pipes

System Calls and Functions

- `dup`, `dup2`
- `pipe`

10.1   SHELL PROGRAMMING

How do the commands

```
ls > my.files
who | sort > userlist
```

work? How does the shell tell a program to send its output to a file instead of the screen? How does the shell connect the output stream of one process to the input stream of another process? What does the term *standard input* really mean?

In this chapter, we focus on a particular form of interprocess communication: *input/output (I/O) redirection* and *pipes*. We start by seeing how I/O redirection and pipes help in writing shell scripts. We then look at underlying features of the operating system that make I/O redirection work. Finally, we write our own programs that change input and output streams for processes.

10.2   A SHELL APPLICATION: WATCH FOR USERS

Consider the following problem: You have a list of pals that use the same Unix machine you do. You want a program that notifies you when people log in or log out of the system so you can watch for your pals.

You *could* write a C program that uses the utmp file and interval timers. The program would open the utmp file, make a list of users, and then sleep for a while, rescan the utmp file, and report any changes. How much time and how much code would that take?

A simpler solution is to write a shell script. Unix already has a program that lists current users: who. Unix also includes programs to sleep and to process lists of strings. Here is a Unix script that reports all logins and logouts:

```
logic                                        shell code
--------------------------------             -----------------------

get list of users (call it prev)            who | sort > prev
while true                                   while true ; do
   sleep                                        sleep 60
   get list of users (call it curr)             who | sort > curr
   compare lists                                echo "logged out:"
      in prev, not in curr -> logout            comm -23 prev curr
                                                echo "logged in:"
      in curr, not in prev -> login             comm -13 prev curr
   make prev = curr                             mv curr prev
repeat                                        done
```

In this script, we combine seven Unix tools, one while loop, and a generous helping of I/O redirection to build a program that solves the problem. Let us look at the details of the programs and the connections among these programs.

The first line in the script builds a list, sorted by username, of all users logged in when the script starts running. The who command outputs a list of users, and the sort command reads a list as input and outputs a sorted version of that list.

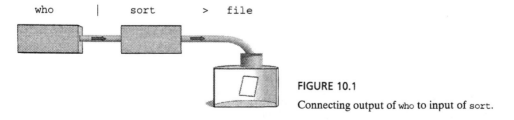

FIGURE 10.1

Connecting output of who to input of sort.

The line who | sort > prev tells the shell to run the commands who and sort at the same time, and to send the output of who directly to the input to sort. (See Figure 10.1.) The who command does not have to finish analyzing the utmp file before sort begins reading and sorting input. The two processes are scheduled to run in small time slices, sharing CPU time with other processes on the system. Furthermore, the `sort > prev` part of the line tells the shell to send the output of `sort` into a file called `prev`, creating the file if it does not exist and replacing its contents if it does.

After sleeping for a minute, the script creates a new list of users in the file called `curr`. How can we compare two sorted lists of log-in records? The Unix tool `comm`, depicted in Figure 10.2, finds lines common to two sorted files. Given two files, there are three subsets: lines in set 1 only, lines in set 2 only, and lines in both sets. The `comm` command compares two sorted lists and prints out three columns, one for each of these subsets. Command-line options allow you to suppress any of the columns. For example, the two commands

```
comm -23 prev curr    # drop columns 2 and 3 => show lines only in prev
```

and

```
comm -13 prev curr    # drop columns 1 and 3 => show lines only in curr
```

produce exactly the two sets we want: those log-in records in the previous list, but not in the current list (logouts), and those log-in records not in the previous list, but only in the current list (logins).

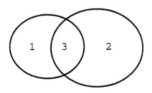

FIGURE 10.2

`comm` compares two lists and outputs three sets.

Finally, the command `mv  curr  prev` replaces the list called `prev` with the list called `curr`.

Lessons

This `watch.sh` script demonstrates three important ideas:

(a) Power of shell scripts—easier and quicker than C
(b) Flexibility of software tools—each tool does one specific, general task
(c) Use and value of I/O redirection and pipes

`watch.sh` shows how to use the `>` operator to treat files as variables of arbitrary size and structure. In the same way one writes

```
x = func_a(func_b(y));    /* store output of func_a of func_b in x */
```

in C, one writes

```
prog_b | prog_a > x       # store output of combination in x
```

in sh.

Questions

How does all this work? What role does the shell play in connecting processes? What role does the kernel play? What role do the individual programs play?

10.3 FACTS ABOUT STANDARD I/O AND REDIRECTION

All Unix I/O redirection is based on the principle of standard streams of data. Consider the sort tool. sort reads bytes from one stream of data, writes the sorted results to another stream, and reports any errors to a third stream. Ignoring for now the question of where these standard streams of data go, the sort utility has the basic shape shown in Figure 10.3. The three channels for data flow are as follows:

standard input—the stream of data to process

standard output—the stream of result data

standard error—a stream of error messages

FIGURE 10.3

A software tool reads input and writes output and errors.

10.3.1 Fact One: Three Standard File Descriptors

All Unix tools use the three-stream model shown in Figure 10.3. The model is implemented via a simple rule. Each of these three streams is a specific file descriptor. Figure 10.4 shows the details.

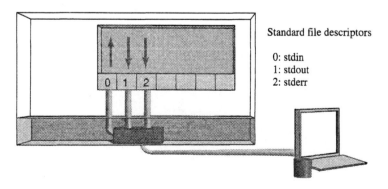

FIGURE 10.4

Three special file descriptors.

FACT: All Unix tools use file descriptors 0, 1, and 2.

Standard input *means* file descriptor 0, standard output *means* file descriptor 1, and standard error *means* file descriptor 2. Unix tools expect to find file descriptors 0, 1, and 2 already open for reading, writing, and writing, respectively.

10.3.2   Default Connections: the `tty`

When you run a Unix tool from the command line of the shell, stdin, stdout, and stderr are usually connected to your terminal. Therefore, the tool reads from the keyboard and writes output and error messages to the screen. For example, if you type sort and press the Enter key, your terminal will be connected to the sort tool. Type as many lines of input as you like. When you indicate end of file by pressing Ctrl-D on a line by itself, the sort program sorts the input and writes the result to stdout.

Most Unix tools process data from files or from standard input. If the tool is given file names on the command line, it reads input from those files. If there are no files named on the command line, the program reads from standard input.

10.3.3   Output Goes Only to `stdout`

On the other hand, most programs do not accept names for output files; they always write results to file descriptor 1 and errors to file descriptor 2.[1] If you want to send the output of a process to a file or to the input of another process, you change where the file descriptor goes.

10.3.4   The Shell, Not the Program, Redirects I/O

You tell the shell to attach file descriptor 1 to a file by using the output redirection notation: cmd > filename. The shell connects that file descriptor to the named file.

The program continues to write to file descriptor 1, unaware of the new data destination. The following program, called listargs.c, shows that the program does not even see the redirection notation on the command line:

```
/* listargs.c
 *              print the number of command line args, list the args,
 *              then print a message to stderr
 */
#include        <stdio.h>

main( int ac, char *av[] )
{
        int     i;

        printf("Number of args: %d, Args are:\n", ac);
```

---

[1]The commands sort and dd allow stdout overrides, but they have good reasons.

```
           for(i=0;i<ac;i++)
                    printf("args[%d] %s\n", i, av[i]);

           fprintf(stderr,"This message is sent to stderr.\n");
      }
```

listargs prints to standard output the list of command-line arguments. Notice that listargs does not print the redirection symbol and filename:

```
$ cc listargs.c -o listargs
$ ./listargs testing one two
args[0] ./listargs
args[1] testing
args[2] one
args[3] two
This message is sent to stderr.
$ ./listargs testing one two > xyz
This message is sent to stderr.
$ cat xyz
args[0] ./listargs
args[1] testing
args[2] one
args[3] two
$ ./listargs testing >xyz one two 2> oops
$ cat xyz
args[0] ./listargs
args[1] testing
args[2] one
args[3] two
$ cat oops
This message is sent to stderr.
```

These examples demonstrate some important facts about output redirection in the shell. The most important fact is that the shell does not pass the redirection symbol and filename to the command.

The second fact is that the redirection request can appear *anywhere* in the command and does not require spaces around the redirection symbol. Even a command like > listing ls is acceptable. Thus, the > sign does not terminate the command and arguments; it is just an added request.

The final fact is that many shells provide notation for redirecting other file descriptors. For example, 2>filename redirects file descriptor 2, that is, standard error, to the named file.

10.3.5   Understanding I/O Redirection

We saw in watch.sh that I/O redirection is an integral part of Unix programming. We saw in listargs.c that the shell, not the tool, redirects input and output.

But *how* does the shell do I/O redirection? How can we write programs that redirect I/O? Our project for this chapter is to write programs that do three basic redirection operations:

who > userlist	attach `stdout` to a file
sort < data	attach `stdin` to a file
**who	sort**	attach `stdout` to stdin

10.3.6   Fact Two: The "Lowest-Available-`fd`" Principle

What is a file descriptor anyway? A file descriptor is a remarkably simple concept: It is an array index. Each process has a collection of files it has open. Those open files are kept in an array. A file descriptor is simply an index of an item in that array. Figure 10.5 illustrates the "lowest-available-file-descriptor" rule.

Unix always assigns new connections to the lowest available file descriptor.

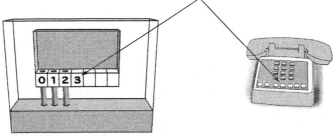

FIGURE 10.5

The "lowest-available-file-descriptor" rule.

FACT: When you open a file, you *always get* the lowest available spot in the array.

Making a new connection with file descriptors is like receiving a connection on a multiline phone. Callers dial a main number, and the internal phone system assigns each new connection an internal line. On many such systems, the next incoming call is assigned the *lowest available line*.

10.3.7   The Synthesis

We now have two basic facts. First, we have the convention that all Unix processes use file descriptors 0, 1, and 2 for the standard input, output, and error channels. Second, we have the fact that the kernel assigns the lowest available file descriptor when a process requests a new file descriptor. By combining these two facts, we can understand how I/O redirection works, and we can write programs that perform I/O redirection.

10.4   HOW TO ATTACH `stdin` TO A FILE

We now examine in detail how a program redirects standard input so that data come from a file. To be precise, processes do not read from files; processes read from file descriptors. If we attach file descriptor 0 to a file, that file becomes the source for standard input.

We examine three methods for attaching standard input to a file. Some of these methods are not appropriate for files, but are essential when we work with pipes.

10.4.1   Method 1: Close Then Open

The first method is the *close-then-open* technique. This technique is like hanging up to free a particular line and then picking up the telephone so you get that line. Here are the steps:

Starting, we have a typical configuration. The three standard streams are connected to the terminal driver. Data flow in through file descriptor 0 and data flow out through file descriptors 1 and 2. (See Figure 10.6.)

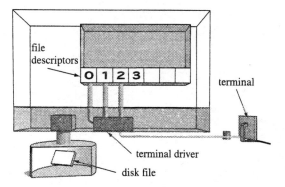

FIGURE 10.6

Typical starting configuration.

Then, close(0), the first step, is to hang up the connection to standard input. We call `close(0)` to break the connection from standard input to the terminal driver. Figure 10.7 shows how the first element in the array of file descriptors is now unused.

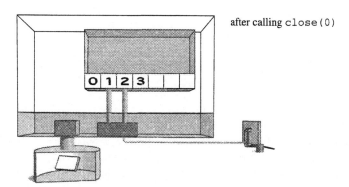

after calling `close(0)`

FIGURE 10.7

`stdin` is now closed.

Finally, open(filename,O_RDONLY), the last step, is to open the file you want to attach to `stdin`. The lowest number available file descriptor is 0, so the file you open will be attached at standard input. (See Figure 10.8.) Any functions that read from standard input will read from that file.

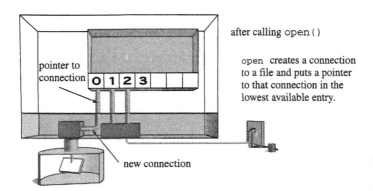

after calling `open()`

`open` creates a connection to a file and puts a pointer to that connection in the lowest available entry.

pointer to connection

new connection

FIGURE 10.8

`stdin` now attached to file.

The following program uses the *close-then-open* method:

```
/* stdinredir1.c
 *        purpose: show how to redirect standard input by replacing file
 *                 descriptor 0 with a connection to a file.
 *         action: reads three lines from standard input, then
 *                 closes fd 0, opens a disk file, then reads in
 *                 three more lines from standard input
 */
#include        <stdio.h>
#include        <fcntl.h>

main()
{
        int     fd ;
        char    line[100];

        /* read and print three lines */

        fgets( line, 100, stdin ); printf("%s", line );
        fgets( line, 100, stdin ); printf("%s", line );
        fgets( line, 100, stdin ); printf("%s", line );

        /* redirect input */

        close(0);
        fd = open("/etc/passwd", O_RDONLY);
        if ( fd != 0 ){
                fprintf(stderr,"Could not open data as fd 0\n");
                exit(1);
        }
```

```
                    /* read and print three lines */

                    fgets( line, 100, stdin ); printf("%s", line );
                    fgets( line, 100, stdin ); printf("%s", line );
                    fgets( line, 100, stdin ); printf("%s", line );
            }
```

stdinreader1 reads and prints three lines from standard input, redirects standard input, and then reads and prints three more lines from standard input. stdinreader1 reads the first three lines from the keyboard, and then reads the next three lines from the passwd file:

```
$ ./stdinredir1
line1
line1
testing line2
testing line2
line 3 here
line 3 here
root:x:0:0:root:/root:/bin/bash
bin:x:1:1:bin:/bin:
daemon:x:2:2:daemon:/sbin:
$
```

Nothing else special is going on. Just hang up the line and dial the new number. When the connection is made, you are now hearing from a new source of standard input.

10.4.2 Method 2: open..close..dup..close

Consider this situation: the telephone rings, you pick up the upstairs extension, but you realize you want to take the call on the downstairs phone. You tell someone downstairs to pick up that phone, giving you two connections to the caller, then you hang up the upstairs phone, leaving the only active connection on the downstairs phone. Does that sound familiar? The idea in this method is to duplicate the connection from the upstairs phone to the downstairs phone so you can hang up the upstairs phone without losing the connection.

The Unix system call dup, depicted in Figure 10.9, makes a second connection to an existing file descriptor. The method requires four steps:

open(file)   The first step is to open the file to which stdin should be attached. This call returns a file descriptor, which is not 0, since 0 is currently open.

close(0)   The next step is to close file descriptor 0. File descriptor 0 is now unused.

dup(fd)   The dup(fd) system call makes a duplicate of fd. The duplicate uses the *lowest number unused file descriptor*. Therefore, the duplicate of the connection to the file is at spot 0 in the array of open files. We have thereby attached the disk file to file descriptor 0.

fd = open("f", O_RDONLY);   close(0);

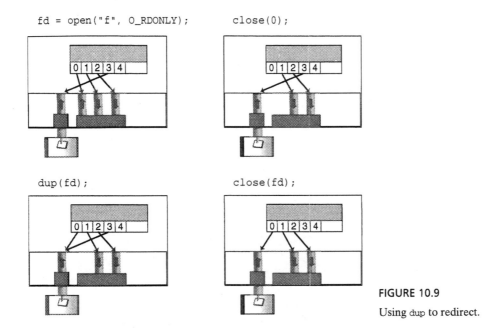

dup(fd);   close(fd);

FIGURE 10.9

Using dup to redirect.

close(fd)   Finally, we `close(fd)`, the original connection to the file, leaving only
the connection on file descriptor 0. Compare this method to the tech-
nique of moving a phone call from one extension to another.

This program, `stdinredir2.c`, uses method 2:

```
/* stdinredir2.c
 *        shows two more methods for redirecting standard input
 *        use #define to set one or the other
 */
#include        <stdio.h>
#include        <fcntl.h>

/* #define      CLOSE_DUP                   /* open, close, dup, close */
/* #define      USE_DUP2            /* open, dup2, close */

main()
{
        int     fd ;
        int     newfd;
        char    line[100];

        /* read and print three lines */

        fgets( line, 100, stdin ); printf("%s", line );
        fgets( line, 100, stdin ); printf("%s", line );
        fgets( line, 100, stdin ); printf("%s", line );

        /* redirect input */
```

```
        fd = open("data", O_RDONLY);       /* open the disk file   */
#ifdef CLOSE_DUP
        close(0);
        newfd = dup(fd);                   /* copy open fd to 0     */
#else
        newfd = dup2(fd,0);                /* close 0, dup fd to 0 */
#endif
        if ( newfd != 0 ){
                fprintf(stderr,"Could not duplicate fd to 0\n");
                exit(1);
        }
        close(fd);                         /* close original fd     */

        /* read and print three lines */

        fgets( line, 100, stdin ); printf("%s", line );
        fgets( line, 100, stdin ); printf("%s", line );
        fgets( line, 100, stdin ); printf("%s", line );
}
```

This four-step method is included for the pedagogical purpose of demonstrating the
dup system call, an essential tool when working with pipes. A simpler method combines
the close(0) and dup(fd) steps into a single system call, dup2.

10.4.3 System Call Summary: dup

dup, dup2	
PURPOSE	Copy a file descriptor
INCLUDE	#include <unistd.h>
USAGE	newfd = dup(oldfd); newfd = dup2(oldfd, newfd);
ARGS	oldfd file descriptor to copy newfd copy of oldfd
RETURNS	-1 if error newfd new file descriptor

dup creates a copy of file descriptor *oldfd*. dup2 makes file descriptor *newfd* the copy of
oldfd. The two file descriptors refer to the same open file. Both calls return the new file
descriptor or −1 on error.

10.4.4 Method 3: open..dup2..close

The code for stdinredir2.c includes #ifdef-ed code to replace the close(0) and
dup(fd) system calls with dup2(fd,0). dup2(orig,new) makes a duplicate of file

descriptor *old* at file descriptor *new*, even if it has to close an existing connection on *new* first.

10.4.5   But the Shell Redirects `stdin` for Other Programs

These samples show how a program can attach its standard input to a file. In practice, of course, if a program wants to read a file, it can just open the file directly rather than changing standard input. The real value of these samples is to show how one program can change standard input for another program.

10.5   REDIRECTING I/O FOR ANOTHER PROGRAM: `who > userlist`

When a user types `who > userlist`, the shell runs the command `who` with the standard output of `who` attached to the file called `userlist`. How does that work?

The secret is the split second between `fork` and `exec`. After `fork`, the child process is still running the shell code, but is about to call `exec`. `exec` will replace the program running in the process, but it will not change either the attributes or the connections of the process. That is, after `exec`, the process will have the same user ID it had before, the process will have the same priority it had before, and the process *will have the same file descriptors it had before* the `exec`. To repeat, a program gets the open files of the process into which it is loaded. Figure 10.10 illustrates the redirection of output for a child.

The child inherits from the parent the pointers to open files. The child redirects standard output:

```
close(1);
creat("f");
exec();
```

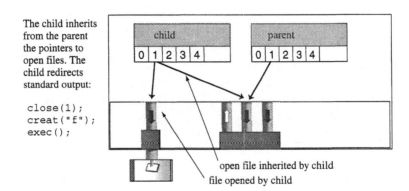

FIGURE 10.10

The shell redirects output for a child.

Let us watch a process use this principle to redirect standard output:

1. *Start here*

In Figure 10.11, a process is running in user space. File descriptor 1 is attached to an open file called *f* as shown. To make the picture clearer, other open files are not shown.

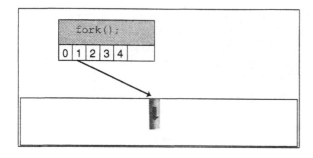

FIGURE 10.11

A process about to fork and its standard output.

2. *After parent calls fork*

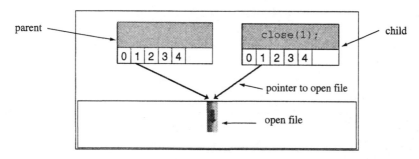

FIGURE 10.12

Standard output of child is copied from parent.

In Figure 10.12, a new process appears. This process runs the same code as the original process, but knows it is a child process. The child process contains the same code, the same data, and the same set of open files as its parent. Therefore the item in spot 1 in the array of open files refers, also, to file *f*. The child calls `close(1)`.

3. *After child calls* `close(1)`

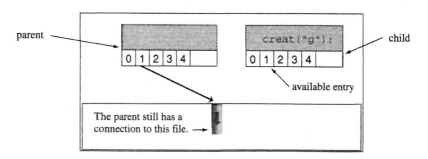

FIGURE 10.13

The child can close its standard output.

In Figure 10.13, the parent process has not called `close(1)`, so file descriptor 1 in the parent still connects to file *f*. In the child process, file descriptor 1 is the lowest unused file descriptor. The child now opens a file called g.

4. *After child calls* `creat("g",m)`

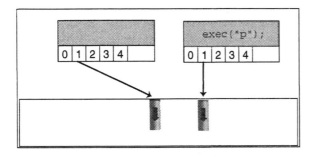

FIGURE 10.14

Child opens a new file, getting `fd = 1`.

In Figure 10.14, file descriptor 1 is now attached to g. Standard output in the child is redirected to g. The child now calls exec to run who.

5. *After child execs a new program*

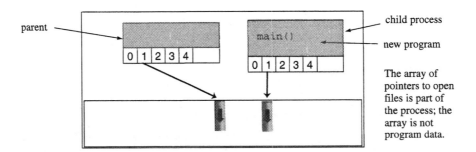

FIGURE 10.15

Child runs a program with new standard output.

In Figure 10.15, the child executes the who program. The code and data for the shell are removed from the child process and are replaced by the code and data for the who program. The *file descriptors* are retained across the exec. Open files are not part of the code nor data of a program; they are attributes of a process.

The who command writes the list of users to file descriptor 1. Unbeknownst to who, that stream of output bytes flows into file g.

The program whotofile.c demonstrates the method:

```
/* whotofile.c
 *        purpose: show how to redirect output for another program
 *           idea: fork, then in the child, redirect output, then exec
 */
```

```
#include          <stdio.h>

main()
{
        int      pid ;
        int      fd;

        printf("About to run who into a file\n");

        /* create a new process or quit */
        if( (pid = fork() ) == -1 ){
                perror("fork"); exit(1);
        }
        /* child does the work */
        if ( pid == 0 ){
                close(1);                            /* close, */
                fd = creat( "userlist", 0644 );      /* then open */
                execlp( "who", "who", NULL );        /* and run     */
                perror("execlp");
                exit(1);
        }
        /* parent waits then reports */
        if ( pid != 0 ){
                wait(NULL);
                printf("Done running who.  results in userlist\n");
        }

}
```

10.5.1 Summary of Redirection to Files

Three basic facts make it easy under Unix to attach standard input, standard output, and standard error to disk files:

(a) Standard input, output, and error are file descriptors 0, 1, and 2.
(b) The kernel always uses the lowest numbered unused file descriptor.
(c) The set of file descriptors is passed unchanged across exec calls.

The shell uses the interval in the child between fork and exec to attach standard data streams to files.

The shell also supports notation of the following form:

```
who >> userlog
sort < data
```

Writing the code to perform these two operations is left as an exercise.

10.6   PROGRAMMING PIPES

We saw how to write a program that attaches standard output to a file. We now examine how to use pipes to connect the standard output of one process to the standard input of another process. Figure 10.16 shows how pipes work. A pipe is a one-way data

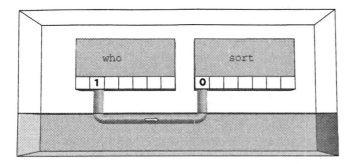

FIGURE 10.16

Two processes connected by a pipe.

channel in the kernel. A pipe has a reading end and a writing end. To write who | sort, we need two skills: how to create a pipe and how to connect standard input and output to a pipe.

10.6.1   Creating a Pipe

A pipe is illustrated in Figure 10.17. Use the pipe system call, summarized as follows, to create a pipe:

pipe	
PURPOSE	Create a pipe
INCLUDE	#include <unistd.h>
USAGE	result = pipe(int array[2])
ARGS	array an array of two ints
RETURNS	-1 if error
	0 if success

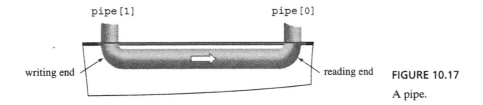

pipe [1]   pipe [0]

writing end   reading end

FIGURE 10.17

A pipe.

pipe creates the pipe and connects its two ends to two file descriptors. array[0] is the file descriptor of the reading end, and array[1] is the file descriptor of the writing end. The internals of the pipe, like the internals of an open file, are hidden in the kernel. The process sees two file descriptors.

The pair of before and after shots in Figure 10.18 shows a process creating a pipe. The *before* shot shows the standard set of file descriptors. The *after* shot shows the newly created pipe in the kernel and the two connections to that pipe in the process. Notice that pipe, like open, uses the lowest-numbered available file descriptors.

Before pipe

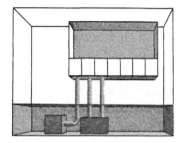

The process has some usual files open.

After pipe

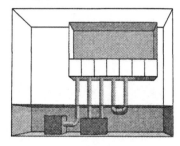

The kernel creates a pipe and sets file descriptors.

FIGURE 10.18

A process creates a pipe.

The program, pipedemo.c, creates a pipe and then uses the pipe to send data to itself:

```
/*  pipedemo.c  * Demonstrates: how to create and use a pipe
 *              * Effect: creates a pipe, writes into writing
 *                  end, then runs around and reads from reading
 *                  end.  A little weird, but demonstrates the idea.
 */
#include        <stdio.h>
#include        <unistd.h>

main()
{
        int     len, i, apipe[2];       /* two file descriptors */
        char    buf[BUFSIZ];            /* for reading end      */

        /* get a pipe */
        if ( pipe ( apipe ) == -1 ){
                perror("could not make pipe");
                exit(1);
        }
        printf("Got a pipe! It is file descriptors: { %d %d }\n",
                                        apipe[0], apipe[1]);

        /* read from stdin, write into pipe, read from pipe, print */
```

```
while ( fgets(buf, BUFSIZ, stdin) ){
        len = strlen( buf );
        if ( write( apipe[1], buf, len) != len ){        /* send */
                perror("writing to pipe");                /* down */
                break;                                    /* pipe */
        }
        for ( i = 0 ; i<len ; i++ )                       /* wipe */
                buf[i] = 'X' ;
        len = read( apipe[0], buf, BUFSIZ ) ;             /* read */
        if ( len == -1 ){                                 /* from */
                perror("reading from pipe");              /* pipe */
                break;
        }
        if ( write( 1 , buf, len ) != len ){              /* send  */
                perror("writing to stdout");              /* to    */
                break;                                    /* stdout */
        }
    }
}
```

Figure 10.19 depicts the flow of bytes from keyboard to process, from process to pipe, from pipe to process, and from process back to terminal.

We now know how to create a pipe and how to write data into a pipe and how to read data from a pipe. In practice, one rarely writes a program that sends data to itself. By combining pipe with fork, though, we can connect two processes.

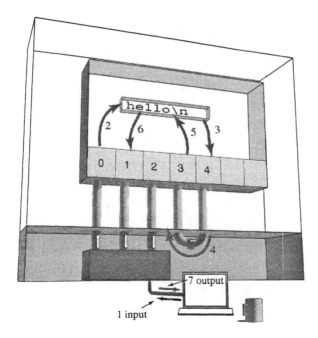

FIGURE 10.19

Data flow in pipedemo.c.

10.6.2 Using `fork` to Share a Pipe

When a process creates a pipe, the process has connections to both ends of the pipe. When that process calls `fork`, the child process, a copy of the parent, also has connections to the pipe, as shown in Figure 10.20. Parent and child can write bytes to the writing end of the pipe, and parent and child can read bytes from the reading end of the pipe. (See Figure 10.21.) Both processes can read and write, but a pipe is most effective when one process writes data and the other process reads the data.

Sharing a pipe:

A process calls `pipe`. The kernel creates a pipe and adds to the array of file descriptors pointers to the ends of the pipe.

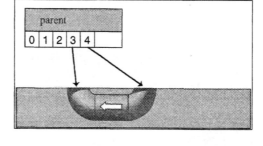

The process then calls `fork`. The kernel creates a new process, and copies into that process the array of file desriptors from the parent.

Both processes have access to both ends of one pipe.

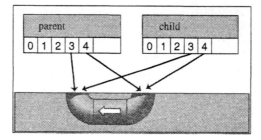

FIGURE 10.20

Sharing a pipe.

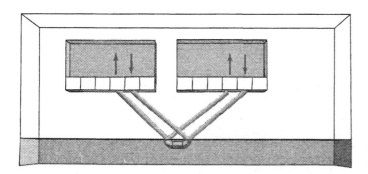

FIGURE 10.21

Interprocess data flow.

This program, pipedemo2.c, shows how to combine pipe and fork to create a pair of processes that communicate through a pipe:

```
/* pipedemo2.c  * Demonstrates how pipe is duplicated in fork()
 *              * Parent continues to write and read pipe,
 *                but child also writes to the pipe
 */
#include         <stdio.h>

#define CHILD_MESS      "I want a cookie\n"
#define PAR_MESS        "testing..\n"
#define oops(m,x)       { perror(m); exit(x); }

main()
{
        int     pipefd[2];              /* the pipe     */
        int     len;                    /* for write    */
        char    buf[BUFSIZ];            /* for read     */
        int     read_len;

        if ( pipe( pipefd ) == -1 )
                oops("cannot get a pipe", 1);

        switch( fork() ){
                case -1:
                        oops("cannot fork", 2);

                /* child writes to pipe every 5 seconds */
                case 0:
                        len = strlen(CHILD_MESS);
                        while ( 1 ){
                                if (write( pipefd[1], CHILD_MESS, len) != len )
                                        oops("write", 3);
                                sleep(5);
                        }

                /* parent reads from pipe and also writes to pipe */
                default:
                        len = strlen( PAR_MESS );
                        while ( 1 ){
                                if ( write( pipefd[1], PAR_MESS, len)!=len )
                                        oops("write", 4);
                                sleep(1);
                                read_len = read( pipefd[0], buf, BUFSIZ );
                                if ( read_len <= 0 )
                                        break;
                                write( 1 , buf, read_len );
                        }
        }
}
```

10.6.3 The Finale: Using `pipe`, `fork`, and `exec`

We now know all the ideas and skills required to write a program that connects the output of `who` to the input of `sort`. We know how to create a pipe, we know how to share a pipe between two processes, we know how to change the standard input of a process, and we know how to change the standard output of a process.

We combine all these skills to write a general-purpose program called `pipe` that takes the names of two programs as arguments. The examples

```
pipe who sort
pipe ls  head
```

show two uses of `pipe`. The logic of the program is as follows:

```
                    pipe(p)
                    fork()
                      |
        +------------+--------------+
      child                     parent
        |                          |
      close(p[0])              close(p[1])
      dup2(p[1],1)             dup2(p[0],0)
      close(p[1])              close(p[0])
      exec "who"               exec "sort"
```

Here is the code:

```c
/* pipe.c
 *         * Demonstrates how to create a pipeline from one process to another
 *         * Takes two args, each a command, and connects
 *           av[1]'s output to input of av[2]
 *         * usage: pipe command1 command2
 *           effect: command1 | command2
 *         * Limitations: commands do not take arguments
 *         * uses execlp() since known number of args
 *         * Note: exchange child and parent and watch fun
 */
#include        <stdio.h>
#include        <unistd.h>

#define oops(m,x)       { perror(m); exit(x); }

main(int ac, char **av)
{
        int     thepipe[2],                 /* two file descriptors */
                newfd,                      /* useful for pipes     */
```

```
                    pid;                             /* and the pid          */

        if ( ac != 3 ){
                fprintf(stderr, "usage: pipe cmd1 cmd2\n");
                exit(1);
        }
        if ( pipe( thepipe ) == -1 )                /* get a pipe            */
                oops("Cannot get a pipe", 1);
        /* ------------------------------------------------------------ */
        /*      now we have a pipe, now let's get two processes          */

        if ( (pid = fork()) == -1 )                  /* get a proc           */
                oops("Cannot fork", 2);

        /* ------------------------------------------------------------ */
        /*      Right Here, there are two processes                      */
        /*              parent will read from pipe                       */
        if ( pid > 0 ){                     /* parent will exec av[2]     */
                close(thepipe[1]);       /* parent doesn't write to pipe  */

                if ( dup2(thepipe[0], 0) == -1 )
                        oops("could not redirect stdin",3);

                close(thepipe[0]);      /* stdin is duped, close pipe     */
                execlp( av[2], av[2], NULL);
                oops(av[2], 4);
        }

        /*      child execs av[1] and writes into pipe                   */
        close(thepipe[0]);                  /* child doesn't read from pipe */

        if ( dup2(thepipe[1], 1) == -1 )
                oops("could not redirect stdout", 4);

        close(thepipe[1]);                   /* stdout is duped, close pipe  */
        execlp( av[1], av[1], NULL);
        oops(av[1], 5);
}
```

The pipe.c program uses the same ideas and techniques the shell uses to create pipelines. The shell, though, does not run an external program like pipe.c. The shell has to create the pipe, then fork to create the two processes, then redirect standard input and output to the pipe, and finally exec the two programs.

10.6.4 Technical Details: Pipes Are Not Files

In many ways, pipes look like regular files. A process uses write to put data into a pipe and uses read to get data from a pipe. A pipe, like a file, appears as a sequence of bytes without any particular block or record structure. In other ways, pipes differ from files. What, for instance, does end of file mean for a pipe? The following technical details clarify some of these similarities and differences.

Reading from Pipes

1. read *on a pipe blocks*

When a process tries to read from a pipe, the call blocks until some bytes are written into the pipe. What prevents a process from waiting forever?

2. *Reading EOF on a pipe*

When all writers close the writing end of the pipe, attempts to read from the pipe return 0, that is, end of file.

3. *Multiple readers can cause trouble*

A pipe is a queue. When a process reads bytes from a pipe, those bytes are no longer in the pipe. If two processes try to read from the same pipe, one process will get some of the bytes from the pipe, and the other process will get the other bytes. Unless the two processes use some method to coordinate their access to the pipe, the data they read are likely to be incomplete.

Writing to Pipes

4. write *to a pipe blocks until there is space*

Pipes have a finite capacity that is far lower than the file-size limit imposed on disk files. When a process tries to write to a pipe, the call blocks until there is enough space in the pipe. If a process wants to write, say, 1000 bytes, and there is only room for 500 bytes, the call waits until 1000 bytes of space are available. What if the process wanted to write a million bytes? Would the call wait forever?

5. write *guarantees a minimum chunk size*

The POSIX standard states that the kernel will not split up chunks of data into blocks smaller than 512 bytes. Linux guarantees an unbroken buffer size of 4096 for pipes. If two different processes write to a pipe, and each process limits its messages to 512 bytes, the processes are assured their messages will not be split.

6. write *fails if no readers*

If all readers have closed the reading ends of a pipe, then an attempt to write to the pipe can lead to trouble. If data were accepted, where would they go? To avoid losing data, the kernel uses two methods to notify a process that write is futile. The kernel sends SIGPIPE to the process. If that kills the process, no further action is required. Otherwise, write returns −1 and sets errno to EPIPE.

SUMMARY

MAIN IDEAS

- Input/Output redirection allows separate programs to work as a team, each program a specialist.
- The Unix convention is that programs read input from file descriptor 0, write results to file descriptor 1, and report errors to file descriptor 2. Those three file descriptors are called standard input, standard output, and standard error.

- When you log in to Unix, the log-in procedure sets up file descriptors 0, 1, and 2. These connections, and all open file descriptors, are passed from parent to child and across the exec system call.
- System calls that create file descriptors always use the lowest-numbered free file descriptor.
- Redirecting standard input, output, or error means changing where file descriptors 0, 1, or 2 connect. There are several techniques for redirecting standard I/O.
- A pipe is a data queue in the kernel with each end attached to a file descriptor. A program creates a pipe with the `pipe` system call.
- Both ends of a pipe are copied to a child process when the parent calls `fork`.
- Pipes can only connect processes that share a common parent.

WHAT NEXT?

The traditional Unix pipe carries data between processes in one direction. What if two processes wanted to pass data back and forth? What if two processes were not related, or if two processes were on different computers? In the next several chapters, we look at pipes in more detail and then study network programming. The idea of a pipe generalizes to the idea of a socket.

EXPLORATIONS

10.1 *Meaning of* >> The >> notation tells the shell to append output to a file. Does the shell use auto-append mode (see Chapter 5), or does it simply seek to the end of the file and start writing there? Devise an experiment using shell scripts to answer the question.

10.2 In `pipe.c`, the parent process runs the program that consumes data, and the child process runs the program that produces data. What difference would it make if those roles were reversed? By changing the test `if ( pid > 0 )` to `if ( pid == 0 )`, the roles will be reversed. What happens? Why?

10.3 What changes do you need to make to your shell to include pipes? First, how would you modify the flow of control to identify and handle commands that end with a pipe sign? Second, what if there are several commands separated by pipe signs?

10.4 In `pipe.c`, the reading process, `sort`, closes its copy of the writing end of the pipe. Change the code so the reading process does *not* close the writing end of the pipe. Now run the program and explain its behavior.

10.5 *Adding* > *and* < *to your shell* We examined earlier in this chapter the notation to attach standard input or standard output to a file. We saw that the redirection symbol and filename may appear anywhere in the command line. We also saw that the symbol and filename are not part of the list of arguments passed to the new program.

Where in the logic of our small shell should we identify the request to change input or output to a disk file?

Where in the logic of our small shell should the redirection be performed?

What if a user typed `set > varlist` ? Does the shell allow you to redirect the output of built-in commands? How can you add that to our shell?

10.6 *Protecting users* What if a user types `sort <data >data` . What is the problem with this request? What do standard Unix shells do about it? How can your shell handle this problem?

10.7 We examined methods for attaching the standard input or standard output of a process to a file. All our examples have assumed regular plain disk files. Can I/O redirection work for files that represent devices? That is, what if you `close(0)` and `open("/dev/tty",0)`? What does the shell do with the command `who > /dev/tty`?

10.8 In `pipe.c`, we call `fork` and `exec`, but we do not call `wait`. Why not?

10.9 How is `dup` like `link`? Discuss pointers.

PROGRAMMING EXERCISES

10.10 Modify the `watch.sh` script so it has nicer features.

   (a) This version prints out logins and logouts for all users. A more useful version would accept as a command-line argument a name of a file that contains a list of users to watch.

   (b) This version prints out something each time through the loop, even if nothing has changed. Modify the program so it prints out the *new logins* and *new logouts* messages only if there is something to show.

   (c) The `who` command lists in addition to username, the log-in time and the terminal name. That may be more information than you want. If a user connects using a second window, that may not be interesting to you. Write a version of the program that reports when a watched user changes from "is logged on" to "is not logged on," regardless of terminal.

   (d) This version stores its data in files called `prev` and `curr` in the current directory and leaves those files there when the program stops running. This design is poor for several reasons. What are some of the reasons? Revise the script to use temporary files and to remove those files at exit. Read about the `trap` command in the shell. Examine the use of the `mktemp` command.

10.11 Modify the `whotofile.c` sample program so it appends the output of `who` to a file. Make sure your program works if the file does not exist.

10.12 Write a program called `sortfromfile.c` that redirects the input of the `sort` command so it reads from a file. The filename is specified on the command line.

10.13 Extend `pipe.c` to handle three-part pipelines. This new version should accept three program names as arguments and run them as a pipeline. The command

```
pipe3 who sort head
```

should have the same effect as `who | sort | head`.

10.14 Extend the `pipe3` program in the previous problem to handle an arbitrary number of arguments.

10.15 *process tee* The `tee` utility lets you redirect data to a file and also pass the data to the next command in a pipeline. For example,

```
who | tee userlist | sort > list2
```

produces an unsorted file and a sorted file: `userlist` and `list2`. The argument to `tee` is the name of a file; read the manual for more details. Write a program called `progtee` that redirects data to a program and also passes the data to the next command in a pipeline. For example, the pipeline

```
who | progtee mail smith | sort | progtee mail -s "hello" root > list2
```

sends an unsorted list to smith, sends a sorted list to root, and puts a copy of the sorted list into the file list2.

10.16 *isatty* Programs that write to standard output do not usually care if the file descriptor leads to a terminal or to a disk file. The text suggests that a process has no way of knowing where the file descriptor leads. This is false. The library function isatty(fd) returns a true value if *fd* refers to a terminal. isatty uses the system call fstat. Read about fstat and use that information to write a function isaregfile that returns a true value if its argument is a file descriptor connected to a regular file.

# CHAPTER 11

Connecting to Processes Near and Far
Servers and Sockets

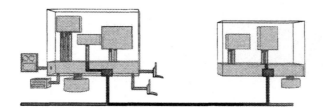

OBJECTIVES

Ideas and Skills

- The client/server model
- Using pipes for two-way communication
- Coroutines
- The file/process similarity
- Sockets: Why, What, How?
- Network services
- Using sockets for client/server programs

System Calls and Functions

- fdopen
- popen
- socket
- bind
- listen
- accept
- connect

11.1   PRODUCTS AND SERVICES

Unix programmers use pipes to create digital assembly lines, the way manufacturers use conveyor belts to carry products from one worker to the next.

Not all businesses are factories, and some forms of communication are bidirectional. Consider dry cleaners, lawyers, and veterinarians. You drop off clothes at the cleaner, you send your pet to the vet, you mail documents to a lawyer, and, unlike a worker in the automobile factory who passes the car to the next worker, you expect to get something back. In these examples, we consider work done by the other person to be a *service*, and we consider ourselves *clients* for that service.

What does this have to do with Unix? Unix pipes carry data from one process to another. Processes and pipes can simulate not only an assembly line, producing finished goods, but also a service industry. In this chapter, we focus on interprocess data flow as the basis for *client/server* programming.

11.2   INTRODUCTORY METAPHOR: A BEVERAGE INTERFACE

Programs consume information. Some people consume soft drinks. Imagine a vending machine that dispenses cups of carbonated beverage, as shown in Figure 11.1. You insert a coin, push a button, and beverage emerges. What happens inside the dispenser? There might be a tank of carbonated water and a separate tank of drink concentrate, and pressing the button would activate a process to mix the raw materials and deliver dynamically generated beverage. On the other hand, there could be a single bottle of premixed beverage attached to a simple pump, and pressing the button simply transfers beverage to the cup.

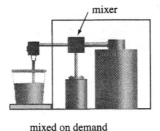
mixer

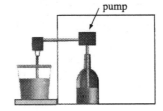
pump

mixed on demand   delivered from storage

FIGURE 11.1
Dynamically generated or static beverage?

Unix, like the soda dispenser, presents one interface, even though data come from different types of sources (see Figure 11.2):

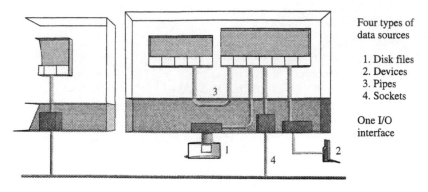

Four types of
data sources

1. Disk files
2. Devices
3. Pipes
4. Sockets

One I/O
interface

FIGURE 11.2

One interface, different sources.

(1,2) Disk/Device Files

Use open to connect, use read and write to transfer data.

(3) Pipes

Use pipe to create, use fork to share, and use read and write to transfer data.

(4) Sockets

Use socket, listen, and connect to connect, use read and write to transfer data.

Unix encapsulates in the file abstraction both the source and the means of production of data. In Chapter 2, we looked at reading data from files. In Chapter 5, we extended the idea of a file to include devices. Now we see how reading data from processes is similar to reading data from files.

11.3   bc: A UNIX CALCULATOR

Every version of Unix includes a version of the bc calculator. bc has variables, loops, and functions, and, as we saw in Chapter 1, bc handles very long numbers:

```
$ bc
17^123
2214202463012020735932057376423695752334560321698733173224049701694\
2928229966374967509063558720253911709279946320639381879900372206855\
0536286573569713
```

The trailing backslashes indicate continuation.

But bc Is Not a Calculator

A calculator program parses its input, performs the operations, and then prints the result. Most versions of bc parse the input but do not perform the operations.[1] Instead, bc

---

[1]The GNU version of bc does the math, too.

runs the dc calculator program and communicates with it through pipes. dc is a stack-based calculator requiring the user to enter both values before specifying the operation. For example, the user writes *2 2 +* to add 2 and 2.

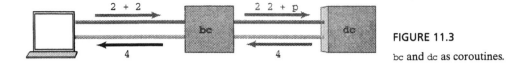

FIGURE 11.3

bc and dc as coroutines.

Figure 11.3 shows how bc processes *2+2*. The user types 2+2 then presses the Enter key. bc reads that expression from standard input, parses out the values and the operation, then sends the sequence of commands "2", "2", "+", and "p" to dc, which stacks up the two values, applies the plus operation, and then prints to standard output the value on the top of the stack.

bc reads the result through the pipe it attached to the standard output of dc and then forwards that message to the user. bc does not even keep variables; if the user types x=2+2, then bc tells dc to do the math and store the result in register *x* in dc. The command bc -c shows what the parser sends to the calculator. Even the GNU version of bc converts user input into stack-based expressions.

Ideas from bc

1. *Client/Server Model*

   The bc/dc pair of programs is an example of the client/server model of program design. dc provides a service: calculation. dc has a well-defined language, reverse Polish notation, and the two processes communicate through stdin and stdout.

   bc provides a user interface *and* uses the services dc provides. bc is called a *client* of dc.

   These two components are completely separate programs. You could replace the version of dc, and bc would still work. Similarly, you could create a nice graphical interface instead of bc and still use dc as the calculation engine. You could even replace dc with a program that parses the dc language and then passes the work to yet another program, perhaps on another, faster computer.

2. *Bidirectional Communication*

   Unlike the assembly-line model of data processing, the client/server model often requires one process to communicate with both the standard input and the standard output of another process. Traditional Unix pipes carry data in one direction only.[2] Figure 11.3 shows two pipes from bc to dc. The top pipe carries calculator commands to the standard input of dc, and the bottom pipe carries the standard output of dc back to bc.

---

[2]Some pipes can carry data in two directions. (See exercise 11.11.)

3. *Persistent Service*

Unlike the shell we wrote, in which each user command creates a new process, the
bc program keeps a single dc process running. bc uses that same instance of dc
over and over again by sending it commands in response to each line of user input.
This relationship differs from the standard *call-return* mechanism we use in function calls.

The bc/dc pair are called *coroutines* to distinguish them from *subroutines*. Both
processes continue to run, but control passes from one to the other as each completes its part of the job. bc has the job of parsing and printing, and dc has the job
of computing.

11.3.1 Coding bc: `pipe, fork, dup, exec`

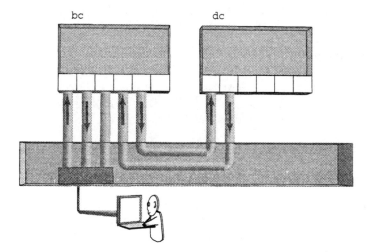

FIGURE 11.4

bc, dc, and kernel.

Figure 11.4 shows the data connections in the kernel that join the user to bc and bc to
dc. We use the figure as a guide for building the code as follows:

(a) Create two pipes.

(b) Create a process to run dc.

(c) In the new process, redirect stdin and stdout to the pipes, then exec dc.

(d) In the parent, read and parse user input, write commands to dc, read response
from dc, and send response to user.

Here is code for tinybc.c, a simple version of bc that uses sscanf to parse input
and speaks with dc through two pipes:

```
/**       tinybc.c        * a tiny calculator that uses dc to do its work
 **                       * demonstrates bidirectional pipes
 **                       * input looks like number op number which
 **                           tinybc converts into number \n number \n op \n p
```

```
**                      and passes result back to stdout
**
**              +-----------+              +----------+
**      stdin  >0              >== pipetodc ====>        |
**             |  tinybc  |              |   dc -   |
**      stdout <1              <== pipefromdc ==<        |
**              +-----------+              +----------+
**
**                  * program outline
**                          a. get two pipes
**                          b. fork (get another process)
**                          c. in the dc-to-be process,
**                                  connect stdin and out to pipes
**                                  then execl dc
**                          d. in the tinybc-process, no plumbing to do
**                                  just talk to human via normal i/o
**                                  and send stuff via pipe
**                          e. then close pipe and dc dies
**                  * note: does not handle multiline answers
**/
#include        <stdio.h>

#define oops(m,x)       { perror(m); exit(x); }

main()
{
        int     pid, todc[2], fromdc[2];        /* equipment     */

        /* make two pipes */

        if ( pipe(todc) == -1 || pipe(fromdc) == -1 )
                oops("pipe failed", 1);

        /* get a process for user interface */

        if ( (pid = fork()) == -1 )
                oops("cannot fork", 2);
        if ( pid == 0 )                         /* child is dc  */
                be_dc(todc, fromdc);
        else {
                be_bc(todc, fromdc);            /* parent is ui */
                wait(NULL);                     /* wait for child */
        }
}

be_dc(int in[2], int out[2])
/*
 *      set up stdin and stdout, then execl dc
 */
{
    /* setup stdin from pipein  */
        if ( dup2(in[0],0) == -1 )      /* copy read end to 0    */
                oops("dc: cannot redirect stdin",3);
```

```
        close(in[0]);                       /* moved to fd 0       */
        close(in[1]);                       /* won't write here    */

    /* setup stdout to pipeout */
        if ( dup2(out[1], 1) == -1 )    /* dupe write end to 1  */
                oops("dc: cannot redirect stdout",4);
        close(out[1]);                      /* moved to fd 1       */
        close(out[0]);                      /* won't read from here */

    /* now execl dc with the - option */
        execlp("dc", "dc", "-", NULL );
        oops("Cannot run dc", 5);
}

be_bc(int todc[2], int fromdc[2])
/*
 *      read from stdin and convert into to RPN, send down pipe
 *      then read from other pipe and print to user
 *      Uses fdopen() to convert a file descriptor to a stream
 */
{
        int     num1, num2;
        char    operation[BUFSIZ], message[BUFSIZ], *fgets();
        FILE    *fpout, *fpin, *fdopen();

        /* setup */
        close(todc[0]);                 /* won't read from pipe to dc  */
        close(fromdc[1]);               /* won't write to pipe from dc */

        fpout = fdopen( todc[1],   "w" );       /* convert file desc-  */
        fpin  = fdopen( fromdc[0], "r" );       /* riptors to streams  */
        if ( fpout == NULL || fpin == NULL )
                fatal("Error converting pipes to streams");

        /* main loop */
        while ( printf("tinybc: "), fgets(message,BUFSIZ,stdin) != NULL ){

                /* parse input */
                if ( sscanf(message,"%d%[-+*/^]%d",&num1,operation,
                  &num2)!=3){
                        printf("syntax error\n");
                        continue;
                }

                if ( fprintf( fpout , "%d\n%d\n%c\np\n", num1, num2,
                                *operation ) == EOF )
                                        fatal("Error writing");
                fflush(  fpout );
                if ( fgets( message, BUFSIZ, fpin ) == NULL )
                        break;
                printf("%d %c %d = %s", num1, *operation , num2, message);
        }
        fclose(fpout);          /* close pipe             */
```

```
        fclose(fpin);              /* dc will see EOF      */
}

fatal( char mess[])
{
        fprintf(stderr, "Error: %s\n", mess);
        exit(1);
}
```

Here is tinybc in action:

```
$ cc tinybc.c -o tinybc ; ./tinybc
tinybc: 2+2
2 + 2 = 4
tinybc: 55^5
55 ^ 5 = 503284375
tinybc:
```

Look at this output carefully and identify which parts come from which programs. tinybc generates the prompt and the restatement of the arithmetic expression. The result of the computation is a string generated by dc; tinybc only reads that string from the pipe and includes it in the output.

11.3.2 Remarks on Coroutines

What other Unix tools can be used as coroutines? Can the sort utility be used as a coroutine for a program? No. sort reads all the data until end of file before it can generate output. The only way to send end of file through a pipe is to close the writing end. Once you close the writing end, though, you cannot send another lot of data to be sorted.

dc, on the other hand, processes data and commands line by line. Interaction with dc is simple and predictable. When you ask dc to print a value, you get back one line of text. When you tell dc to push a value, you get no response.

For a program to be part of a client-server coroutine system, the program must have a clear way of indicating the end of a message, and the program must use simple, predictable requests and replies.

11.3.3 fdopen: Making File Descriptors Look like Files

In tinybc.c we introduce the library function fdopen. fdopen works like fopen, returning a FILE *, but takes a file descriptor, not a filename, as an argument.

Use fopen to open something with a filename. fopen opens device files as well as regular disk files. Use fdopen when you have a file descriptor but no filename, as in the case of a pipe, and want to convert that connection into a FILE * so you can use standard, buffered I/O operations. Notice how tinybc.c uses fprintf and fgets to send data through the pipes to dc.

Using fdopen makes a remote process feel even more like a file. In the next section, we examine popen, a function that, by encapsulating calls to pipe, fork, dup, and exec, completes the illusion that programs and files are pretty much the same thing.

11.4   popen: MAKING PROCESSES LOOK LIKE FILES

In this section, we continue to study how a program can obtain services by connecting to another process. We examine the popen library function. We see what popen does and how popen works, and then we write our own version.

11.4.1 What popen Does

fopen opens a buffered connection to a file:

```
FILE *fp;                        /* a pointer to a struct */
fp = fopen( "file1", "r" );      /* args are filename, connection type */
c = getc(fp);                    /* read char by char */
fgets(buf, len, fp);             /* line by line        */
fscanf(fp,"%d%d%s",&x,&y,x);     /* token by token      */
fclose(fp);                      /* close when done     */
```

fopen takes two string arguments: the name of the file and the type of connection (e.g., "r", "w", "a", ...).popen looks and works very much like fopen. popen opens a buffered connection to a process:

```
FILE *fp;                        /* same type of struct */

fp = popen("ls", "r");           /* args are program name, connection type */
fgets(buf, len, fp);             /* exactly the same functions            */
pclose(fp);                      /* close when done */
```

Figure 11.5 shows similarities between popen and fopen. Both functions use the same syntax, and both functions return the same type of value. The first argument to popen is the name of the command to open; it can be any shell command. The second argument can be either "r" or "w", but never "a".

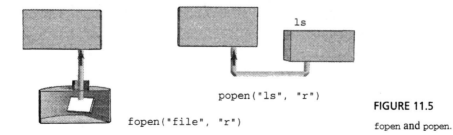

popen("ls", "r")

fopen("file", "r")

FIGURE 11.5

fopen and popen.

popen examples

The following program, in which the who|sort command is a source of data, uses popen to obtain a sorted list of current users:

```
/* popendemo.c
 *       demonstrates how to open a program for standard i/o
 *       important points:
 *               1. popen() returns a FILE *, just like fopen()
```

```
*                  2. the FILE * it returns can be read/written
*                     with all the standard functions
*                  3. you need to use pclose() when done
*/
#include        <stdio.h>
#include        <stdlib.h>

int main()
{
        FILE    *fp;
        char    buf[100];
        int     i = 0;

        fp = popen( "who|sort", "r" );            /* open the command  */

        while ( fgets( buf, 100, fp ) != NULL ) /* read from command */
                printf("%3d %s", i++, buf );    /* print data        */

        pclose( fp );                             /* IMPORTANT!        */
        return 0;
}
```

This second example uses popen to connect to the mail program and notify some users of system trouble:

```
/* popen_ex3.c
 *       shows how to use popen to write to a process that
 *       reads from stdin.  This program writes email to
 *       two users.  Note how easy it is to use fprintf
 *       to format the data to send.
 */
#include         <stdio.h>

main()
{
        FILE    *fp;

        fp = popen( "mail admin backup", "w" );
        fprintf( fp, "Error with backup!!\n" );
        pclose( fp );
}
```

pclose is Required

When you are done reading from or writing to the connection created by popen, use pclose, not fclose. A process needs to be waited for, or it becomes a zombie. pclose calls wait.

11.4.2 Writing popen: Using fdopen

How does popen work, and how do we write it? popen runs a program and returns a connection to the standard input or standard output of that program.

We need a new process to run the program, so we use fork. We need a connection to that process, so we use pipe. We need to make a file descriptor into a buffered stream, so we use fdopen. Finally, we need to be able to run any shell command in that process, so we use exec, but what do we execute?. The only program that can run any shell command is the shell itself: /bin/sh. Conveniently, sh supports a -c option that tells the shell to run a command and then exit. For example,

```
sh -c "who|sort"
```

tells sh to run the single command line who|sort. (See also Figure 11.6.)
We combine pipe, fork, dup2, and exec as shown in this flowchart:

```
                        pipe(p)
                        fork()
                          |
      +-------------+-------------+
close(p[1]);                 close(p[0]);
fp = fdopen(p[0],"r")        dup(p[1],1);
return fp;                   close(p[1]);
                             execl("/bin/sh","sh","-c",cmd,NULL);
```

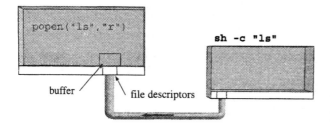

FIGURE 11.6

Reading from a shell command.

An implementation of that flowchart is popen.c:

```
/*  popen.c -  a version of the Unix popen() library function
 *       FILE *popen( char *command, char *mode )
 *               command is a regular shell command
 *               mode is "r" or "w"
 *               returns a stream attached to the command, or NULL
 *               execls "sh" "-c" command
 *    todo: what about signal handling for child process?
 */
#include        <stdio.h>
#include        <signal.h>

#define READ    0
#define WRITE   1

FILE *popen(const char *command, const char *mode)
{
        int     pfp[2], pid;            /* the pipe and the process    */
```

```
FILE    *fdopen(), *fp;         /* fdopen makes a fd a stream   */
int     parent_end, child_end;  /* of pipe                      */

if ( *mode == 'r' ){            /* figure out direction         */
        parent_end = READ;
        child_end = WRITE ;
} else if ( *mode == 'w' ){
        parent_end = WRITE;
        child_end = READ ;
} else return NULL ;

if ( pipe(pfp) == -1 )                  /* get a pipe           */
        return NULL;
if ( (pid = fork()) == -1 ){            /* and a process        */
        close(pfp[0]);                  /* or dispose of pipe   */
        close(pfp[1]);
        return NULL;
}

/* --------------- parent code here ------------------- */
/*    need to close one end and fdopen other end         */

if ( pid > 0 ){
        if (close( pfp[child_end] ) == -1 )
                return NULL;
        return fdopen( pfp[parent_end] , mode );   /* same mode */
}

/* --------------- child code here -------------------- */
/*    need to redirect stdin or stdout then exec the cmd  */

if ( close(pfp[parent_end]) == -1 )     /* close the other end  */
        exit(1);                        /* do NOT return        */

if ( dup2(pfp[child_end], child_end) == -1 )
        exit(1);

if ( close(pfp[child_end]) == -1 )      /* done with this one   */
        exit(1);

                                        /* all set to run cmd   */
execl( "/bin/sh", "sh", "-c", command, NULL );
exit(1);
}
```

This version of popen does not do anything about signals. Is that a problem?

11.4.3 Access to Data: Files, APIs, and Servers

fopen gets data from a file, and popen gets data from a process. Let us focus on the general question of getting data and compare three methods. As an example, we compare three methods for getting the list of people logged on to a system.

Method 1: Getting Data from Files   You can get data by reading from a file. In Chapter 2, we wrote a version of who that reads the list of current users from the utmp file.

File-based information services are not perfect. Client programs rely on a particular file format and specific member names in structures. The lines

```
/* Backwards compatibility hacks.   */
#define ut_name          ut_user
```

in the Linux header file for the `utmp` structure show what happens.

Method 2: Getting Data from Functions   You can get data by calling a function. A library function hides data formats and file locations behind a standard function interface. Unix provides a function interface to the `utmp` file. The manual page for `getutent` describes functions that read the `utmp` database. The underlying storage structure may change, but programs that use the interface still work.

Application programming interface (API)-based information services are not always the right solution, either. There are two methods for using system library functions. A program might use *static linking* and include the actual function code. Those functions may use filenames or file formats that are no longer correct. On the other hand, a program might call functions in *shared libraries*, but these libraries are not always installed on a system, or the version on a system may not match the version the program needs.

Method 3: Getting Data from Processes   A third method is to get data by reading from a process. The `bc/dc` and `popen` examples showed how to create a connection to another process. A program that wants the list of users can call `popen` to connect to the `who` program. The `who` command, not your program, is responsible for knowing the correct filename and file format and for using the appropriate libraries.

Calling separate programs for data provides other benefits. Server programs can be written in any language: shell scripts, compiled C code, Java, Perl. The most dramatic benefit of implementing system services as separate programs is that the client program can run on one machine and the server program can run on a different machine. All we need is some way of connecting to a process on a different computer.

11.5   SOCKETS: CONNECTING TO REMOTE PROCESSES

Pipes allow processes to send data to other processes as easily as they send data to files, but pipes have two significant limitations. A pipe is created in one process and is shared by calling `fork`. Therefore, pipes can only connect related processes, and pipes can only connect processes on the same computer. Unix provides another method of interprocess communication—*sockets*:

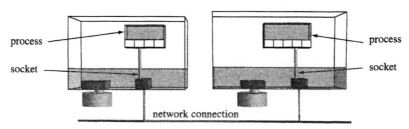

FIGURE 11.7

Connecting to a remote process.

Sockets allow processes to create pipelike connections to unrelated processes and even to processes on other computers. (See Figure 11.7.) In this section, we study the basic ideas of sockets and see how to use sockets to connect clients and servers on different computers. The idea is as simple as calling a telephone number to get the time of day.

11.5.1   An Analogy: "At the Tone, the Time Will Be..."

Many cities have a time telephone number. You dial that number, and the machine that picks up the call tells you the time in that city. How does it work? What if you wanted to set up your own time service? You could use the low-tech solution depicted in Figure 11.8. In the figure, that's you on the right in the office. You are the server providing the time service. You put a clock on the wall. The steps you follow to set up your time service match exactly the steps a Unix program follows to set up a socket-based service. Therefore, we describe these steps carefully.

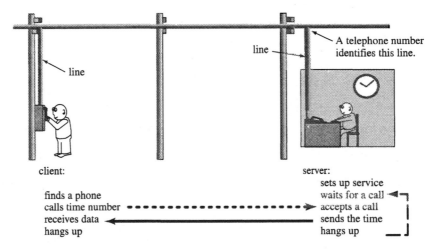

FIGURE 11.8

A time service.

Setting Up and Operating the Service

How do you set up and operate a time service once you buy and install your clock?

Setting Up the Service   Setting up your service consists of three steps:

1. *Get a phone line*

First, you need to have a line run from the telephone network to a jack on the wall by your desk. This wire and the jack allow you to connect to the network so that calls can be routed to your desk. In fancier language, the jack is an *endpoint of communication*. The next time you have a phone line installed in your home, tell the company or electrician that you need an endpoint of communication.

2. *Get a phone number for that line*

Clients need a number to call to reach your endpoint of communication. The telephone network identifies each wall jack with a telephone number. For the purposes of this analogy, it is important to imagine that you are in a large business that offers several services in addition to your time service. Therefore, your jack is identified by a telephone number *and* an extension number.

For example, your number might be 617–999–1234, extension 8080. The telephone number identifies the building that contains your office, and the extension (8080) identifies your particular telephone in that building. Got that part? One number for the building, a second number for your service. This is important.

3. *Arrange for incoming calls*

You may have used pay telephones marked *no incoming calls*. Your service does not want that type of telephone. You tell the telephone network your line should accept incoming calls. You might set up a queue for incoming calls. You could have a message that tells callers how important their calls are to you and then plays music. The queue idea applies to sockets, the music does not.

Operating the Service   Operating the time service consists of a loop with the following three steps:

4. *Wait for a call*

Sit there doing nothing until a call comes in. In technical terms, you *block* on a call. When a call arrives, you unblock and accept the call.

5. *Provide the service*

In your case, you look at the clock, then you send that number down the wire by speaking.

6. *Hang up*

Your work is done for this call, so you hang up.

Those six steps, three steps of setup and three steps per call, are the details of running a time service over a telephone network.

Using the Service

How does a client use your service? A client follows these four steps:

1. *Get a phone line*

The client also needs an endpoint of communication. The client orders a phone line from the telephone network.

2. *Connect to your number*

The client now uses the line to request a connection through the telephone network to your line. The client connects to the business number and extension that identifies your service. The combination of business number and extension is called the *network address* of your service. In technical terms, the telephone number of the business is the *host address*, and your extension is the *port number* or just *port*. In the preceding example, the host address is 617–999–1234, and the port is 8080.

3. *Use the service*

The two endpoints of communication (the client's and the server's) are now connected. Either party may send data through this connection to the other endpoint. In the case of a time service, the server sends data through the connection, and the client receives the information. A more complicated service, such as a catalog-order line, requires a more complicated interaction between client and server. We explore more complex services later.

4. *Hang up*

The interaction is complete. The client hangs up.

Important Concepts

The time-server example includes four concepts we use in socket programming:

client and server

We discussed these ideas several times. The server is the program that provides a service. A server, in Unix terms, is a program, not a computer. Typical names for a computer are computer, host, system, machine, and box. A server process waits for a request, processes the request, then loops back to take the next request. A client process, on the other hand, does not loop. A client makes a connection, exchanges some data with the server, and then continues.

hostname and port

A server on the Internet is a process running on some computer. The computer is called the *host*. Machines often are assigned names like *sales.xyzcorp.com*; this is called the *hostname* of the machine. The server has a port number on that host. The combination of host and port identifies a server.

address family

Your time service has a telephone number. It might also have a street address and zip code. It also has a longitude and latitude, another set of numbers. Each of these sets of numbers is an address for your service. It would not work, though, to use your longitude and latitude as telephone number and extension.

Each of these addresses belongs to an *address family*. The telephone number and extension have a meaning inside the telephone-network address family, which we could symbolize as AF_PHONE. Similarly, the longitude and latitude make sense in the global-coordinate-system address family, which we could symbolize as AF_GLOBAL.

protocol

A *protocol* is the rules of interaction between the client and the server. In the time service, the protocol is simple: the client calls, the server answers, the server states the time, and the server hangs up.

What if you ran a directory-assistance service instead? The protocol would be a little more complicated. You, the server, would answer and send an initial greeting (*"Phoneco directory assistance. What city?"*). The client would respond with the name of a city. The server then asks for a name (*"What listing?"*). The client responds with the name of a person or business. The server then sends back the telephone number or a message that no such listing exists in that city. Some directory-assistance servers will offer, for a fee, to dial the number for you. That exchange of messages follows the *directory-assistance protocol*, known as DAP to readers of this paragraph.

Every client/server system must define a protocol.

11.5.2 Internet Time, DAP, and Weather Servers

The dial-the-time and directory-assistance server examples are more than pedagogical metaphors; they have exact equivalents on the Internet. Try this:

```
$ telnet mit.edu 13
Trying 18.7.21.69...
Connected to mit.edu.
Escape character is '^]'.
Mon Aug 13 22:36:44 2001
Connection closed by foreign host.
$
```

Somewhere on a machine at MIT is a time server waiting to take calls on port 13. When we call that server using the telnet program, the server picks up the call, checks the clock on the system, sends the current time back over the wire, and then hangs up. Exactly like your dial-the-time service. It even uses the same simple protocol. Try connecting to port 13 on other hosts. You can find out what time it is on machines around the world.

The telnet program is like a telephone. It makes a connection to a port on a remote host, and then it transfers bytes from your keyboard to the connection and from the connection to your display.

What about directory assistance? The directory-assistance server usually listens for calls on port 79. For example, we might have

```
$ telnet princeton.edu 79
Trying 128.112.128.81...
Connected to princeton.edu.
Escape character is '^]'.
smith
-------------------------------------------
        alias: 000012345
         name: Waldo Smith
   department: Special Student
        email: waldos@Princeton.EDU
     emailbox: waldos@mail.Princeton.EDU
        netid: waldos
-------------------------------------------
```

```
        alias: 000333333
         name: Ignatz E Smith
   department: Undergraduate Class of 1997
        email: ismith@Princeton.EDU
     emailbox: ismith@mail.Princeton.EDU
        netid: ismith
                 .
                 .
                 .
```

When a call comes in, the server picks up the call. The protocol specifies that the client type a name and then press the return key. The server sends back all matching entries, then hangs up.

What about the weather? Try the following:

```
telnet rainmaker.wunderground.com 3000
```

The protocol for this weather server is more complicated but friendlier.

11.5.3   Lists of Services: Well-Known Ports

How did I know to use port 13 for the time and port 79 for directory assistance? The same way people in the United States know to dial 911 for emergencies and 411 for directory assistance—these are *well-known ports*. The file /etc/services is a list of well-known services and their port numbers:

```
$ more /etc/services
#       $NetBSD: services,v 1.18 1996/03/26 00:07:58 mrg Exp $
#
# Network services, Internet style
#
# Note that it is presently the policy of IANA to assign a single well-known
# port number for both TCP and UDP; hence, most entries here have two entries
# even if the protocol doesn't support UDP operations.
# Updated from RFC 1340, "Assigned Numbers" (July 1992).  Not all ports
# are included, only the more common ones.
#
#       from: @(#)services      5.8 (Berkeley) 5/9/91
#
tcpmux          1/tcp           # TCP port service multiplexer
echo            7/tcp
echo            7/udp
discard         9/tcp           sink null
discard         9/udp           sink null
systat          11/tcp          users
daytime         13/tcp
daytime         13/udp
--More--(13%)
```

You can see in this listing that the *daytime* service uses port 13. Explore this file to see the standard services on Internet machines. Look for the ftp, telnet, finger, and http entries.

All these servers running on Internet hosts are based on the ideas and steps we saw in the telephone-based time service. We now translate these ideas into Unix system calls to write our own version of the time server and time client.

11.5.4   Writing `timeserv.c`: A Time Server

Our telephone-based time server involved six steps. Each step corresponds to a system call. This table shows the translation:

action	syscall
1. Get a phone line	socket
2. Assign a number	bind
3. Allow incoming calls	listen
4. Wait for a call	accept
5. Transfer data	read/write
6. Hang up	close

Here is the code:

```
/* timeserv.c - a socket-based time of day server
 */

#include  <stdio.h>
#include  <unistd.h>
#include  <sys/types.h>
#include  <sys/socket.h>
#include  <netinet/in.h>
#include  <netdb.h>
#include  <time.h>
#include  <strings.h>
#define   PORTNUM  13000    /* our time service phone number */
#define   HOSTLEN  256
#define   oops(msg)        { perror(msg) ; exit(1) ; }

int main(int ac, char *av[])
{
        struct  sockaddr_in   saddr;    /* build our address here */
        struct  hostent          *hp;   /* this is part of our    */
        char    hostname[HOSTLEN];       /* address                */
        int     sock_id,sock_fd;         /* line id, file desc     */
        FILE    *sock_fp;                /* use socket as stream   */
        char    *ctime();                /* convert secs to string */
        time_t  thetime;                 /* the time we report     */
        /*
         * Step 1: ask kernel for a socket
         */
```

```
    sock_id = socket( PF_INET, SOCK_STREAM, 0 );     /* get a socket */
    if ( sock_id == -1 )
            oops( "socket" );

/*
 * Step 2: bind address to socket.  Address is host,port
 */

bzero( (void *)&saddr, sizeof(saddr) ); /* clear out struct    */

gethostname( hostname, HOSTLEN );        /* where am I ?        */
hp = gethostbyname( hostname );          /* get info about host */
                                         /* fill in host part   */
bcopy( (void *)hp->h_addr, (void *)&saddr.sin_addr, hp->h_length);
saddr.sin_port = htons(PORTNUM);         /* fill in socket port */
saddr.sin_family = AF_INET ;             /* fill in addr family */

    if ( bind(sock_id, (struct sockaddr *)&saddr, sizeof(saddr)) != 0 )
            oops( "bind" );

/*
 * Step 3: allow incoming calls with Qsize=1 on socket
 */

    if ( listen(sock_id, 1) != 0 )
            oops( "listen" );

/*
 * main loop: accept(), write(), close()
 */

    while ( 1 ){
            sock_fd = accept(sock_id, NULL, NULL); /* wait for call */
             printf("Wow! got a call!\n");
            if ( sock_fd == -1 )
                    oops( "accept" );        /* error getting calls */

            sock_fp = fdopen(sock_fd,"w");   /* we'll write to the  */
            if ( sock_fp == NULL )           /* socket as a stream  */
                    oops( "fdopen" );        /* unless we can't     */

            thetime = time(NULL);            /* get time            */
                                             /* and convert to strng */
            fprintf( sock_fp, "The time here is .." );
            fprintf( sock_fp, "%s", ctime(&thetime) );
            fclose( sock_fp );               /* release connection  */
    }
}
```

And here is an explanation of how the program works:

Step 1:   Ask kernel for a socket

A *socket* is an endpoint of communication. Like the telephone jack at the wall, a socket is a place from which calls can be made and a place to which calls can be directed. The socket system call creates a socket:

socket	
PURPOSE	Create a socket
INCLUDE	#include <sys/types.h> #include <sys/socket.h>
USAGE	sockid = socket(int domain, int type, int protocol)

ARGS	domain communication domain.
	                PF_INET is for Internet sockets
	type type of socket.
	                SOCK_STREAM looks like a pipe
	protocol protocol used within the socket.
	                0 is default.

RETURNS	-1 if error sockid a socket id if successful

socket creates an endpoint for communication and returns an identifier for that socket. There are various sorts of communication systems, each of which is called a *domain* of communication. The Internet is one domain. We shall see later that the Unix kernel is another domain. Linux supports communication in several other domains.

The type of a socket specifies the type of data flow the program plans to use. The SOCK_STREAM type works like a bidirectional pipe. Data written in one end can be read from the other end as a continuous sequence of bytes. We examine SOCK_DGRAM in a later chapter.

The last argument, *protocol*, refers to the protocol used within the network code in the kernel, not the protocol between the client and server. A value of 0 selects the standard protocol.

Step 2:   Bind address to socket. Address is host, port

The next step is to assign a network address to our socket. In the Internet domain, an address consists of a host and a port number. We cannot use port 13; that is reserved for the *real* time server. Instead, we use port 13000. You can select any port number you like for a server, as long as it is not too low and not already in use. Low-numbered ports may be used only by system services, not by regular users. Check your system for the restricted range. Port numbers are 16-bit quantities, so there are a lot of them. bind is summarized as follows:

---

bind

PURPOSE	Bind an address to a socket
INCLUDE	`#include <sys/types.h>` `#include <sys/socket.h>`
USAGE	`result = bind(int sockid, struct sockaddr *addrp,` `                        socklen_t addrlen)`
ARGS	sockid the id of the socket addrp a pointer to a struct containing the address addrlen the length of the struct
RETURNS	-1 if error 0 if success

---

bind assigns an address to a socket. This address works like the telephone number assigned to the jack on the wall in your office; other processes use that address when they want to connect to your server. Each address family has its own format. The Internet address family (AF_INET) uses host and port. An address is a struct with the host and port number as members. Our program first zeros the struct, then fills in the host address, then fills in the port number, and, finally, fills in the address family. Consult the manual pages for the functions used to construct each of these numbers.

When all those parts are filled in, the address is attached to the socket. Other types of sockets use addresses with different members.

Step 3: Allow incoming calls with queue size=1 on socket

A server accepts incoming calls, so our program must call listen:

---

listen

PURPOSE	Listen for connections on a socket
INCLUDE	`#include <sys/socket.h>`
USAGE	`result = listen(int sockid, int qsize)`
ARGS	sockid socket that will accept calls qsize backlog of incoming connections
RETURNS	-1 if error 0 if success

---

listen asks the kernel to allow the specified socket to receive incoming calls. Not all types of sockets can receive incoming calls. SOCK_STREAM can. The second argument specifies the size of the queue for incoming calls. In our code, we request a queue of one call. The maximum queue size depends on the socket implementation.

Step 4:   Wait For/Accept a Call

Once the socket is created, assigned an address, and set up to receive incoming calls, the program is ready to begin its work. The server now waits until a call comes in. It uses accept:

accept	
PURPOSE	Accept a connection on a socket
INCLUDE	`#include <sys/types.h>` `#include <sys/socket.h>`
USAGE	`fd = accept(int sockid, struct sockaddr *callerid,` `                                      socklen_t *addrlenp)`
ARGS	sockid accept a call on this socket callerid pointer to struct for address of caller addrlenp pointer to storage for length of address of caller
RETURNS	-1 if error fd a file descriptor open for reading and writing

accept suspends the current process until an incoming connection on the specified socket is established. accept returns a file descriptor opened for reading and writing. That file descriptor is a connection to a file descriptor in the calling process.

The accept call supports a form of *caller ID*. The socket in the caller has an address. For Internet connections, the address is a host and port number. If the *callerid* and *addrlenp* pointers are not null, the kernel puts the address of the caller into the struct pointed to by *callerid* and puts the length of that struct into the value pointed to by *addrlenp*.

Just as a human can use caller-ID information to decide how to handle an incoming call, a network program can use the address of the calling process to decide how to handle an incoming connection.

Step 5:   Transfer Data

The file descriptor returned by accept is a regular file descriptor, the sort of thing we have been using since we learned about open back in Chapter 2. In timeserv.c, we use fdopen to make this file descriptor into a buffered data stream so we can use fprintf. We could have used plain old write.

Step 6:   Close Connection

The file descriptor returned by accept may be closed with the standard close system call. When one process closes its end of the socket, the process on the other end will see an end-of-file result if it tries to read data. Pipes work the same way.

11.5.5 Testing `timeserv.c`

We can now compile and run our time server:

```
$ cc timeserv.c -o timeserv
$ timeserv&
29362
$
```

We started our server with a trailing ampersand, so the shell runs it but does not call `wait`. The server is blocked at the `accept` system call. We can connect to it with `telnet`:

```
$ telnet `hostname` 13000
Trying 123.123.123.123
Connected to somesite.net
Escape character is '^]'.
Wow! got a call!
The time here is ..Tue Aug 14 11:36:30 2001
Connection closed by foreign host.
$
$ telnet `hostname` 13000
Trying 123.123.123.123
Connected to somesite.net
Escape character is '^]'.
Wow! got a call!
The time here is ..Tue Aug 14 11:36:53 2001
Connection closed by foreign host.
$
```

We have made two connections, and the server responded both times. The server will continue to run until we kill it:

```
$ kill 29362
```

`telnet` works as a client for this server, but it is not always a suitable way to connect to a server. We now write a special client for this server.

11.5.6 Writing `timeclnt.c`: A Time Client

Our telephone-based time client uses four steps, each corresponding to a system call:

action	syscall
1. Get a phone line	socket
2. Call the server	connect
3. Transfer data	read/write
4. Hang up	close

Here is the code:

```
/* timeclnt.c - a client for timeserv.c
 *              usage: timeclnt hostname portnumber
 */
#include        <stdio.h>
#include        <sys/types.h>
#include        <sys/socket.h>
#include        <netinet/in.h>
#include        <netdb.h>

#define         oops(msg)       { perror(msg); exit(1); }
main(int ac, char *av[])
{
        struct sockaddr_in  servadd;        /* the number to call */
        struct hostent      *hp;            /* used to get number */
        int    sock_id, sock_fd;            /* the socket and fd  */
        char   message[BUFSIZ];             /* to receive message */
        int    messlen;                     /* for message length */
    /*
     * Step 1: Get a socket
     */

        sock_id = socket( AF_INET, SOCK_STREAM, 0 );    /* get a line  */
        if ( sock_id == -1 )
                oops( "socket" );                       /* or fail     */
    /*
     * Step 2: connect to server
     *         need to build address (host,port) of server  first
     */
        bzero( &servadd, sizeof( servadd ) );   /* zero the address    */

        hp = gethostbyname( av[1] );            /* lookup host's ip #  */
        if (hp == NULL)
                oops(av[1]);                    /* or die              */
        bcopy(hp->h_addr, (struct sockaddr *)&servadd.sin_addr, hp->h_length);

        servadd.sin_port = htons(atoi(av[2]));  /* fill in port number */

        servadd.sin_family = AF_INET ;          /* fill in socket type */

                                                /* now dial    */
        if ( connect(sock_id,(struct sockaddr *)&servadd, sizeof(servadd)) !=0)
                oops( "connect" );
    /*
     * Step 3: transfer data from server, then hangup
     */

        messlen = read(sock_id, message, BUFSIZ);       /* read stuff  */
        if ( messlen == - 1 )
                oops("read") ;
```

```
        if ( write( 1, message, messlen ) != messlen )   /* and write to */
                oops( "write" );                           /* stdout        */
        close( sock_id );
}
```

And here is an explanation of how the program works:

Step 1:   Ask Kernel for a Socket

The client needs a socket to connect to the network, just as a client for your telephone time service needs a phone line to connect to the phone network. The socket for the client also has to be an Internet socket (AF_INET) and has to be a stream socket (SOCK_STREAM).

Step 2:   Connect to Server

The client connects to the time server. The connect system call is the network equivalent of making a telephone call.

connect	
PURPOSE	Connect to a socket
INCLUDE	#include <sys/types.h> #include <sys/socket.h>
USAGE	result = connect(int sockid, struct sockaddr *serv_addrp, socklen_t addrlen);
ARGS	sockid socket to use for connection serv_addrp pointer to struct containing server address addrlen length of that struct
RETURNS	-1 if error 0 if success

connect attempts to connect the socket specified by *sockid* to the socket identified by the socket address pointed to by *serv_addrp*. If the attempt succeeds, connect returns 0. In that case, the *sockid* is now a valid file descriptor open for reading and writing. Data written into this file descriptor are sent to the socket at the other end of the connection, and data written into the other end may be read from this file descriptor.

Steps 3 and 4:   Transfer Data and Then Hang Up

After a successful connect, a process may read and write data from this file descriptor as though it were connected to a regular file or pipe. In the time client/server system, timeclnt simply reads one line from the server.

After reading the time, the client closes the file descriptor and exits. The client could have just exited, and the kernel would have closed this open file descriptor.

11.5.7 Testing `timeclnt.c`

We have not seen any pictures for several pages, so you may have forgotten what all this code is supposed to do. A look at Figure 11.9 will remind you. The server process runs on one computer. A client process on another computer connects to the server over the network. The server sends data to the client by calling `write`. The client receives that message by calling `read`.

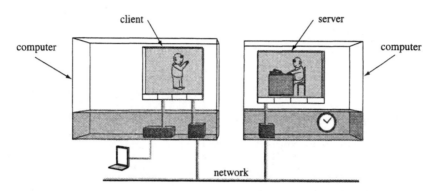

FIGURE 11.9

Processes on different computers.

A real test of our software involves running the two programs on different computers. I am not sure how clear this looks in a book, but here goes:

```
$ hostname                          # check current machine
computer1.mysite.net                # the first machine
$ cc timeserv.c -o timeserv         # build server
$ ./timeserv &                      # and run it
[1] 10739
$
$ scp timeclnt.c bruce@computer2:# send client code elsewhere
bruce@computers2's password:
timeclnt.c              |           1 KB |   1.8 kB/s | ETA: 00:00:00 | 100%

$ ssh bruce@computer2
bruce@computer2's password:
No mail.
computer2:bruce$ cc timeclnt.c -o timeclnt
computer2:bruce$ ./timeclnt computer1 13000Wow! got a call!
The time here is ..Tue Aug 14 02:44:31 2001
computer2:bruce$
```

The server is compiled and set running on computer1. I then copy the client code to computer2 and log in to computer2. On computer2, I compile the client and ask it to connect to the server running on computer1 listening at port 13000. The message I see is sent over the network from the server on `computer1` to the client on `computer2`. That client sends the message to standard output.

Am I really seeing the output on `computer2`? I am connected to `computer2` from `computer1`, so the terminal on which the message appears is actually attached to `computer1`. See the exercise that asks you to think about what is *really* going on.

These `timeserv/timeclnt` programs let us see what time it is on another computer. Checking the time on another computer also allows computers to keep their clocks synchronized. One machine on a network can serve as the authority on time. Other machines can use this sort of client/server system to reset their clocks periodically.

11.5.8 Another Server: `remote ls`

Our next project is to write a program that lists files on a remote computer. You may have accounts on two systems. What if you wanted to list files you have on the other machine? You could log in to the other machine and run `ls`. A quicker, more convenient method would be a *remote ls* program, we can call it `rls`. You would specify a hostname and a directory:

```
$ rls computer2.site.net /home/me/code
```

Of course, `rls` needs a server process running on the other machine to receive the request, do the work, and return the result. The system looks like that shown in Figure 11.10. A server runs on one computer. A client on another computer connects to the server and sends the name of a directory. The server sends back to the client a list of the files in that directory. The client displays the list by writing to standard output. This two-process system provides access to directories on a different computer.

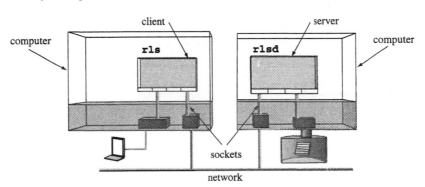

FIGURE 11.10

A `remote ls` system.

Planning the `remote ls` System

We need three things to implement the `rls` system:

(a) a protocol
(b) a client program
(c) a server program

The Protocol

The protocol consists of a request and a reply. First, the client sends a single line containing the name of a directory. The server reads that line. Next, the server opens and reads that directory and sends back to the client the list of files. The client reads the list of files, line by line, until the server closes the connection, which generates an end-of-file condition.

The Client: `rls`

```
/* rls.c - a client for a remote directory listing service
 *          usage: rls hostname directory
 */
#include        <stdio.h>
#include        <sys/types.h>
#include        <sys/socket.h>
#include        <netinet/in.h>
#include        <netdb.h>

#define         oops(msg)        { perror(msg); exit(1); }
#define         PORTNUM          15000

main(int ac, char *av[])
{
      struct sockaddr_in  servadd;         /* the number to call */
      struct hostent      *hp;             /* used to get number */
      int     sock_id, sock_fd;            /* the socket and fd  */
      char    buffer[BUFSIZ];              /* to receive message */
      int     n_read;                      /* for message length */

      if ( ac != 3 ) exit(1);

  /** Step 1: Get a socket **/

      sock_id = socket( AF_INET, SOCK_STREAM, 0 );     /* get a line */
      if ( sock_id == -1 )
            oops( "socket" );                          /* or fail    */

  /** Step 2: connect to server **/
      bzero( &servadd, sizeof(servadd) );      /* zero the address   */
      hp = gethostbyname( av[1] );             /* lookup host's ip # */
      if (hp == NULL)
            oops(av[1]);                        /* or die             */
      bcopy(hp->h_addr, (struct sockaddr *)&servadd.sin_addr, hp->h_length);

      servadd.sin_port = htons(PORTNUM);       /* fill in port number */
      servadd.sin_family = AF_INET ;           /* fill in socket type */

      if ( connect(sock_id,(struct sockaddr *)&servadd, sizeof(servadd)) !=0)
            oops( "connect" );

  /** Step 3: send directory name, then read back results **/
```

```
        if ( write(sock_id, av[2], strlen(av[2])) == -1)
                oops("write");
        if ( write(sock_id, "\n", 1) == -1 )
                oops("write");

        while( (n_read = read(sock_id, buffer, BUFSIZ)) > 0 )
                if ( write(1, buffer, n_read) == -1 )
                        oops("write");
        close( sock_id );
}
```

Note the differences between this client and the time client. The rls client first writes the directory name into the socket. Our protocol states that the client sends a line, so we append a newline character. Next, the client enters a loop, copying data from the socket to standard output until end of file. rls.c uses low-level write and read to transfer data to and from the server. The loop uses a standard buffer size to be efficient. Next, we write the server.

The Server: rlsd

The server has to get a socket, bind, listen, and then accept a call. After accepting a call, the server reads the name of a directory from the socket and then lists the contents of that directory. How does the server list a directory? We could copy our version of ls from Chapter 3, but we can use a simpler method: Just use popen to read the output from the regular version of ls. (See Figure 11.11.)

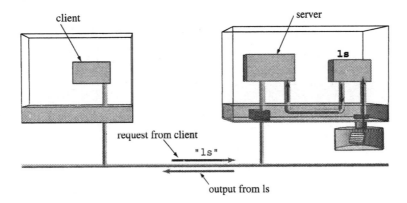

FIGURE 11.11

Using popen("ls") to list remote directories.

The following code uses popen toward that end:

```
/* rlsd.c - a remote ls server - with paranoia
 */

#include <stdio.h>
```

```
#include   <unistd.h>
#include   <sys/types.h>
#include   <sys/socket.h>
#include   <netinet/in.h>
#include   <netdb.h>
#include   <time.h>
#include   <strings.h>

#define    PORTNUM  15000   /* our remote ls server port */
#define    HOSTLEN  256
#define    oops(msg)       { perror(msg) ; exit(1) ; }

int main(int ac, char *av[])
{
        struct  sockaddr_in   saddr;    /* build our address here */
        struct  hostent           *hp;  /* this is part of our    */
        char    hostname[HOSTLEN];       /* address               */
        int     sock_id,sock_fd;         /* line id, file desc     */
        FILE    *sock_fpi, *sock_fpo;    /* streams for in and out */
        FILE    *pipe_fp;                /* use popen to run ls    */
        char    dirname[BUFSIZ];         /* from client            */
        char    command[BUFSIZ];         /* for popen()            */
        int     dirlen, c;

    /** Step 1: ask kernel for a socket **/

        sock_id = socket( PF_INET, SOCK_STREAM, 0 );     /* get a socket */
        if ( sock_id == -1 )
                oops( "socket" );

    /** Step 2: bind address to socket.  Address is host,port **/

        bzero( (void *)&saddr, sizeof(saddr) ); /* clear out struct    */
        gethostname( hostname, HOSTLEN );        /* where am I ?        */
        hp = gethostbyname( hostname );          /* get info about host */
        bcopy( (void *)hp->h_addr, (void *)&saddr.sin_addr, hp->h_length);
        saddr.sin_port = htons(PORTNUM);         /* fill in socket port */
        saddr.sin_family = AF_INET ;             /* fill in addr family */
        if ( bind(sock_id, (struct sockaddr *)&saddr, sizeof(saddr)) != 0 )
                oops( "bind" );

    /** Step 3: allow incoming calls with Qsize=1 on socket **/

        if ( listen(sock_id, 1) != 0 )
                oops( "listen" );

    /*
     * main loop: accept(), write(), close()
     */

        while ( 1 ){
                sock_fd = accept(sock_id, NULL, NULL); /* wait for call */
                if ( sock_fd == -1 )
                        oops("accept");
```

```
                    /* open reading direction as buffered stream */
                    if( (sock_fpi = fdopen(sock_fd,"r")) == NULL )
                            oops("fdopen reading");

                    if ( fgets(dirname, BUFSIZ-5, sock_fpi) == NULL )
                            oops("reading dirname");
                    sanitize(dirname);

                    /* open writing direction as buffered stream */
                    if ( (sock_fpo = fdopen(sock_fd,"w")) == NULL )
                            oops("fdopen writing");

                    sprintf(command,"ls %s", dirname);
                    if ( (pipe_fp = popen(command, "r")) == NULL )
                            oops("popen");

                    /* transfer data from ls to socket */
                    while( (c = getc(pipe_fp)) != EOF )
                            putc(c, sock_fpo);
                    pclose(pipe_fp);
                    fclose(sock_fpo);
                    fclose(sock_fpi);
            }
    }

    sanitize(char *str)
    /*
     * it would be very bad if someone passed us an dirname like
     * "; rm *"  and we naively created a command  "ls ; rm *"
     *
     * so..we remove everything but slashes and alphanumerics
     * There are nicer solutions, see exercises
     */
    {
            char *src, *dest;

            for ( src = dest = str ; *src ; src++ )
                    if ( *src == '/' || isalnum(*src) )
                            *dest++ = *src;
            *dest = '\0';
    }
```

Notice that our server uses standard buffered streams for reading and for writing. The server uses fgets to read the directory name from the client. After calling popen, the server transfers data using getc and putc just as though it were copying a file. Of course, the server is actually copying data from one process to a process on another computer.

Note the sanitize function. Any server that runs commands based on arguments and data it receives over the Internet *must* be written extremely carefully. Our server expects to receive the name of a directory from the client. The server appends that string to the command ls. For example, if the client sends the string "/bin", our server creates and executes the string "ls /bin", which is fine. If, though, someone sends the string "; rm *" to our server, our server would create and execute the string "ls; rm *".

To reduce the risk of damage, our program makes sure the string it receives does not overflow the input buffer, does not overflow the buffer for the command, and does not allow any special characters in the directory name, although limiting the directory name to alphanumeric is too restrictive. The popen function is too risky for network services because it passes a string to a shell. It is a poor idea to write any network servers that pass strings to a shell. I included this example for two reasons: first, to show another use of popen, and second, to alert you to this danger. It is a serious one.

11.6   SOFTWARE DAEMONS

Unix server programs, like most Unix programs, have short, concise names. Many server programs have names that end in the letter *d*, such as httpd, inetd, syslogd, atd. The *d* in these names stands for *daemon*, so the name syslogd identifies the program as the *system log daemon*. A daemon is a term for an attendant spirit, sort of a supernatural helper that floats around waiting to help out. On your system, type ps -el or ps -ax and look for processes running programs with names that end in the letter *d*. You can then read the manual pages about those commands. By doing so, you can learn more about the way Unix uses client/server programming to manage many basic operations.

Most daemon processes are started when the system comes up. Shell scripts in a directory with a name like /etc/rc.d[3] start these servers in the background, where they run detached from any terminals, ready to provide data or services.

SUMMARY

MAIN IDEAS

- Some programs are constructed as separate processes that send data back and forth. In a client/server system, a server process provides processing or data to client processes.
- A client/server system consists of a communication system and a protocol. Clients and servers can communicate through pipes or sockets. A protocol is a set of rules for the structure of a conversation.
- The popen library function can make any shell command into a server program and makes access to the server look like access to buffered files.
- A pipe is a connected pair of file descriptors. A socket is an unconnected communication endpoint, a potential file descriptor. A client process creates a communication link by connecting its socket to a server socket.
- Connections between sockets may extend from one computer to another. Each socket is identified by a machine number and a port number.

---

[3]The exact directory name depends on the version of Unix.

- Connections to pipes and sockets use file descriptors. File descriptors provide programs with a single interface for communication with files, devices, and other processes.

WHAT NEXT?

In this chapter, we looked at the client/server model of program design. We saw two methods for connecting processes: pipes and sockets. In the next chapter, we focus on the design principles of client/server programming, and we write more complex applications. In particular, we combine socket programming with our knowledge of file systems and process control to write a Web server.

EXPLORATIONS

11.1 *The pizza-delivery-order protocol* What if you ran a pizza-delivery service instead of a time or directory-assistance service? The protocol would be more complicated. Describe the sequence of messages passed between server and client for a pizza-delivery service. Note that this protocol contains a loop that allows the client to add several items to the order.

11.2 popen *and signals* The version of popen provided in the text does not do anything about signals. Is that correct? A child inherits the signal-handling settings from its parent. Answer this question by considering the three cases of signal handling for the parent: terminate, ignore, and call a function.

11.3 *Data flow in testing* timeserv The sample run of the time server and time client showed that I used ssh to log in to computer2 from computer1. I was still logged into computer1, but I was running a shell on computer2. From that shell, I compiled and ran the time client.

My terminal is really connected to computer1. Redraw figure 11.11 so it includes my shell on computer1, my shell on computer2, my terminal, and the correct flow of data from timeclnt to my terminal. Pretty complex data flow, isn't it?

11.4 *Sockets are not files* We saw earlier that disk files and device files both support the standard file interface, but connections to disk files have one set of properties, and connections to device files have a very different set of properties. What special properties do sockets have? Look at the manual page for setsockopt for details.

11.5 stderr *and servers* The remote directory lister runs the ls command. What happens when ls encounters an error? For example, the directory specified may not exist or may not be readable by the server. What happens to the error messages ls generates? Consider two ways to handle error messages from ls. First, how would you send error messages back to the client? Second, how would you record error messages in a log and tell the user about the problem?

PROGRAMMING EXERCISES

11.6 Add the -c option to tinybc. Once you have added this option, the following command should work:

```
printf "2 + 2\n4 * 4\n" | tinybc -c | dc
```

11.7 Add the -c option to your shell. What changes do you need to make?

11.8   Write `pclose`. The function takes as an argument the `FILE *` returned from `popen`. The `fdopen` function has allocated memory for the buffer and for bookkeeping details. The `fclose` function deallocates that memory and closes the underlying file descriptor. What else does `pclose` have to do? What if another child process dies between the call to `popen` and `pclose`?

11.9   *caller ID* Our time server does not use the caller-ID feature the `accept` system call provides. Modify `timeserv.c` so that it prints a message such as, *Got a call from 123.123.123.123 (computer2.mysite.net)* when it receives a request.

Read the manual and header files to learn about the functions and structures you need for this project.

11.10   Write a program that uses `sort` as a subroutine. Your program should read lines of data into an array of strings. The program should then create two pipes and then create a process to run `sort`. Send the sequence of lines of input to `sort` through one pipe, then close that pipe. Read the results from `sort` through the other pipe, and put the results back into the array. Print the array.

11.11   *Bidirectional pipes* Versions of Unix based on System V provide bidirectional pipes. You can test if a version of Unix supports these by running this program:

```
/*
 * testbpd.c  - test bidirectional pipes
 */

main()
{
        int     p[2];
        if ( pipe(p) == -1 ) exit(1);
        if ( write(p[0], "hello", 5) == -1 )
                perror("write into pipe[0] failed");
        else
                printf("write into pipe[0] worked\n");
}
```

Internally, a bidirectional pipe contains two queues, one from `pipe[0]` to `pipe[1]` and one going the other way. Writing data into one end of a pipe adds it to the queue that goes to the other end, and reading data from one end of a pipe pulls bytes from the queue leading from the other end.

If your system does not support bidirectional pipes, you can create a pair using this call:

```
#include <sys/types.h>
#include <sys/socket.h>
int apipe[2];       /* a pipe */
socketpair(AF_UNIX, SOCK_STREAM, PF_UNSPEC, apipe);
```

Recode `tinybc.c` so it uses a single bidirectional pipe rather than using two unidirectional pipes.

11.12   *IP blocking* Modify `timeserv.c` so it only responds to clients calling from a specific host IP number. The server accepts the call and checks the address of the client. If the client is not at the specified IP number, the server hangs up, otherwise, the server sends back the time message.

Enhance this blocking feature so the server reads a list of acceptable IP numbers from a file. Describe some practical applications of this technique.

11.13 *More secure* Using `popen` in a server is extremely risky. There are two ways to address the risks. The first is to write a more flexible, but still secure version of the `sanitize` function. For example, there is no problem with directory names that contain periods, dashes, spaces, and many other characters. A directory name can contain asterisks and semicolons. It is just that the shell assigns special meanings to those characters. Write a more useful, but still safe string-cleaning function.

The other method is to drop `popen` and use `fork`, `exec`, `dup`, etc. Rewrite `rlsd.c` using this method. Do you need to use `wait`? Why or why not?

11.14 *A finger server* Write a version of the directory-assistance server we saw running at port 79. The server should accept a username as a single line of input and then send back to the client a list of matching records from the local user list.

11.15 *Time-server proxy* A proxy is a program that accepts your request, forwards it to another server, and then sends the response from that server back to you. Like a dry cleaner storefront, the shop does not do the cleaning; it just transfers the clothes to and from the cleaning plant.

Write a time-server proxy. Your program should accept connections on the standard port. To process the connection, your program should then open a connection to a "real" time server, get the time from that server, and send the response back to your client.

11.16 *Caches and proxies* Read about proxy servers in the previous problem. The time only changes once per second, so if your proxy server gets lots of connections milliseconds apart, there is no reason for your proxy to call a server for the time. Write a *caching proxy* time server that stores the time it read from the server and only makes a new call when that string is more than a second old. (See `gettimeofday`.)

11.17 *More caches and proxies* Admittedly, the caching time server in the previous exercise is a silly idea. Explain why using a cache for a finger server makes sense. Write a finger server that keeps a cache of user information.

The time server has a natural lifetime for items in the cache, but how do you decide how long to keep user information in the finger-server cache?

11.18 *A bakery number server* Some bakery shops have a machine that dispenses numbers to customers. A sign over the counter that says "Now Serving" displays the number of the next customer to be served. Devise a client-server pair to implement the bakery number system. The server issues sequential numbers. A user runs the client program to obtain a number from the server.

11.19 *Using* `popen` Every C programmer knows that `argv[0]` usually contains the name of the program being run. There is another, slightly roundabout, way a process can obtain its name. A program can use `popen` and search the output of the `ps` command for its own process ID number. Write a program that uses this method.

# CHAPTER 12

Connections and Protocols
Writing a Web Server

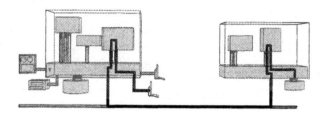

OBJECTIVES

Ideas and Skills

- Server sockets: purpose and construction
- Client sockets: purpose and construction
- Client/server protocol
- Server design: using `fork` for multiple requests
- The zombie problem
- HTTP

12.1 SPOTLIGHT ON SERVERS

Using the World Wide Web is easy. Type a Web location into a browser or click on a link, and a Web page is delivered from a remote computer. How does the Web work? Is calling up a page from a Web site similar to getting the current time from a time server?

Most socket-based client/server systems are pretty similar. E-mail, file transfer, remote log-in, distributed databases, and many other Internet services appear different on the screen, but all work the same way.

Once you understand one stream-socket client/server system, you can understand most of the other ones. In this chapter, we look at operations and design principles common to network programs, and we then apply those abstractions to build a Web server.

12.2   THREE MAIN OPERATIONS

We saw in Chapter 11 that stream-based client/server systems look like the illustration shown in Figure 12.1. Clients and servers are processes. A server sets up a service, then

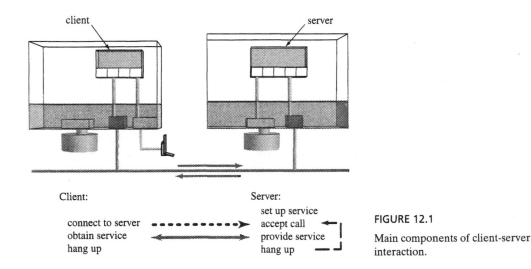

FIGURE 12.1

Main components of client-server interaction.

enters a loop taking and handling calls. A client connects to a server, sends, receives, or exchanges data with the server, and then exits. This interaction consists of three main operations:

1. Server sets up a service
2. Client connects to a server
3. Server and client do business

We first look at each of these operations separately.

12.3   OPERATIONS 1 AND 2: MAKING A CONNECTION

A stream-based system requires a connection. We review the steps to make the connection and then abstract those steps into a pair of library functions.

12.3.1   Operation 1: Setting Up a Server Socket

First, the server sets up a service, as shown in Figure 12.2. Note that every stream-based server sets up a service with these three steps:

(a) *Create a socket*

```
sock = socket(PF_INET, SOCK_STREAM, 0)
```

(b) *Give the socket an address*

```
bind(sock, &addr, sizeof(addr))
```

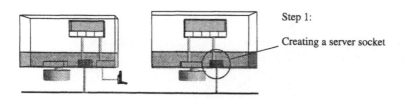

Step 1:

Creating a server socket

FIGURE 12.2

Creating a server socket.

(c) *Arrange to take incoming calls*

```
listen(sock, queue_size)
```

Rather than retype these steps for every server we write, we combine this three-step procedure into a single function: `make_server_socket`. Code for this function is included in the file called `socklib.c` listed later in this chapter. When we write servers, we can just call this function. The details are as follows:

```
sock = make_server_socket(int portnum)

returns -1 if error,
     or a server socket listening at port "portnum"
```

12.3.2 Operation 2: Connecting to a Server

Next, a client connects to a server. (See Figure 12.3.) Stream-based network clients connect to servers with these two steps:

(a) *Create a socket*

```
sock = socket(PF_INET, SOCK_STREAM, 0)
```

(b) *Use the socket to connect to a server*

```
connect(sock, &serv_addr, sizeof(serv_addr))
```

We abstract these two steps into a single function: `connect_to_server`, included in `socklib.c` listed later in this chapter. When we write clients, we can just call this function. The details are as follows:

```
fd = connect_to_server(hostname, portnum)

returns -1 if error,
```

Step 2:

Create and connect a client socket

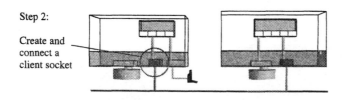

FIGURE 12.3

Connecting to a server.

or a fd open for reading and writing connected to the
socket at port "portnum" on host "hostname"

12.3.3 `socklib.c`

Here is the code to `socklib.c`:

```
/*  socklib.c
 *
 *      This file contains functions used lots when writing internet
 *      client/server programs.  The two main functions here are:
 *
 *      int make_server_socket( portnum )       returns a server socket
 *                                      or -1 if error
 *      int make_server_socket_q(portnum,backlog)
 *
 *      int connect_to_server(char *hostname, int portnum)
 *                                      returns a connected socket
 *                                      or -1 if error
 */
#include        <stdio.h>
#include        <unistd.h>
#include        <sys/types.h>
#include        <sys/socket.h>
#include        <netinet/in.h>
#include        <netdb.h>
#include        <time.h>
#include        <strings.h>

#define   HOSTLEN   256
#define   BACKLOG   1

int make_server_socket(int portnum)
{
        return make_server_socket_q(portnum, BACKLOG);
}
int make_server_socket_q(int portnum, int backlog)
{
        struct  sockaddr_in   saddr;    /* build our address here */
        struct  hostent       *hp;      /* this is part of our   */
        char    hostname[HOSTLEN];      /* address               */
        int     sock_id;                /* the socket            */

        sock_id = socket(PF_INET, SOCK_STREAM, 0);  /* get a socket */
        if ( sock_id == -1 )
                return -1;

        /** build address and bind it to socket **/

        bzero((void *)&saddr, sizeof(saddr));    /* clear out struct    */
        gethostname(hostname, HOSTLEN);          /* where am I ?        */
```

```
        hp = gethostbyname(hostname) ;              /* get info about host  */
                                                    /* fill in host part    */

        bcopy( (void *)hp->h_addr, (void *)&saddr.sin_addr, hp->h_length);
        saddr.sin_port = htons(portnum);            /* fill in socket port  */
        saddr.sin_family = AF_INET ;                /* fill in addr family  */
        if ( bind(sock_id, (struct sockaddr *)&saddr, sizeof(saddr)) != 0 )
                return -1;

        /** arrange for incoming calls **/

        if ( listen(sock_id, backlog) != 0 )
                return -1;
        return sock_id;
}

int connect_to_server(char *host, int portnum)
{
        int sock;
        struct sockaddr_in  servadd;        /* the number to call */
        struct hostent      *hp;            /* used to get number */

        /** Step 1: Get a socket **/

        sock = socket( AF_INET, SOCK_STREAM, 0 );   /* get a line    */
        if ( sock == -1 )
                return -1;

        /** Step 2: connect to server **/

        bzero( &servadd, sizeof(servadd) );     /* zero the address     */
        hp = gethostbyname( host );             /* lookup host's ip #   */
        if (hp == NULL)
                return -1;
        bcopy(hp->h_addr, (struct sockaddr *)&servadd.sin_addr, hp->
          h_length);
        servadd.sin_port = htons(portnum);      /* fill in port number  */
        servadd.sin_family = AF_INET ;          /* fill in socket type  */

        if ( connect(sock,(struct sockaddr *)&servadd, sizeof(servadd))
          !=0)
                return -1;

        return sock;
}
```

12.4   OPERATION 3: CLIENT/SERVER CONVERSATION

We now have a single function to create a server socket, and we have a single function to connect to a server socket. How do we use these new functions in practice? What do the client and server say to each other? In this section, we look at the general form of a client program, the general form of a server program, and some design choices for building a server.

The Generic Client

A network client calls a server and obtains service. A typical client looks like the following:

```
main()
{
    int fd;

    fd = connect_to_server(host, port);        /* call the server   */
    if ( fd == -1 )
        exit(1);                               /* or die            */
    talk_with_server(fd);                      /* chat with server  */
    close(fd);                                 /* hang up when done */
}
```

The function `talk_with_server` handles the conversation with the server. Details of that function depend on the application. For example, an e-mail client talks to the mail server about the mail, while a weather-forecast client talks about the weather.

The Generic Server

A typical server looks like this:

```
main()
{
    int sock, fd;                    /* socket and connection */

    sock = make_server_socket(port);
    if ( sock == -1 )
        exit(1);

    while(1){
        fd = accept(sock, NULL, NULL);         /* take next call    */
        if ( fd == -1 )
            break;                             /* or die            */
        process_request(fd);                   /* chat with client  */
        close(fd);                             /* hang up when done */
    }
}
```

The function `process_request` handles the conversation with the client. Details of that function depend on the application. For example, an e-mail server tells the client about letters, and a weather server tells the client about the weather.

12.4.1 `timeserv/timeclnt` using `socklib.c`

How do we use these two generic templates to a build client/server systems? For instance, what does our time client/server system look like in this framework? Figure 12.4 gives us some idea of the relationship. To recode the time client and server programs using `socklib.c`, we write the functions that conduct the conversation—`talk_with_server` for the time client and `process_request` for the time server:

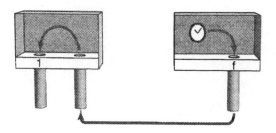

FIGURE 12.4

Time server and client version 1.

```
talk_with_server(fd)                    process_request(fd)
{                                       {
    char buf[LEN];                          time_t now;
    int  n;                                 char *cp;

    n=read(fd,buf,LEN);                     time(&now);
    write(1,buf,n);                         cp  = ctime(&now);
}                                           write(fd, cp, strlen(cp));

                                        }
```

The server calls time to obtain the time from the kernel and ctime to convert that number into a printable string. The server writes that string into the socket, sending it to the socket in the client. The client reads the string from the socket and writes that string to standard output. This new version follows the same logic as the previous version, but the design is more modular, and the code is cleaner.

12.4.2 A Second Version of the Server: Using **fork**

Consider now a second version of the time server. Instead of computing the current time, the server calls the Unix date command. Figure 12.5 shows the relationship involved; the code is as follows:

```
process_request(fd)
/*
 * send the date out to the client via fd
 */
{
        int    pid = fork();

        switch(pid){
            case -1: return;              /* cannot provide service  */
```

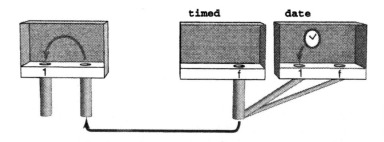

timed   date

FIGURE 12.5

Server forks to run date.

```
          case  0: dup2(fd, 1);        /* child runs date        */
                   close(fd);          /* by redirecting stdout   */
                   execl("/bin/date","date",NULL);
                   oops("execlp");     /* or quits                */
          default: wait(NULL);         /* parent wait for child   */
     }
}
```

As the diagram shows, the server forks to produce a new process. That child redirects standard output to the socket and then execs date. The date command figures out the date and writes the result to standard output, thereby sending the string to the client. We call wait in this program. A shell typically calls wait after calling fork, but does it make sense here? We explore this question in the next section.

12.4.3   Server Design Question: DIY or Delegate?

These time servers show two types of server design:

> Do it yourself—the server takes the call and does the work itself.
>
> Delegate—the server takes the call and then forks a process to do the work.

What are the advantages and disadvantages of each method?

Do It Yourself for Quick, Simple Tasks   Computing the current date and time requires one system call to time and a library call to ctime. Using fork and exec to run date requires at least three system calls and a whole new process. For some servers, the most efficient method is for the server to do the work and to adjust the connection queue size with listen. The make_server_socket_q function in socklib.c accepts a queue size as an argument.

Delegate for Slower, More Complex Tasks   Servers that do time-consuming tasks or wait for resources should delegate work. Like a telephone receptionist at a business who picks up a call, passes the connection to the next sales or service person, and then loops back to take the next call, a server can call fork to create a new process to handle each call. By doing so, a server can handle many requests simultaneously.

To serve several clients at once, the server should not wait for the child to finish handling the request. If the parent does not call wait, though, its children become zombies. How can a server prevent zombies?

Using SIGCHLD for Zombie Prevention   Rather than wait for children to die, a process can arrange to receive a signal when a child dies. Chapter 8 explained that the kernel sends SIGCHLD to the parent when a child process exits or is killed, but unlike other signals we discussed, SIGCHLD is ignored by default. A parent process may set a signal handler for SIGCHLD. That handler can call wait. The naive solution looks like the following:

```
/* naive use of SIGCHLD handler with wait() - buggy */
main()
{
```

```
int     sock, fd;
void    child_waiter(int), process_request(int);

signal( SIGCHLD, child_waiter );
if ( (sock = make_server_socket( PORTNUM )) == -1 )
        oops( "make_server_socket" );

while( 1 ) {
        fd = accept(sock,NULL,NULL );
        if ( fd == -1 )
                break;
        process_request(fd);
        close(fd);
    }
}
void child_waiter(int signum)
{
        wait(NULL);
}
void process_request(int fd)
{
        if ( fork() == 0 ){             /* child               */
                dup2( fd, 1 );          /* moves socket to fd 1 */
                close(fd);              /* closes socket        */
                execlp("date","date",NULL);  /* exec date       */
                oops("execlp date");
        }
}
```

Consider the flow of control in this program. A call comes in, the parent forks, and then the parent returns at once to accept the next call, leaving the child to process the request. When the child exits, the parent receives SIGCHLD, jumps to the handler function, and calls wait. The child is removed from the process table, and the parent returns from the signal handler to main. Sounds perfect. There are two problems, one simple and one subtle.

The simple problem is that the jump to the signal handler interrupts the accept system call. When interrupted by a signal, accept returns −1, and sets errno to EINTR. Our code treats a value of −1 from accept as an error and breaks from the main loop. We just modify main to distinguish between a real error and an interrupted system call. We leave this change as an exercise.

The subtler problem concerns how Unix handles multiple signals. What happens if several child processes all exit at almost exactly the same time? Imagine that three instances of SIGCHLD are sent to the parent. The first signal to arrive causes the parent to jump to the handler. The parent then calls wait to ensure the child is removed from the process table. OK so far?

While the parent is executing the signal handler, the other two signals arrive. Unix blocks, but does not queue signals. Therefore, the second signal is blocked and the third one is *lost*. If other children exit while the parent is in the handler, signals from those processes are lost, too.

The signal handler calls wait exactly once, so each lost signal means one fewer call to wait, which means one more zombie. The solution is for the signal handler to call wait enough times to mop up all terminated processes. The waitpid call solves the problem:

```
void child_waiter(int signum)
{
    while( waitpid(-1, NULL, WNOHANG) > 0 )
        ;
}
```

waitpid provides a superset of the functions of wait. waitpid accepts as its first argument the ID number of the process you want it to wait for. The value of -1 tells waitpid to wait for all children. The second argument is the pointer to the integer to receive the status. This server does not care what happens to its children. A more thorough server might use that information to track errors.

The last argument to waitpid specifies options. The WNOHANG option tells waitpid not to wait if there are no zombies.

This loop repeats until all finished children are waited for. Even if several children exit at once and generate scores of SIGCHLD signals, all those children will be found.

12.5 WRITING A WEB SERVER

We now know enough to write a Web server. A Web server is an extension of the directory-listing server we wrote. The extra parts are a cat server and an exec server.

12.5.1 What a Web Server Does

A Web server is a simple concept. A Web server is a program that performs the three most common user operations:

(a) list directories

(b) cat files

(c) run programs

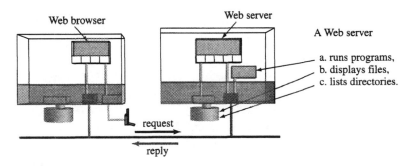

FIGURE 12.6

A Web server offers remote ls, cat, exec.

Logic of the Web Server and Client

A Web server provides these three operations to users on other machines through a stream socket connection. (See Figure 12.6.) Users on other machines run a client program to connect to our server and send a request, and the Web server sends back the requested information. The following list illustrates the process:

client		**server**
user selects a link		
`connect` to server	——>	`accept` a call
`write` a request	——>	`read` a request
		handle request:
		directory: list it
		regular file: `cat` it
		`.cgi` file: run it
		not exist: error message
`read` the reply	<——	`write` a reply
hangup		
display the reply		
`html`: render it		
image: draw it		
sound: play it		
repeat		

12.5.2 Planning Our Web Server

What operations do we need to code?

(a) *Set up the server*

> We can use `make_server_socket` from `socklib.c`.

(b) *Accept a call*

> Use `accept` to get the file descriptor to the client. We can use `fdopen` to make that file descriptor into a buffered stream.

(c) *Read a request*

> What does a request look like? How does the client ask for something? We need to study this one more.

(d) *Handle the request*

> We know how to list directories, `cat` files, and run programs. We can use `opendir` and `readdir`, `open` and `read`, `dup2` and `exec`.

(e) *Send a reply*

> What does a reply look like? What does the client expect to see? This one also requires more study.

This looks encouraging. We already know almost all the ideas and skills required to write a Web server. The one thing we need to learn is the Web-server protocol.

12.5.3 The Protocol of a Web Server

Interaction between a Web client (typically a browser) and a Web server consists of a request from the client and a reply from the server. The format of the request and the format of the reply are specified by the *hypertext transfer protocol* known as HTTP. HTTP, like the protocol for the time servers and finger servers of the last chapter, uses plain text. As we did with time servers and finger servers, we can use telnet to talk to Web servers. Web servers listen at port 80. Here is an actual transcript:

```
$ telnet www.prenhall.com 80
Trying 165.193.123.253...
Connected to www.prenhall.com.
Escape character is '^]'.
GET /index.html HTTP/1.0

HTTP/1.1 200 OK
Server: Netscape-Enterprise/3.6 SP3
Date: Tue, 22 Jan 2002 16:11:14 GMT
Content-type: text/html
Last-modified: Fri, 08 Sep 2000 20:20:06 GMT
Content-length: 327
Accept-ranges: bytes
Connection: close

<HTML><HEAD>
<META HTTP-EQUIV="Refresh" CONTENT="0; URL=http://vig.prenhall.com/">
</HEAD><BODY></BODY></HTML>
<!-- ------------------------------------------------------------ -->
<!--                      Caught you peeking!                     -->
<!-- ------------------------------------------------------------ -->
Connection closed by foreign host.
$
```

Here, I send a one-line request and receive a multiline response. What are the details?

The HTTP Request: GET

I used telnet to connect to the Web server at a specific host. telnet created a socket and called connect. The server accepted the connection creating a data channel from my keyboard through the sockets to the server process.

I then typed the request

```
GET /index.html HTTP/1.0
```

An HTTP request consists of a single line containing three strings. The first string is the command, the second string is the argument, and the third string is the version of the protocol the client speaks. In the example shown here, I type the GET command with an argument of /index.html and I claim to speak HTTP version 1.0.

HTTP includes several other commands. Most Web requests use GET since most of the time users click on links in order to get pages. The GET command may be followed by several lines of additional arguments. We keep this request simple. We indicate the end of the list of arguments by a blank line. We used the same convention in the prompting shell we wrote earlier. In fact, a Web server is just a Unix shell with cat and ls as built-in commands.

The HTTP Reply: OK

The server reads the request, examines it, and sends back a reply. The reply has two parts: a header and the content. The header begins with a status line, as follows:

```
HTTP/1.1 200 OK
```

The status line consists of two or more strings. The first string is the version of the protocol the server is speaking, and the second string is a response code number. The response code in this example is 200. The textual phrase associated with that code is "OK". We requested a file called /info.html, and the server said we could have that file. If there had not been a file with that name, the response code would have been 404 and the message would be something like "Not found".

The rest of the header consists of several lines containing additional information about the response. In this example, additional information includes the name of the server, the time of the response, the type of the data the server is sending, and the type of the connection used for the response. A response header may contain many lines of information. The server indicates the end of the header by sending a blank line. That blank line appears after the line that reads Connection: close.

The rest of the reply is the content of the response. In this case, the server sent back the contents of the file /index.html.

Summary of HTTP

The basic structure of the interaction between a Web client and a Web server is as follows:

Client sends request

```
GET filename HTTP/version
```
optional arguments
a blank line

Server sends reply

```
HTTP/version status-code status-message
```
additional information
a blank line
content

The complete description of the protocol is available on line in a document called *RFC1945* for version 1.0, and *RFC2068* for version 1.1.

Our Web server has to accept an HTTP request from clients and then send back HTTP replies. The plain text formats of these requests and replies are easy to read and process with standard C input/output and string functions.

12.5.4   Writing a Web Server

Our Web server will support the GET command only. Our server will read the request line, skip the additional arguments, then process the request and send back a reply. The main loop of our Web server looks like the following:

```
while(1){

    fd = accept(sock, NULL, NULL);    /* take a call         */
    fpin = fdopen(fd, "r");           /* make it a FILE *     */

    fgets(fpin, request, LEN);        /* read client request */
    read_until_crnl(fpin);            /* skip over arguments */
    process_rq(request, fd);          /* reply to client      */

    fclose(fpin);                     /* hang up connection   */
}
```

Error checking at each system call and function has been omitted for clarity.

Processing the Request   Processing the request consists of identifying the command and then acting on the argument:

```
process_rq(char *rq, int fd)
{
    char cmd[11], arg[513];

    if ( fork() != 0 )                /* if child, do work   */
        return;                       /* if parent, return   */

    sscanf(rq, "%10s %512s", cmd, arg);
    if ( strcmp(cmd, "GET") != 0 )    /* check command        */
        cannot_do(fd);

    else if ( not_exist(arg) )        /* does the arg exist */
        do_404(arg, fd);              /*   n: tell user       */

    else if ( isadir(arg) )           /* is it a directory? */
        do_ls(arg, fd);               /*   y: list contents */

    else if ( ends_in_cgi(arg) )      /* name is X.cgi?       */
        do_exec(arg, fd);             /*   y: execute it      */

    else                              /* otherwise            */
        do_cat(arg, fd);              /*    display contents */
}
```

This server creates a new child to handle each request. The child then splits the request into a command and an argument. If the command is not GET, the server sends back the HTTP code for nonimplemented commands. If the command is GET, the server expects to see the name of a directory, an executable program ending with the string *.cgi*, or the name of a regular file. If there is no such directory or file with the specified name, the server reports the error.

If there is a file or directory by that name, the server decides which of the three operations to perform: ls, exec, or cat.

The Directory-Listing Function   The function do_ls handles the requests to list directories:

```
do_ls(char *dir, int fd)
{
        FILE    *fp ;
        fp = fdopen(fd,"w");            /* make socket into a FILE * */
        header(fp, "text/plain");       /* send HTTP reply header    */
        fprintf(fp,"\r\n");             /* and end of header mark     */
        fflush(fp);                     /* force to socket            */

        dup2(fd,1);                            /* make socket stdout    */
        dup2(fd,2);                            /* make socket stderr    */
        close(fd);                             /* close socket          */
        execl("/bin/ls","ls","-l",dir,NULL);   /* ls -l does the work */
        perror(dir);                           /* or it doesn't         */
        exit(1);                               /* child exits           */
}
```

We do not use popen in this function as we did in the directory lister in the previous chapter. By calling ls directly, we eliminate the problems caused by passing an arbitrary string from a user to the shell popen runs.

The Other Functions   The rest of the code is included later in the chapter. The program works, but it is incomplete and insecure. Some of the needed repairs are as follows:

(a) zombie elimination

(b) buffer overflow protection

(c) CGI programs should see several environment variables set

(d) HTTP header should have more information

On the other hand, the program is a complete Web server in about 230 lines of C code, including comments and blank lines.

12.5.5 Running the Web Server

Compile the code and then run the program at a port:

```
$ cc webserv.c socklib.c -o webserv
$ ./webserv 12345
```

You can now visit your Web server at http://yourhostname:12345/. Put an html file in that directory and open it with http://yourhostname:12345/filename.html. Create the following shell script:

```
#!/bin/sh
# hello.cgi - a cheery cgi page
printf "Content-type: text/plain\n\nhello\n";
```

Call it hello.cgi, chmod it to 755, and then use your browser to invoke the script with http://yourhostname:12345/hello.cgi.

12.5.6 Webserv Source Code

Here is the code for this simple Web server:

```
/* webserv.c - a minimal web server (version 0.2)
 *       usage: ws portnumber
 *    features: supports the GET command only
 *              runs in the current directory
 *              forks a new child to handle each request
 *              has MAJOR security holes, for demo purposes only
 *              has many other weaknesses, but is a good start
 *       build: cc webserv.c socklib.c -o webserv
 */
#include        <stdio.h>
#include        <sys/types.h>
#include        <sys/stat.h>
#include        <string.h>

main(int ac, char *av[])
{
        int     sock, fd;
        FILE    *fpin;
        char    request[BUFSIZ];

        if ( ac == 1 ){
                fprintf(stderr,"usage: ws portnum\n");
                exit(1);
        }
        sock = make_server_socket( atoi(av[1]) );
        if ( sock == -1 ) exit(2);

        /* main loop here */

        while(1){
                /* take a call and buffer it */
                fd = accept( sock, NULL, NULL );
                fpin = fdopen(fd, "r" );

                /* read request */
                fgets(request,BUFSIZ,fpin);
```

```
                        printf("got a call: request = %s", request);
                        read_til_crnl(fpin);

                        /* do what client asks */
                        process_rq(request, fd);

                        fclose(fpin);
        }
}
/* ------------------------------------------------------------ *
   read_til_crnl(FILE *)
   skip over all request info until a CRNL is seen
   ------------------------------------------------------------ */
read_til_crnl(FILE *fp)
{
        char    buf[BUFSIZ];
        while( fgets(buf,BUFSIZ,fp) != NULL && strcmp(buf,"\r\n") != 0 )
                ;
}

/* ------------------------------------------------------------ *
   process_rq( char *rq, int fd )
   do what the request asks for and write reply to fd
   handles request in a new process
   rq is HTTP command:  GET /foo/bar.html HTTP/1.0
   ------------------------------------------------------------ */

process_rq( char *rq, int fd )
{
        char    cmd[BUFSIZ], arg[BUFSIZ];

        /* create a new process and return if not the child */
        if ( fork() != 0 )
                return;

        strcpy(arg, "./");                      /* precede args with ./ */
        if ( sscanf(rq, "%s%s", cmd, arg+2) != 2 )
                return;

        if ( strcmp(cmd,"GET") != 0 )
                cannot_do(fd);
        else if ( not_exist( arg ) )
                do_404(arg, fd );
        else if ( isadir( arg ) )
                do_ls( arg, fd );
        else if ( ends_in_cgi( arg ) )
                do_exec( arg, fd );
        else
                do_cat( arg, fd );
}

/* ------------------------------------------------------------ *
   the reply header thing: all functions need one
```

```
       if content_type is NULL then don't send content type
       ---------------------------------------------------- */

header( FILE *fp, char *content_type )
{
        fprintf(fp, "HTTP/1.0 200 OK\r\n");
        if ( content_type )
                fprintf(fp, "Content-type: %s\r\n", content_type );
}

/* ---------------------------------------------------- *
   simple functions first:
        cannot_do(fd)        unimplemented HTTP command
    and do_404(item,fd)      no such object
       ---------------------------------------------------- */

cannot_do(int fd)
{
        FILE    *fp = fdopen(fd,"w");

        fprintf(fp, "HTTP/1.0 501 Not Implemented\r\n");
        fprintf(fp, "Content-type: text/plain\r\n");
        fprintf(fp, "\r\n");

        fprintf(fp, "That command is not yet implemented\r\n");
        fclose(fp);
}

do_404(char *item, int fd)
{
        FILE    *fp = fdopen(fd,"w");
        fprintf(fp, "HTTP/1.0 404 Not Found\r\n");
        fprintf(fp, "Content-type: text/plain\r\n");
        fprintf(fp, "\r\n");

        fprintf(fp, "The item you requested: %s\r\nis not found\r\n",
                        item);

        fclose(fp);
}

/* ---------------------------------------------------- *
   the directory listing section
   isadir() uses stat, not_exist() uses stat
   do_ls runs ls. It should not
       ---------------------------------------------------- */

isadir(char *f)
{
        struct stat info;
        return ( stat(f, &info) != -1 && S_ISDIR(info.st_mode) );
}
not_exist(char *f)
```

```
        {
                struct stat info;
                return( stat(f,&info) == -1 );
        }

        do_ls(char *dir, int fd)
        {
                FILE    *fp ;

                fp = fdopen(fd,"w");
                header(fp, "text/plain");
                fprintf(fp,"\r\n");
                fflush(fp);

                dup2(fd,1);
                dup2(fd,2);
                close(fd);
                execlp("ls","ls","-l",dir,NULL);
                perror(dir);
                exit(1);
        }

        /* ------------------------------------------------------ *
           the cgi stuff.  function to check extension and
           one to run the program.
           ------------------------------------------------------ */

        char * file_type(char *f)
        /* returns 'extension' of file */
        {
                char    *cp;
                if ( (cp = strrchr(f, '.' )) != NULL )
                        return cp+1;
                return "";
        }

        ends_in_cgi(char *f)
        {
                return ( strcmp( file_type(f), "cgi" ) == 0 );
        }

        do_exec( char *prog, int fd )
        {
                FILE    *fp ;

                fp = fdopen(fd,"w");
                header(fp, NULL);
                fflush(fp);
                dup2(fd, 1);
                dup2(fd, 2);
                close(fd);
                execl(prog,prog,NULL);
                perror(prog);
        }
```

```
/* ------------------------------------------------------- *
    do_cat(filename,fd)
    sends back contents after a header
   ------------------------------------------------------- */
do_cat(char *f, int fd)
{
        char    *extension = file_type(f);
        char    *content = "text/plain";
        FILE    *fpsock, *fpfile;
        int     c;

        if ( strcmp(extension,"html") == 0 )
                content = "text/html";
        else if ( strcmp(extension, "gif") == 0 )
                content = "image/gif";
        else if ( strcmp(extension, "jpg") == 0 )
                content = "image/jpeg";
        else if ( strcmp(extension, "jpeg") == 0 )
                content = "image/jpeg";

        fpsock = fdopen(fd, "w");
        fpfile = fopen( f , "r");
        if ( fpsock != NULL && fpfile != NULL )
        {
                header( fpsock, content );
                fprintf(fpsock, "\r\n");
                while( (c = getc(fpfile) ) != EOF )
                        putc(c, fpsock);
                fclose(fpfile);
                fclose(fpsock);
        }
        exit(0);
}
```

12.5.7 Comparing Web Servers

A Web server is a program that allows users on other computers to list directories, read files, and run programs. All Web servers perform the same basic operations, and all must conform to the core HTTP rules.

What distinguishes one server from another? Some servers are easier to configure and operate than others. Some servers provide more security features than others. Some servers process requests faster or use less memory. One of the important features for busy Web sites is the efficiency of a server. How many requests can it handle at once? How many system resources does the server require for each request?

The Web server in this chapter creates a new process for each request. Is this the most efficient method? Requests to read from files and directories can take a long time, so the server should not wait for those to complete, but do we need a whole new process?

A third method exists for running several operations at the same time. A program can run several tasks in one process by using something called *threads* of execution. We study threads in a later chapter.

SUMMARY

MAIN IDEAS

- Client/server socket-based programs follow a standard framework. The server accepts and processes requests. Clients place requests.
- Servers set up server sockets. Server sockets have specific addresses and are set up to receive connections.
- Clients create and use client sockets. A client does not care about the address of its socket.
- A server may handle requests in one of two ways. A server may process the request itself, or a server may use fork to create a process to handle the request.
- A Web server is a popular socket-based application. A Web server processes three main types of requests: to send back the contents of a file, to send back a listing of a directory, and to run a program. The protocol of request and reply is called HTTP.

WHAT NEXT?

The telephone-call model is not the only way clients and servers communicate. Some people shop by mail from catalogs, sending out orders and getting back merchandise. Using a message-based communication system, each shopper can deal with several stores at once, and each store can deal with several shoppers at once. In the next chapter, we look at network programming that uses a postcard model: *datagram* sockets.

EXPLORATIONS

12.1   The sample client code for the time client calls read and write once. What if the amount of data delivered by the server arrived in several shipments or exceeded the size of the buffer? How should the client be modified to handle data that require several calls to read? In the server, what if the call to write returns a value less than the length of the string?

12.2   *wait vs. waitpid* The revised version of the SIGCHLD handler uses waitpid and a loop. Could we have instead used regular wait in a loop to handle the multiple signal problem?

PROGRAMMING EXERCISES

12.3   Modify the generic server so it restarts the call to accept if it is interrupted by a signal.

12.4   Modify the Web server so it keeps a log of all requests and the status of the response.

12.5   When a Web server receives a request for a CGI program, the server puts a number of variables into the environment of the CGI program. Find out what those variables are, and add some of them to the Web server. The shell programming chapter explains how to add variables to the environment.

12.6   *cgi-bin* Web servers use two main systems for identifying which requests run programs. The server presented in the chapter identifies programs by the *.cgi* extension. The other method is by path. Typically, if the file requested has the directory name `cgi-bin` in the path, the program is run. For example, the request for `/cgi-bin/counter` would, under this system, be run by the server. Modify the server to support this system.

12.7 *Response headers* Modify the Web server so it sends back more information in the header. The sample connection in the text shows a typical collection of header items. Add those items to the Web server.

12.8 *The HEAD method* Modify the Web server to support the HEAD request. Read the HTTP specification for details.

12.9 *The POST method* Modify the Web server to support the POST request. Read the HTTP specification for details.

PROJECTS

Based on the material in this chapter, you can learn about and write versions of the following Unix programs:

```
httpd, telnetd, fingerd, ftpd
```

# CHAPTER 13

Programming with Datagrams
A License Server[1]

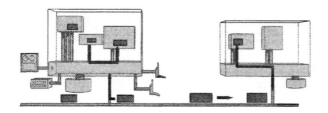

OBJECTIVES

Ideas and Skills

- Programming with datagrams, datagram sockets
- TCP vs. UDP
- License server
- Software tickets
- Designing robust systems
- Designing distributed systems
- Unix domain sockets

System Calls

- socket
- sendto, recvfrom

---

[1] This chapter is based on a lecture written and presented by Lawrence deLuca while he was a teaching assistant at Harvard Extension School. The lecture was based on a product he helped develop.

13.1   SOFTWARE CONTROL

Running a program requires memory, a process, CPU time, and some system resources. An operating system takes care of those things, but some programs require one more thing: permission from the owner of the program.

In legal terms, you need a license to use some programs, and some licenses come with restrictions. A license may, for example, limit the number of users allowed to run the program at the same time. A ten-user license may cost one amount while a fifty-user license may cost another amount. Some vendors rent software licenses and want programs to stop running when the rental term ends. Software use is also limited for reasons other than legal ownership. A computer lab at a school might limit the times of day during which computer games may be run.

Some software owners use the honor system to limit the use of their programs; they print the terms of the license on a screen or a piece of paper and ask users to obey the contract. Other software owners enforce licensing rules with technology.

One technological method for enforcing software licenses is to write programs that enforce their own licenses. A popular technique is to design application programs that ask permission from a *license server*, a process that tells the application program if it is allowed to run. The license server knows and enforces the rules of the license. (See Figure 13.1.)

FIGURE 13.1

A license server gives permission.

Asking permission and granting permission require communication between the licensed program and the license server.

How does a license server work? In this chapter, we examine a specific model of client/server license control. By studying this solution, we shall learn about another kind of socket—the *datagram* socket—another address domain—the *Unix domain*—a network protocol that maintains the *state* of a system, and some techniques for designing security and robustness into a client/server system.

13.2   A BRIEF HISTORY OF LICENSE CONTROL

Techniques for controlling the use of software have evolved over the years.

In the era of stand-alone personal computers, restricted software came on special disks or came with *key disks* with secret coding hidden on the tracks. The secret coding was difficult to copy, and the program would only run when that disk was in the disk drive. If you lost the special disk or spilled coffee on it, you could not run the program. People soon figured out how to copy the special disks, so software vendors invented hardware keys. Hardware keys are adapters that plug into a parallel port, serial port, or

USB port; the licensed program only runs if it finds the adapter plugged into the computer. If you lose the hardware key or leave the key at work when you take your computer home, you can not run the program.

Networked computers and multiuser systems pose new problems. If ten users want to run the same program on one machine or network, does each user have to plug a hardware key into a port on the server? Vendors of software that runs on servers want a way to enforce licenses that is reliable and does not burden legitimate users with additional inconveniences.

Networking and multiuser systems provide a new solution, the license server. The licensed program checks, not for a disk or key, but for permission from a server process. A license server is immune to coffee spills, cannot be left in your other briefcase, and can be shared by several users on the same computer. Server processes can also include sophisticated logic to control how many people may use the program, when the program is used, where it may be used, and even how the program is used. As more computers join the Internet, server-controlled access to software and data is increasing.

Our Project

Our license server will enforce an *n*-user limit. That is, the server allows only a certain number of simultaneous instances of the program to run.

13.3   A NONCOMPUTER EXAMPLE: MANAGING COMPANY CARS

A company purchases a license that sets a limit for the number of simultaneous users of a program. The company may have more employees than the number of users allowed by the license, but not all employees need to use the program at the same time. What design can we use for a program to enforce these terms?

The physical world is full of systems for sharing a fixed number of items among a larger number of users. We look there for a model. Consider the problem of sharing company cars among employees. A company has a certain number of cars that are kept in a lot and a larger number of employees. How can we manage access to cars?

13.3.1   Description of Car Key Management

We can control use of cars by controlling access to the car keys. When you want to use a car, you try to get a key. If no keys are in the key box, then you can't use a car. If there are keys available, you take one, sign for it, and then use the car. When you are done, you put the key back in the box and cross your name off the list of people holding keys. The process is depicted in Figure 13.2.

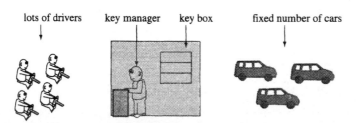

lots of drivers   key manager   key box   fixed number of cars

FIGURE 13.2

Controlling access to cars.

What is the point of the sign-out list? The purpose of the system is to limit access to the cars, so the existence of available keys should be sufficient. People are not perfect, and a driver may forget to return the key even though the car is back on the lot. The key manager can identify forgotten keys by calling the drivers on the sign-out list to make sure they are still using the car.

The car-access management system looks like a useful model for managing access to software. Before translating the model into software equivalents, we need to describe the key system in more detail.

Components of Key Management System

(a) Central Location of Keys—where to go for keys

(b) Key Manager—someone to enforce the policy

(c) Keys—the things you need to get

(d) Sign-Out List—general record keeping and for recovering keys

13.3.2   Managing Cars in Client/Server Terms

Having listed the components of the car key system, we next describe the system in the language of client/server programming.

Server and Clients

First, who is the client and who is the server? The key manager holds a resource that drivers need. In network programming terms, the key manager is the server, and the drivers are clients.

The Protocol

Second, what is the protocol? What are the transactions? This car-key-management protocol (CKMP) contains two main transactions:

Get Keys

Client: Hi, I'd like a key.
Server: Here is key 5. *or* Sorry, no more keys.

Give Back

Client: I'm done with key 5.
Server: Thanks.

The Communication System

Third, how do the client and server communicate? In the car key system, people exchange brief messages by speaking to each other.

The Data Structures

Finally, what data structures do the drivers and key manager need? The key manager keeps a sign-out sheet with one entry for each key. When a driver takes a key, the manager writes the name of the driver in that entry, and when the driver returns the key, the manager erases the name from that entry. The following table illustrates a key sign-out sheet:

Key Sign-out Sheet	
key#	**driver**
1	adam@sales
2	
3	carol@support
4	

A key is free if there is no name on the sign-out sheet for that key. A key is taken if there is a name on the sign-out sheet.

13.4   LICENSE MANAGEMENT

We now translate the key management system into a license management system.

13.4.1   The License Server System: What Does It Do?

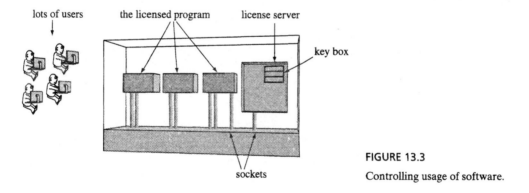

FIGURE 13.3

Controlling usage of software.

Figure 13.3 shows a collection of people who might want to run the licensed program. Our system works as follows:

(a) A user U starts the licensed program P.

(b) Program P asks the server S for permission to run.

(c) Server S checks the number of people currently running P.

(d) If the limit is not reached, S grants permission, and program P runs.

(e) If the limit has been reached, S denies permission, and program P tells U to try later.

The license server system differs slightly from the car key server system. In the car system, the driver asks the key manager for permission; in the software system, the program asks the server for permission. It is as though a driver goes to a car and the car asks the key manager for a key.[2]

The creator of the licensed program writes both of the programs: the application and the server. The two programs work as a system. The server grants permission to the application program to run and also enforces the terms of the license. If the license server is not running, the application program cannot obtain permission and will refuse to run.

We have the car key system as a model. How do we translate the details of that system into software? How will the licensed program ask the server for permission? How will the server grant permission? What is the software equivalent of a car key?

13.4.2 The License Server System: How Does It Work?

The Ticket Model

> The key manager gives out keys. What does the license server give out? Consider movie theaters and ball parks. You pay money for permission to enter the theater, and you get a ticket. Our license server will issue digital *tickets*. What does a ticket look like? Clients and servers exchange strings of text, so the ticket should be a string of text. We shall use the following format:
>
> ```
> pid.ticketnumber   e.g.   6589.3
> ```
>
> Each ticket consists of the PID of the process holding the ticket and the ticket number. We include the PID on tickets we issue for the same reasons airlines print your name on tickets they sell you. Attaching your name to an air ticket ensures that only you can use the ticket and helps if you lose the ticket. Can processes lose tickets?

Server and Clients

> First, who is the client and who is the server? The license server holds a resource that programs need: tickets. In network programming terms, the license server is the server, and the application is the client.

The Protocol

> Second, what is the protocol? What are the transactions? Our ticket management protocol contains the following two main transactions:

Get Keys

> Client: HELO mypid
> Server: TICK ticketid *or* FAIL no tickets

---

[2]This idea is not far fetched. As appliances become smarter and more connected, your radio may soon ask a server if it has permission to play your favorite song.

Give Back

> Client: GBYE ticketid
>
> Server: THNX message

We define a text-based protocol consisting of simple four-character commands with arguments, similar in flavor to the commands used by Web clients and servers.

The Communication System

Third, how will these short text messages travel between client and server? We consider this question in a later section.

The Data Structures

Finally, what data structures do the clients and server need? We use an array of integers for the sign-out list. Each entry in the array corresponds to one ticket. When a client takes a ticket, the manager writes the PID of the client in that entry. When the client returns the ticket, the manager erases the PID from that entry. The following table is illustrative:

\ Ticket signout sheet	
tick#	**process**
1	1234
2	0
3	6589
4	0

If an element in the array contains 0, that ticket is free. If an array element contains a PID, that ticket is in use.

13.4.3 A Communication System

How do the clients ask for tickets, and how does the server issue tickets? We need some form of interprocess communication. The clients and server exchange short messages. The license server has to receive, process, and reply to requests from many clients. What techniques are available? Signals are short, but too short. Pipes only connect related processes. Sockets are the obvious answer, but it turns out that we have a choice with sockets. We know about stream sockets, pipe-like connections between unrelated processes. Another type of socket is called a *datagram socket*. Datagram, or UDP, sockets are a better choice for this project.

13.5   DATAGRAM SOCKETS

Stream sockets carry data from one process to another the way the telephone network carries sound from one person to another. You make a connection and then use that connection for an ongoing, bidirectional, pipelike flow of bytes.

Datagram communication is like sending postcards from one mailbox to another. You do not make a connection. Instead, you send messages to addresses. The other process receives messages at an address.

Stream sockets use a network protocol called TCP, which stands for *transmission control protocol*. Datagram sockets use UDP, which stands for *user datagram protocol*. How do these two types of sockets differ? When are stream sockets a good choice, and when are datagram sockets a good choice? How do we use datagram sockets in a program?

13.5.1   Streams vs. Datagrams

How do sockets really work? How does data travel through the Internet? What does the kernel do when we write data to a stream socket, and how does that differ from what the kernel does when we write data to a datagram socket?

The continuous, seamless flow of data from one stream socket to another is an illusion. Internet connections divide your data stream into separate packets. Network data transfer looks more like the process shown in Figure 13.4.

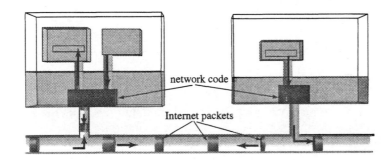

network code

Internet packets

FIGURE 13.4

Internet packets carry data.

Dividing a chunk of information into smaller packets happens in the physical world, too. Imagine you want to send a 100-page document by express overnight delivery. What if the delivery company requires you to use their special envelopes that hold only 20 pieces of paper. You split that document into five packages, each individually wrapped and addressed. Then you drop those five separate packages into the mailbox, and the delivery service carries them (you hope) to the destination. At the receiving end, someone has to unpack those five envelopes and put the five stacks of paper into the correct order to reassemble your original document.

The Internet works like that delivery service. Data flowing through the Internet has to fit into containers of limited size. Large chunks of data are broken into smaller fragments to be sent through the network. If you want a large chunk of data to arrive in one piece, someone at the receiving end has to put the fragments into the correct order.

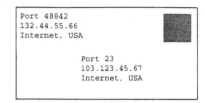

```
Port 48842
132.44.55.66
Internet, USA

            Port 23
            103.123.45.67
            Internet, USA
```

FIGURE 13.5

Communication can be connected or unconnected.

Stream sockets do all the work of splitting, ordering, and reassembling for you. Datagram sockets do not. The following table lists the differences between the two techniques:

TCP		UDP
Streams	**vs.**	**Datagrams**
Fragment/Reassemble		No
Ordering		No
Reliable		May not arrive
Connected		Multiple senders

Inside a stream socket, the kernel breaks chunks of data into clearly numbered fragments. The kernel on the receiving machine puts the fragments in order, recreating the exact sequence of bytes written by the sender. Inside a datagram socket, the kernel does not label the data for ordering or reassembly at the destination.

A stream socket guarantees delivery, a datagram socket does not. The receiving end of a stream socket checks the fragment sequence numbers to make sure it has the complete shipment. The receiving end notifies the sender of missing fragments and arranges for copies of the missing parts to be sent again. A datagram socket does not check for missing packets and does not demand retransmission. If a packet is lost in the Internet, it just does not arrive. TCP does much more work than UDP. UDP is faster, simpler, and puts less load on the network.

A UDP socket receives messages the way a mailbox does: Senders put your address on cards, the postal service gets them to your mailbox, and you pull them out of the mailbox. A TCP socket requires an explicit accept, read, then close just to read one message from a remote process.

UDP is a good fit for our application. Clients send short notes to request permission, and the server sends back short notes granting or denying permission. The clients and server exchange these notes without the complications of setting up connections. These short notes do not need fragmentation and reassembly. Reliability is not even essential. If a request or a ticket is lost, the user can launch the application again. In any event, the server and the clients are likely to be on the same machine or on the same section of a network, so there is little risk of losing packets.

UDP is a bad choice for Web servers or e-mail servers. Web pages and e-mail messages can be large documents. Those streams of bytes must arrive complete and in the correct order. UDP is a good choice for streams of music and video where a missing note or frame may not even be noticed.

13.5.2 Programming with Datagrams

A datagram is the network equivalent of a postcard. A datagram has three main parts: a destination address, a return address, and a message. (See Figure 13.6.)

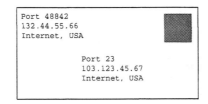

```
Port 48842
132.44.55.66
Internet, USA

        Port 23
        103.123.45.67
        Internet, USA
```

sender	destination	data

FIGURE 13.6

The three parts of a datagram.

A datagram socket is a delivery box for datagrams. The sender specifies the address of the destination socket. The network carries the datagram from the sender to the specified socket. The receiving process picks up datagrams from the socket. Programs use sendto to send a datagram to a socket and recvfrom to pick up a datagram from a socket. (See Figure 13.7.)

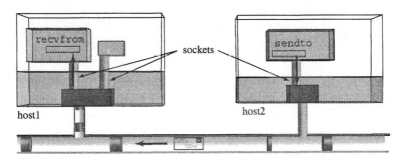

One host may contain many active sockets. Each socket is assigned an identifying number called a "port number." Packets are addressed to a port on a host.

FIGURE 13.7

Using sendto and recvfrom.

Receiving Datagrams   The program dgrecv.c is a simple datagram-based server. dgrecv.c sets up a socket at a port specified on the command line and then loops, receiving and printing datagrams sent by clients:

```
/*************************************************************************
 * dgrecv.c   - datagram receiver
 *                usage: dgrecv portnum
 *                action: listens at the specfied port and reports messages
 */

#include        <stdio.h>
#include        <stdlib.h>
#include        <sys/types.h>
#include        <sys/socket.h>
#include        <netinet/in.h>

#define oops(m,x)   { perror(m);exit(x);}

int   make_dgram_server_socket(int);
int   get_internet_address(char *, int,  int *, struct sockaddr_in *);
void say_who_called(struct sockaddr_in *);

int main(int ac, char *av[])
{
        int     port;                   /* use this port         */
        int     sock;                   /* for this socket       */
        char    buf[BUFSIZ];            /* to receive data here  */
        size_t  msglen;                 /* store its length here */
        struct  sockaddr_in    saddr;   /* put sender's address here */
        socklen_t saddrlen;             /* and its length here   */

        if ( ac == 1 || (port = atoi(av[1])) <= 0 ){
                fprintf(stderr,"usage: dgrecv portnumber\n");
                exit(1);
        }

    /*  get a socket and assign it a port number */

        if( (sock = make_dgram_server_socket(port)) == -1 )
                oops("cannot make socket",2);

    /* receive messaages on that socket */
        saddrlen = sizeof(saddr);
        while( (msglen = recvfrom(sock,buf,BUFSIZ,0,&saddr,&saddrlen) )>0) {
                buf[msglen] = '\0';
                printf("dgrecv: got a message: %s\n", buf);
                say_who_called(&saddr);
        }
        return 0;
}
void say_who_called(struct sockaddr_in *addrp)
{
        char    host[BUFSIZ];
        int     port;

        get_internet_address(host,BUFSIZ,&port,addrp);
        printf("  from: %s:%d\n", host, port);
}
```

The support functions make_dgram_server_socket and get_internet_address are defined in the file dgram.c listed later. Receiving a message at a datagram socket is simpler than receiving a message at a stream socket. The recvfrom call blocks until a datagram arrives. When a datagram arrives, the content of the message, the return address, and the length of the return address are copied into buffers.

Sending Datagrams   The program dgsend.c sends datagrams. dgsend.c creates a socket and then uses that socket to send a message to a socket at a hostname and port number specified on the command line:

```c
/*********************************************************************
 * dgsend.c  - datagram sender
 *                  usage: dgsend hostname portnum "message"
 *                  action: sends message to hostname:portnum
 */

#include        <stdio.h>
#include        <stdlib.h>
#include        <sys/types.h>
#include        <sys/socket.h>
#include        <netinet/in.h>

#define oops(m,x)   { perror(m);exit(x);}

int make_dgram_client_socket();
int make_internet_address(char *,int, struct sockaddr_in *);

int main(int ac, char *av[])
{
        int     sock;                   /* use this socket to send   */
        char    *msg;                   /* send this messag          */
        struct  sockaddr_in   saddr;    /* put sender's address here */

        if ( ac != 4 ){
                fprintf(stderr,"usage: dgsend host port 'message'\n");
                exit(1);
        }
        msg = av[3];

    /* get a datagram socket */
        if( (sock = make_dgram_client_socket()) == -1 )
                oops("cannot make socket",2);

    /* combine hostname and portnumber of destination into an address */

        make_internet_address(av[1], atoi(av[2]), &saddr);

    /* send a string through the socket to that address */

        if ( sendto(sock, msg, strlen(msg), 0, &saddr, sizeof(saddr)) == -1 )
                oops("sendto failed", 3);
        return 0;
}
```

The single call to sendto sends the contents of a buffer to a socket at the specified address.

Supporting Functions   Details of making the sockets and socket addresses are wrapped in functions in dgram.c:

```
/**************************************************************
 *          dgram.c
 *          support functions for datagram based programs
 */

#include         <stdio.h>
#include         <unistd.h>
#include         <sys/types.h>
#include         <sys/socket.h>
#include         <netinet/in.h>
#include         <arpa/inet.h>
#include         <netdb.h>
#include         <string.h>

#define   HOSTLEN  256

int make_internet_address();

int make_dgram_server_socket(int portnum)
{
        struct   sockaddr_in   saddr;    /* build our address here */
        char     hostname[HOSTLEN];      /* address               */
        int      sock_id;                /* the socket            */

        sock_id = socket(PF_INET, SOCK_DGRAM, 0);  /* get a socket */
        if ( sock_id == -1 ) return -1;

        /** build address and bind it to socket **/

        gethostname(hostname, HOSTLEN);           /* where am I ?         */
        make_internet_address(hostname, portnum, &saddr);

        if ( bind(sock_id, (struct sockaddr *)&saddr, sizeof(saddr)) != 0 )
                return -1;

        return sock_id;
}
int make_dgram_client_socket()
{
        return socket(PF_INET, SOCK_DGRAM, 0);
}

int make_internet_address(char *hostname, int port, struct sockaddr_in
   *addrp)
/*
 * constructor for an Internet socket address, uses hostname and port
 *   (host,port) -> *addrp
 */
```

```
{
        struct hostent  *hp;

        bzero((void *)addrp, sizeof(struct sockaddr_in));
        hp = gethostbyname(hostname);
        if ( hp == NULL ) return -1;
        bcopy((void *)hp->h_addr, (void *)&addrp->sin_addr, hp->h_length);
        addrp->sin_port = htons(port);
        addrp->sin_family = AF_INET;
        return 0;
}
int
get_internet_address(char *host, int len, int *portp, struct sockaddr_in
    *addrp)
/*
 * extracts host and port from an internet socket address
 *    *addrp -> (host,port)
 */
{
        strncpy(host, inet_ntoa(addrp->sin_addr), len );
        *portp = ntohs(addrp->sin_port);
        return 0;
}
```

Creating a datagram socket is similar to setting up a stream socket. The two differences are that we set the type of socket to SOCK_DGRAM and we do not need to call listen.

Compile and Test

```
$ cc dgrecv.c dgram.c -o dgrecv
$ ./dgrecv 4444 &
[1] 19383
$ cc dgsend.c dgram.c -o dgsend
$ ./dgsend host2 4444 "testing 123"
dgrecv: got a message: testing 123
  from: 10.200.75.200:1041
$ ps
  PID TTY          TIME CMD
14599 pts/3    00:00:00 bash
19383 pts/3    00:00:00 dgrecv
19393 pts/3    00:00:00 ps
$
```

We compile and start the server listening at port 4444. We then compile and use the client to send a string to port 4444. The server receives the message, and then prints the message, and then prints out the return address of the message. The client socket has a host address and port number. The kernel assigned an arbitrary port number of 1041 to the client socket. ps shows that the server continues to run.

13.5.3 Summary of `sendto` and `recvfrom`

---

sendto

PURPOSE	Send a message from a socket

INCLUDE	`#include <sys/types.h>`
	`#include <sys/socket.h>`

USAGE	`nchars = sendto( int socket, const void *msg, size_t len,`
	`                 int flags,`
	`                 const struct sockaddr *dest,`
	`                 socklen_t dest_len);`

ARGS		
	socket	a socket id
	msg	an array of chars to send
	len	the number of chars to send
	flags	a set of bits setting transmission properties
		use 0 for normal
	dest	a pointer to the address of the remote socket
	dest_len	length to the address

RETURNS	-1	if error
	nchars	number of chars sent

`sendto` sends a datagram from one socket to a destination socket. The first three arguments are analogous to the arguments to `write`: the socket to send through, the array of `chars` to send, and the number of `chars` to send. `sendto`, like `write`, returns the number of `chars` actually sent. The *flags* argument specifies various properties of the transmission; consult your on-line manual page for the options your version of Unix supports. The last two arguments specify the address of the destination socket. A socket address is a struct; for Internet addresses, it contains the IP address of the host and the port number. Other address types contain other members.

---

recvfrom

PURPOSE	Receive a message from a socket

INCLUDE	`#include <sys/types.h>`
	`#include <sys/socket.h>`

USAGE	`nchars = recvfrom( int socket, const void *msg, size_t len,`
	`                   int flags,`
	`                   const struct sockaddr *sender,`
	`                   socklen_t *sender_len);`

ARGS		
	socket	a socket id
	msg	an array of chars
	len	number of chars to receive
	flags	a set of bits setting properties of reception
		use 0 for normal
	sender	a pointer to the address of the remote socket
	sender_len	pointer to an int containing size
		of the address of the remote socket

RETURNS	-1	if error
	nchars	number of chars received

---

recvfrom reads a datagram from a socket. The first three arguments to recvfrom are analogous to the arguments to read: the socket to read from, an array of chars to hold the received data, and the number of chars to read. recvfrom, like read, returns the number of chars actually read. The *flags* argument specifies various properties of the reception; consult your on-line manual page for the options your version of Unix supports. Use the last two arguments to obtain the address of the sender. The address of the sender's socket will be stored in a struct pointed to by the first argument, and the length of that address will be stored in the integer pointed to by the second argument. The length of the address must be provided to recvfrom; it will modify that value if the actual address is a different size. If these pointers are null, the address of the sender is not recorded.

13.5.4 Replying to Datagrams

Sample programs dgsend.c and dgrecv.c show how to send data from a client to a server. How can a server send a response back to a client? In the physical world, suppose someone sends you a postcard inviting you to dinner. How do you know where to send your reply? That's easy: You send the reply to the return address on the invitation.

The program dgrecv2.c receives messages from clients and replies by sending a thank-you note to the sender's address:

```
/******************************************************************
 * dgrecv2.c   - datagram receiver
 *                 usage: dgrecv portnum
 *                 action: receives messages, prints them, sends reply
 */

#include        <stdio.h>
#include        <stdlib.h>
#include        <sys/types.h>
#include        <sys/socket.h>
#include        <netinet/in.h>

#define oops(m,x)   { perror(m);exit(x);}

int make_dgram_server_socket(int);
int get_internet_address(char *, int,  int *, struct sockaddr_in *);
void say_who_called(struct sockaddr_in *);
void reply_to_sender(int,char *,struct sockaddr_in *, socklen_t);

int main(int ac, char *av[])
{
        int     port;                   /* use this port            */
        int     sock;                   /* for this socket          */
        char    buf[BUFSIZ];            /* to receive data here     */
        size_t  msglen;                 /* store its length here    */
        struct  sockaddr_in   saddr;    /* put sender's address here */
        socklen_t saddrlen;             /* and its length here      */

        if ( ac == 1 || (port = atoi(av[1])) <= 0 ){
                fprintf(stderr,"usage: dgrecv portnumber\n");
```

```
                        exit(1);
                }

        /*  get a socket and assign it a port number */

                if( (sock = make_dgram_server_socket(port)) == -1 )
                        oops("cannot make socket",2);

        /* receive messaages on that socket */

                saddrlen = sizeof(saddr);
                while( (msglen = recvfrom(sock,buf,BUFSIZ,0,&saddr,&saddrlen))>0 ) {
                        buf[msglen] = '\0';
                        printf("dgrecv: got a message: %s\n", buf);
                        say_who_called(&saddr);
                        reply_to_sender(sock,buf,&saddr,saddrlen);
                }
                return 0;
        }
void
reply_to_sender(int sock,char *msg,struct sockaddr_in *addrp, socklen_t len)
{
        char    reply[BUFSIZ+BUFSIZ];
        sprintf(reply, "Thanks for your %d char message\n",  strlen(msg));
        sendto(sock,  reply,  strlen(reply), 0, addrp, len);
}
void say_who_called(struct sockaddr_in *addrp)
{
        char    host[BUFSIZ];
        int     port;

        get_internet_address(host,BUFSIZ,&port,addrp);
        printf("  from: %s:%d\n", host, port);
}
```

The sender program, of course, has to be modified to receive the reply. That change is left as an exercise.

13.5.5 Summary of Datagrams

Datagrams are short messages sent from one socket to another. The sender uses the sendto system call to specify a message, its length, and its destination. The receiver uses recvfrom to receive the message from the socket. Datagrams match closely the underlying structure of the addressed packets that flow through the Internet. Datagrams, therefore, place less load on kernel network code and on network traffic. Datagrams may get lost in transit, and they may arrive out of order. For those two reasons, datagram sockets are best suited to applications in which simplicity, efficiency, and speed are more important than data integrity and consistency.

Messages for our license-server protocol are simple. The ease of having one server receive short requests, process them, and send back replies makes datagrams a suitable solution.

13.6   LICENSE SERVER VERSION 1.0

We return to the software license-server project. Our server limits the number of instances of a program that may run at once. When a user tries to run the restricted program, the process asks the server for permission.

If not too many people are using the program, the license server grants permission by sending a *ticket* to the process. If the maximum number of instances are running, the server sends a message to the process saying no tickets are available, and the
program politely tells the user to try again later or to purchase a license that allows
more simultaneous users. The licensed program and the server communicate by sending datagrams back and forth.

The logic of the two programs and their interaction look like this:

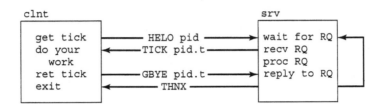

The client and server programs are each composed of two files: a short file containing main and a larger file containing ticket-management functions. We examine the
client and then the server.

13.6.1 Client Version 1

```
/*************************************************************************
 * lclnt1.c
 * License server client version 1
 *   link with lclnt_funcs1.o dgram.o
 */

#include <stdio.h>

int main(int ac, char *av[])
{
        setup();
        if (get_ticket() != 0 )
                exit(0);

        do_regular_work();

        release_ticket();
        shut_down();

}
/*************************************************************************
 * do_regular_work   the main work of the application goes here
 */
do_regular_work()
```

```
        {
                printf("SuperSleep version 1.0 Running - Licensed Software\n");
                sleep(10);        /* our patented sleep algorithm */
        }
```

The top-level code for the client follows our outline closely. The client gets a ticket, does its job, releases the ticket, and then exits. The sample licensed program here is a special version of the Unix sleep utility. People not satisfied with the standard version may purchase licenses to use this version. Of course, they have to run our special license server or else our sleep program refuses to run. The supporting functions are in lclnt_funcs1.c:

```
/***************************************************************************
 * lclnt_funcs1.c: functions for the client of the license server
 */

#include <stdio.h>
#include <sys/types.h>
#include <sys/socket.h>
#include <netinet/in.h>
#include <netdb.h>

/*
 * Important variables used throughout
 */
static int pid = -1;                    /* Our PID */
static int sd = -1;                     /* Our communications socket */
static struct sockaddr serv_addr;       /* Server address */
static socklen_t serv_alen;             /* length of address */
static char ticket_buf[128];            /* Buffer to hold our ticket */
static have_ticket = 0;                 /* Set when we have a ticket */

#define MSGLEN          128             /* Size of our datagrams */
#define SERVER_PORTNUM  2020            /* Our server's port number */
#define HOSTLEN         512
#define oops(p) { perror(p); exit(1) ; }

char *do_transaction();

/*
 * setup:  get pid, socket, and address of license server
 * IN      no args
 * RET     nothing, dies on error
 * notes:  assumes server is on same host as client
 */
setup()
{
        char    hostname[BUFSIZ];

        pid = getpid();                               /* for ticks and msgs   */
        sd  = make_dgram_client_socket();             /* to talk to server    */
        if ( sd == -1 )
                oops("Cannot create socket");
```

```
        gethostname(hostname, HOSTLEN);            /* server on same host */
        make_internet_address(hostname, SERVER_PORTNUM, &serv_addr);
        serv_alen = sizeof(serv_addr);
}

shut_down()
{
        close(sd);
}

/***************************************************************************
 * get_ticket
 * get a ticket from the license server
 * Results: 0 for success, -1 for failure
 */
int get_ticket()
{
        char *response;
        char buf[MSGLEN];

        if(have_ticket)                            /* don't be greedy      */
                return(0);

        sprintf(buf, "HELO %d", pid);              /* compose request      */

        if ( (response = do_transaction(buf)) == NULL )
                return(-1);

        /* parse the response and see if we got a ticket.
         *    on success, the message is: TICK ticket-string
         *    on failure, the message is: FAIL failure-msg
         */
        if ( strncmp(response, "TICK", 4) == 0 ){
                strcpy(ticket_buf, response + 5);     /* grab ticket-id */
                have_ticket = 1;                      /* set this flag  */
                narrate("got ticket", ticket_buf);
                return(0);
        }

        if ( strncmp(response,"FAIL",4) == 0)
                narrate("Could not get ticket",response);
        else
                narrate("Unknown message:", response);

        return(-1);
} /* get_ticket */

/***************************************************************************
 * release_ticket
 * Give a ticket back to the server
 * Results: 0 for success, -1 for failure
 */
int release_ticket()
{
```

```
        char buf[MSGLEN];
        char *response;

        if(!have_ticket)                            /* don't have a ticket   */
                return(0);                          /* nothing to release    */

        sprintf(buf, "GBYE %s", ticket_buf);     /* compose message      */
        if ( (response = do_transaction(buf)) == NULL )
                return(-1);

        /* examine response
         * success: THNX info-string
         * failure: FAIL error-string
         */
        if ( strncmp(response, "THNX", 4) == 0 ){
                narrate("released ticket OK","");
                return 0;
        }
        if ( strncmp(response, "FAIL", 4) == 0)
                narrate("release failed", response+5);
        else
                narrate("Unknown message:", response);
        return(-1);
} /* release_ticket */

/***************************************************************************
 * do_transaction
 * Send a request to the server and get a response back
 * IN   msg_p              message to send
 * Results: pointer to message string, or NULL for error
 *                         NOTE: pointer returned is to static storage
 *                         overwritten by each successive call.
 * note: for extra security, compare retaddr to serv_addr (why?)
 */
char *do_transaction(char *msg)
{
        static char buf[MSGLEN];
        struct sockaddr retaddr;
        socklen_t       addrlen=sizeof(retaddr);
        int ret;

        ret = sendto(sd, msg, strlen(msg), 0, &serv_addr, serv_alen);
        if ( ret == -1 ){
                syserr("sendto");
                return(NULL);
        }

        /* Get the response back */
        ret = recvfrom(sd, buf, MSGLEN, 0, &retaddr, &addrlen);
        if ( ret == -1 ){
                syserr("recvfrom");
                return(NULL);
        }
```

```
                   /* Now return the message itself */
                   return(buf);
        } /* do_transaction */

        /***********************************************************************
         * narrate:  print messages to stderr for debugging and demo purposes
         * IN msg1, msg2 : strings to print along with pid and title
         * RET      nothing, dies on error
         */
        narrate(char *msg1, char *msg2)
        {
                   fprintf(stderr,"CLIENT [%d]: %s %s\n", pid, msg1, msg2);
        }
        syserr(char *msg1)
        {
                   char     buf[MSGLEN];
                   sprintf(buf,"CLIENT [%d]: %s", pid, msg1);
                   perror(buf);
        }
```

get_ticket and release_ticket are the major functions in the file. Both follow the same outline: compose a short request, send the message to the server, wait for a response from the server, and then examine and act on the response.

get_ticket requests a ticket by sending the command HELO followed by its process ID. The server approves the request by sending back a message of the form TICK ticket-id. The server denies the request by sending back a message of the form FAIL explanation.

release_ticket returns a ticket by sending the command GBYE ticket-id. If the ticket is OK, the server replies with a message of the form THNX greeting. If the ticket is not valid, the server replies with a message of the form FAIL explanation.

Why would a ticket be invalid? We consider problems and their solutions later.

13.6.2 Server Version 1

```
        /***********************************************************************
         * lserv1.c
         * License server server program version 1
         */

        #include <stdio.h>
        #include <sys/types.h>
        #include <sys/socket.h>
        #include <netinet/in.h>
        #include <signal.h>
        #include <sys/errno.h>
        #define MSGLEN          128                 /* Size of our datagrams */

        int main(int ac, char *av[])
        {
                   struct sockaddr_in client_addr;
```

```
              socklen_t addrlen=sizeof(client_addr);
              char      buf[MSGLEN];
              int       ret;
              int       sock;

              sock = setup();

              while(1) {
                      addrlen = sizeof(client_addr);
                      ret = recvfrom(sock,buf,MSGLEN,0,&client_addr,&addrlen);
                      if ( ret != -1 ){
                              buf[ret] = '\0';
                              narrate("GOT:", buf, &client_addr);
                              handle_request(buf,&client_addr,addrlen);
                      }
                      else if ( errno != EINTR )
                              perror("recvfrom");
              }
      }
```

The top-level code for the license server is a loop that receives request datagrams, acts on the request, and sends a reply. Code to handle the requests is in lserv_funcs1.c:

```
/****************************************************************************
 * lsrv_funcs1.c
 * functions for the license server
 */

#include <stdio.h>
#include <sys/types.h>
#include <sys/socket.h>
#include <netinet/in.h>
#include <netdb.h>
#include <signal.h>
#include <sys/errno.h>

#define SERVER_PORTNUM   2020          /* Our server's port number */
#define MSGLEN           128           /* Size of our datagrams */
#define TICKET_AVAIL     0             /* Slot is available for use */
#define MAXUSERS         3             /* Only 3 users for us */
#define oops(x) { perror(x); exit(-1); }

/****************************************************************************
 * Important variables
 */
int ticket_array[MAXUSERS];     /* Our ticket array */
int sd = -1;                    /* Our socket */
int num_tickets_out = 0;        /* Number of tickets outstanding */

char *do_hello();
char *do_goodbye();
```

```
/***************************************************************************
 * setup() - initialize license server
 */
setup()
{
        sd = make_dgram_server_socket(SERVER_PORTNUM);
        if ( sd == -1 )
                oops("make socket");
        free_all_tickets();
        return sd;
}
free_all_tickets()
{
        int     i;

        for(i=0; i<MAXUSERS; i++)
                ticket_array[i] = TICKET_AVAIL;
}

/***************************************************************************
 * shut_down() - close down license server
 */
shut_down()
{
        close(sd);
}

/***************************************************************************
 * handle_request(request, clientaddr, addrlen)
 *    branch on code in request
 */
handle_request(char *req,struct sockaddr_in *client, socklen_t addlen)
{
        char    *response;
        int     ret;

        /* act and compose a response */
        if ( strncmp(req, "HELO", 4) == 0 )
                response = do_hello(req);
        else if ( strncmp(req, "GBYE", 4) == 0 )
                response = do_goodbye(req);
        else
                response = "FAIL invalid request";

        /* send the response to the client */
        narrate("SAID:", response, client);
        ret = sendto(sd, response, strlen(response),0, client, addlen);
        if ( ret == -1 )
                perror("SERVER sendto failed");
}
```

```
/******************************************************************************
 * do_hello
 * Give out a ticket if any are available
 * IN   msg_p                      message received from client
 * Results: ptr to response
 *     NOTE: return is in static buffer overwritten by each call
 */
char *do_hello(char *msg_p)
{
        int x;
        static char replybuf[MSGLEN];

        if(num_tickets_out >= MAXUSERS)
                return("FAIL no tickets available");

        /* else find a free ticket and give it to client */

        for(x = 0; x<MAXUSERS && ticket_array[x] != TICKET_AVAIL; x++)
                ;

        /* A sanity check - should never happen */
        if(x == MAXUSERS) {
                narrate("database corrupt","",NULL);
                return("FAIL database corrupt");
        }

        /* Found a free ticket.  Record "name" of user (pid) in array.
         *      generate ticket of form: pid.slot
         */
        ticket_array[x] = atoi(msg_p + 5); /* get pid in msg */
        sprintf(replybuf, "TICK %d.%d", ticket_array[x], x);
        num_tickets_out++;
        return(replybuf);
} /* do_hello */

/******************************************************************************
 * do_goodbye
 * Take back ticket client is returning
 * IN   msg_p                      message received from client
 * Results: ptr to response
 *     NOTE: return is in static buffer overwritten by each call
 */
char *do_goodbye(char *msg_p)
{
        int pid, slot;          /* components of ticket */

        /* The user's giving us back a ticket.  First we need to get
         * the ticket out of the message, which looks like:
         *
         *      GBYE pid.slot
         */
        if((sscanf((msg_p + 5), "%d.%d", &pid, &slot) != 2) ||
           (ticket_array[slot] != pid)) {
```

```
                narrate("Bogus ticket", msg_p+5, NULL);
                return("FAIL invalid ticket");
        }

        /* The ticket is valid.  Release it. */
        ticket_array[slot] = TICKET_AVAIL;
        num_tickets_out--;
        /* Return response */
        return("THNX See ya!");
} /* do_goodbye */

/***************************************************************************
 * narrate() - chatty news for debugging and logging purposes
 */
narrate(char *msg1, char *msg2, struct sockaddr_in *clientp)
{
        fprintf(stderr,"\t\tSERVER: %s %s ", msg1, msg2);
        if ( clientp )
                fprintf(stderr,"(%s:%d)", inet_ntoa(clientp->sin_addr),
                                          ntohs(clientp->sin_port) );
        putc('\n', stderr);
}
```

The three important functions here are as follows:

handle_request

> Requests consist of a four-character command followed by an argument. The server checks the command and calls the corresponding function. Even if the command is invalid, the server has to send some response or the client will remain blocked waiting for a reply.

do_hello

> The HELO command is a request for a ticket. The server searches the array of tickets for a free spot. An entry with a PID of zero indicates a free ticket. The server uses a separate variable, num_tickets_out to save time. The server could search the table in response to each request, but this variable tells when the table is full.

do_goodbye

> The GBYE command is a request to return a ticket. A ticket is a string consisting of a PID and a ticket number. The server compares the PID and ticket number to the data in the ticket_array sign-out list. If the numbers agree, the server crosses the name off the list and thanks the client. If the numbers do not match, something is wrong.

If you worked at an airline check-in counter and a customer presented an airplane ticket stamped with a number and name that did not match the record in the airline database, you might ask, "Where did you get this ticket, and who are you, anyway?" We discuss the problem of bogus tickets later. First, we test this version.

13.6.3 Testing Version 1

We compile the server and set it running in the background:

```
$ cc lserv1.c lserv_funcs1.c dgram.c -o lserv1
$ ./lserv1 &
[1] 25738
```

We compile the client and launch four of them at once:

```
$ cc lclnt1.c lclnt_funcs1.c dgram.c -o lclnt1
$ ./lclnt1 &./lclnt1 &./lclnt1 &./lclnt1 &
            SERVER: GOT: HELO 25912 (10.200.75.200:1053)
                SERVER: SAID: TICK 25912.0 (10.200.75.200:1053)
CLIENT [25912]: got ticket 25912.0
SuperSleep version 1.0 Running - Licensed Software
                SERVER: GOT: HELO 25913 (10.200.75.200:1054)
                SERVER: SAID: TICK 25913.1 (10.200.75.200:1054)
CLIENT [25913]: got ticket 25913.1
SuperSleep version 1.0 Running - Licensed Software
                SERVER: GOT: HELO 25915 (10.200.75.200:1055)
                SERVER: SAID: TICK 25915.2 (10.200.75.200:1055)
CLIENT [25915]: got ticket 25915.2
SuperSleep version 1.0 Running - Licensed Software
                SERVER: GOT: HELO 25914 (10.200.75.200:1059)
                SERVER: SAID: FAIL no tickets available (10.200.75.200:1059)
CLIENT [25914]: Could not get ticket FAIL no tickets available
                SERVER: GOT: GBYE 25912.0 (10.200.75.200:1053)
                SERVER: SAID: THNX See ya! (10.200.75.200:1053)
CLIENT [25912]: released ticket OK
                SERVER: GOT: GBYE 25913.1 (10.200.75.200:1054)
                SERVER: SAID: THNX See ya! (10.200.75.200:1054)
CLIENT [25913]: released ticket OK
                SERVER: GOT: GBYE 25915.2 (10.200.75.200:1055)
                SERVER: SAID: THNX See ya! (10.200.75.200:1055)
CLIENT [25915]: released ticket OK
```

The output is more dramatic when you run it live. Nonetheless, you can see the server receiving the requests and passing out tickets and the clients getting their tickets and starting work; and you can see that poor process 25914 missed out. All the tickets were gone when he showed up. Notice that process 25915 got one. If you run this test several times, you are likely to see different results.

13.6.4 How'd We Do?

License server version 1 appears to work well. The server handles requests and maintains a list of which processes hold which tickets. Clients obtain tickets successfully from the server, do their work, and return tickets when done. It looks ideal. But the world is not ideal, and software and users do not always do what you expect or want. What can go wrong? How do we respond when they do?

13.7   REAL-WORLD PROGRAMMING

Our license server system works correctly as long as both processes cooperate. Sometimes, software runs into trouble. What would happen if the SuperSleep application was killed by a user, or if it produced a segmentation fault and was killed by the kernel? What would happen to its ticket? What would happen if the license server process crashed? What would happen if the license server was then restarted?

Programs for the real world must be prepared for disruptions. We consider two cases: when the client crashes and when the server crashes.

13.7.1   Handling Client Crashes

If a client crashes, the client will not return its ticket. (See Figure 13.8.)

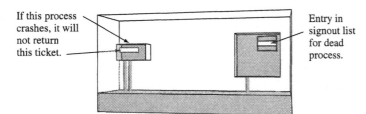

If this process crashes, it will not return this ticket.

Entry in signout list for dead process.

FIGURE 13.8

A client takes a ticket to its grave.

In the car system, an employee may quit, be fired, go home, or die still holding a key to a company car. How do these events affect the system? The sign-out list still shows that ticket or car key in use. Other processes or employees will not be given that ticket. If enough processes crash, the sign-out list could be full even though nobody is running the program.

The car key manager can reclaim lost keys by calling the people holding the keys. At some regular interval, the car manager goes through the sign-out list and calls each driver to ask, "Are you still using that key?" If nobody responds, the car manager erases that name from the list. The more frequently the manager checks in with the people holding keys, the more accurate the list will be.

The license server can use the same technique. At some regular interval, the license server can go through the array of tickets and check if each process listed there still exists. If a process no longer exists, the license server can erase that name from the list, releasing that ticket. The more frequently the license server executes this function, the more accurate the list will be.

Reclaiming Lost Tickets: Scheduling

Where do we put the code to reclaim lost tickets? How do we call it? Our server has to do two independent operations: wait for incoming requests from clients and also, at regular intervals, reclaim lost tickets. Scheduling actions is easy; use `alarm` and `signal` to call a function at regular intervals. We used this technique in the bouncing message program in an earlier chapter.

Our new, revised program flow is shown in Figure 13.9.

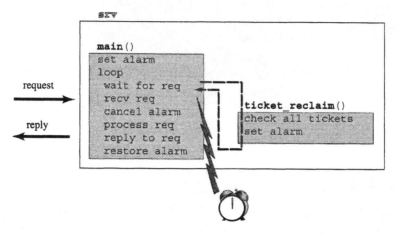

FIGURE 13.9

Use alarm to schedule ticket cleanup.

When we design a program that does two things at once, we must be careful about interference of functions. Could there be trouble if our server, in the middle of processing a client request, were called away by SIGALRM to reclaim tickets? Do those two operations share any variables or data structures? Yes, issuing and returning tickets modifies the sign-out list, and reclaiming tickets might modify the sign-out list. Can interference between these two functions damage the integrity of these data structures? This question is left as an exercise. To be safe, we turn off alarms while processing requests.

Reclaiming Lost Tickets: Coding

We want to reclaim tickets from processes that die. How can we tell if a process has died? We could use popen to run ps and then search the output of ps for PIDs of processes holding tickets. A faster, simpler solution, though, is to use a special feature of the kill system call.

You can determine whether a process exists by sending signal number zero to that process. The kernel will not send a signal, but will return an error and set errno to ESRCH if the process does not exist. We use that fact in the new function ticket_reclaim, which appears in lserv_funcs2.c:

```
#define RECLAIM_INTERVAL 60            /* reclaim every 60 seconds */
/***********************************************************************
 * ticket_reclaim
 * go through all tickets and reclaim ones belonging to dead processes
 * Results: none
 */
void ticket_reclaim()
{
        int     i;
```

```
        char    tick[BUFSIZ];

        for(i = 0; i < MAXUSERS; i++) {
                if((ticket_array[i] != TICKET_AVAIL) &&
                   (kill(ticket_array[i], 0) == -1) && (errno == ESRCH)) {
                        /* Process is gone - free up slot */
                        sprintf(tick, "%d.%d", ticket_array[i],i);
                        narrate("freeing", tick, NULL);
                        ticket_array[i] = TICKET_AVAIL;
                        num_tickets_out--;
                }
        }
        alarm(RECLAIM_INTERVAL);            /* reset alarm clock */
}
```

Next, we add code to main to schedule the ticket reclaim function and to turn off the alarm during normal processing. This revised main appears in lserv2.c:

```
int main(int ac, char *av[])
{
    struct sockaddr client_addr;
    socklen_t addrlen=sizeof(client_addr);
    char    buf[MSGLEN];
    int     ret, sock;
    void    ticket_reclaim();        /* version 2 addition */
    unsigned time_left;

    sock = setup();
    signal(SIGALRM, ticket_reclaim);  /* run ticket reclaimer */
    alarm(RECLAIM_INTERVAL);           /* after this delay      */

    while(1) {
            addrlen = sizeof(client_addr);
            ret = recvfrom(sock,buf,MSGLEN,0,&client_addr,&addrlen);
            if ( ret != -1 ){
                    buf[ret] = '\0';
                    narrate("GOT:", buf, &client_addr);
                    time_left = alarm(0);
                    handle_request(buf,&client_addr,addrlen);
                    alarm(time_left);
            }
            else if ( errno != EINTR )
                    perror("recvfrom");
    }
}
```

With these minor additions, our license server reclaims unused tickets on a regular schedule. Do we need to reclaim tickets on a regular schedule? Why not reclaim tickets only when the table fills up and a client is denied permission. Would that be better?

13.7.2 Handling Server Crashes

A server crash has two serious consequences. First, the sign-out list is lost; there is no record of which processes hold which tickets. Second, no clients can run, because the program that grants permission is not available. The obvious solution is to start the server again. (See Figure 13.10.)

tickets issued by previous server

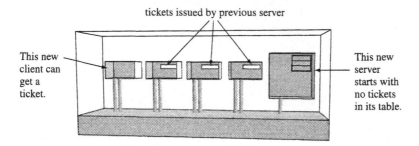

This new client can get a ticket.

This new server starts with no tickets in its table.

FIGURE 13.10

Server restarted after server crash.

Restarting the server allows new clients to run, but introduces two new problems.

The first new problem is that the ticket array in the restarted server is empty; the server has a fresh set of untaken tickets. The ticket array in the crashed server might have been full, but this new server gladly gives permission to another bunch of clients. Repeatedly killing and restarting the license server is like printing money.

The other new problem is that as clients holding tickets issued by the previous instance of the server release their tickets, they will be told they are holding bogus tickets.

Ticket Validation

A solution to both these problems is *ticket validation*. Ticket validation means that each client sends a copy of its ticket to the server at regular intervals. The client sends a datagram saying, "Here is my ticket. Is it still good?" (See Figure 13.11.)

FIGURE 13.11

Client validates ticket.

The ticket contains the array index and the PID. The server checks the table. If that slot is empty, the server might assume the ticket was issued by an earlier incarnation of itself. The server would add that entry to the table. Gradually, as the clients present their tickets for validation, the table is repopulated.

Rebuilding the table in the server through ticket validation solves the lost table problem but can lead to other problems. If a new client asks for a ticket before the table is fully restored, the server might issue a ticket number already issued to another client. When the client holding that older ticket presents its ticket for validation, the server has to reject it.

A different solution is for the server to reject all tickets that do not appear in the table. Clients with rejected tickets just ask for a new ticket. Is that better?

Adding Validation to the Protocol

Ticket validation is a new transaction for our protocol:

> Client: VALD tickid
>
> Server: GOOD *or* FAIL invalid ticket

We have to change the client and the server to add ticket validation.

Adding Ticket Validation to the Client

We add ticket validation to the client by adding a validation function and by calling that function from the main part of the program. The flow in the client is now like that shown in Figure 13.12.

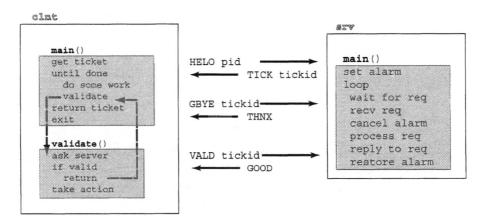

FIGURE 13.12

Client validates ticket now and then.

The client can schedule validation according to any system that makes sense for the program. The client could set a timer and validate on a regular schedule. If the client program is a spreadsheet, it might validate after a certain number of recalculations. A licensed version of pong might validate after each ball.

The SuperSleep client program could split the 10 seconds of sleep into two 5-second intervals with a call to the validation code in the middle. This change is left as an exercise.

Ticket Validation in the Server

Adding ticket validation to the server requires two changes. The new file lserv_funcs2.c contains the changes. First, we add a function to validate tickets:

```
/***********************************************************************
 * do_validate
 * Validate client's ticket
 * IN  msg_p                        message received from client
 * Results: ptr to response
 *    NOTE: return is in static buffer overwritten by each call.
 */
static char *do_validate(char *msg)
{
    int pid, slot;            /* components of ticket */

    /* msg looks like VALD pid.slot - parse it and validate */

    if (sscanf(msg+5,"%d.%d",&pid,&slot)==2 && ticket_array[slot]==pid)
        return("GOOD Valid ticket");

    /* bad ticket */
    narrate("Bogus ticket", msg+5, NULL);
    return("FAIL invalid ticket");
}
```

Then, we add one more test to handle_request:

```
handle_request(char *req,struct sockaddr_in *client, socklen_t addlen)
{
    char    *response;
    int     ret;

    /* act and compose a response */
    if ( strncmp(req, "HELO", 4) == 0 )
            response = do_hello(req);
    else if ( strncmp(req, "GBYE", 4) == 0 )
            response = do_goodbye(req);
    else if ( strncmp(req, "VALD", 4) == 0 )
            response = do_validate(req);
    else
            response = "FAIL invalid request";

    /* send the response to the client */
    narrate("SAID:", response, client);
    ret = sendto(sd, response, strlen(response),0, client, addlen);
    if ( ret == -1 )
            perror("SERVER sendto failed");
}
```

13.7.3 Testing Version 2

We now compile and test these new versions of our client and server. The test involves killing clients and killing servers and starting new clients and servers. Keep your eye on the process ID numbers and the messages from the programs. For testing purposes, the client sleeps for two 15-second intervals, and the server reclaims tickets every 5 seconds. The results of the test are as follows:

```
$ cc lserv2.c lserv_funcs2.c dgram.c -o lserv2
$ cc lclnt2.c lclnt_funcs2.c dgram.c -o lclnt2
$ ./lserv2 &                    # start a server
[1] 30804
$ ./lclnt2 & ./lclnt2 & ./lclnt2 &   # start three clients
[2] 30805
[3] 30806
[4] 30807
$               SERVER: GOT: HELO 30805 (10.200.75.200:1085)
                SERVER: SAID: TICK 30805.0 (10.200.75.200:1085)
CLIENT [30805]: got ticket 30805.0
SuperSleep version 1.0 Running - Licensed Software
                SERVER: GOT: HELO 30806 (10.200.75.200:1086)
                SERVER: SAID: TICK 30806.1 (10.200.75.200:1086)
CLIENT [30806]: got ticket 30806.1
SuperSleep version 1.0 Running - Licensed Software
                SERVER: GOT: HELO 30807 (10.200.75.200:1087)
                SERVER: SAID: TICK 30807.2 (10.200.75.200:1087)
CLIENT [30807]: got ticket 30807.2
SuperSleep version 1.0 Running - Licensed Software

$ kill 30806                # kill a client
[3]- Terminated                ./lclnt2
                SERVER: freeing 30806.1
                SERVER: GOT: VALD 30805.0 (10.200.75.200:1085)
                SERVER: SAID: GOOD Valid ticket (10.200.75.200:1085)
CLIENT [30805]: Validated ticket:  GOOD Valid ticket
                SERVER: GOT: VALD 30807.2 (10.200.75.200:1087)
                SERVER: SAID: GOOD Valid ticket (10.200.75.200:1087)
CLIENT [30807]: Validated ticket:  GOOD Valid ticket

$ kill 30804                # kill the server
[1]  Terminated                ./lserv2

$ ./lserv2 &                # start a new server
[5] 30808
$
                SERVER: GOT: GBYE 30805.0 (10.200.75.200:1085)
                SERVER: Bogus ticket 30805.0
                SERVER: SAID: FAIL invalid ticket (10.200.75.200:1085)
CLIENT [30805]: release failed invalid ticket
                SERVER: GOT: GBYE 30807.2 (10.200.75.200:1087)
                SERVER: Bogus ticket 30807.2
                SERVER: SAID: FAIL invalid ticket (10.200.75.200:1087)
CLIENT [30807]: release failed invalid ticket

$ ./clnt2                   # start a new client
                SERVER: GOT: HELO 30809 (10.200.75.200:1087)
                SERVER: SAID: TICK 30809.0 (10.200.75.200:1087)
CLIENT [30809]: got ticket 30809.0
SuperSleep version 1.0 Running - Licensed Software
                SERVER: GOT: VALD 30809.0 (10.200.75.200:1087)
                SERVER: SAID: GOOD Valid ticket (10.200.75.200:1087)
```

```
CLIENT [30809]: Validated ticket:  GOOD Valid ticket
                SERVER: GOT: GBYE 30809.0 (10.200.75.200:1087)
                SERVER: SAID: THNX See ya! (10.200.75.200:1087)
CLIENT [30809]: released ticket OK
[2]   Done                      ./lclnt2
[4]-  Done                      ./lclnt2
$
$ ps
  PID TTY          TIME CMD
23509 pts/3     00:00:00 bash
30808 pts/3     00:00:00 lserv2
30810 pts/3     00:00:00 ps
$
```

Whew! That test went well. Try these programs yourself to see how the interactions work.

13.8   DISTRIBUTED LICENSE SERVERS

The licensed program and the license server communicate through sockets, and sockets can connect processes on different hosts. In theory, the client can run on one machine, and the server can run on another machine, the same way Web browsers and Web servers run on different machines. Are there any problems running the clients and server on different machines? Yes.

Problem 1: Duplicate Process ID Numbers

Process ID numbers are unique within a machine, but not across a network. There is nothing wrong or uncommon in the picture shown in Figure 13.13:

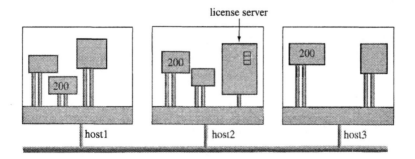

FIGURE 13.13

PIDs are not unique across a network.

Tickets and the ticket table contain a ticket number and a PID. In the situation shown in Figure 13.13, the license server would think it had issued three tickets to the same process. That ought to be an error. A process needs only one ticket to run. Asking for additional tickets could be a sign of a bug in the client.

We can solve the duplicate PID problem by extending the format of the tickets and the contents of the ticket table to include something that identifies the host running the server.

Problem 2: Reclaiming Tickets

The server reclaims lost tickets by using `kill(pid,0)` to send signal 0 to processes holding tickets. With a revised ticket table, the server now knows on which host the client is running.

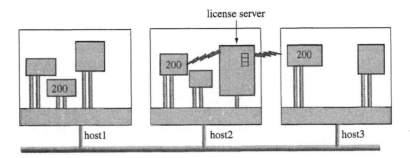

FIGURE 13.14

A process cannot signal to another host.

The server, though, cannot send signals to processes on other machines. (See Figure 13.14.) If the license server wants to send a signal to a process on *host3*, the license server must generate the request on *host3*.

Why not run instances of the license server on each host on the network? Each local server could then watch for lost tickets. (See Figure 13.15.)

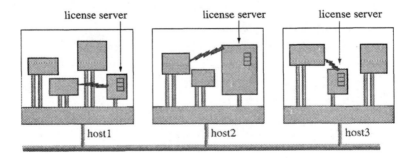

FIGURE 13.15

Running local copies of `lserv`.

Local servers solve the problem of getting signals to other hosts, but they raise the following questions: Which server issues tickets? How does that main server communicate with the local servers? To whom does a client send its ticket for validation?

Problem 3: A Host Crashes

What happens if one of the machines, not just the program, stops running? How can the main server, if it is still running, reclaim tickets? How can the client programs, if they are still running, validate their tickets? If the host with the main server crashes, who issues tickets?

Models for a Distributed License Management System How can one build a license management system that serves several machines at once? Here are three methods. Consider the design details, strengths, and weaknesses of each. Be sure to consider how each design responds if a client, server, computer, or the network crashes.

Solution 1: Local servers talk to a central server

Each machine has a local server, like the one we wrote. Each client talks to its local server. The local server passes the request back to the central server. The central server sends back a ticket or a denial. The local server records and passes the response back to the client. The local server could also enforce any local limitations such as the maximum number of instances on that machine or the time of day when the program may run.

Solution 2: Everyone talks to a central server

The clients send requests directly to a server on a particular host. Local servers run on each host, but those servers do not talk to local clients. Instead, the local servers act as agents of the central server to reclaim tickets.

Solution 3: Local servers talk to local servers

Each machine has a local server, like the one we wrote, and each client talks to its local server. There is no central server. All the local servers talk to one another. Each time a client asks for a ticket, the local server asks all the other servers how many tickets they have given out. If the total of all those numbers is less than the license-imposed limit, the local server issues a ticket.

13.9   UNIX DOMAIN SOCKETS

Our license server uses the standard host-ID, port-number addressing system for its sockets. Using these Internet addresses, a server on one machine can receive requests from clients on other machines on the local or wider network.

What if, as in two of the models for a distributed license system, clients only need to communicate with a server on their own machine? Can a socket be used for internal communication only?

13.9.1   Filenames as Socket Addresses

There are two kinds of connections—stream and datagram—and there are also two types of socket addresses—Internet addresses and local addresses. An Internet address consists of a host ID and a port number. A local address, usually called a *Unix domain address*, is a filename. No host, no port, just a filename (such as /dev/log, /dev/printer, or /tmp/lserversock).

The two socket names /dev/log and /dev/printer are used on many Unix systems. /dev/log is used by a server (syslogd) that acts as a scribe for the system. Programs that want to record a message in the system log send datagrams to the socket with the address /dev/log. The socket with Unix address /dev/printer, is used by some printing systems.

13.9.2 Programming with Unix Domain Sockets

To learn about client/server systems that use Unix domain sockets, we write a log system. The wtmp file is an example of a log system. The wtmp file records all logins, logouts, and other connections. Log systems are used by security and system maintenance programs to record suspicious activity. A log server is a scribe; clients send messages to the server, and the server adds those messages to a file only it can modify. The log server can keep the file any place it likes in any format it likes, and none of its clients need to know any of those details.

We use a Unix domain address for the datagram socket of our log server. Only clients on the same machine can send datagrams to that socket. What follows is the client and server code for a log-file system that uses Unix domain sockets. The server creates a socket and binds an address:

```
/***********************************************************************
 * logfiled.c  -   a simple logfile server using Unix Domain Datagram Sockets
 *                 usage: logfiled >>logfilename
 */

#include         <stdio.h>
#include         <sys/types.h>
#include         <sys/socket.h>
#include         <sys/un.h>
#include         <time.h>

#define MSGLEN  512
#define oops(m,x) { perror(m); exit(x); }
#define SOCKNAME "/tmp/logfilesock"

int main(int ac, char *av[])
{
        int     sock;                   /* read messages here   */
        struct sockaddr_un addr;        /* this is its address  */
        socklen_t addrlen;
        char    msg[MSGLEN];
        int     l;
        char    sockname[] = SOCKNAME ;
        time_t  now;
        int     msgnum = 0;
        char    *timestr;

        /* build an address */
        addr.sun_family = AF_UNIX;                      /* note AF_UNIX */
```

```
       strcpy(addr.sun_path, sockname);           /* filename is address */
       addrlen = strlen(sockname) + sizeof(addr.sun_family);

       sock = socket(PF_UNIX, SOCK_DGRAM, 0);  /* note PF_UNIX  */
       if ( sock == -1 )
               oops("socket",2);

       /* bind the address */
       if ( bind(sock, (struct sockaddr *) &addr, addrlen) == -1 )
               oops("bind", 3);
       /* read and write */
       while(1)
       {
               l = read(sock, msg, MSGLEN);     /* read works for DGRAM */
               msg[l] = '\0';                    /* make it a string     */
               time(&now);
               timestr = ctime(&now);
               timestr[strlen(timestr)-1] = '\0';        /* chop newline */

               printf("[%5d] %s %s\n", msgnum++, timestr, msg);
               fflush(stdout);
       }
}
```

We still use socket and bind to create a server socket. The type of socket is
SOCK_DGRAM, and the family for the address is PF_UNIX.[3] The socket address is a filename. We use read rather than recvfrom because we do not need to reply.

The client is even shorter:

```
/**********************************************************************
 * logfilec.c - logfile client - send messages to the logfile server
 *              usage: logfilec "a message here"
 */

#include        <stdio.h>
#include        <sys/types.h>
#include        <sys/socket.h>
#include        <sys/un.h>

#define SOCKET   "/tmp/logfilesock"
#define oops(m,x) { perror(m); exit(x); }

main(int ac, char *av[])
{
        int                sock;
        struct sockaddr_un addr;
        socklen_t          addrlen;
        char               sockname[] = SOCKET ;
        char               *msg = av[1];
```

---

[3]PF_LOCAL may be used instead of PF_UNIX.

```
if ( ac != 2 ){
        fprintf(stderr,"usage: logfilec 'message'\n");
        exit(1);
}
sock = socket(PF_UNIX, SOCK_DGRAM, 0);
if ( sock == -1 )
        oops("socket",2);

addr.sun_family = AF_UNIX;
strcpy(addr.sun_path, sockname);
addrlen = strlen(sockname) + sizeof(addr.sun_family) ;

if ( sendto(sock,msg, strlen(msg), 0, &addr, addrlen) == -1 )
        oops("sendto",3);
}
```

We use socket to create the socket and sendto to send the message. The server receives the message and then prints the message, preceded by a message number and time stamp.

Here is a simple test:

```
$ cc logfiled.c -o logfiled
$ ./logfiled >> visitorlog&
1500
$ cc logfilec.c -o logfilec
$ ./logfilec 'Nice system.  Swell software!'
$ ./logfilec "Testing this log thing."
$ ./logfilec "Can you read this?"
$ cat vistorlog
[    0] Mon Aug 20 18:25:34 2001 Nice system.  Swell software!
[    1] Mon Aug 20 18:25:44 2001 Testing this log thing.
[    2] Mon Aug 20 18:25:48 2001 Can you read this?
```

This pair of short programs shows how to use Unix domain sockets and demonstrates the idea of a log server. Another nice feature of this system is that it implements the autoappend mode without using O_APPEND. The server takes one message at a time and appends that message to the file. Even if several clients send messages at once, the underlying socket mechanism serializes delivery to the socket.

13.10 SUMMARY: SOCKETS AND SERVERS

Sockets are a powerful, versatile tool for carrying data between processes. We have seen two types of sockets and two types of socket addresses:

socket	domain	
	PF_INET	**PF_UNIX**
SOCK_STREAM	connected, intermachine	connected, local
SOCK_DGRAM	datagrams, intermachine	datagrams, local

In the past few chapters, we studied projects using three of these four combinations. Keep this chart in mind when you think about Unix programs and when you design your own projects. What sort of messages are you sending? How far do you want them to go?

SUMMARY

MAIN IDEAS

- Datagrams are short messages sent from one socket to another. Datagram sockets are not connected; each message contains a destination address. Datagram (UDP) sockets are simpler, faster, and put less load on the system than stream (TCP) sockets.
- A license server is a program that enforces rules for use of licensed programs. A license server issues permission, in the form of short tickets, to programs.
- A license server has to remember what tickets were issued to what processes. It has to keep an internal database. In this way, the license server differs from our Web server.
- Servers that record the state of a system must be designed to be able to handle client crashes and server crashes.
- Some license servers serve several machines on a network. Several designs are possible, each having strengths and weaknesses.
- Sockets can have two sorts of addresses: network or local. Sockets with local addresses are called *Unix domain sockets* or *named sockets*. These sockets use filenames as addresses and can only exchange data with sockets on the same machine.

WHAT NEXT?

We examined two methods that servers use to handle multiple requests. The license server receives requests as datagrams and responds to messages one at a time. A Web server receives requests as data streams and uses `fork` to respond to several messages in parallel. Servers have a third choice; a single process can use a technique called *threads* to run several function calls at the same time. Next, we look at the ideas and techniques of threads.

EXPLORATIONS

13.1   In the examples using stream sockets, the server did not use the client's address when it replied to a request. How did the server know how to get the message back to the client?

13.2   How did process 25915 beat process 25914 to a ticket? Consider the sequence of operations between the creation of each client process and the arrival of the request at the server. In a multitasking system, processes take turns running. Where could the processes be interrupted to cause the result shown in the test run?

13.3   How could you use one license server to manage the use of two or more programs? One method is to modify the protocol so each request includes the name of the program to run. Describe the changes to the protocol, data structures, and program logic to add support for several products.

13.4   Is there any potential for damage to the list of tickets if the `ticket_reclaim` function were invoked during the routine handling of a client request? Consider each of the functions that modify the array and the counter. At what points in the code are the state of the array and the value of the counter inconsistent? How does the handler modify the array and counter? How would an unexpected change in those values affect the regular handling functions?

13.5   *PID rollover* Process ID numbers are assigned as processes are created. Consider the following sequence of events. A client with PID 7777 gets a ticket and then dies abruptly. Soon after the death of the client, a different user runs a program and gets a new process, which just happens to be assigned PID 7777. When the `ticket_reclaim` function runs, it finds a process with PID 7777. The ticket assigned to 7777 is not recycled, even though 7777 is running an unrelated program and is not holding a ticket. How much of a problem does this situation pose? How can the system be modified to prevent it from happening?

13.6   One method to prevent loss of the ticket_array is for the server to write the data in the table to a disk file. How would you change the server to implement this data-backup scheme? Suppose the customer was killing the server intentionally to generate new tickets. How would your file-backup scheme work in such a situation?

13.7   A client holding a ticket from an earlier version of the server that waits too long to validate the ticket may find no more tickets available when it reapplies for a ticket. Devise a response to this situation. The client should not be allowed to continue, because that would violate the limit of simultaneous sessions, but the client should not just quit abruptly.

13.8   Compare the three models of distributed license control according to the set of questions listed in the text.

13.9   *Writing to sockets* We used `write` and `sendto` to transmit data from one socket to another. Read the manual to learn about `send` and `sendmsg`. What are the differences among all these methods?

13.10   The connection between automobile management and datagrams is more than metaphorical. Imagine that each of the company cars contains a GPS device so the car can determine its location, a computer, and a cellular modem that connects the computer to the Internet. Imagine also that the ignition for these cars is controlled, not by a cut metal key, but by a magnetic card reader in the dashboard. Devise a system that allows employees to sign up and use company cars and also allows the car fleet manager to keep track of the driver and location of each car.

PROGRAMMING EXERCISES

13.11   Modify the `dgrecv.c` program to print, in addition to the address of the sender, the time when the message was received and also a message number. The message numbers start at zero. The output should now look like this:

```
dgrecv: got a message: testing 123
   from: 10.200.75.200:1041
     at: Sun Aug 19 10:22:27 EDT 2001
   msg#: 23
```

13.12   Write, by adding to `dgsend.c`, a client program for `dgrecv2.c`.

13.13   *Printing server status* The license server stores the table containing the information on which clients hold which tickets. What if you wanted the server to print the table? Seeing the table could help you debug or test the server. A standard technique for communicating with server processes is to use signals.

Modify lserv1 so it responds to SIGHUP by printing the contents of the table to standard output. You can test this feature by using the kill -HUP serverpid command.

13.14   *Garbage collection method 2* Modify the license server so it calls ticket_reclaim only when a client is denied permission. What are the advantages and disadvantages of this solution?

13.15   Modify lclnt2.c so it sleeps for five seconds and then validates its ticket. If the ticket is valid, the client sleeps for five more seconds and then wraps up. If the ticket is not valid, the client should try to get another ticket. If it succeeds, it proceeds normally. If it fails, it tells the user there has been a problem with the license server and then quits.

13.16   Modify the small shell or the bounce program from the earlier chapters to use the license server. Where do you add ticket validation? What do you tell the user if, due to server crash, the ticket becomes invalid?

13.17   Modify the client and server code to support tickets that include the IP address of the host. How do you have to change the ticket table? Make sure to include changes for the validation function.

13.18   Implement one of the three models of distributed license control.

13.19   One problem with the log system is that the messages are anonymous. Modify the system so messages in the log include the username of the person who sent the message.

13.20   *Reading from sockets* We use read in the log-file server. Write two new versions of the server, one that uses recvfrom and one that uses recv. How do these methods for getting data differ? Read the manual for details.

13.21   What changes would you have to make to the license server and client code to use Unix domain sockets? Explain why the client has to use bind.

13.22   *Network dealer* In the first chapter, we discussed Internet bridge games. In any distributed card game, the software must simulate a single stack of cards, making sure that no two clients hold the same card.

Write a pair of programs cardd and cardc that use datagram sockets to manage a deck of cards. The server program starts by shuffling a deck of cards. The client program can be run from the command line to get cards from the dealer. This sample run

```
$ cardc get 5
4D AH 2D TD KC
```

shows a user requesting five cards and being dealt a four of diamonds, an ace of hearts, a two of diamonds, a ten of diamonds, and a king of clubs.

Make sure your program does not deal the same card twice and that the protocol has a way to indicate when the dealer runs out of cards. What other transactions would be useful additions to the protocol?

PROJECTS

Based on the material in this chapter, you can learn about and write versions of the following Unix programs:

```
talk, rwho, streaming video servers
```

C H A P T E R   1 4

Threads
Concurrent Functions

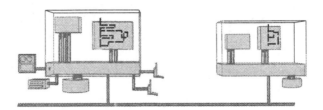

OBJECTIVES

Ideas and Skills

- Threads of execution
- Multithreaded programs
- Creating and destroying threads
- Sharing data between threads safely using mutex locks
- Synchronizing data transfer using condition variables
- Passing multiple arguments to a thread

System Calls and Functions

- `pthread_create`, `pthread_join`
- `pthread_mutex_lock`, `pthread_mutex_unlock`
- `pthread_cond_wait`, `pthread_cond_signal`

14.1   DOING SEVERAL THINGS AT ONCE

I don't know about you, but I am really bugged by Web pages filled with flashing, danc-ing, twirling, animated images and advertisements. Annoying though these pages may be, they do raise an interesting technical question: How can one program do several things at the same time?

Animated images are not the only example on the Web of a program doing several things at once. Your Web browser had to download and uncompress those images from various servers around the world, and if your Web browser is like most, it downloaded those images in parallel, not one after the other. How can a Web browser download and uncompress several images at once?

The browser is not the only process doing several things at once. The Web server had to read those images from the disk and send them back in parallel while it was handling connections to perhaps hundreds of Web browsers. How does the server do all these transmissions at once?

Don't Be Silly! We Already Know about Multitasking!

We already studied these questions. In the video game chapter, we saw how to use one interval timer and two counters to control animation in two dimensions at once. In other chapters, the shell and the Web server use fork and exec to create new processes to run several concurrent programs. Why not use those ideas?

Using fork and exec, we can run several programs at the same time. What if we want to run several *functions* at the same time or several invocations of the same function at once?

In this chapter, we study *threads*. A thread is to functions what a process is to programs, an environment in which to run. We shall write programs that run several functions at once, all within the same process.

Our main project will be a program to fill a text screen with animated messages. We shall build up to that project by revising the Web server project to handle simultaneous requests for directory listings and file contents without starting new processes.

14.2 THREADS OF EXECUTION

What is a *thread*? What does it do? How do we create one? We begin by studying a traditional program that executes code instruction by instruction, one after the other. Then, by making two small changes, we turn the program into one that executes two functions in parallel.

14.2.1 A Single-Threaded Program

Consider this program:

```
/* hello_single.c - a single threaded hello world program */

#include  <stdio.h>
#define NUM     5

main()
{
        void    print_msg(char *);

        print_msg("hello");
        print_msg("world\n");
}
```

```
void print_msg(char *m)
{

        int i;
        for(i=0 ; i<NUM ; i++){
                printf("%s", m);
                fflush(stdout);
                sleep(1);
        }

}
```

In `hello_single.c`, `main` makes two function calls, one after the other. Each function invocation executes a loop. The output reflects the internal flow of control:

```
$ cc hello_single.c -o hello_single
$ ./hello_single
hellohellohellohellohelloworld
world
world
world
world
$
```

Each message is followed by a 1-second delay, and the program takes 10 seconds to run. Figure 14.1 shows the flow of execution through the program.

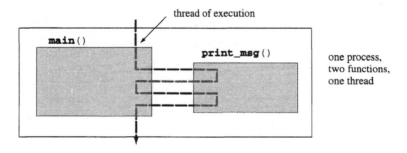

FIGURE 14.1

Single thread of execution.

The path of execution enters `main`. It then enters `print_msg`, returns from `print_msg` to the next instruction in `main`, goes back to `print_msg` for a second invocation of that function, and returns to `main`, where there are no more instructions, so it returns from `main`.

That unbroken path tracing the order of execution of instructions is called a *thread of execution*. Traditional programs have a single thread of execution. Even programs with `goto`s and recursive subroutines have a single, although sometimes knotted, thread of execution.

14.2.2 A Multithreaded Program

What if we want to run both invocations of print_msg at the same time, the way we use fork to run two processes simultaneously? A revised picture might look like that shown in Figure 14.2.

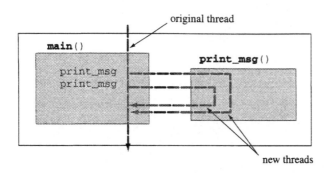

FIGURE 14.2

Multiple Threads of Execution.

A single thread of execution enters main. That thread then starts a new thread that runs to print_msg. The original thread continues to the next instruction where it starts another thread that runs to print_msg for the second invocation. Finally, the original thread waits for the two threads to join it before returning from main.

People do this sort of multithreaded task management all the time. A parent who has to run several errands could do them in sequence or, instead, could take a couple of kids along and have one buy milk at the grocery store, the other return books to the library, and then wait for both to return before going home.

A thread is like a kid you bring along to run a function for you. If you want to run several errands at once, you bring along several kids. If a program wants to run several functions at once, it creates several threads. This program, hello_multi.c, follows the flow of control depicted in Figure 14.2:

```
/* hello_multi.c - a multi-threaded hello world program */
#include   <stdio.h>
#include   <pthread.h>

#define NUM      5

main()
{
        pthread_t t1, t2;                  /* two threads */

        void    *print_msg(void *);

        pthread_create(&t1, NULL, print_msg, (void *)"hello");
        pthread_create(&t2, NULL, print_msg, (void *)"world\n");
        pthread_join(t1, NULL);
        pthread_join(t2, NULL);

}
```

```
void *print_msg(void *m)
{
        char *cp = (char *) m;
        int i;
        for(i=0 ; i<NUM ; i++){
                printf("%s", m);
                fflush(stdout);
                sleep(1);
        }
        return NULL;
}
```

Notice the changes to the original program. First, we include a new header file. pthread.h contains data-type definitions and function prototypes. Second, we define two variables of type pthread_t: t1 and t2. These two threads are like the two kids the parent brings along in the car to run errands.

Each branch point in the flow of control in the diagram has a corresponding line of code. Let us look at each instruction in detail:

```
pthread_create(&t1, NULL, print_msg, (void *)"hello")
```

This function call is the equivalent of saying, "Kid one, please run errand print_msg with argument hello." The first argument is the address of the thread. The second argument is a pointer to attributes of the thread. A NULL pointer indicates default thread attributes. The third argument is the function you want the thread to execute, and the last argument is a pointer to the argument you want passed to that function.

That single instruction creates a new thread with the specified attributes. That new thread runs the function print_msg with the argument "hello".

```
pthread_create(&t2, NULL, print_msg, (void *)"world\n")
```

This function call creates a new thread with default attributes. That new thread of execution runs print_msg with the argument "world\n".

```
pthread_join(t1, NULL)
```

Like the parent waiting for the two children to return from their errands, the main function here waits for the paths of the two threads to return. The function pthread_join takes two arguments. The first argument is the thread to wait for, and the second argument points to a location to receive a return value from the thread. If the pointer is NULL, any return value is discarded.

```
pthread_join(t2, NULL)
```

The main function waits for the other thread to finish.

We can now compile and run this program:

```
$ cc hello_multi.c -lpthread -o hello_multi
$ ./hello_multi
helloworld
helloworld
helloworld
helloworld
helloworld
$
```

This program takes only five seconds to run because the two loops run in parallel. Differences in scheduling of the threads can cause your output to differ from the output shown. Notice how flexible threads can be. Here we are running two instances of the same function at once, only the argument is different. We could have just as easily called two different functions and run those in parallel.

14.2.3 Function Summaries

pthread_create		
PURPOSE	Create a new thread	
INCLUDE	#include <pthread.h>	
USAGE	int pthread_create(pthread_t *thread,	
		pthread_attr_t *attr,
		void *(*func)(void *),
		void *arg);
ARGS	thread	a pointer to a variable of type pthread_t
	attr	a pointer to a variable of type pthead_attr_t or NULL.
	func	the function this new thread will run
	arg	the argument to be passed to func
RETURNS	0	if successful
	errcode	if not successful

pthread_create creates a new thread of execution and calls *func*(*arg*) within that thread. The new thread is given attributes specified by the *attr* argument. *func* is a function that accepts one pointer as an argument and returns one pointer as a value. The argument and return values are both defined as pointers of type void * to allow them to point to any type of value.

If *attr* is NULL, default attributes are used. We discuss attributes of threads in a later section. pthread_create returns 0 on success and a nonzero error code otherwise.

	pthread_join	
PURPOSE	Wait for termination of a thread	
INCLUDE	#include <pthread.h>	
USAGE	int pthread_join(pthread_t thread, void **retval)	
ARGS	thread	the thread to wait for
	retval	points to a variable to receive the return value from the thread
RETURNS	0	if thread terminates
	errcode	if an error

pthread_join blocks the calling thread until the thread specified by *thread* termi-nates. If *retval* is not null, the return value from the thread is stored where *retval* points.

pthread_join returns 0 when the thread terminates. pthread_join returns a nonzero error code in case of an error. It is an error for a thread to wait for a thread that does not exist, to wait for a thread someone else is waiting for, or to wait for itself.

Programming with threads is like assigning several people to do several tasks. If you manage the project correctly, you can get work done faster, but you have to make sure that your workers do not get in each other's ways and that they perform tasks in the correct sequence. We now look at techniques for thread cooperation and coordination.

14.3   INTERTHREAD COOPERATION

Processes communicate with each other using pipes, sockets, signals, exit/wait, and the environment. Threads have it easy. Threads execute functions in a single process, so like any functions in the same process, threads share global variables. Threads can commu-nicate by setting and reading these global variables. Simultaneous access to memory is a powerful, yet dangerous, feature of threads.

14.3.1 Example 1: **incrprint.c**

```
/* incprint.c - one thread increments, the other prints */

#include   <stdio.h>
#include   <pthread.h>

#define NUM      5

int     counter = 0;

main()
```

```
        {
                pthread_t  t1;                          /* one thread */
                void       *print_count(void *); /* its function */
                int        i;

                pthread_create(&t1, NULL, print_count, NULL);
                for( i = 0 ; i<NUM ; i++ ){
                        counter++;
                        sleep(1);
                }

                pthread_join(t1, NULL);
        }
        void *print_count(void *m)
        {
                int i;
                for(i=0 ; i<NUM ; i++){
                        printf("count = %d\n", counter);
                        sleep(1);
                }
                return NULL;
        }
```

This program, incprint.c, uses two threads. The original thread executes a loop incrementing counter once per second. Before the original thread enters the loop, it creates a new thread. That new thread runs a function that prints the value of counter. Both functions, main and print_count, run in the same process, so both have access to counter. Figure 14.3 shows the two functions and the global variable.

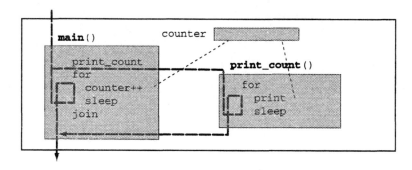

FIGURE 14.3

Two threads share a global variable.

When main changes the value of counter, print_counter sees that new value at once. There is no need to send the new value through a pipe or socket. We compile and run the program:

```
$ cc incprint.c -lpthread -o incprint
$ ./incprint
count = 1
count = 2
count = 3
count = 4
count = 5
```

The program appears to work perfectly. One function modifies a variable, the other function reads and displays the value. This example shows that functions running in separate threads share global variables. Our next example is more interesting.

14.3.2 Example 2: `twordcount.c`

Before computers, students made sure their term papers were long enough by counting the number of words manually. Imagine a student with a 10-page paper. That student could count the number of words in all 10 pages one by one, or she could find 10 other students and give each student a different page of words to count. Counting all 10 pages in parallel should be much faster.

The Unix wc program counts lines, words, and characters in one or more files. Typically, it is single threaded. How can we design a multithreaded program to count and print the total number of words in two files?

Version 1: Two Threads, One Counter

Our first version creates a separate thread to count each file. Both threads increment the same counter as they detect words. The idea is illustrated in Figure 14.4.

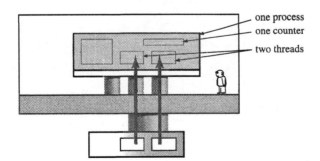

FIGURE 14.4

A common counter for two threads.

Here is the code for this version, `twordcount1.c`:

```
/* twordcount1.c - threaded word counter for two files. Version 1 */

#include   <stdio.h>
#include   <pthread.h>
#include   <ctype.h>

int        total_words ;
```

```
main(int ac, char *av[])
{
        pthread_t t1, t2;                    /* two threads */
        void      *count_words(void *);

        if ( ac != 3 ){
                printf("usage: %s file1 file2\n", av[0]);
                exit(1);
        }
        total_words = 0;
        pthread_create(&t1, NULL, count_words, (void *) av[1]);
        pthread_create(&t2, NULL, count_words, (void *) av[2]);
        pthread_join(t1, NULL);
        pthread_join(t2, NULL);
        printf("%5d: total words\n", total_words);
}
void *count_words(void *f)
{
        char *filename = (char *) f;
        FILE *fp;
        int  c, prevc = '\0';

        if ( (fp = fopen(filename, "r")) != NULL ){
                while( ( c = getc(fp)) != EOF ){
                        if ( !isalnum(c) && isalnum(prevc) )
                                total_words++;
                        prevc = c;
                }
                fclose(fp);
        } else
                perror(filename);
        return NULL;
}
```

count_words considers the end of a word to be an alphanumeric character followed by
a nonalphanumeric character. That logic misses the last word in the file, but counts
"U.S.A." as three words. We compile and test as follows:

```
$ cc twordcount1.c -lpthread -o twc1
$ ./twc1 /etc/group /usr/dict/words
45614: total words
$ wc -w /etc/group /usr/dict/words
    58 /etc/group
 45402 /usr/dict/words
 45460 total
```

twordcount1 produces different results from the regular version of wc, because the two
programs use different rules for the end of a word.

Stepping on Toes   There is a more subtle problem in this program than the rule for end of word: Both threads increment the same counter, potentially at the same time. How can that cause trouble? The C language does not specify how the operation total_words++ is carried out by the computer. The computer might be executing

```
total_words = total_words + 1
```

That is, the program fetches the current value of the counter into a register, adds one to that value, then stores the result from the register back into memory.

What happens if both threads increment the counter using the fetch-add-store sequence at the same time?

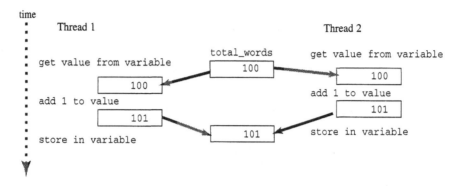

FIGURE 14.5

Two threads increment the same counter.

Figure 14.5 shows that both threads fetch the same value, increment the register, and then store the new value. Two increments take place, but the value of the counter increases only by one. How can we prevent threads from interfering with each other? We explore two solutions.

Version 2: Two Threads, One Counter, One Mutex

A public locker, the kind at airports and bus terminals, is open to everyone until someone claims it. When a person drops in some coins and takes the key, nobody else has access to that storage space. Later, when that person returns and unlocks the storage space, anyone else can claim it. If our two threads are to share a common counter safely, they need a way to put a lock on that variable.

The threads system includes variables called *mutual exclusion locks*, which cooperating threads use to prevent simultaneous access to any variable, function, or other resource. This revised version, twordcount2.c, shows how to create and use a *mutex*:

```
/* twordcount2.c - threaded word counter for two files.    */
/*                 version 2: uses mutex to lock counter    */

#include  <stdio.h>
#include  <pthread.h>
#include  <ctype.h>
```

```
int             total_words ;    /* the counter and its lock */
pthread_mutex_t counter_lock = PTHREAD_MUTEX_INITIALIZER;

main(int ac, char *av[])
{
        pthread_t t1, t2;                  /* two threads */
        void      *count_words(void *);

        if ( ac != 3 ){
                printf("usage: %s file1 file2\n", av[0]);
                exit(1);
        }
        total_words = 0;
        pthread_create(&t1, NULL, count_words, (void *) av[1]);
        pthread_create(&t2, NULL, count_words, (void *) av[2]);
        pthread_join(t1, NULL);
        pthread_join(t2, NULL);
        printf("%5d: total words\n", total_words);
}
void *count_words(void *f)
{
        char *filename = (char *) f;
        FILE *fp;
        int  c, prevc = '\0';

        if ( (fp = fopen(filename, "r")) != NULL ){
                while( ( c = getc(fp)) != EOF ){
                        if ( !isalnum(c) && isalnum(prevc) ){
                                pthread_mutex_lock(&counter_lock);
                                total_words++;
                                pthread_mutex_unlock(&counter_lock);
                        }
                        prevc = c;
                }
                fclose(fp);
        } else
                perror(filename);
        return NULL;
}
```

The program now looks like Figure 14.6.

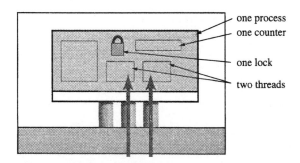

FIGURE 14.6

Two threads use a mutex to share a counter.

We add only three lines to the program. First we define a global variable, counter_lock, of type pthread_mutex_t, and we assign it an initial value. Then we change count_words so that it sandwiches the step that increments the counter between a call to pthread_mutex_lock and a call to pthread_mutex_unlock.

The two threads can now share the counter safely. If one thread calls pthread_mutex_lock when the other thread has locked the mutex, that thread blocks until the mutex is unlocked. As soon as the mutex is unlocked, the call to pthread_mutex_lock unblocks, and the thread can increment the counter. After incrementing the counter, the thread unlocks the mutex and loops back to process more data.

Any number of threads can wait for a mutex to become unlocked. When a thread unlocks a mutex, the threads system passes control to exactly one of the waiting threads. A mutex is only useful, though, if all threads cooperate. If a thread wants to increment the counter without waiting for the mutex, nobody can stop it.

---

pthread_mutex_lock

PURPOSE	Wait for and lock a mutex
INCLUDE	#include <pthread.h>
USAGE	int pthread_mutex_lock(pthread_mutex_t *mutex)
ARGS	mutex a pointer to a mutual exclusion object
RETURNS	0 for success
	errcode for errors

---

pthread_mutex_lock locks the specified mutex. If the mutex is unlocked, it becomes locked and owned by the calling thread, and pthread_mutex_lock returns a value of 0 at once. If the mutex is already locked by another thread, the calling thread is suspended until the mutex is unlocked. If there is an error, pthread_mutex_lock returns an error code.

---

pthread_mutex_unlock

PURPOSE	Unlock a mutex
INCLUDE	#include <pthread.h>
USAGE	int pthread_mutex_unlock(pthread_mutex_t *mutex)
ARGS	mutex a pointer to a mutual exclusion object
RETURNS	0 for success
	errcode for errors

`pthread_mutex_unlock` releases the lock on the specified mutex. If there are threads blocked on the specified mutex, one of them will acquire the lock to the mutex. `pthread_mutex_unlock` returns 0 if it succeeds, and it returns a nonzero error code if there is a problem.

We only considered the case in which everything goes well. What happens if a thread tries to unlock a mutex it did not lock? What happens if a thread tries to lock a mutex it already locked? What if a thread exits without unlocking a mutex? Different implementations of the threads system may handle these situations in different ways. Check your local manual pages for details.

Do We Need a Mutex?   If both threads might try to modify the same variable at the same time, they have to use a mutex to prevent interference. Using a mutex makes the program run slower. Checking the lock, setting the lock, and releasing the lock for every word in both files adds up to a lot of operations. A more efficient solution is to give each thread its own counter.

Version 3: Two Threads, Two Counters, Multiple Arguments to Threads

In this next version of the word-counting program, we eliminate the need for a mutex by giving each thread its own counter. When the threads are done, we add together the values in those two counters.

How do we get those counters to the threads, and how do the threads pass their counts back? In a regular, one-thread program, the word-counting function would return the number of words to its calling function. A thread can return a value by calling `pthread_exit`, and that value can be obtained with `pthread_join`. The manual has the details. We shall use a different, slightly easier method.

Instead of having a thread send back a value, the calling thread can pass to the function a pointer to a variable and let the function increment that variable. Passing this pointer poses a problem: We are already passing the name of the file to the thread, and `pthread_create` only lets us pass a single argument. How can we pass the filename and the counter to the thread? Easy, we create a struct with two members and pass the address of that struct. Here is the code:

```
/* twordcount3.c - threaded word counter for two files.
 *                 - Version 3: one counter per file
 */

#include   <stdio.h>
#include   <pthread.h>
#include   <ctype.h>

struct arg_set {                    /* two values in one arg */
            char *fname;    /* file to examine      */
            int  count;     /* number of words      */
};

main(int ac, char *av[])
{
        pthread_t      t1, t2;          /* two threads */
        struct arg_set args1, args2;    /* two argsets */
        void           *count_words(void *);
```

```
        if ( ac != 3 ){
                printf("usage: %s file1 file2\n", av[0]);
                exit(1);
        }
        args1.fname = av[1];
        args1.count = 0;
        pthread_create(&t1, NULL, count_words, (void *) &args1);

        args2.fname = av[2];
        args2.count = 0;
        pthread_create(&t2, NULL, count_words, (void *) &args2);

        pthread_join(t1, NULL);
        pthread_join(t2, NULL);
        printf("%5d: %s\n", args1.count, av[1]);
        printf("%5d: %s\n", args2.count, av[2]);
        printf("%5d: total words\n", args1.count+args2.count);
}
void *count_words(void *a)
{
        struct arg_set *args = a;        /* cast arg back to correct type */
        FILE *fp;
        int  c, prevc = '\0';

        if ( (fp = fopen(args->fname, "r")) != NULL ){
                while( ( c = getc(fp)) != EOF ){
                        if ( !isalnum(c) && isalnum(prevc) )
                                args->count++;
                        prevc = c;
                }
                fclose(fp);
        } else
                perror(args->fname);
        return NULL;

}
```

We solve the problem of passing two arguments by defining a struct that contains the name of the file and the number of words in that file. In main, we define two of these structs as local variables, initialize the structs, and pass addresses of the structs to the threads. (See Figure 14.7.) Passing pointers to local structs not only eliminates the need for a mutex, but also gets rid of global variables.

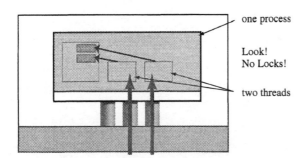

one process

Look!
No Locks!

two threads

FIGURE 14.7

Each thread has a pointer to its own struct.

Each invocation of count_words receives a pointer to a different struct, so the threads read different files and increment different pointers. The structs are local variables in main, so the memory allocated to the counters persists until control leaves main.

14.3.3 Interthread Cooperation: Summary

The data space of a process contains all its variables. All threads running in that process can have access to those variables. If those variables never change, threads can read and use the values without chance of error.

If any threads in the process modify a variable, all threads that use that variable must cooperate on a method to prevent data corruption. Only one thread should use that variable at a time.

The three versions of the word-counting program show three approaches to sharing values between threads. The first approach, taken in twordcount1.c, is to allow threads to modify the same variable without any cooperation. That program works most of the time but is not correct.

The second approach, taken in twordcount2.c, is to use a mutual exclusion object, a *mutex*, to make sure only one thread increments the shared counter at a time. This program works all the time but makes many calls to the functions to check, set, and release the lock.

The third approach, in twordcount3.c, is to get rid of a shared counter and create separate counters, one for each thread. The threads no longer share a variable, so they no longer need to cooperate with each other. The threads still cooperate with the original thread, though. In particular, the original thread should not read the counter from a thread until the thread is done. In this case, the original thread uses pthread_join to block until the counting threads are done. When a counting thread finishes, the call to pthread_join unblocks, effectively unlocking access to the counter and telling main it is time to read the value.

This third version also shows how to pass several arguments to the function in a thread. We create one struct that contains all the arguments and then pass the address of that struct. The thread may read and modify any of the members in that struct. Other functions with access to that struct will see the new values. Of course, if more than one thread changes those values, a mutex must be used to prevent data corruption.

14.4   COMPARING THREADS WITH PROCESSES

Processes have been part of Unix since the beginning. Threads were added later. The model of a process is clear and uniform. Threads evolved from a variety of sources; there are different types of threads with different attributes. The examples we have looked at use an interface called *POSIX threads*. We have ignored questions of efficiency and scheduling; the answers to these questions depend on the version of Unix and the version of threads you use.

Processes differ from threads in fundamental ways. Each process has its own data space, file descriptors, and process ID number. Threads share one data space, set of file descriptors, and process ID number. The implications are significant to a programmer.

Shared Data Space Consider a database system that stores a large, complex tree-structured database in memory. Multiple threads can read this shared set of data easily. Multiple queries from clients can be served from one process. Variables do not change. Sharing this data space causes no problems.

Now consider a program that uses `malloc` and `free` to manage memory. One thread allocates a chunk of memory to store a string. When that thread is not looking, a different thread calls `free` to deallocate that chunk of memory. The original thread is suddenly holding a pointer to deallocated memory, or perhaps worse, a chunk of memory that had been reallocated to hold different data.

Threading can also introduce memory hoarding. Afraid to deallocate a chunk of memory on the off chance that a thread somewhere is still using the pointer, a programmer might err on the side of caution and never free memory.

Functions that, in a single-threaded model, return pointers to static local variables cannot work in a multithreaded model. The same function might be active in several threads at once.

In short, unless the number of shared variables is small and well defined, a multithreaded application can be a debugging nightmare.

Shared File Descriptors File descriptors are automatically duplicated by `fork` so that the child process has a new set of file descriptors. If the child process closes a file descriptor inherited from the parent, that file descriptor is still open for the parent.

In a multithreaded program, it is possible to pass the same file descriptor to two different threads. Both those values refer to the same file descriptor, though. If a function in one thread closes the file, that file descriptor is closed for all threads in the process. Other threads may still need the connection.

***fork, exec, exit,* Signals** All threads share the same process. If one thread calls `exec`, the kernel replaces the current program with a new one. All running threads are gone, and that might surprise the other threads. If one thread calls `exit`, the entire process finishes. What if a thread causes a segmentation violation or other system error and the thread crashes? The whole process dies, not just one thread.

`fork` creates a new process that contains an exact replica of the code and data of the calling process. If a function in one thread calls `fork`, do the other threads get duplicated in the new process? No. Only the thread that called `fork` is running in the new process. What if another thread was in the middle of modifying some data when the `fork` occurred? In what condition will that data be in the new process?

Signals are more complicated with threads. Processes can receive all sorts of signals. Who receives the signal, all the threads? What about signals caused by segmentation violations or bus errors? Who gets those? The manual explains the details of threads and signals.

Experiment on Your Own This chapter introduces you to the basic ideas of threads and the major problems and design concerns to think about if you want to use threads. A good exercise is to code two solutions to the same problem, one with threads and one with processes. Which is easier to design, code, and debug? Which one runs faster? Which one is more portable across versions of Unix?

14.5   INTERTHREAD NOTIFICATION

We take one more look at the multithreaded word-count program. Imagine you are the Director of Elections for a large city. Small precincts finish counting sooner because they have fewer votes to count. You do not announce the grand total until all the numbers are in, but you want to see each report as it arrives.

Counting words in files is like counting votes in precincts. Some files are larger than others and take longer to count. It is interesting to see what would happen with

```
twordcount really-big-file tiny-file
```

The original thread uses `pthread_wait` to wait for the first thread to finish and then for the second thread to finish. In this example, the second thread will have results long before the first thread is done. How can the quicker thread notify the original thread?

How Can One Thread Notify Another Thread?   When a counting thread finishes its work, how can it notify the original thread that its results are ready? With processes, the `wait` system call returns when *any* child process terminates. Is there a similar mechanism for threads? Can one thread wait for *any* thread to finish? No. Threads do not work that way. Threads do not have a parent, so there is no obvious thread to notify.

14.5.1 Notifying Election Central

When a precinct finishes counting its votes, it delivers its results to the central office. Consider the following system for getting results from a precinct to the central office (it sounds weird, but it is exactly how threads notify one another of events):

(a) Election Central sets up a vote report mailbox. This mailbox has space for only one vote report at a time. This mailbox has a flag that can be raised and then snaps right back.

(b) Election Central waits until the flag is raised.

(c) Precinct head puts the precinct report in the vote-report mailbox.

(d) Precinct head raises the flag on the mailbox (called *signaling*).

(e) Election Central sees the flag raised. Election Central responds by executing the following steps:

Election Central takes the precinct report from the mailbox.

Election Central processes the data on the precinct report.

Election Central goes back to waiting (loop back to step (b)).

This scheme can seem tricky at first, but it makes sense. The sender puts data into a storage container and then raises a flag to notify the receiver that information is available.

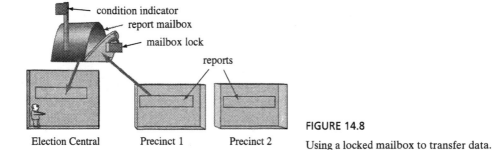

FIGURE 14.8

Using a locked mailbox to transfer data.

Figure 14.8 shows Election Central and two precincts. Each precinct delivers a report to the mailbox and then notifies Election Central. Election Central then consumes the report. The technical term for raising the flag is *signaling* the flag, and we say the receiver *waits* for the flag to be signaled. Operating these flags has nothing to do with regular Unix signals; only the word and basic idea are the same.

The figure also shows one more thing: a lock on the report mailbox. The mailbox has space for only one report, so it is crucial that only one person has access to the mailbox at any one time. The lock makes the procedure slightly more complicated, but completely reliable. The complete procedure, with locks, is as follows:

(a) Election Central sets up a vote report mailbox.

This mailbox has space for only one vote report at a time.

This mailbox has a flag that can be raised and then snaps right back.

This mailbox has a mutex that can be locked and unlocked.

(b) EC unlocks the box and waits until the flag is signaled.

(c) PH waits until it can lock the mailbox.

If the mailbox is not empty, PH unlocks the mailbox and waits until the flag is signaled before locking the mailbox again.

PH puts the precinct report in the mailbox.

(d) PH signals the flag on the mailbox.

PH releases the lock on mailbox.

(e) Election Central stops waiting because the flag was signaled.

EC locks the mailbox.

EC takes the precinct report from the mailbox.

EC processes the data on the precinct report.

EC signals the flag in case a PH is waiting.

EC returns to Step (b).

14.5.2   Programming with Condition Variables

We now translate the vote-counting system into a word-counting program. The vote-counting system used three items: a storage container, a flag, and a lock. These items correspond to three items in the world of threads programming: a variable, a condition object, and a mutex. Figure 14.9 shows the three threads and the three variables. One variable will hold a pointer to a word count, one variable will hold a condition object, and one variable will hold a mutex.

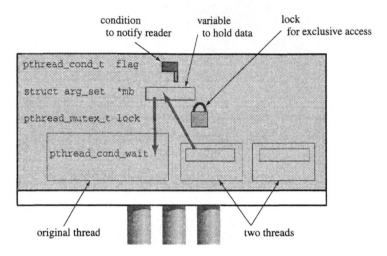

FIGURE 14.9

Using a locked variable to transfer data.

Now for the logic of the program. The original thread launches the two counting threads and then waits for results to come in. In particular, the original thread calls pthread_cond_wait to wait for the flag to be signaled. This call blocks the original thread.

When a counting thread finishes counting, that thread is ready to deliver the result by storing a pointer in the mailbox global variable. First, the thread has to acquire a lock for the mailbox. Then the thread checks the mailbox. If the mailbox is not empty, the thread unlocks the mailbox and waits for the flag to be signaled before locking the mailbox again. Then, the thread delivers the result to the mailbox. Finally, the counting thread signals the condition variable flag by calling pthread_cond_signal.

Signaling this flag wakes up the original thread, which was blocked on that flag by calling pthread_cond_wait. The newly awakened original thread rushes to open the mailbox. It tries to obtain a lock for that mailbox, but the lock is still held by the counting thread.

When the counting thread releases the lock with pthread_mutex_unlock, the original thread gets the lock. Now that it holds the lock, the original thread takes the report out of the mailbox, reports the result to the screen, adds the number to its total, signals the flag in case a counting thread is waiting, and then loops back to call pthread_cond_wait, which atomically unlocks the mutex and blocks the thread until the flag is signaled again.

The steps described in the preceding paragraphs correspond exactly to those described in the vote-reporting system, and they also correspond to the instructions in the code for twordcount4.c:

```
/* twordcount4.c - threaded word counter for two files.
 *              - Version 4: condition variable allows counter
 *                          functions to report results early
 */

#include  <stdio.h>
#include  <pthread.h>
#include  <ctype.h>

struct arg_set {                /* two values in one arg*/
                char *fname;    /* file to examine    */
                int  count;     /* number of words    */
};

struct arg_set  *mailbox;
pthread_mutex_t lock = PTHREAD_MUTEX_INITIALIZER;
pthread_cond_t  flag = PTHREAD_COND_INITIALIZER;

main(int ac, char *av[])
{
        pthread_t      t1, t2;             /* two threads */
        struct arg_set args1, args2;    /* two argsets */
        void           *count_words(void *);
        int            reports_in = 0;
        int            total_words = 0;

        if ( ac != 3 ){
                printf("usage: %s file1 file2\n", av[0]);
                exit(1);
        }
        pthread_mutex_lock(&lock);      /* lock the report box now */

        args1.fname = av[1];
        args1.count = 0;
        pthread_create(&t1, NULL, count_words, (void *) &args1);

        args2.fname = av[2];
        args2.count = 0;
        pthread_create(&t2, NULL, count_words, (void *) &args2);

        while( reports_in < 2 ){
                printf("MAIN: waiting for flag to go up\n");
                pthread_cond_wait(&flag, &lock); /* wait for notify */
                printf("MAIN: Wow! flag was raised, I have the lock\n");
                printf("%7d: %s\n", mailbox->count, mailbox->fname);
                total_words += mailbox->count;
                if ( mailbox == &args1)
                        pthread_join(t1,NULL);
                if ( mailbox == &args2)
                        pthread_join(t2,NULL);
                mailbox = NULL;
                pthread_cond_signal(&flag);
                reports_in++;
        }
```

```
                printf("%7d: total words\n", total_words);
        }
        void *count_words(void *a)
        {
                struct arg_set *args = a;      /* cast arg back to correct type */
                FILE *fp;
                int  c, prevc = '\0';

                if ( (fp = fopen(args->fname, "r")) != NULL ){
                        while( ( c = getc(fp)) != EOF ){
                                if ( !isalnum(c) && isalnum(prevc) )
                                        args->count++;
                                prevc = c;
                        }
                        fclose(fp);
                } else
                        perror(args->fname);
                printf("COUNT: waiting to get lock\n");
                pthread_mutex_lock(&lock);       /* get the mailbox */
                printf("COUNT: have lock, storing data\n");
                if ( mailbox != NULL )
                    pthread_cond_wait (&flag, &lock);
                mailbox = args;                  /* put ptr to our args there */
                printf("COUNT: raising flag\n");
                pthread_cond_signal(&flag);      /* raise the flag */
                printf("COUNT: unlocking box\n");
                pthread_mutex_unlock(&lock);     /* release the mailbox */
                return NULL;
        }
```

A sample run shows the flow of events:

```
$ cc twordcount4.c -lpthread -o twc4
$ ./twc4 /etc/group /usr/dict/words
COUNT: waiting to get lock
MAIN: waiting for flag to go up
COUNT: have lock, storing data
COUNT: raising flag
COUNT: unlocking box
MAIN: Wow! flag was raised, I have the lock
    195: /etc/group
MAIN: waiting for flag to go up
COUNT: waiting to get lock
COUNT: have lock, storing data
COUNT: raising flag
COUNT: unlocking box
MAIN: Wow! flag was raised, I have the lock
  45419: /usr/dict/words
  45614: total words
```

The printed page does not capture the excitement of election night, but the first report came in quickly, and a perceptible delay preceded the second report.

14.5.3 Functions for Condition Variables

The flag on the mailbox used by one thread to notify another thread is a *condition variable*. Threads use the following calls to communicate through condition variables:

pthread_cond_wait	
PURPOSE	Blocks a thread on a condition variable
INCLUDE	#include <pthread.h>
USAGE	int pthread_cond_wait(pthread_cond_t *cond, pthread_mutex_t *mutex);
ARGS	cond pointer to a condition variable mutex pointer to a mutex
RETURNS	0 if successful errcode if not successful

pthread_cond_wait causes the calling thread to block until another thread signals the condition variable *cond*. pthread_cond_wait is always used with a mutex. pthread_cond_wait atomically releases the specified mutex and then waits on the condition. Results are undefined if you do not lock the mutex before calling this function. Before returning to the calling thread, pthread_cond_wait automatically relocks the specified mutex.

pthread_cond_signal	
PURPOSE	Unblocks a thread waiting on a condition variable
INCLUDE	#include <pthread.h>
USAGE	int pthread_cond_signal(pthread_cond_t *cond);
ARGS	cond pointer to a condition variable
RETURNS	0 if successful errcode if not successful

pthread_cond_signal signals the condition variable *cond*, thereby unblocking one thread waiting on that condition variable. If no threads are waiting on the variable, nothing happens. If several threads are waiting, only one will be unblocked.

14.5.4 Back to the Web

We have now seen the basic ideas and skills for POSIX threads. We know how to create threads, how to wait for threads to finish, how threads can share data safely, and how threads can notify other threads of events. We know enough to use threads for a Web server and for complicated animation.

14.6   A THREADED WEB SERVER

We wrote a Web server in an earlier chapter. That server used `fork` to create new processes to handle client requests. Web servers perform three operations: send back directory listings, send back contents of files, and send back output of CGI programs.

A server needs a new process to run a CGI program, but a server does not need a new process to list a directory or to read a file.

14.6.1 Changes to Our Web Server

We modify the original Web server in a few ways. Most importantly, we replace calls to `fork` with calls to `pthread_create`. Client requests are no longer handled in separate processes; instead they are handled in separate threads.

We make two other changes. First, we remove the CGI feature. We can add it back later. Second, we write an internal version of the function to list directories. The original version used `exec` to run the standard `ls` command.

14.6.2 Threads Allow a New Feature

Using threads instead of processes lets us add a new feature to the server: internal statistics. People who run servers always like to know how long the server has been running, the number of requests received, and the volume of data sent out to the world.

The requests all share the same memory space, so we can use shared variables to keep these statistics. How can a user access these statistics? We add a special URL to the server: `status`. When a remote user requests that URL, the server sends back its internal statistics.

14.6.3 Preventing Zombie Threads: Detached Threads

We now consider one more technical detail. All the programs thus far in this chapter called `pthread_join` for each thread. Threads use system resources. If we did not call `pthread_join`, those resources would not be reclaimed, similar to calling `malloc` without calling `free`.

In the word-count program, the original thread has to wait for the counting threads so it can collect totals. The Web server has no reason to wait for the threads that handle requests. Those threads do not return any useful information.

We can create threads that do not have to be joined. These *detached threads* deallocate their resources automatically when the function finishes, and they do not even allow other threads to join them. To create a detached thread, we pass a special attribute value to `pthread_create`:

```
                /* creating a detached thread */

                pthread_t       t;
                pthread_attr_t attr_detached;

                pthread_attr_init(&attr_detached);
                pthread_attr_setdetached(&attr_detached, PTHREAD_CREATE_DETACHED);

                pthread_create(&t, &attr_detached, func, arg);
```

14.6.4 The Code

The complete code for a multithreaded Web server is as follows:

```
/* twebserv.c - a threaded minimal web server (version 0.2)
 *      usage: tws portnumber
 * features: supports the GET command only
 *           runs in the current directory
 *           creates a thread to handle each request
 *           supports a special status URL to report internal state
 * building: cc twebserv.c socklib.c -lpthread -o twebserv
 */

#include <stdio.h>
#include <sys/types.h>
#include <sys/stat.h>
#include <string.h>

#include <pthread.h>
#include <stdlib.h>
#include <unistd.h>

#include <dirent.h>
#include <time.h>

/* server facts here */

time_t   server_started ;
int      server_bytes_sent;
int      server_requests;

main(int ac, char *av[])
{
        int             sock, fd;
        int             *fdptr;
        pthread_t       worker;
        pthread_attr_t  attr;

        void *handle_call(void *);

        if ( ac == 1 ){
                fprintf(stderr,"usage: tws portnum\n");
                exit(1);
        }
        sock = make_server_socket( atoi(av[1]) );
```

```
            if ( sock == -1 ) { perror("making socket"); exit(2); }

            setup(&attr);

            /* main loop here: take call, handle call in new thread  */

            while(1){
                    fd = accept( sock, NULL, NULL );
                    server_requests++;

                    fdptr = malloc(sizeof(int));
                    *fdptr = fd;
                    pthread_create(&worker,&attr,handle_call,fdptr);
            }
}

/*
 * initialize the status variables and
 * set the thread attribute to detached
 */
setup(pthread_attr_t *attrp)
{
        pthread_attr_init(attrp);
        pthread_attr_setdetachstate(attrp,PTHREAD_CREATE_DETACHED);

        time(&server_started);
        server_requests = 0;
        server_bytes_sent = 0;
}

void *handle_call(void *fdptr)
{
        FILE    *fpin;
        char    request[BUFSIZ];
        int     fd ;

        fd = *(int *)fdptr;
        free(fdptr);                            /* get fd from arg  */

        fpin = fdopen(fd, "r");                 /* buffer input */
        fgets(request,BUFSIZ,fpin);             /* read client request */
        printf("got a call on %d: request = %s", fd, request);
        skip_rest_of_header(fpin);

        process_rq(request, fd);                /* process client rq */

        fclose(fpin);
}

/* ------------------------------------------------------- *
   skip_rest_of_header(FILE *)
   skip over all request info until a CRNL is seen
   ------------------------------------------------------- */
skip_rest_of_header(FILE *fp)
{
        char    buf[BUFSIZ];
```

```
                while( fgets(buf,BUFSIZ,fp) != NULL && strcmp(buf,"\r\n") != 0 )
                        ;
}
/* ------------------------------------------------------ *
   process_rq( char *rq, int fd )
   do what the request asks for and write reply to fd
   handles request in a new process
   rq is HTTP command:  GET /foo/bar.html HTTP/1.0
   ------------------------------------------------------ */
process_rq( char *rq, int fd)
{
        char    cmd[BUFSIZ], arg[BUFSIZ];

        if ( sscanf(rq, "%s%s", cmd, arg) != 2 )
                return;
        sanitize(arg);
        printf("sanitized version is %s\n", arg);

        if ( strcmp(cmd,"GET") != 0 )
                not_implemented();
        else if ( built_in(arg, fd) )
                ;
        else if ( not_exist( arg ) )
                do_404(arg, fd);
        else if ( isadir( arg ) )
                do_ls( arg, fd );
        else
                do_cat( arg, fd );
}
/*
 * make sure all paths are below the current directory
 */
sanitize(char *str)
{
        char    *src, *dest;

        src = dest = str;

        while( *src ){
                if( strncmp(src,"/../",4) == 0 )
                        src += 3;
                else if ( strncmp(src,"//",2) == 0 )
                        src++;
                else
                        *dest++ = *src++;
        }
        *dest = '\0';
        if ( *str == '/' )
                strcpy(str,str+1);
        if ( str[0]=='\0' || strcmp(str,"./")==0 || strcmp(str,"./..")==0 )
                strcpy(str,".");
```

```
        }

        /* handle built-in URLs here.  Only one so far is "status" */
        built_in(char *arg, int fd)
        {
                FILE    *fp;

                if ( strcmp(arg,"status") != 0 )
                        return 0;
                http_reply(fd, &fp, 200, "OK", "text/plain",NULL);

                fprintf(fp,"Server started: %s", ctime(&server_started));
                fprintf(fp,"Total requests: %d\n", server_requests);
                fprintf(fp,"Bytes sent out: %d\n", server_bytes_sent);
                fclose(fp);
                return 1;
        }

        http_reply(int fd, FILE **fpp, int code, char *msg, char *type, char *content)
        {
                FILE    *fp = fdopen(fd, "w");
                int     bytes = 0;

                if ( fp != NULL ){
                        bytes = fprintf(fp,"HTTP/1.0 %d %s\r\n", code, msg);
                        bytes += fprintf(fp,"Content-type: %s\r\n\r\n", type);
                        if ( content )
                                bytes += fprintf(fp,"%s\r\n", content);
                }
                fflush(fp);
                if ( fpp )
                        *fpp = fp;
                else
                        fclose(fp);
                return bytes;
        }

        /* ------------------------------------------------------------ *
           simple functions first:
                not_implemented(fd)        unimplemented HTTP command
                and do_404(item,fd)        no such object
           ------------------------------------------------------------ */
        not_implemented(int fd)
        {
                http_reply(fd,NULL,501,"Not Implemented","text/plain",
                                "That command is not implemented");
        }

        do_404(char *item, int fd)
        {
                http_reply(fd,NULL,404,"Not Found","text/plain",
                                "The item you seek is not here");
```

```
}
/* --------------------------------------------------------- *
   the directory listing section
   isadir() uses stat, not_exist() uses stat
   --------------------------------------------------------- */
isadir(char *f)
{
        struct stat info;
        return ( stat(f, &info) != -1 && S_ISDIR(info.st_mode) );
}

not_exist(char *f)
{
        struct stat info;
        return( stat(f,&info) == -1 );
}

do_ls(char *dir, int fd)
{
        DIR            *dirptr;
        struct dirent *direntp;
        FILE           *fp;
        int            bytes = 0;

        bytes = http_reply(fd,&fp,200,"OK","text/plain",NULL);
        bytes += fprintf(fp,"Listing of Directory %s\n", dir);

        if ( (dirptr = opendir(dir)) != NULL ){
                while( direntp = readdir(dirptr) ){
                        bytes += fprintf(fp, "%s\n", direntp->d_name);
                }
                closedir(dirptr);
        }
        fclose(fp);
        server_bytes_sent += bytes;
}
/* --------------------------------------------------------- *
   functions to cat files here.
   file_type(filename) returns the 'extension': cat uses it
   --------------------------------------------------------- */
char * file_type(char *f)
{
        char    *cp;
        if ( (cp = strrchr(f, '.' )) != NULL )
                return cp+1;
        return "";
}

/* do_cat(filename,fd): sends header then the contents */
do_cat(char *f, int fd)
```

```
{
        char    *extension = file_type(f);
        char    *type = "text/plain";
        FILE    *fpsock, *fpfile;
        int     c;

        int     bytes = 0;

        if ( strcmp(extension,"html") == 0 )
                type = "text/html";
        else if ( strcmp(extension, "gif") == 0 )
                type = "image/gif";
        else if ( strcmp(extension, "jpg") == 0 )
                type = "image/jpeg";
        else if ( strcmp(extension, "jpeg") == 0 )
                type = "image/jpeg";

        fpsock = fdopen(fd, "w");
        fpfile = fopen( f , "r");
        if ( fpsock != NULL && fpfile != NULL )
        {
                bytes = http_reply(fd,&fpsock,200,"OK",type,NULL);
                while( (c = getc(fpfile) ) != EOF ){
                        putc(c, fpsock);
                        bytes++;
                }
                fclose(fpfile);
                fclose(fpsock);
        }
        server_bytes_sent += bytes;
}
```

Note that the program works, but has one problem: The statistics feature uses shared variables, and those shared variables are not protected with locks. Adding the mutex locks is left as an exercise.

14.7 THREADS AND ANIMATION

A Web server does not need threads; it can use fork to handle concurrent requests. A Web browser, on the other hand, can not easily animate multiple images and advertisements without threads. Our next use of threads is to control animation.

In the video-game chapter, we used an interval timer to control animation. The timer sent SIGALRM at regular intervals, and the signal handler used counters to decide when to move the image.

14.7.1 Advantages of Threads

The signal-handler and interval-timer technique works, but threads provide a better match between external and internal structure. Externally, users see two independent flows of activity: animation and keyboard control. (See Figure 14.10.)

Animation settings are used by the animation thread.

Animation settings are modified by the keyboard handling thread.

FIGURE 14.10

An animated image and keyboard controls.

Internally, threads let us separate the animation code from the keyboard-input code. The threads share the variables that define the position and velocity of the animation, as shown in Figure 14.11.

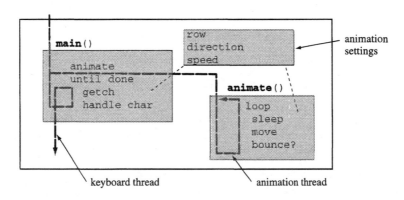

FIGURE 14.11

An animation thread and keyboard thread.

Hidden somewhere, of course, an interval timer controls the animation, but a threaded solution lets us focus on program components.

Threads offer a second advantage over signal handlers and timers. Modern threads libraries may run different threads on separate processor chips, providing true simultaneous execution. For animations that require computing complicated trajectories, rotations, or texture mapping, running each thread on its own processor produces faster, smoother action.

14.7.2   Threaded **bounce1d.c**

Compare the original version of bounce1d.c with this new, two-thread version, tbounce1d.c:

```
/* tbounce1d.c: controlled animation using two threads
 *      note    one thread handles animation
 *              other thread handles keyboard input
 *      compile cc tbounce1d.c -lcurses -lpthread -o tbounce1d
 */

#include        <stdio.h>
#include        <curses.h>
#include        <pthread.h>
#include        <stdlib.h>
#include        <unistd.h>

/* shared variables both threads use. These need a mutex. */

#define MESSAGE " hello "

int     row;    /* current row          */
int     col;    /* current column       */
int     dir;    /* where we are going   */
int     delay;  /* delay between moves   */

main()
{
        int     ndelay;         /* new delay            */
        int     c;              /* user input           */
        pthread_t msg_thread;   /* a thread             */
        void    *moving_msg();

        initscr();              /* init curses and tty  */
        crmode();
        noecho();
        clear();

        row   = 10;             /* start here           */
        col   = 0;
        dir   = 1;              /* add 1 to row number  */
        delay = 200;            /* 200ms = 0.2 seconds  */

        if ( pthread_create(&msg_thread,NULL,moving_msg,MESSAGE) ){
                fprintf(stderr,"error creating thread");
                endwin();
                exit(0);
        }

        while(1) {
                ndelay = 0;
                c = getch();
                if ( c == 'Q' ) break;
                if ( c == ' ' ) dir = -dir;
                if ( c == 'f' && delay > 2 ) ndelay = delay/2;
                if ( c == 's' ) ndelay = delay * 2 ;
                if ( ndelay > 0 )
                        delay = ndelay ;
```

```
          }
          pthread_cancel(msg_thread);
          endwin();
  }

  void *moving_msg(char *msg)
  {
          while( 1 ) {
                  usleep(delay*1000);    /* sleep a while      */
                  move( row, col );      /* set cursor position */
                  addstr( msg );         /* redo message       */
                  refresh();             /* and show it        */

                  /* move to next column and check for bouncing  */

                  col += dir;            /* move to new column  */

                  if ( col <= 0 && dir == -1 )
                          dir = 1;
                  else if (  col+strlen(msg) >= COLS && dir == 1 )
                          dir = -1;
          }
  }
```

How does this new version differ from the original, signal-driven model? The main difference is that the main function creates a new thread to execute the moving_msg function. That moving_msg function executes a simple loop: sleep, move, check for bounce, repeat. Meanwhile, in another part of the same process, main executes a simple loop: getch, process, repeat.

This revised program still uses global variables for the state of the ball. We had to use global variables in the interrupt-based version because we can not pass arguments to a signal handler. Threads, on the other hand, can accept arguments. We can improve this program by creating a struct of settings as we did in versions 3 and 4 of the threaded word-count program.

14.7.3 Multiple Animations: `tanimate.c`

How can we animate several messages at once? The multithreaded word-count program ran concurrent instances of the word-counting function, each with its own filename and counter. We use the same principle to run several concurrent animations.

This threaded animation program, tanimate.c, is an extension of tbounce1.c. tanimate.c accepts up to ten command-line strings and animates each of its arguments on a separate line, each with its own direction and speed. Sort of like a Web page. For example, the command

tanimate 'Buy this' 'Drive this car' 'Spend Money here' Consume 'Buy!'

produces a screen containing multiple bouncing, animated messages, as shown in Figure 14.12.

FIGURE 14.12

Multiple bouncing messages.

A user may bounce any of the messages by pressing the digits "0", "1", . . .
You can animate any list of strings, even those from other Unix tools. Try these:

tanimate `ls`
tanimate `users`
tanimate `date`

tanimate runs an animation function in several threads. Each instance of the function
is passed a different set of arguments. The arguments specify the message, row, direction, and speed:

```
/* tanimate.c: animate several strings using threads, curses, usleep()
 *
 *      bigidea one thread for each animated string
 *              one thread for keyboard control
 *              shared variables for communication
 *      compile cc tanimate.c -lcurses -lpthread -o tanimate
 *      to do   needs locks for shared variables
 *              nice to put screen handling in its own thread
 */
#include         <stdio.h>
#include         <curses.h>
#include         <pthread.h>
#include         <stdlib.h>
#include         <unistd.h>

#define MAXMSG   10              /* limit to number of strings   */
#define TUNIT    20000           /* timeunits in microseconds */

struct   propset {
                 char    *str;   /* the message */
                 int     row;    /* the row      */
                 int     delay;  /* delay in time units */
                 int     dir;    /* +1 or -1      */
         };

pthread_mutex_t mx = PTHREAD_MUTEX_INITIALIZER;

int main(int ac, char *av[])
{
```

```
        int         c;              /* user input          */
        pthread_t   thrds[MAXMSG];  /* the threads         */
        struct propset props[MAXMSG]; /* properties of string */
        void        *animate();     /* the function        */
        int         num_msg ;       /* number of strings   */
        int         i;

        if ( ac == 1 ){
                printf("usage: tanimate string ..\n");
                exit(1);
        }

        num_msg = setup(ac-1,av+1,props);

        /* create all the threads */
        for(i=0 ; i<num_msg; i++)
              if ( pthread_create(&thrds[i], NULL, animate, &props[i])){
                        fprintf(stderr,"error creating thread");
                        endwin();
                        exit(0);
              }
        /* process user input */
        while(1) {
                c = getch();
                if ( c == 'Q' ) break;
                if ( c == ' ' )
                        for(i=0;i<num_msg;i++)
                                props[i].dir = -props[i].dir;
                if ( c >= '0' && c <= '9' ){
                        i = c - '0';
                        if ( i < num_msg )
                                props[i].dir = -props[i].dir;
                }
        }

        /* cancel all the threads */
        pthread_mutex_lock(&mx);
        for (i=0; i<num_msg; i++ )
                pthread_cancel(thrds[i]);
        endwin();
        return 0;
}

int setup(int nstrings, char *strings[], struct propset props[])
{
        int num_msg = ( nstrings > MAXMSG ? MAXMSG : nstrings );
        int i;

        /* assign rows and velocities to each string */
        srand(getpid());
        for(i=0 ; i<num_msg; i++){
                props[i].str = strings[i];      /* the message  */
                props[i].row = i;               /* the row      */
```

```
                props[i].delay = 1+(rand()%15); /* a speed      */
                props[i].dir = ((rand()%2)?1:-1);      /* +1 or -1     */
        }

        /* set up curses */
        initscr();
        crmode();
        noecho();
        clear();
        mvprintw(LINES-1,0,"'Q' to quit, '0'..'%d' to bounce",num_msg-1);

        return num_msg;
}

/* the code that runs in each thread */
void *animate(void *arg)
{
        struct propset *info = arg;             /* point to info block */
        int     len = strlen(info->str)+2;      /* +2 for padding      */
        int     col = rand()%(COLS-len-3);      /* space for padding   */

        while( 1 )
        {
                usleep(info->delay*TUNIT);

                pthread_mutex_lock(&mx);        /* only one thread     */
                    move( info->row, col );     /* can call curses     */
                    addch(' ');                 /* at a the same time  */
                    addstr( info->str );        /* Since I doubt it is */
                    addch(' ');                 /* reentrant           */
                    move(LINES-1,COLS-1);       /* park cursor         */
                    refresh();                  /* and show it         */
                pthread_mutex_unlock(&mx);      /* done with curses    */

                /* move item to next column and check for bouncing    */

                col += info->dir;

                if ( col <= 0 && info->dir == -1 )
                        info->dir = 1;
                else if (  col+len >= COLS && info->dir == 1 )
                        info->dir = -1;
        }
}
```

14.7.4 Mutexes and `tanimate.c`

Compile and try tanimate.c. The code has three major sections: an initialization, a
function to animate a message, and a loop to read and process user input. The user-
input loop runs in the original thread; the animate function runs in several threads.
tanimate can have as many as eleven threads running at once. Running eleven threads
in parallel demands cooperation. What are the shared resources, and how do we prevent
interference?

Data Interference: Dynamic Initialization of a Mutex The animation function uses and modifies values in a struct that represent the position, speed, and direction of motion. When the user bounces a message, the user-input thread changes the `dir` member of the struct. A shared, changing variable needs a mutex to prevent data corruption. Do we add one mutex for all the direction variables, or do we create a mutex for each `dir` variable?

The better choice is to create a mutex in each struct. The animation thread and the user-input thread use that mutex when they read or modify shared data in the struct. The revised struct now looks like the following:

```
struct  propset {
                char    *str;    /* the message */
                int     row;     /* the row      */
                int     delay;   /* delay in time units */
                int     dir;     /* +1 or -1      */
          pthread_mutex_t lock;   /* a mutex for dir */
        };
```

The initialization in `setup` now looks like this:

```
for(i=0 ; i<num_msg; i++){
          props[i].str = strings[i];       /* the message  */
          props[i].row = i;                 /* the row       */
          props[i].delay = 1+(rand()%15); /* a speed       */
          props[i].dir = ((rand()%2)?1:-1);        /* +1 or -1    */

        pthread_mutex_init(&props[i].lock,NULL);
    }
```

The other changes to the code are left as exercises.

Screen Interference: Critical Sections Direction variables are not the only shared resources. The screen and the curses functions that modify the screen are shared by all the animation threads. We use a mutex `mx` to prevent simultaneous access to curses functions.

To see why this lock is needed, consider the screen-control calls in `animate`: `move`, `addch`, `addstr` .. `refresh`. What would happen if two threads executed that sequence concurrently? For example, what if the two threads called curses in alternation: `move`, `move`, `addch`, `addch`, `addstr`, `addstr`...

The first thread would move the cursor to one screen location, and the second thread would move the cursor somewhere else. Then the first thread would add some text, thinking the cursor was where it asked curses to put it, but that text would actually go where the second thread put it.

The curses library does not know about threads. Use of these functions must not be interrupted by another thread; these functions are not reentrant. To make sure only one thread uses the curses functions at a time, we use a mutex.

The curses library contains internal data structures. In the same way we use a mutex to prevent corruption of our own data structures, we use a mutex to prevent corruption of data structures managed by system libraries.

14.7.5 A Thread for Curses

A mutex is not the only way to protect curses from data corruption. A different method is to create a new thread to handle all the calls to screen-control functions. (See Figure 14.13.)

You can think of this screen-control thread like the public relations department in a large business. Any department that wants to send information to the media sends a request to the public relations department. The people there take care of getting the message out.

A screen-control thread works like the PR department; any thread that wants a message displayed on the screen sends a request to the SMT (screen-management thread).

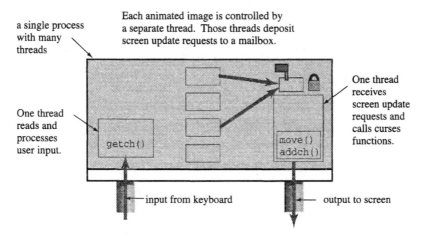

FIGURE 14.13

A separate thread speaks to curses.

The threads send requests to put text on the screen, so each request can be a struct containing a row, a column, and a string. The animation threads deliver these messages, and the screen-management thread receives and acts on the messages.

This system with several producers of requests and one consumer is similar to the design of the threaded word-count program. We need a storage variable to hold the messages, a mutex to prevent corruption of that storage, and a condition variable to signal the SMT when an animation thread drops off a message.

Centralizing and abstracting screen management makes the program more flexible. To replace curses with a different display system, we change only the functions used by the SMT. The SMT could even speak to a remote graphics server through a pipe or socket without the animation threads knowing the difference. This project is left as an exercise.

SUMMARY

MAIN IDEAS

- A thread of execution is the flow of control through a program. The pthreads library allows a program to run several functions at the same time.
- Functions running at the same time have their own local variables but share all global variables and dynamically allocated data.
- When threads share a variable, they need to make sure they do not get in each other's way. Threads may use a mutex lock to make sure only one thread is using a shared variable at a time.
- When threads need to coordinate or synchronize their action, they may use a condition variable. One thread waits for the condition variable to change in a specific way, and the other thread signals the variable to change.
- Threads need to use a mutex lock to prevent simultaneous access to functions that operate on shared resources. Functions that are not reentrant must be protected this way.

WHAT NEXT?

A program can be built from several processes that communicate and cooperate through pipes, files, sockets, and signals. A program can also be built from several threads that communicate and cooperate through shared variables, files, locks and signals. In the last chapter, we focus on interprocess communication. How many methods does Unix provide, and how can one decide which method is the best choice for an application?

EXPLORATIONS

14.1 Experiment with basic operations on threads by making some changes to `hello_multi.c`. First, add another message or two to see how easy it is to add new threads of execution to a program.

Then, change `print_msg` so the number of repetitions is equal to the length of the string it prints. Print a message after each call to `pthread_join` to see what is going on. Explain the results.

14.2 *piping to* `tanimate` It might be amusing to allow `tanimate` to read its list of strings from standard input, one line per string, so that a command like

```
who | tanimate
```

would work. Adding this feature is not trivial. Explain why not. To add this feature, you need to read the lines from standard input and then redirect standard input to the terminal so that curses can read characters in noncanonical mode. Hint: Open `/dev/tty` and `dup` it to standard input.

14.3 In the video-game chapter, we looked at using signal masks to prevent interruptions during critical sections of code. Compare signal masks and signal handlers to threads and mutex locks and condition variables.

PROGRAMMING EXERCISES

14.4   *Threads creating threads* In `hello_multi.c`, the original thread creates the two printing threads. Write a new version in which the thread that prints "hello" starts a thread to print "world\n". Which thread waits for the "world\n" thread to rejoin it? Why?

14.5   `twordcount1.c` uses three threads: the original thread and the two threads to count the words, but the original thread does not do much work. Write a version of the program in which the original thread counts the words in the first file and creates a second thread to count the number of words in the second file. Is this any faster? Is it a better design?

14.6   *Error handling* The `count_words` function reports an error if it cannot open the named file. The other thread, though, continues to run. Is this a good idea? Modify the program so `count_words` calls `exit` if it cannot open the file.

14.7   *Scaling to more files* How can you extend the methods presented in `twordcount2.c` and `twordcount3.c` so that the programs can accept many files on the command line? Modify both programs so they accept an arbitrary number of command-line filenames. Which version is easier to extend so that it can handle more files? Which one is more efficient?

14.8   *Processes vs. threads*

   (a)   Write a version of the word-count program that uses `fork` to create a new process for each file. You need to devise a system for the child processes to send their results back to the parent for tabulation. Do not use the exit value, as that number cannot exceed 255. One advantage of using `fork` is that you can run the regular `wc -w` command to count words in the file.

   (b)   Write a version of the word-count program that is single threaded.

   (c)   Compare these three versions (processes, multithreads, one thread) on the bases of ease of design, ease of coding, speed of execution, and portability. Any surprises?

14.9   *Handling several files* Expand `twordcount4.c` to handle more than two files on the command line.

14.10   `twordcount4.c` has global variables. Remove the global variables by making them local to `main` and passing pointers to them as members of the struct used to hold the arguments for the threads.

14.11   Add mutex locks to `twebserv.c` to protect the statistics variables.

14.12   Remove all global variables from `tbounce1d.c` by defining a struct that contains all the properties of a bouncing message.

14.13   The shared state variables in `tbounce1d.c` need a mutex. What race conditions can occur in this program, and what are the effects on the program when the two threads interfere?

14.14   The single-string animation program included speed control. The user could press "s" and "f" to increase and decrease the delay between moves. Add speed control to the multimessage version.

14.15   All the messages in `tanimate.c` move horizontally. Change the program so that some strings move up and down and some strings move left and right. How do you handle collisions?

14.16   Modify `tanimate` to use a separate thread for screen management. The threads that represent the messages have to send messages to the screen thread. Devise a system for interthread communication.

14.17   *MT finger server* Write a multithreaded server for the finger service. The server accepts one line of input. It then looks up that string in the database of users and sends back information about records matching that string. The server should include the following features:

(a) Loads entire user database into memory.

(b) Starts a new, detached thread for each request.

(c) The server records the number of *hits* per record.

(d) The special request STATUS returns statistics.

(e) The server refreshes its internal database if it receives SIGHUP.

14.18 *A curses server* The end of the tanimate section included a discussion of separating the display functions from the timing and data-handling logic. Write a client/server version of tanimate that uses datagram sockets to send simple requests from the tanimate program to a general-purpose curses server.

The curses server supports a simple protocol consisting of two commands:

```
CLEAR                      clears the display
DRAW R C Any string        puts "Any string" at row R, column C
```

The revised version of tanimate no longer calls curses functions. Instead, it sends messages to the curses server. The curses server receives these messages and draws the strings.

When you get this working, explore the ideas and design of the X11 window system Unix uses.

C H A P T E R   1 5

IPC Roundup
Can We Talk?

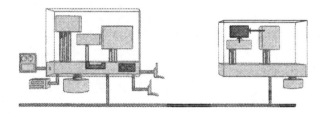

OBJECTIVES

Ideas and Skills

- Blocking on input from several sources: `select` and `poll`
- Named pipes
- Shared memory
- File locks
- Semaphores
- IPC overview

System Calls and Functions

- `select`, `poll`
- `mkfifo`
- `shmget`, `shmat`, `shmctl`, `shmdt`
- `semget`, `semctl`, `semop`

Commands

- `talk`
- `lpr`

15.1   PROGRAMMING CHOICES

Long ago, when two people wanted to communicate, their choices were few: talk or throw rocks. Modern people have more choices: cell phone, e-mail, regular mail, overnight express, bicycle courier, voice mail, pager, sticky note on monitor, talk in person, or throw rocks. Each method has strengths and weaknesses. How does one choose? Why are there so many?

Unix programmers also must choose among several types of interprocess communication. Each method has advantages and disadvantages. How do you choose?

We begin by studying talk, a Unix command people use to type to each other. We then compare and discuss various other Unix methods for getting information from one process to another process.

15.2 THE talk COMMAND: READING FROM MULTIPLE INPUTS

The Unix talk command is a form of interperson communication; talk lets people type back and forth between two terminals. talk even works over the Internet to connect terminals on different computers. (See Figure 15.1.)

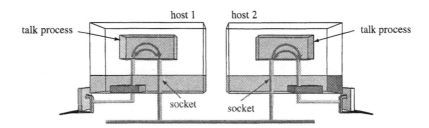

FIGURE 15.1

talk connects terminals over the net.

talk divides the screen into a top region and a bottom region and operates in character-by-character terminal mode. As users type, the characters appear in both screens simultaneously. Characters you type appear in the top half of the screen, and characters the other person types appear in the bottom half. talk uses sockets, as shown in Figure 15.2.

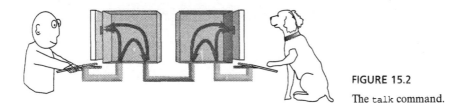

FIGURE 15.2

The talk command.

The talk program reads in characters and writes them to their destinations, but unlike other programs we studied, talk waits for input from two file descriptors at once.

15.2.1 Reading from Two File Descriptors at Once

talk receives data from the keyboard and from the socket. Characters from the keyboard are copied to the top half of the screen and sent out through the socket. Characters read from the socket are added to the bottom half of the screen.

talk users may type at any speed and in any order. talk must be prepared to read a character from either source at any time. Other programs rely on clear protocols. A server waits for a request with `read` or `recvfrom` and then sends a reply with `write` or `sendto`, but people do not always take turns when they talk. What can `talk` do? `talk` certainly cannot do this:

```
while( 1 ){
        read(fd_kbd, &c, 1);      /* read from keyboard      */
        waddch(topwin, c);        /* add to screen           */
        write(fd_sock, &c, 1);    /* send to other person    */
        read(fd_sock, &c, 1);     /* read from other person  */
        waddch(botwin, c);        /* add to screen           */
}
```

What would happen if the person on the other end of the line types a lot, but the person at the keyboard types nothing? The program blocks at the first `read` call and never picks up any data from the other person. The method coded above only works if the users take turns typing characters.

Why not make the file descriptors *nonblocking*? We could set the `O_NONBLOCK` flag on the file descriptors by calling `fcntl`. Using nonblocking mode causes calls to `read` to return immediately, returning zero when no character is available. A nonblocking method works, but uses too much processor time. Each `read` is a system call, and the program may execute kernel code to check for input hundreds or thousands of times before receiving a single character.

15.2.2 The `select` System Call

Unix provides the `select` system call designed precisely for programs that want to block on input from more than one file descriptor. The principle is simple:

(a) Make a list of file descriptors you want to watch.

(b) Pass that list to `select`.

(c) `select` blocks until data arrive at any of those descriptors.

(d) `select` sets bits in a variable to tell you which descriptors have input.

This program `selectdemo.c` waits for input to arrive on two devices:

```
/* selectdemo.c : watch for input on two devices AND timeout
 *          usage: selectdemo dev1 dev2 timeout
 *          action: reports on input from each file, and
 *                  reports timeouts
 */

#include <stdio.h>
#include <sys/time.h>
#include <sys/types.h>
#include <unistd.h>
#include <fcntl.h>

#define oops(m,x) { perror(m); exit(x); }

main(int ac, char *av[])
{
        int     fd1, fd2;          /* the fds to watch        */
        struct timeval timeout;    /* how long to wait        */
```

```
        fd_set  readfds;           /* watch these for input */
        int     maxfd;             /* max fd plus 1         */
        int     retval;            /* return from select    */

        if ( ac != 4 ){
                fprintf(stderr,"usage: %s file file timeout", *av);
                exit(1);
        }
        /** open files **/
        if ( (fd1 = open(av[1],O_RDONLY)) == -1 )
                oops(av[1], 2);
        if ( (fd2 = open(av[2],O_RDONLY)) == -1 )
                oops(av[2], 3);
        maxfd = 1 + (fd1>fd2?fd1:fd2);

        while(1) {
                /** make a list of file descriptors to watch **/
                FD_ZERO(&readfds);          /* clear all bits  */
                FD_SET(fd1, &readfds);       /* set bit for fd1 */
                FD_SET(fd2, &readfds);       /* set bit for fd2 */

                /** set timeout value **/
                timeout.tv_sec = atoi(av[3]);  /* set seconds */
                timeout.tv_usec = 0;           /* no useconds */

                /** wait for input **/
                retval = select(maxfd,&readfds,NULL,NULL,&timeout);
                if( retval == -1 )
                        oops("select",4);
                if ( retval > 0 ){
                        /** check bits for each fd **/
                        if ( FD_ISSET(fd1, &readfds) )
                                showdata(av[1], fd1);
                        if ( FD_ISSET(fd2, &readfds) )
                                showdata(av[2], fd2);
                }
                else
                    printf("no input after %d seconds\n", atoi(av[3]));
        }
}
showdata(char *fname, int fd)
{
        char buf[BUFSIZ];
        int  n;

        printf("%s: ", fname, n);
        fflush(stdout);
        n = read(fd, buf, BUFSIZ);
        if ( n == -1 )
                oops(fname,5);
        write(1, buf, n);
        write(1, "\n", 1);
}
```

The code follows the four steps we outlined. A list of file descriptors is stored as bits in a variable of type `fd_set`. Macros `FD_ZERO`, `FD_SET`, and `FD_ISSET` clear all bits, set one bit, and test one bit in an `fd_set`. We want to watch two data sources at once, so we call `FD_SET` for both descriptors.

select also accepts a timeout value. `select` returns if no data arrive during the specified time. In `selectdemo.c`, we accept a number of seconds as a command-line argument. I tested it with the following code:

```
$ cc selectdemo.c -o selectdemo
$ ./selectdemo /dev/tty /dev/mouse 10
hello
/dev/tty: hello

no input after 4 seconds
no input after 4 seconds
testing
/dev/tty: testing
I moved the mouse
/dev/mouse: (
/dev/mouse:
/dev/mouse: ÿ
```

This sample run shows how a program can wait until input arrives from the keyboard or from the mouse. A more interesting program would process, rather than print, the input.

Summary of select

select	
PURPOSE	Synchronous I/O Multiplexing
INCLUDE	`#include <sys/time.h>`

USAGE	`int = select( int numfds,`
	`              fd_set *read_set`
	`              fd_set *write_set`
	`              fd_set *error_set,`
	`              struct timeval *timeout);`
	`void FD_ZERO(fd_set *fdset)`
	`void FD_SET(int fd, fd_set *fdset)`
	`void FD_CLR(int fd, fd_set *fdset)`
	`void FD_ISSET(int fd, fd_set *fdset)`

ARGS	`numfds` maximum fd number to watch + 1 `read_set` wait for incoming data on these fds `write_set` wait until ok to write on these fds `error_set` wait until an exception on these fds `timeout` return after this time regardless
RETURNS	`-1` if error `0` on timeout `num` number of file descriptors meeting criteria

select watches several file descriptors at the same time and returns when something interesting happens on any of them. More precisely, select watches for events on three sets of file descriptors. select watches one set to see if any are ready to read, one set to see if any are ready to write, and one set to see if any exceptions occur. Each set of file descriptors is recorded in an array of bits. numfds is equal to one greater than the largest file descriptor to watch.

select returns when any of the conditions specified by its arguments is met or when the timeout value passes. select returns an integer value indicating the number of file descriptors that meet the conditions.

A null pointer for any argument tells select to ignore that condition.

15.2.3 `select` and `talk`

We shall not write talk in this chapter. Locating the other user and setting up the connection requires several steps. For example, locating the other user requires searching the utmp file. We have studied all the ideas and techniques required for all the other steps. What are those steps? What system calls do they require?

15.2.4 `select` vs. `poll`

If you do not like select, you can use poll instead. select was developed at Berkeley, and poll was developed at Bell Labs. Both perform a similar role. Most versions of Unix these days support both.

15.3 COMMUNICATION CHOICES

The talk command is a good example of a Unix systems program: a synthesis of cooperating, communicating processes. The two processes in talk read and write just as though the information were stored in regular disk files.

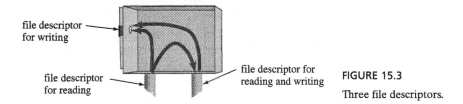

FIGURE 15.3

Three file descriptors.

File descriptors in talk are attached to keyboards, screens, and sockets (see Figure 15.3), but they could be connected to other processes or to other devices. Data transfer between the processes is as important a part of talk as the operations within the processes. Selecting a communication method is as important as selecting the right algorithm or data structure.

15.3.1 One Problem, Three Solutions

The Problem: Getting Data from Server to Client   How do you decide which communication method to use? Consider the time/date server we wrote using stream sockets. One process knows what time it is, and the other process wants to know the time. (See Figure 15.4.) How do we get the information from one process to the other?

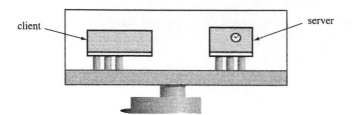

FIGURE 15.4

One process has information the other one wants.

Three Solutions: File, Pipe, Shared Memory   Figure 15.5 shows three methods: one method we know about and two new ones. The familiar method is a file, and the two new methods are a *named pipe* and a *shared memory segment*. Respectively, these methods transfer data through the disk, through the kernel, and through user space. What are the details, strengths, and weaknesses of each?

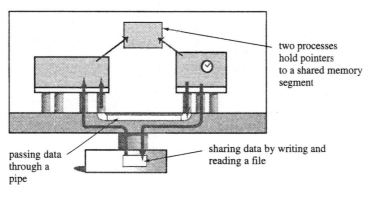

two processes hold pointers to a shared memory segment

passing data through a pipe

sharing data by writing and reading a file

FIGURE 15.5

Three ways to transfer data.

15.3.2 IPC with Files

Processes can communicate through files. One process writes to a file, other processes read from that file.

A Time/Date Server Using a File   We do not have to write C; a simple shell script works:

```
#!/bin/sh
# time server - file version

    while true ; do
        date > /tmp/current_date
        sleep 1
    done
```

The server writes the current date and time into a file every second. The output redirection operation, >, truncates and then rewrites the file.

A Time/Date Client Using a File The client reads the contents of the file:

```
#!/bin/sh
# time client - file version

  cat /tmp/current_date
```

Remarks on IPC with Files

Access: Clients must be able to read the file. Using standard file access permissions, we give the server write access and limit clients to read access.

Multiple Clients: Any number of clients may read data from the file at the same time. Unix does not limit the number of processes that may open a file at once.

Race Conditions: The server updates the file by truncating and then replacing the contents with the new date and time. If a client reads the file at the instant between the truncate and rewrite, the client will receive empty or partial results.

Avoiding Race Conditions: The server and clients could use some sort of mutex. We look at file-locking methods later. Alternatively, if the server uses `lseek` and `write` instead of `creat`, the file will never be empty. `write` is an atomic operation.

15.3.3 Named Pipes

Regular pipes can only connect related processes. A regular pipe is created by a process and vanishes when the last process closes it.

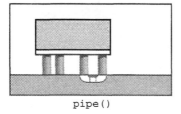

| pipe() | mkfifo() |

FIGURE 15.6

FIFOs are independent of processes.

A *named pipe*, also called a *FIFO*, can connect unrelated processes and exists independently of processes. (See Figure 15.6.) A FIFO is like an unconnected garden hose lying on the lawn. Anyone can put one end of the hose to his ear, and another person can walk up to the hose and speak into the other end. Unrelated people may communicate through a hose, and the hose exists even if nobody is using it. A FIFO is a pipe identified by a filename.

Using FIFOs

1. How do I create a FIFO?

`mkfifo(char *name, mode_t mode)` The library function `mkfifo` creates a FIFO with the specified permission mode. The command `mkfifo` usually calls this function.

2. How do I remove a FIFO?

Use `unlink(fifoname)` to remove a FIFO just as you remove a regular file.

3. How do I listen at a FIFO for a connection?

`open(fifoname, O_RDONLY)`. `open` blocks until a process opens the FIFO for writing.

4. How do I wait to speak into a FIFO?

`open(fifoname, O_WRONLY)`. `open` blocks until a process opens the FIFO for reading.

5. How do two processes speak through a FIFO?

The sending process uses `write`, and the listening process uses `read`. When the writing process calls `close`, the reader sees end of file.

Time/Date Server and Client Using a FIFO These two shell scripts are the server and client for a FIFO-based time/date service:

```
#!/bin/sh
# time server
    while true ; do
      rm -f /tmp/time_fifo
      mkfifo /tmp/time_fifo
      date > /tmp/time_fifo
    done

#!/bin/sh
# time client
    cat /tmp/time_fifo
```

Remarks on IPC with FIFOs

Access: FIFOs use the same file access permission system as regular files. The server can have write permission. Clients can be limited to read permission.

Multiple Readers: A named pipe is a queue, not a regular file. The writer adds bytes to the queue, a reader removes data from the queue. Each client pulls the date/time string from the FIFO, so the server must write the message again.

Race Conditions: The FIFO version of the date/time server does not have race-condition problems. The `read` and `write` system calls are atomic if the size of the message does not exceed the size of the pipe. Reading the message empties the pipe, and writing to the pipe fills it. The kernel blocks the processes until a writer and reader are connected. Locks are not needed.

Servers That Read from FIFOs   The time/date server writes into a FIFO, blocking until some client opens the FIFO for reading. In some applications, the server reads from a FIFO, waiting for the client to write data into the pipe. What is an example where the server waits for client input?

15.3.4   Shared Memory

How do bytes travel through a file or FIFO? write copies data from process memory to a kernel buffer. read copies data from a kernel buffer to process memory.

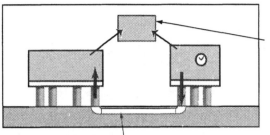

Using shared memory allows one process to put data directly into the memory space of another process.

Using a pipe requires copying data twice.

FIGURE 15.7

Two processes share a block of memory.

Why should processes copy data in and out of the kernel if both processes are on the same machine, living in different parts of user space? Two processes on the same machine may exchange or share data by using a *shared memory segment*—a part of user-space memory to which both processes have pointers. (See Figure 15.7.) Depending on access permission settings, both processes may read and write the data in that piece of memory. The information is shared, not copied, between the processes. Shared memory is to processes what global variables are to threads.

Facts about Shared Memory Segments

- A shared memory segment lives in memory independent of a process.
- A shared memory segment has a name, called a *key*.
- A key is an integer.
- A shared memory segment has an owner and permission bits.
- Processes may *attach* a segment, obtaining a pointer to the segment.

Using a Shared Memory Segment

1. How do I get a shared memory segment?

   ```
   int seg_id = shmget( key, size-of-segment, flags )
   ```

   If the segment exists, shmget locates it. If the segment does not exist, you specify in the flags value a request to create the segment and the initial permission mode. A lot like open.

2. How do I attach to a shared memory segment?

```
void ptr = *shmat( seg_id, NULL, flags )
```

shmat makes the shared segment part of the address space of the process and returns a pointer to the segment. Use the flags to specify whether you want the segment to be read only.

3. How do I read and write data to a shared memory segment?

```
strcpy( ptr, "hello" );
```

memcpy(), ptr[i], other regular pointer operations

A Time/Date Server Using Shared Memory

```c
/* shm_ts.c : the time server using shared memory, a bizarre application */

#include        <stdio.h>
#include        <sys/shm.h>
#include        <time.h>

#define TIME_MEM_KEY    99                      /* like a filename    */
#define SEG_SIZE        ((size_t)100)           /* size of segment    */
#define oops(m,x)   { perror(m); exit(x); }

main()
{
        int     seg_id;
        char    *mem_ptr, *ctime();
        long    now;
        int     n;

        /* create a shared memory segment */

        seg_id = shmget( TIME_MEM_KEY, SEG_SIZE, IPC_CREAT|0777 );
        if ( seg_id == -1 )
                oops("shmget", 1);

        /* attach to it and get a pointer to where it attaches */

        mem_ptr = shmat( seg_id, NULL, 0 );
        if ( mem_ptr == ( void *) -1 )
                oops("shmat", 2);

        /* run for a minute */
        for(n=0; n<60; n++ ){
                time( &now );                   /* get the time */
                strcpy(mem_ptr, ctime(&now));   /* write to mem */
                sleep(1);                       /* wait a sec   */
        }


        /* now remove it */
        shmctl( seg_id, IPC_RMID, NULL );
}
```

A Time/Date Client Using Shared Memory

```
/* shm_tc.c : the time client using shared memory, a bizarre application */

#include        <stdio.h>
#include        <sys/shm.h>
#include        <time.h>

#define TIME_MEM_KEY    99              /* kind of like a port number */
#define SEG_SIZE        ((size_t)100)           /* size of segment      */
#define oops(m,x)   { perror(m); exit(x); }

main()
{
        int     seg_id;
        char    *mem_ptr, *ctime();
        long    now;

        /* create a shared memory segment */

        seg_id = shmget( TIME_MEM_KEY, SEG_SIZE, 0777 );
        if ( seg_id == -1 )
                oops("shmget",1);

        /* attach to it and get a pointer to where it attaches */

        mem_ptr = shmat( seg_id, NULL, 0 );
        if ( mem_ptr == ( void *) -1 )
                oops("shmat",2);

        printf("The time, direct from memory: ..%s", mem_ptr);

        shmdt( mem_ptr );                       /* detach, but not needed here */
}
```

Remarks on IPC with Shared Memory

Access: Clients for this server must be able to read the shared memory segment. Shared memory segments have a file permission system that works just like the system for files. A shared memory segment has an owner and has access bits for user, group, and other. A shared memory block can be protected so the server has write permission and the clients have read access only.

Multiple Clients: Any number of clients may read data from the shared segment at the same time.

Race Conditions: The server updates the shared memory by calling strcpy, a regular library function that runs in user space. If a client reads the memory segment when the server is copying a new string to the segment, the client may read a combination of the old and new strings.

Avoiding Race Conditions: The server and clients must use some system to lock the resource. The kernel provides an interprocess locking mechanism called *semaphores*; we study them in a later section.

15.3.5 Comparing Communication Methods

The original problem was to get a string from one process to another. All three methods work. Clients get the data they want from the server. We now have four versions of this client-server system. We could even write versions that use datagrams or Unix domain addresses. How do you decide on a method? What criteria matter?

Speed

Sending data through files and named pipes requires more operations. The kernel copies data to kernel space then back to user space. For files, the kernel may copy data to the disk and then may later copy data from the disk. Actually, storing data in memory can be more complicated than it first appears. A virtual memory system allows sections of user space to be swapped out to a disk, so a shared memory segment can also involve writing and reading the disk.

Connected or Unconnected

Files and shared memory segments work like billboards. The data producer posts the information and goes away. Data consumers may read at any time, and many may read the message at the same time. A FIFO requires a connection; reader and writer must both have the FIFO open before the kernel will transfer data, and only one client may read the message. Stream sockets are connected, whereas datagram sockets are not. In some applications, these distinctions matter.

Range

How far do you want your messages to travel? Shared memory and named pipes only connect processes on the same machine. A file can be stored on a shared file server and can connect processes on different machines. Sockets with Internet addresses can connect processes on different machines, sockets with Unix addresses can not. Do you want the range to be wide or limited?

Restricted Access

Do you want everyone to be able to speak with your server or do you want to limit access to specific users? Files, FIFOs, shared memory, and Unix address sockets provide standard Unix file system permissions. Internet sockets do not.

Race Conditions

Shared memory and shared files are trickier to program than pipes and sockets. Pipes and sockets are queues managed by the kernel. A writer puts data into one end, a reader takes data from the other end. The processes do not have to worry about the internal structure.

Access to shared files and shared memory is not managed by the kernel. If a process reads a file while another process is busy rewriting the file, the reading process may get inconsistent or incomplete data. In the next sections, we study file locks and semaphores.

15.4   INTERPROCESS COOPERATION AND COORDINATION

What about those pesky race conditions? Clients and servers can share the same files
or memory. How can we prevent them from getting in each others' ways? How can
they coordinate their actions? In this section, we look at techniques that processes use
with shared resources: *file locks* and *semaphores*.

15.4.1   File Locks

Two Kinds of Locks

Consider two sorts of problems. First, what happens if the server is in the middle of
rewriting the file when a client tries to read the file? The client will find the file empty
or incomplete. Our date/time server is not likely to encounter this problem, but a
weather forecast server, with longer messages, probably would. Therefore, when the
server is rewriting the file, clients must wait for the server to finish.

Consider now the opposite situation. What happens if a client is in the middle of
reading the file line by line when, suddenly, the server grabs the file from the client,
truncates it, and starts writing new data. The client will see the file changing in front of
its eyes. Therefore, when a client is reading the file, the server must wait for the client to
finish. Other clients do not need to wait; there is no risk if several processes read the
file at once.

To prevent both sorts of problems, we need two kinds of file locks. The first type,
a *write lock*, says, "I am writing the file, and everyone should wait until I am done." The
second type, a *read lock*, says, "I am reading the file. Writers should wait until I am done
reading, but anyone else can read it."

Programming with File Locks

Unix provides three ways to apply locks to open files: `flock`, `lockf`, and `fcntl`. The
most flexible and portable of the three is `fcntl`.

Using `fcntl` *to Lock Files*

1. How do I set a read lock on an open file?

> Use `fcntl(fd, F_SETLKW, &lockinfo )`

The first argument is the file descriptor to the file. The second argument,
`F_SETLKW`, says you are willing to wait for another process to release a lock if necessary. The third argument points to a variable of type `struct flock`. The following code sets a read lock on a file descriptor:

```
set_read_lock(int fd)
{
  struct flock lockinfo;
  lockinfo.l_type    = F_RDLCK;    /* a read lock on a region */
  lockinfo.l_pid     = getpid();   /* for ME                  */
  lockinfo.l_start   = 0;          /* starting 0 bytes from.. */
```

```
        lockinfo.l_whence  = SEEK_SET;    /* start of file           */
        lockinfo.l_len     = 0;           /* extending until EOF      */

        fcntl(fd, F_SETLKW, &lockinfo);
}
```

2. How do I set a write lock on an open file?

Use `fcntl(fd, F_SETLKW, &lockinfo )`

with `lockinfo.l_type = F_WRLCK;`

3. How do I release a lock I hold?

Use `fcntl(fd, F_SETLKW, &lockinfo )`

with `lockinfo.l_type = F_UNLCK;`

4. How do I lock only part of a file?

Use `fcntl(fd, F_SETLKW, &lockinfo )`

with `lockinfo.l_start` equal to the offset of the start and `lockinfo.l_len` equal to the length of the region.

Code for a File-Based Time Server:

```
/* file_ts.c - write the current date/time to a file
 *     usage: file_ts filename
 *    action: writes the current time/date to filename
 *     note: uses fcntl()-based locking
 */

#include <stdio.h>
#include <sys/file.h>
#include <fcntl.h>
#include <time.h>

#define  oops(m,x)   { perror(m); exit(x); }

main(int ac, char *av[])
{
        int     fd;
        time_t  now;
        char    *message;

        if ( ac != 2 ){
                fprintf(stderr,"usage: file_ts filename\n");
                exit(1);
        }
        if ( (fd = open(av[1],O_CREAT|O_TRUNC|O_WRONLY,0644)) == -1 )
                oops(av[1],2);

        while(1)
```

```
                {
                        time(&now);
                        message = ctime(&now);               /* compute time      */

                        lock_operation(fd, F_WRLCK);    /* lock for writing  */
                        if ( lseek(fd, 0L, SEEK_SET) == -1 )
                                oops("lseek",3);
                        if ( write(fd, message, strlen(message)) == -1 )
                                oops("write", 4);

                        lock_operation(fd, F_UNLCK);    /* unlock file       */
                        sleep(1);                        /* wait for new time */
                }
        }

        lock_operation(int fd, int op)
        {
                struct flock lock;

                lock.l_whence = SEEK_SET;
                lock.l_start = lock.l_len = 0;
                lock.l_pid = getpid();
                lock.l_type = op;

                if ( fcntl(fd, F_SETLKW, &lock) == -1 )
                        oops("lock operation", 6);
        }
```

Code for a File-Based Time Client:

```
/* file_tc.c - read the current date/time from a file
 *      usage: file_tc filename
 *      uses: fcntl()-based locking
 */

#include <stdio.h>
#include <sys/file.h>
#include <fcntl.h>

#define  oops(m,x)   { perror(m); exit(x); }
#define  BUFLEN 10

main(int ac, char *av[])
{
        int     fd, nread;
        char    buf[BUFLEN];

        if ( ac != 2 ){
                fprintf(stderr,"usage: file_tc filename\n");
                exit(1);
        }

        if ( (fd= open(av[1],O_RDONLY)) == -1 )
                oops(av[1],3);
```

```
            lock_operation(fd, F_RDLCK);

               while( (nread = read(fd, buf, BUFLEN)) > 0 )
                        write(1, buf, nread );

            lock_operation(fd, F_UNLCK);

            close(fd);
       }

       lock_operation(int fd, int op)
       {
            struct flock lock;

            lock.l_whence = SEEK_SET;
            lock.l_start = lock.l_len = 0;
            lock.l_pid = getpid();
            lock.l_type = op;

            if ( fcntl(fd, F_SETLKW, &lock) == -1 )
                    oops("lock operation", 6);
       }
```

File Locks: Summary

Calls to fcntl with F_SETLKW block until the kernel allows the process to set the specified lock. Clients must set a read lock before reading the data. If the server holds a write lock, the clients are suspended until the server is done. The server must set a write lock before updating the file. If a client holds a read lock, the server is suspended until all clients release their read locks.

Important Note: Processes Can Ignore Locks

In our discussion of file locks, we assumed the client and server programs wait for, set, and release locks when they read or modify shared data. Can a process ignore the locks and read or change the file, even when another process holds a lock? Yes. Unix locks allow processes to cooperate, Unix does not force cooperation.

15.4.2 Semaphores

The shared memory segment in the shared memory version of the time/date client and server plays the same role as the file in the file-based version. How do we prevent interference? Are there read and write locks for memory segments? No, but processes can use a more flexible mechanism to cooperate: *semaphores*.

A semaphore is a kernel variable accessible to all processes on the system. Processes can use these kernel variables to coordinate access to shared memory and other resources. The threads chapter explains how threads can use a condition variable to notify another thread when something interesting happens. Condition objects are global within a process. Semaphores are global within the system.

How can we use these global variables for our time server and clients?

Counters and Operations

The server writes to the shared segment and should wait until no clients are reading. The clients read from the segment and should wait until no server is writing. We can translate these rules into statements about values of variables:

- Clients wait until the number_of_writers == 0
- Server waits until the number_of_readers == 0

Semaphores are systemwide global variables; we can use one to represent the number of readers and one to represent the number of writers. Managing these variables requires two operations.

A reader, for example, must wait until the number of writers equals zero, and then immediately increment the number of readers. When a reader finishes reading data, it decrements the number of readers.

Similarly, the writer waits for the number of readers to equal zero and then increments the number of writers. The two operations of waiting for the reader count to reach zero and incrementing the writer count must happen indivisibly. That is, the pair must be atomic. Processes that communicate through semaphores can use several variables and apply several operations atomically.

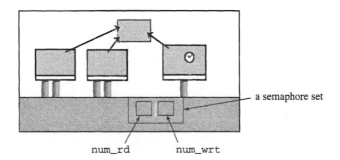

a semaphore set

num_rd   num_wrt

FIGURE 15.8

A semaphore set: num_readers, num_writers.

That's what semaphores are all about. A process can perform a set of actions on a set of semaphores, all at once.

Sets of Semaphores, Sets of Actions

The time-server system uses two semaphores (see Figure 15.8), and the readers and writers both perform two action sets.

Before modifying shared memory, the server must perform this action set:

[0] wait for num_readers to become 0
[1] add 1 to num_writers

When the server finishes, the server must perform this action set:

[0] subtract 1 from num_writers

Before reading from shared memory, a client must perform these actions:

[0] wait for num_writers to become 0
[1] add 1 to num_readers

When the client finishes, the client must perform this action set:

[0] subtract 1 from num_readers

The Server: shm_ts2.c

We add semaphores to shm_ts.c, our earlier program, to get shm_ts2.c:

```
/* shm_ts2.c - time server shared mem ver2 : use semaphores for locking
 * program uses shared memory with key 99
 * program uses semaphore set with key 9900
 */

#include         <stdio.h>
#include         <sys/shm.h>
#include         <time.h>
#include         <sys/types.h>
#include         <sys/sem.h>
#include         <signal.h>

#define TIME_MEM_KEY    99                      /* like a filename    */
#define TIME_SEM_KEY    9900
#define SEG_SIZE        ((size_t)100)           /* size of segment    */
#define oops(m,x)   { perror(m); exit(x); }

union semun { int val ; struct semid_ds *buf ; ushort *array; };
int     seg_id, semset_id;                      /* global for cleanup() */
void    cleanup(int);

main()
{
        char    *mem_ptr, *ctime();
        time_t  now;
        int     n;

        /* create a shared memory segment */

        seg_id = shmget( TIME_MEM_KEY, SEG_SIZE, IPC_CREAT|0777 );
        if ( seg_id == -1 )
                oops("shmget", 1);

        /* attach to it and get a pointer to where it attaches */

        mem_ptr = shmat( seg_id, NULL, 0 );
        if ( mem_ptr == ( void *) -1 )
                oops("shmat", 2);

        /* create a semset: key 9900, 2 semaphores, and mode rw-rw-rw */
```

```
            semset_id = semget( TIME_SEM_KEY, 2, (0666|IPC_CREAT|IPC_EXCL) );
            if ( semset_id == -1 )
                    oops("semget", 3);

            set_sem_value( semset_id, 0, 0);          /* set counters */
            set_sem_value( semset_id, 1, 0);          /* both to zero */

            signal(SIGINT, cleanup);

            /* run for a minute */
            for(n=0; n<60; n++ ){
                    time( &now );                     /* get the time */
                            printf("\tshm_ts2 waiting for lock\n");
                    wait_and_lock(semset_id);         /* lock memory  */
                            printf("\tshm_ts2 updating memory\n");
                    strcpy(mem_ptr, ctime(&now));     /* write to mem */
                            sleep(5);
                    release_lock(semset_id);          /* unlock       */
                            printf("\tshm_ts2 released lock\n");
                    sleep(1);                         /* wait a sec   */
            }

            cleanup(0);
    }

void cleanup(int n)
{
        shmctl( seg_id, IPC_RMID, NULL );         /* rm shrd mem  */
        semctl( semset_id, 0, IPC_RMID, NULL);    /* rm sem set   */
}

/*
 * initialize a semaphore
 */
set_sem_value(int semset_id, int semnum, int val)
{
        union semun  initval;
        initval.val = val;
        if ( semctl(semset_id, semnum, SETVAL, initval) == -1 )
                oops("semctl", 4);
}

/*
 * build and execute a 2-element action set:
 *     wait for 0 on n_readers AND increment n_writers
 */
wait_and_lock( int semset_id )
{
        struct sembuf actions[2];         /* action set           */

        actions[0].sem_num = 0;           /* sem[0] is n_readers  */
        actions[0].sem_flg = SEM_UNDO;    /* auto cleanup         */
        actions[0].sem_op  = 0 ;          /* wait til no readers  */
```

```
            actions[1].sem_num = 1;           /* sem[1] is n_writers  */
            actions[1].sem_flg = SEM_UNDO;    /* auto cleanup          */
            actions[1].sem_op  = +1 ;         /* incr num writers      */

            if ( semop( semset_id, actions, 2) == -1 )
                    oops("semop: locking", 10);
    }
    /*
     * build and execute a 1-element action set:
     *     decrement num_writers
     */
    release_lock( int semset_id )
    {
            struct sembuf actions[1];         /* action set            */

            actions[0].sem_num = 1;           /* sem[0] is n_writerS   */
            actions[0].sem_flg = SEM_UNDO;    /* auto cleanup          */
            actions[0].sem_op  = -1 ;         /* decr writer count     */

            if ( semop( semset_id, actions, 1) == -1 )
                    oops("semop: unlocking", 10);
    }
```

The server does five things with the semaphore set:

1. *Create the semaphore set*

    ```
    semset_id = semget(key_t key, int numsems, int flags)
    ```

    semget creates a semaphore set containing numsems semaphores. shm_ts2 creates a set with two semaphores. The set has permission mode 0666. semget returns an ID for the semaphore set.

2. *Set both semaphores to 0*

    ```
    semctl(int semset_id, int semnum, int cmd, union semun arg)
    ```

    We use semctl to control a semaphore set. The first argument is the ID of the set. The second argument is the number of a specific semaphore in the set. The third argument is the control command. If the control command requires an argument, the fourth argument is that argument. In shm_ts2 we use the SETVAL command to assign each semaphore an initial value of 0.

3. *Wait until no readers, then increment* num_writers

    ```
    semop(int semid, struct sembuf *actions, size_t numactions)
    ```

    semop applies a set of actions to a set of semaphores. The first argument identifies the semaphore set. The second argument is an array of actions. The last argument is the size of the array of actions. Each action in the set is a struct that says, "Do operation sem_op to semaphore number sem_num with options sem_flg." The entire set of actions is performed as a group. That's the point.

    The wait_and_lock function has to perform two actions: wait for the number of readers to reach zero and then increment the number of writers. We create an array of two actions. Action zero says, "Wait for zero on semaphore 0." Action one says, "Add 1 to semaphore 1." The process blocks until both these actions can be performed. As soon as the reader count is zero, the writer count is incremented, and semop returns.

The SEM_UNDO flag tells the kernel to undo these operations when the process exits. In this application, incrementing the writer count effectively locks the memory segment. If the process died before decrementing the count, other processes could never use the shared memory segment.

4. *Decrement* num_writers

In release_lock, we only have one thing to do: decrement the count of writers. We call semop with an array containing this one action. If a client is waiting for the writer count to reach zero, that client resumes execution.

5. *Delete the semaphore*

```
semctl(semset_id, 0, IPC_RMID, 0)
```

When done, the server calls semctl again, this time to delete the semaphore.

The Client: shm_tc2.c

The client is simpler. shm_tc2 neither initializes the semaphores nor deletes them:

```
/* shm_tc2.c - time client shared mem ver2 : use semaphores for locking
 * program uses shared memory with key 99
 * program uses semaphore set with key 9900
 */

#include        <stdio.h>
#include        <sys/shm.h>
#include        <time.h>
#include        <sys/types.h>
#include        <sys/ipc.h>
#include        <sys/sem.h>

#define TIME_MEM_KEY    99              /* kind of like a port number */
#define TIME_SEM_KEY    9900            /* like a filename            */
#define SEG_SIZE        ((size_t)100)        /* size of segment       */
#define oops(m,x)   { perror(m); exit(x); }
union semun { int val ; struct semid_ds *buf ; ushort *array; };

main()
{
        int     seg_id;
        char    *mem_ptr, *ctime();
        long    now;

        int     semset_id;                     /* id for semaphore set */

        /* create a shared memory segment */

        seg_id = shmget( TIME_MEM_KEY, SEG_SIZE, 0777 );
```

```
                if ( seg_id == -1 )
                        oops("shmget",1);

                /* attach to it and get a pointer to where it attaches */

                mem_ptr = shmat( seg_id, NULL, 0 );
                if ( mem_ptr == ( void *) -1 )
                        oops("shmat",2);

                /* connect to semaphore set 9900 with 2 semaphores */

                semset_id = semget( TIME_SEM_KEY, 2, 0);
                wait_and_lock( semset_id );

                printf("The time, direct from memory: ..%s", mem_ptr);

                release_lock( semset_id );
                shmdt( mem_ptr );                  /* detach, but not needed here */
        }
        /*
         * build and execute a 2-element action set:
         *    wait for 0 on n_writers AND increment n_readers
         */
        wait_and_lock( int semset_id )
        {
                union semun    sem_info;         /* some properties       */
                struct sembuf actions[2];        /* action set            */

                actions[0].sem_num = 1;          /* sem[1] is n_writers   */
                actions[0].sem_flg = SEM_UNDO;   /* auto cleanup          */
                actions[0].sem_op  = 0 ;         /* wait for 0            */
                actions[1].sem_num = 0;          /* sem[0] is n_readers   */
                actions[1].sem_flg = SEM_UNDO;   /* auto cleanup          */
                actions[1].sem_op  = +1 ;        /* incr n_readers        */

                if ( semop( semset_id, actions, 2) == -1 )
                        oops("semop: locking", 10);
        }

        /*
         * build and execute a 1-element action set:
         *    decrement num_readers
         */
        release_lock( int semset_id )
        {
                union semun    sem_info;         /* some properties       */
                struct sembuf actions[1];        /* action set            */

                actions[0].sem_num = 0;          /* sem[0] is n_readers   */
                actions[0].sem_flg = SEM_UNDO;   /* auto cleanup          */
                actions[0].sem_op  = -1 ;        /* decr reader count     */

                if ( semop( semset_id, actions, 1) == -1 )
                        oops("semop: unlocking", 10);
        }
```

Compile and Test These Programs:

```
$ cc shm_ts2.c -o shmserv
$ cc shm_tc2.c -o shmclnt
$ ./shmserv &
[1] 15533
        shm_ts2 waiting for lock
        shm_ts2 updating memory
$       shm_ts2 released lock
        shm_ts2 waiting for lock
        shm_ts2 updating memory
$ ./shmclnt
    shm_ts2 released lock
The time, direct from memory: ..Sat Oct 27 17:36:34 2001
$       shm_ts2 waiting for lock
        shm_ts2 updating memory
$ ./shmclnt
        shm_ts2 released lock
The time, direct from memory: ..Sat Oct 27 17:36:40 2001
$       shm_ts2 waiting for lock
ipcs

------ Shared Memory Segments --------
key        shmid     owner     perms     bytes     nattch     status
0x00000063 30670854  bruce     777       100       1

------ Semaphore Arrays --------
key        semid     owner     perms     nsems     status
0x000026ac 262146    bruce     666       2

------ Message Queues --------
key        msqid     owner     perms     used-bytes  messages

$       shm_ts2 released lock
        shm_ts2 waiting for lock
$ kill -INT 15533
$ semop: unlocking: Invalid argument
```

The test run shows that the client waits for the server to release the lock. Many clients can run at once. Each client waits for the server count to be zero and then increments the client counter. If three clients read from shared memory at the same time, the reader count will be three. The server has to wait until all three clients decrement the reader counter.

The program does not handle all cases, though. In particular, what is to stop two servers from running at the same time? The server only waits until the client count is zero and does not wait for the server counter.

Waiting for a Semaphore to Become Positive

Our client waits until the number-of-writers semaphore equals zero, and our server waits until the number-of-readers semaphore equals zero. In other programs, we might want to wait for a semaphore to equal a positive value. For example, say we wanted to wait until a semaphore had a value of 2. How do we program that?

We use a slightly indirect method: We ask the kernel to subtract 2 from the sema-phore. Semaphores are never allowed be negative, so the kernel blocks the call until the semaphore equals 2 or greater. Notice how clever this is. As soon as the semaphore reaches 2, our process subtracts 2 from the value blocking any other process that wants to subtract 2 from the semaphore.

The sem_op member of the operation works as follows:

sem_op is positive

Action: Increment the semaphore by sem_op.

sem_op is zero

Action: Block until the semaphore equals zero.

sem_op is negative

Action: Block until adding sem_op to the semaphore will not be negative.

15.4.3 Sockets and FIFOs vs. Shared Storage

We wrote four versions of the time/date server and client. The socket version and the FIFO version are simple. A client connects to a server, the server sends some data, and the processes hang up. The shared memory and shared file versions seem simple at first, but they require locks or semaphores to protect the data, and adding locks and semaphores is more work.

Nonetheless, files and shared memory allow many clients to read from one serv-er, allow the clients and servers to run at different times, and allow data to persist if processes crash.

Furthermore, even pipes and sockets involve some sort of locks. Pipes and sock-ets are memory segments holding data moving from source to destination. The kernel, not the process, handles the locks and semaphores that protect data in pipes and sock-ets from corruption.

15.5   A PRINT SPOOLER

A single time/date server sends data to several clients. Some applications work the other way: Multiple clients send data to one server—a print spooler, for example. What design questions apply here?

15.5.1 Many Writers, One Reader

Many users share one printer. (See Figure 15.9.) How can we use client/server design to create a printer-sharing program? Several people may send printing requests at once, but the printer can only print one file at a time. A printing program has to accept many simultaneous inputs and produce a single stream of output to a printer. What does the server do? What do the clients do? How do they communicate?

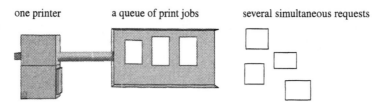

FIGURE 15.9

Many sources of data, one printer.

What are the functional units? What data and messages do these components exchange?

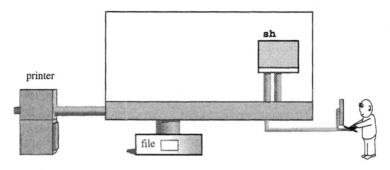

FIGURE 15.10

Getting a file to the printer.

The simplest way to print a file on a Unix system is the command

```
cat filename > /dev/lp1   or   cp filename /dev/lp1
```

where /dev/lp1 is the name of the device file for the printer. Your system may have a different name for the file that connects to the printer, but the only way to send data to a printer or other device on Unix is to open and write to a device file.

Can We Use Write Locks?

We know about write locks and semaphores. Why not write a special printer version of cat or cp that uses a write lock on the device file to prevent simultaneous access?

A lock-based file-copy program works. If one program has a lock on the printer, other instances of the file-copy program block until the first job releases the lock. Which program gets to go next? The kernel unblocks one of the programs, but it may not be the next one that tried to print. It does not seem fair. A second problem with allowing users to copy data to the printer device is that some people may try to cheat and not use the special program. A third problem is that some files require special processing. An image file may need to be converted into graphics commands that the printer understands. Many users do not know which programs to use to convert the data to printable format, and they are likely to get disappointing and frustrating results. Centralization solves all these problems.

15.5.2 A Client/Server Model

The client/server model of program design solves the printing problems we discussed. A server program called the *line printer daemon* has permission to write to the printer device, and other users do not. (See Figure 15.11.) Users run a client program called lpr when they want to print a file. lpr makes a copy of the file and then places that copy in the queue of print jobs. The user may delete or edit the file, since the copy will be printed. Furthermore, the printer daemon program can apply conversion programs so that images and fonts print correctly.

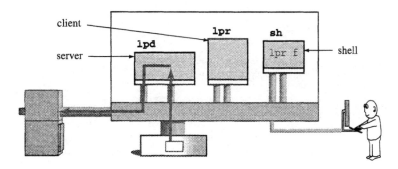

FIGURE 15.11

Client/server printing system.

How do the client and server communicate? What data do they exchange? Does the client send the entire file to the server or does the client merely send the name of the file to the server? What if the server is on a different computer from the client? How does that affect the choice of communication methods? Many different printing systems have been developed for Unix. Some use sockets, some use named pipes, some use only fork and files.

What about cooperation, file locks, and mutual exclusion? Does using a centralized server eliminate the need for locks? Devise a component, communication, and co-operation model for printing that works on one machine and then for printing that works over the Internet. Compare your ideas with the various Unix printing systems.

15.6   IPC OVERVIEW

We have studied many forms of interprocess communication. Here is a summary:

Method	Type	Different Machines	Different Processes P/C	Sib	Unrel	Different Threads
exec/wait	M		*			
environ	M		*			
pipe	S		*	*		*
kill–signal	M		*	*	*	*
inet socket	S	*	?	?	?	?
inet socket	M	*	?	?	?	?
Unix socket	S		?	?	*	?
Unix socket	M		?	?	*	?
named pipe	S		?	?	*	?
shared mem	R		*	*	*	?
msg queue	M		*	*	*	*
files	R	N	*	*	*	?
variables	M					*
file locks	C	N	*	*	*	*
semaphores	C		*	*	*	?
mutexes	C					*
link	C		*	*	*	?

Key:

P/C—parent/child relationship

Sib—sibling relationship

Unrel—unrelated processes

M—sends data in short to medium-sized messages

S—stream of data using read and write

R—random access to data

C—used to synchronize/coordinate tasks

*—appropriate application

?—inappropriate application

N—appropriate with a networked file system

The table does not include the Bell Labs networking tools TLI or their descendants.

Explanations

fork-execv-argv, exit-wait

Used to call a program with a list of arguments and for the called program to return a single integer value back to its caller. The parent process calls fork to create a new process. The program then, in the new process, calls execv to run a new program and pass it an array of strings. The child process sends a value back with exit, and the parent receives that value with wait.

Message oriented, related processes only, within one machine.

environ

The exec system call automatically copies into the new program the array of strings pointed to by a global variable called environ. This method allows a program to pass values to children, their descendants, and programs they run. The environment is copied, so the child cannot change the parent's environment.

Message oriented, one-way, related processes only, within one machine.

pipe

A pipe is a one-way stream of data created by a process. It consists of two file descriptors connected in the kernel. Data written to one of the file descriptors can be read from the other file descriptor. If a process calls fork after creating a pipe, the new process can read or write to the same pipe, passing data from one to the other.

Stream oriented, usually one-way, related processes, within one machine.

kill-signal

A signal is a single, integer-valued message sent from one process (using the kill system call) to another process. The receiving process can arrange, using the signal system call to have a *handler* function invoked when a signal arrives.

Message oriented, one-way at a time, same user ID, within one machine.

Internet Sockets

Internet sockets are connection endpoints established on a machine with a specific *port number*. Bytes are transferred from one process to another by sending them into one socket and receiving them at another socket, much as a person speaks into a telephone in Boston and another person receives the message in Tokyo. Internet sockets come in two main flavors: stream sockets and datagram sockets. Both are bidirectional. Stream sockets work like file descriptors: The programmer uses write and read to send data and receive data. Datagram sockets work like postcards: the writer sends a short buffer of data to a receiver. All transactions are done in buffers of data, not streams.

Message and stream versions, two-way, unrelated, spans machines.

Named Sockets

Named sockets, also called *Unix-domain sockets*, use a filename as an address rather than a hostname–port-number pair. Named sockets are available in stream or datagram versions. Since these use filenames rather than host–port as addresses, they can only connect processes on the same machine.

Message and stream versions, two-way, unrelated, within one machine.

Named Pipes (FIFOs)

A named pipe works just like a regular (unnamed) pipe except it can be used to connect unrelated processes. A named pipe is identified by a filename. The writer opens the file for writing using open, and the reader opens the file for reading using open. They are simpler to use than named sockets, but they only go one way.

Stream oriented, one-way, unrelated, within one machine.

File Locks

Unix allows processes to set locks on sections of files. One process can lock a section of a file so that it can modify that section. Another process that tries to lock that file will be suspended or told the section is locked. These locks allow one process to communicate with another about who is changing or reading a file. The system calls flock, lockf, and fcntl can be used to set and test advisory locks. Compulsory locks are available on some systems.

Message oriented, *n*-way, unrelated, within one machine.

Shared Memory

Each process has its own data space. Any variables a program defines or allocates at run time are available only to that process. A process may, using shmget and shmat, create a chunk of memory that may be shared by more than one process. Data that one process writes to such a shared memory chunk may be read by any other process that has access to that memory chunk. This is the most efficient form of IPC since no transfer of data is required.

Random access, *n*-way, unrelated, within one machine.

Semaphores

Semaphores are systemwide variables that programs can use to coordinate their work. A process can increment, decrement, and wait for semaphores to reach certain values. A semaphore simulates the tickets in the license server. When a process wants to use a resource, it decrements a semaphore. If there are no more tickets, the process blocks until another process increments the semaphore. Semaphores can be used in many other ways.

Message oriented, *n*-way, unrelated, within one machine.

Message Queues

Message queues are like FIFOs, but they do not have filenames. Processes may add messages to a queue, and processes may take messages from a queue. Multiple queues may be shared by multiple processes.

Message oriented, one-way, unrelated, within one machine.

Files

A file may be opened by more than one process at the same time. If one process writes data to a file, another process may read that data. In fact, several processes may have the same file open at the same time. With a carefully planned protocol, complex communication may be implemented using plain old files.

Random access, *n*-way, unrelated, NFS allows cross-machine communication.

15.7 CONNECTIONS AND GAMES

In this chapter, we looked at ways to transfer data between processes. A Unix kernel manages many processes, files, and devices, and it operates the pipes, sockets, files, shared memory, and signals that carry data from place to place. For some programs, creating and managing transfers and connections is the whole idea.

Ken Thompson, the co-inventor of Unix, wrote in 1978:

> *The UNIX kernel is an I/O multiplexer more than a complete operating system. This is as it should be. Because of this outlook, many features are found in most other operating systems that are missing from the UNIX kernel. ... Many of these things are implemented in user software using the kernel as a tool.*[1]

In the first chapter, we talked about bc, a Web server, and an Internet bridge game. Later, we wrote a version of bc and two Web servers. What about writing a network-based bridge game? You can use curses for the user interface and some sort of sockets for the glue. Who are servers? Who are clients? What about locks? All the tools you need are discussed somewhere in these chapters. Unix programming is not as difficult as you think it is, but it is not as easy as you might first imagine.

Speaking of games and networks, recall how Dennis Ritchie described the *Space Travel* game that led to Unix:

> *First written on Multics, ..., it was nothing less than a simulation of the movement of the major bodies of the Solar System, with the player guiding a ship here and there, observing the scenery, and attempting to land on the various planets and moons.*

Guiding a ship here and there, observing scenery, and attempting to land on planets and moons sounds sort of like Web surfing. Maybe surfing is not the best metaphor. People guide their Web browser here and there. Web servers send back scenery from distant places. People use telnet, ssh, and ftp to land on other machines. Perhaps the Internet is an unintended realization of the expansive space Ritchie and Thompson set out to simulate in 1969?

SUMMARY

MAIN IDEAS

- Many programs consist of two or more processes that work as a system, sharing data or passing data from one to the other. Two people using the Unix talk command, for example, run two processes that transfer data from keyboards and sockets to screens and sockets.
- Some processes need to receive data from multiple sources and send data to multiple destinations. The select and poll calls let a process wait for input on multiple file descriptors.

---

[1]"Unix Implementation," *Bell System Technical Journal*, vol. 56, no. 6, 1978.

- Unix provides several methods for transferring data from one process to another. Named pipes and shared memory are two techniques that processes on the same machine can use. Communication methods can be compared on the bases of speed, type of message, required range, ability to restrict access, and potential for data corruption.
- File locks are a technique that processes may use to prevent data corruption in files.
- Semaphores are systemwide variables that processes can use to coordinate action. A process waits for a semaphore to change, and another process can change the semaphore.

WHAT NEXT?

A good way to learn more about Unix systems programming is to continue to read and write programs. The Web has a lot of information, and there are many books that explain details of Unix internals and details of the programming interface. Look at the programs you use every day and at new ones that interest or amuse you. By using, studying, and writing your own version of a program, you can refine and extend your understanding of Unix.

EXPLORATIONS

15.1 *Threads instead of* select Why not use threads to read from two file descriptors in talk? One thread could read from the keyboard, and the other thread could read from the socket. What new complication does a multithreaded solution add to the program?

15.2 *TCP or UDP* The talk program reads and writes single characters most of the time, but uses a stream socket to transfer data. What would be the advantages and disadvantages of using a datagram socket?

15.3 The FIFO-based time server blocks at date > /tmp/time_fifo until a client opens the FIFO for reading. If the server blocks for a long time, does the client receive the time when the server blocked or the time when the server unblocked? Why?

15.4 *Shared memory and files* Read about the mmap call. mmap makes a section of a file look like an array in memory, allowing a program random access to a file without having to use lseek. How does using mmap compare to using files or shared memory as a means of interprocess communication? What are the advantages and disadvantages of mmap compared to these other methods?

15.5 *The talk server* The explanation of talk showed two connected processes. Experiment with talk to see how the connection is made. What other programs have to be involved?

PROGRAMMING EXERCISES

15.6 Read the manual pages on select and poll to determine whether both are supported on your system. On some systems, one is the real system call, and the other is emulated by *using* the real one. Rewrite the selectdemo.c program to use poll.

15.7 Write versions of the time/date server and client that use

    (a) Datagram sockets with Internet addresses

    (b) Stream sockets with Unix domain addresses

15.8 Write a C version of the FIFO-based date/time server and client.

15.9 *Multiple shared memory servers*

(a) Can you run two shared memory servers at the same time? Why or why not? Try it.

(b) Modify `wait_and_lock` in the server so the server waits until the number of servers is zero.

15.10 *Semaphores as file locks* We used file locks to protect the shared file in the file version. Rewrite that program to use semaphores instead of file locks.

15.11 *File locks as semaphores* We use semaphores to protect shared memory in the memory version. Rewrite that program to use file locks instead. You will need a file.

15.12 *Too many readers* The semaphore solution to the shared memory server will not report the correct time if there are too many clients. Consider this pattern: Reader A increases the reader count to 1. Next, reader B increases the reader count to 2. Then reader A finishes, dropping the reader count to 1, but reader C increases the count to 2. Then B finishes, A starts again, C finishes, then B starts again, and so on. At no time is the shared memory not being read. Explain why this prevents the writer from updating the time. Modify the system so the writer can prevent new readers from locking the shared memory segment.

15.13 Write a special printer version of `cp` that uses a write lock to prevent simultaneous access to the output file. Use it on your home machine to print two files at once:

```
printcp file1 /dev/lp1 & printcp file2 /dev/lp1&
```

Index